Living Philosophy

Living Philosophy

An Introduction to Moral Thought
Second Edition

Ray Billington

London and New York

First published in 1988
by Routledge & Kegan Paul Ltd

Reprinted 1989, 1991
Second edition first published in 1993 by Routledge
11 New Fetter Lane, London EC4P 4EE
Simultaneously published in the USA and Canada by Routledge
29 West 35th Street, New York, NY 10001

Set in 10$^1/_2$/12 Plantin
by Florencetype Ltd, Kewstoke, Avon
Printed in Great Britain
by T J Press Ltd, Padstow, Cornwall

© *Ray Billington 1988, 1993*

A catalogue record for this book is available from the British Library

Library of Congress Cataloging in Publication Data

Billington, Ray.
* Living philosophy: An introduction to moral thought*
* Ray Billington. – 2nd ed.*
* Includes bibliographical references and index.*
* 1. Ethics. I. Title.*
* BJ1025.B53 1993   93-19012*
* 170 dc19*

ISBN 0 415 10028 3

Without the strength provided by Alcoholics Anonymous
this book could have been no more than a shadow of
what it has become.
To all members of the Fellowship, known and unknown,
it is therefore dedicated.
My gratitude will be lifelong, but it can be expressed
'a day at a time'.

A truly good man is not aware of his goodness,
And is therefore good.
A foolish man tries to be good,
And is therefore not good.

A truly good man does nothing,
Yet leaves nothing undone.
A foolish man is always doing,
Yet much remains to be done.

Therefore when Tao is lost, there is goodness.
When goodness is lost, there is kindness.
When kindness is lost, there is justice.
When justice is lost, there is ritual.

Therefore the truly great man dwells on what is real
    and not what is on the surface,
On the fruit and not the flower.
Therefore accept the one and reject the other.

– Tao Te Ching

Contents

Preface to the first edition

The initial incentive for writing this book is the presence of students for a course entitled 'Persons and Values', a module of the degree in Humanities offered at the University of the West of England at Bristol. This solemn title may sound somewhat woolly, but the content of the course is quite down-to-earth, being effectively an introduction to applied philosophy, with particular reference to ethics. Over the twenty years of its life, the course has never covered the same ground twice, hence the amount of relevant available material has become, to put it mildly, extensive. If what follows seems therefore discursive, perhaps these details will explain why this is so. I am aware that 'to explain' sometimes means 'to explain away', and can only hope that this is not deemed to be the case here.

As will be noted by perusing the table of contents, the book falls into three main sections. In the first, the general philosophical issues of ethics are given an airing, though not, on the whole, by way of the delineations used by most modern writers on the subject (more of this in a moment).

In the second part, an examination is made of certain schools of philosophy in which moral theory and practice play an important role. I am conscious that the selection here will seem rather arbitrary: Aristotle and Spinoza, to name but two, merit a chapter to themselves, while some readers will think, with an element of justice, that Freud and Marx are scantily covered – a situation unlikely to please their devotees whichever way you look at it. But to be comprehensively comparative in this field would be to miss out on the book's purpose. For those whose appetites are whetted by the second section, there are many histories of ethics to explore, one of the best of which is mentioned in the text.

In the third section, I take up a number of issues which, while not falling directly under the umbrella of ethics, involve certain (to me) fundamental moral questions. They are issues with which any active, thinking person can hardly avoid getting involved, and they bring some of the earlier more theoretical considerations to a point where they must be applied in practice. Each of them, of course, merits a book to itself. All that can be hoped is that the central issues in each topic are touched on sensitively enough to reveal their basic importance within the framework of the book as a whole.

Each chapter ends with one or more case studies. Generally, these concern specific practical moral and/or social problems relating to some of the content of the foregoing chapter. Sometimes they call for an analysis of an issue, raised in the chapter, which would break the flow of the discussion if it were included in the text itself. The most rewarding way of tackling any of the case studies is in a group – whether of fellow-students, interested friends, or members of the family.

In some of the chapters, I have found it impossible to be totally neutral about my own perceptions of life, and the philosophy which has grown out of these. I know well that this is not the modus operandi normally adopted by writers in the field. My response to that (which may sound conceited but I don't think it is) is *tant pis*. Others may be able to write on the subject and remain totally impersonal but, as I perceive philosophy, this attitude would for me be unnatural. If, as I believe, it is the case that philosophy is a living, vibrant entity, the most sure basis for the appreciation of what is worthwhile in life, then it would be quite artificial, I think, for me to neutralise, if not neuter-ise, myself when discussing these issues.

While writing the book I have therefore borne continually in mind the students with whom I have discussed its contents over the years (many of whom may recognise contributions they have made from time to time in the course of seminar discussions). It is through such discussions, rather than by learned tomes and monographs, that philosophy at its best has always been taught, and learned, and – above all – done. If more of 'me' emerges from the ensuing discussions than normally occurs in philosophical discourses, then it must be simply accepted that this is how I conceive the whole of education to be – a process of person to person rather than brain to brain: and if philosophy, of all subjects, doesn't follow this path, there seems little hope elsewhere. This is not, of course, to say that the use of the intellect is not a central factor in such discussions, and I hope that, within the limits I have set myself, this book meets this requirement.

The book's aim is to arouse discussion of moral issues generally, not to bring about the conversion of anyone to a particular school of thought. In this process, I hope I have managed to avoid any casual use of technical philosophical jargon, and that where such words or phrases are used, they are explained either in the text or in the glossary of terms at the end. If I've slipped up on this, I offer my apologies. The reader I have in mind is one who has never before formally read philosophy. The catch-22 situation for such a person is that the majority of books on philosophy assume a certain philosophical awareness on the part of their readers. There are loads of books for second- and third-year students, and annotated tomes galore for those who have reached the research stage. My hope is that this book will be both readable and read not only by first-year students, but also by those mature people who recognise that education is an unending process and pursue this by means of evening and other extension classes; I hope it can be put into the hands of sixth-formers, together with any one else who seeks to use his spare time in broadening the mind as much as in being entertained. (Chapter 9 may be found to be specialist in its appeal, and may well be omitted by some readers.)

What 'living philosophy' means must vary from person to person. I think one common element (or, at least, one that is very widespread) is the ability to accept that it is given to us to understand only a tiny particle of the vast wisdom of the universe. Newton compared his knowledge in relation to that which is unknown as a pebble compared with the rest of the beach. Such humility is healthy, and is the beginning of understanding, both of oneself and of others. Too much of my life has been spent with people who think they have all the answers, and a leading role to play in instructing others in them. In my youth I shared this delusion, but now that I have become a man I have, I hope, put aside these childish notions. A certain acceptance of the frustrations of life seems wise in order to remain relatively sane; and if this can be vitalised with an element of humour, then one is further armed for the battle of coping with it all. John Calder, writing in 'The Guardian' about Samuel Beckett, stated, 'He gives the message that the established religions have all forgotten: that it is by courage to face reality that man achieves dignity; and his kindness to others can find a kind of nobility'. My feeling is that all the moral utterances and ethical tomes of centuries are epitomised in that sentiment. It expresses a living philosophy without which – or something like it – all ethical treatises are merely arid excursions into academia, and the study of the subject no more valuable than dissecting a frog's hindquarters.

Just as Beethoven communicates with people who can't read music, and just as Shakespeare's plays were written mainly for, and appreciated by, illiterate people, so philosophy is essentially an expression of the process whereby 'cor ad cor loquitur'. If philosophy loses this dimension it loses the ground of its being. It must live, or it is nothing.

My indebtedness to a host of writers will be evident in the text. There are others, too numerous to mention, with whom I have discussed most of the matters raised in the book, and with whom I have begun to unravel some of the mysteries. One person in particular needs my special thanks. My former colleague, Glyn Davies, taught alongside me on the 'Persons and Values' course for several years. In that time, I gained more than I can express, more, I imagine, than he is aware, from his own blend of philosophy. His influence is to be found at numerous points in this book in general, and, in particular, in some of the case studies; and the philosophy of experience outlined in the final chapter owes its origins in my mind to the years spent working with him. This book is partly his.

Ray Billington,
Bristol
July, 1986

Preface to the second edition

As Britain's greatest post-World War II prime minister, Harold Wilson, remarked: 'A week is a long time in politics.' Similarly, in the sphere of moral philosophy, five years (the time that has elapsed since *Living Philosophy* was first published) is an eternity. Since 1988, the world has been shattered by the AIDS virus; experiments on human embryos and the transplanting of human organs have ceased to be seven-day wonders; and the world generally has plummeted downhill into an abyss of such self-indulgent violence that it threatens to annihilate the entire human species. One wonders if there is anyone, anywhere, who can declare with sincerity, 'Things are better than they were.'

This revision can therefore be no more than interim: soon – sooner than most people expect – the issues discussed here will seem to be fiddling while Rome burns. Yet, we have to do *something* meantime; somehow or other we must at least make the attempt to understand each other and live side by side. The fact that this is all doomed to failure in the vast death of homo sapiens – the experiment that failed – seems no reason for ceasing to try to make it work.

So in this second edition, much of the material in the first edition has been updated, many case studies discarded as outdated, and about twenty new case studies introduced. Like those of the 1988 edition, I think they reflect what I claim to be the great positive factor of this book: like it or hate it, agree with its assessments or disagree with them, you will at least know precisely what it is you like or lump, accept or reject. But whether or not the issues will still be a matter of concern by the turn of the century is a matter for speculation: if they are, there may well be a further update around 2000. We shall see.

I had wished to make constant changes in the use of the male pronoun throughout this book, in order to accommodate it more to the (justifiable) sexual egalitarianism of our time. This has not been possible, so I hope that readers will bear with me on this matter, and take it as read that the one includes the other.

In the preparation of this second edition I gladly acknowledge the driving force of Avril Sadler. She, more than anyone else, has been the catalyst to stir me out of my lethargy.

Ray Billington
Bristol,
February, 1993

Section One

General theory of ethics

Chapter One

What is philosophy?

To state that you are a philosopher is to risk committing social suicide. When asked one's profession by a stranger, it is usually a conversation-stopper to affirm that one reads or teaches the subject. The image of the philosopher conjured up in many people's eyes is that of a dilettante, an exponent of ideas and ideals unrelated to the real facts of life; an occupier of an ivory tower giving unintelligible answers to insoluble problems.

Yet philosophy is probably the oldest academic discipline known to the human race; one which has occupied the minds of innumerable human beings since time immemorial. From Plato to Wittgenstein, from Aristotle to Russell, fundamental questions about our existence have been asked by philosophers. Why am I here? What is life's meaning or purpose? Is there an ultimate reality? What can I validly talk about? How am I to determine the difference between right and wrong? Much of the casual conversation in places where people talk comes round to such issues at one time or another.

Assuming, then, that one doesn't have to have two heads in order to qualify, and that one can be a relatively normal human being in the process (and normality, so far as human beings are concerned, is invariably relative), what exactly is one engaged in when studying philosophy? The word itself is, not surprisingly (since the subject took off with the Greeks of the classical period, 500–400 BC), of Greek origin. 'Philo' means to love, or like, and 'sophia' means wisdom. It would be no exaggeration to affirm that this etymological definition takes us little further forward. To declare oneself as a lover of wisdom is to do no more than assert one's support of rationality against prejudice, of experience against innocence, which is not saying much. But at least it gives us a clue, a hint, as to the meaning of the word. To study philosophy means that one is at least attempting to look a little more deeply into things than may normally be expected. It suggests that the student of the subject will not, as a rule, accept opinions or arguments only at their face value. He or she will look and reflect beyond the headlines of the daily newspaper, above the reverberations of the self-assured know-all, and will feel uneasy when encountering glib answers to complex questions. Instead, one will look for underlying attitudes which influence opinions, create points of view, and determine ideologies – which, in their own turn, may establish procedures. The philosopher will ask 'Why is this so?' when faced with an affirmation; 'are you sure?', when reacting to a wild statement; 'on what grounds do you go along with this?', when confronted with an attitude. For the philosopher, few points of view are likely to be totally cut and dried, right or wrong.

Of course, this does not mean that many philosophers have not made the claim to possessing 'ultimate truth'. On reading any history of philosophy one will be confronted with a series of men claiming that they have hit on this. Plato, for instance, was convinced that our human ideals reflect the 'forms' of heaven; Descartes was sure that reason conquers all – 'I reflect, therefore I am'; Kant affirmed the infallibility of the good will. However, in recent years, particularly in Britain and America, philosophers have concentrated their attention on the analysis of words and ideas; they have treated philosophy as more a tool than an end in itself. In the right hands, this tool is extremely useful: one of the best books on philosophy that I have read is written by John Hospers and entitled, rather forbiddingly, *Introduction to Philosophical Analysis*. In Hospers's hands the philosophical tool has a sharp edge; unfortunately, in others' it has been dulled, if not completely blunted: either that, or it has become as pedantic as did theology when the debate raged as to how many angels could stand on the head of a pin. As a result, many English readers of philosophy have, over the past forty or so years, felt themselves being dragooned into a narrow, arid approach to the subject, which, for a considerable number of them, has killed it off. In the light of this, it is not to be wondered at that philosophy has, in some circles, become a word to generate the suspicion that the philosopher has divorced himself from the world that people understand and are comfortable with, the world of relationships, of eating, working, and making love. The search for the philosopher's stone seems to have produced a number of petrified philosophers.

Philosophical analysis

Despite these lapses, the analytical process is a good place to start when attempting to describe what philosophy is about. It requires a person to look more deeply at the statements which people bandy about than is normally expected of him. There must be few people who are not willing, at a moment's notice, to give their opinions on any issue with which they are presented. It may be their view on the Government's handling of the economy, the merits of American football compared with other versions, or the rights of the trade unions under capitalism. Whatever the issue (or almost) the general public can be expected to hold forth with what sounds like conviction. Thus most of the British people, according to media reports, supported the Falklands venture; most believe that a spouse-poisoner, if not a dog-poisoner, should be hanged; ask anyone in a bar the answer to what is arguably the greatest social problem facing the Western world today, inner-city riots, and his answer is likely to be breathtaking in its simplicity.

So what does it mean to look more deeply into such matters? The first requirement is obvious, and needs no distinctive contribution from philosophy: that a person should take some trouble to ascertain the facts of a situation before venturing an opinion. This will not always be entirely possible, of course, but it should be enough to prevent the pub bore from mouthing headlines from his *Daily Bigot* as though he himself had actually done some thinking on the issues. Any expert in any field will expect this kind of self-discipline; what follows from it is peculiarly philosophical: acknowledging and identifying the difference between factual statements and value judgments, between truth, as far as this can be arrived at, and opinion. We shall return to this issue specifically in Chapter Three but a few initial remarks can be made at this stage.

Statements of fact are those that can be verified, in that they can be tested and shown to be either sound or unsound. Let me make a few factual statements. My pipe is large, compared with others of its genre (if you doubt this, I suggest we meet some time so that I can discover the extent of your willingness to give me a fill of tobacco). The trees in my garden are bare (fact) which is not surprising because it is the month of December (another fact, though not open to verification by you, the reader). Your spelling is good, bad, or somewhere in between, as the case may be: a simple test would quickly verify which is the case. Many, if not most, of our statements can be verified in one way or another. But, whatever proportion of the whole they may be, there remain numerous statements, which we all constantly make, of the type that cannot be verified: they cannot be divided into the categories 'true' or 'false'.

Suppose, for instance, I state that the Russian, or Marxist, interpretation of history is more valid than that of the Roman Catholic Church: on what basis can the 'truth' or otherwise of such a statement be tested? I have just read a newspaper article in which the author demonstrates, apparently to his own satisfaction, that there is a connection between violence depicted through the media and violence as expressed in real life: how would one set about proving this thesis? I am informed by a certain set of people that all abortions are wrong because they break the Commandment, 'Thou shalt not kill'. Other people, however, assure me equally vehemently that abortions are, and must remain by law, acceptable, because otherwise the woman loses her inalienable right to choose whether or not to continue with the pregnancy. By reference to what set of facts am I supposed to make up my mind on this matter?

The one certain fact about these issues and a million like them is that there are no verifiable facts which might enable us to make up our minds about them. Protagonists for any of these points of view may argue as

3

though there were such solid support for their case, but they are blinded by their strength of conviction. Thus those who oppose abortion on the grounds that it is a form of murder have unilaterally decided that the foetus is in fact a person, even if only a potential person. Their opponents, on the other hand, have decided that a potential person is in fact no more an actual person than a tadpole is a frog, a caterpillar a butterfly, or a fertilised egg a chicken. All these judgments, from whatever side, are not factual but value judgments, based on the understanding of each individual concerned as to which forms of human behaviour are most worthwhile, and which standards are most worth upholding. But all these judgments, admirable though we may often think them to be, and though often expressed with passion, conviction and sincerity, belong in the end not to the realm of hard fact but to that of, at best, belief, at worst, fantasy, with hope occupying the middle ground.

It is possible, then, to make certain statements which may be declared to be 'true'; the earth is round, the Pythagorus theorem is sound, light travels at a certain speed: but the words 'true' or 'false' can never be used when making evaluative statements. It is true that Reagan's term in the US presidency was longer than that of Carter; it is not true that he was a better (or worse) president, even if the majority of Americans think one (or other) is the case. Similarly, it is not true that football is a more manly game than tennis, that breeding animals for food or for their skins is wicked, that homosexuality is unnatural. Many people hold strong views on all these issues, but that does not make them true, since there exists no set of facts by reference to which they can be verified; and this situation is changed not one iota by strength of opinion, articulateness of expression or consistency of thought.

So one of the main tasks of the philosopher through the centuries has been to arbitrate within this confusion of provable and unprovable statements. In the process, he often seems to sit on the fence, to the despair, if not actual contempt, of many. But to expect him to come off his fence and provide his fellows with some kind of hierarchy of values in the form, say, of some latter-day Ten Commandments would be looking for him to exceed his role as a philosopher, and as inappropriate as demanding that a book critic should write a bestseller. The philosopher's task is to analyse statements, not to grade them; he is a teacher, not a preacher. His aim is to increase understanding and tolerance, and the realisation that these two are fellow travellers.

This aspect of philosophy is illustrated by the following conversation:

First philosopher: What do you mean?

Second philosopher: What do you mean, 'What do you mean?'?

This is a philosophical joke and therefore, like a German joke, is no laughing matter. The question, however, is basic. What do I mean when I call someone an imperialist, or a fascist, a reactionary, or simply immoral? Whatever is meant (and it may be no more than an expression of dislike for the person so addressed) an analysis of the words in relation to the person to whom they allegedly apply will almost certainly reveal that they are no more than an expression of my personal values, which to other people may seem to be merely prejudices.

Philosophy within other disciplines

The philosopher then extends this approach into other disciplines. This is not to say that he claims to make academic judgments relating to those disciplines. No philosopher of history, for example, would presume to have anything worthwhile to say, as a philosopher, about the causes of the civil wars in England or America. What he does claim is the right to bring into question the fundamental assumptions of any discipline, whether in theology, art, science, psychology, history, or elsewhere. The student of medicine, for instance, will be taught that his main concern must be to alleviate suffering and preserve life; and most of the general public expect this of their doctors. But the philosopher must pose the question, what should the doctor do, or recommend, when these two desirable aims are in conflict? This leads inevitably to a discussion about the rights and wrongs of euthanasia – an issue which is at the heart of at least one of the case studies presented in this book.

Philosophy of history

Let's have a closer look at the first example used, that of history. One of the basic assumptions in this discipline is that there is such a thing as a historical fact; without this assumption, it is hard to conceive how anyone could study the subject. But what is the nature of such a 'fact'? Is it the same as 'historical truth'? It may well be answered that it is a fact that a certain treaty was signed by certain dignitaries at a certain place on a certain date, and that it is the historian's job to be aware of this. Fine: but is this the stuff of which history is made? These, surely, are no more than the dry bones of the subject: what puts meat on them is the interpretation offered by the historian, the suggestion that event A, carefully chronicled, caused event B, influenced by event C – or not, as the case may be. The chronicles record individual events or incidences, but it is the historian who gives them 'meaning' by (to change the metaphor) weaving them into coherent pattern.

The trouble is that no two examples of such weaving seem to be using the same thread. I was brought up to believe that Richard III was as villainous as Shakespeare depicts him; yet my sense of security here has

5

been undermined by the tome of a recent historian entitled *Good King Richard*. This is just one vivid example of the variety of interpretations offered to the reader whenever historical problems are discussed – interpretations more varied than those of a symphony made by different conductors. What are the 'facts' about the origins of the Second World War? Was Roosevelt's New Deal in 1933 as altruistic in its conception as has generally been portrayed? (The answer to this one seems to depend on whether the historian is of the Democratic or Republican persuasion.)

A current problem should put this issue into full focus. Let us suppose that a number of historians were asked to write a history of Ireland from, say, 1914 to the present. How far do you think any two would agree on their interpretations of any events? Would we not have as many different accounts as there were writers? How could anyone arrive at the 'true' account? Is not a history book in the end rather similar to a daily newspaper: a choice of events made from an almost infinite range of possibilities, a blending of these events according to taste, and an assessment of the characters and motives of those involved as judged by the historian? If this is the case – and it seems axiomatic that it is so – can we set any more credence on a book of so-called historical fact than on one of historical fiction? Is the historian really a failed novelist?

A further assumption often made by students of history is that there is a kind of golden thread running through it, throwing into relief an element of progress; that, in the words of the Russian historian Nicolas Berdyaev, there is a 'meaning' to history. The philosopher will ask whether this is the case, and, if so, what that meaning is. If there is, to use out of context the words of Tennyson, 'one far-off divine event to which the whole creation moves', who can claim the right, and on what basis, to spell this out with authority? If, on the other hand, it is accepted that all that can be learned from history is that nothing can be learned from history, what then is the point of studying history – assuming that there needs to be a 'point' in studying anything?

Aesthetics

There is no distinctive name for the philosophy of history, but philosophy of art has been debated so extensively over the centuries that it has acquired its own nomenclature: aesthetics, a word that relates to art in all its forms – painting, music, literature, sculpture, and so on. The phrase 'work of art' is glibly bandied about, but what quality must a painting, or novel, or musical composition, or whatever, possess in order to merit that distinction? The judgment cannot be left to the artist alone, since he is often the worst critic of his work. Browning wrote a good deal of doggerel as well as poetry (try reading 'Sordello' if you doubt this); Shakespeare, especially in some of his history plays, could be boring; and who listens to half of Haydn's 104 symphonies? (Even as a boy I learned the hard way about the unreliability of self-appreciation when a painting of a sunset, on which I had spent hours of loving effort, was exhibited in the classroom over the title, *A Poached Egg*. This lack of appreciation of my work by the public terminated my artistic career.)

Are the public, then, to be accepted as arbiters of artistic merit, with popularity the supreme test? If so, the greatest painting in the world must be the one gracing the most living-room walls – Trechikov's *Green Chinese Lady*: all the sales of Leonardo, Michelangelo, and Rembrandt combined cannot outnumber this; by the same standard, Paul McCartney emerges as the greatest composer of all time. But public tastes vary, and change: today's treasure may be tomorrow's trash, and vice versa. At his death, G. M. Hopkins was viewed as a minor poet: today he ranks with Tennyson, Browning, and Arnold. Until Mendelssohn rediscovered his works in the nineteenth century, Bach's composition went virtually ignored by the musical public for over a century. And the number of so-called artists, lionised in their time, who are now in oblivion (perhaps waiting to be rediscovered?) is legion. Where generations differ so radically in their assessments, who is to say which has got it right?

Does art require a message, seriousness of purpose? What place would there then be in the artistic hierarchy for the poems of Edward Lear, the music of the Beatles, or even Shakespeare's *Much Ado About Nothing*? What is the role of the expert or critic in any field? If their word had been final, we should not be hearing Beethoven's Seventh Symphony or even, perhaps, Mozart's *Magic Flute*. If seriousness of purpose is to be a major element when assessing what is a work of art, could this bring into the reckoning structures designed for practical use, with a pragmatic purpose? Is the Golden Gate Bridge a work of art?

Philosophy in other fields

Examples of a similar method of enquiry in other disciplines may be briefly mentioned. Two of the main issues in *science* concern laws of nature and the scientist's modus operandi. What is a law of nature? By the sound of it, this must be immutable, unchangeable and unchanging. For centuries it was considered a law of nature that the earth was the centre of the universe; that it was flat, and constituted one of several tiers (three, in Hebraic thought, many more in Indian teachings). Few of us, with our post-Renaissance knowledge, can appreciate how devastating to the general sense of security were the revelations of Copernicus and Galileo, which relegated the earth to the status of a minor planet orbiting a minor star in a mighty universe. Even the claim of homo sapiens to be the crown of all creation became open to doubt. Some people still sing of a Friend 'above the bright blue sky', and affirm their belief in one who 'ascended into heaven': but the words reflect a long-outdated 'law of

7

nature'. How many other so-called laws await similar abandonment? After Einstein and in an age of theoretical physics, can any law of nature be treated as more than a rule of thumb, due to be made redundant as knowledge increases?

According to one philosopher of science, Karl Popper, this is precisely the role of the scientist. In his book, *Conjectures and Refutations*, he argued that scientific procedure is that of devising theories and attempting to disprove them. Indeed, unless they be proved or disproved – that is, unless they are verifiable – he refused to honour laws or theories with the title 'scientific'. Popper's main concern was to expose what he termed 'pseudosciences' which are unverifiable, such as the Marxist claim to have a scientific interpretation of history, or the acceptance of psychoanalysis as a science. Another philosopher of science, Kuhn, acknowledged more than Popper that most scientific research is far removed from such grandiose schemes, focussing itself, as it does, on an infinitesimally narrow problem within a subsidiary part of a sub-section of one of science's many strata. But Popper's proposal seems no less apposite in the narrower than in the broader issues; in fact, to the layman these more limited areas of research seem more conducive to the Popperian method than, for example, the law of gravity and the laws of motion as enunciated by Newton.

In the field of *psychology*, the philosopher raises questions about the theory of the person. Who or what is this self of which I am aware during my waking moments? Is my personal identity consistent and continuous, or is it possible for me to have more than one identity, or to have an identity only intermittently? What image do I hold of myself, and how far is this, or can it be, an accurate perception? In *vocational fields* the philosopher's interest may well centre on the accepted priorities within those vocations. The civil engineer will be asked to reflect on whether the creation of a new airstrip justifies the destruction of a large number of a threatened species of birds: the student of business, whether the profit motive should outweigh all other considerations in business activity: is it right or wrong to covet one's neighbour's customers? By studying jurisprudence, the lawyer will be urged, among many other issues, to ask himself whether the law should be made for man or man for the law. Would it ever be moral to break the law?

Philosophy of religion is generally discussed under the title of metaphysics, but mention should be made here of the issue of religious language. It is (and has for thousands of years been) the case that theologians and philosophers often come into conflict with each other about the literalness of the words and affirmations made in a religious context. How, for instance, (using the Christian religion as a case study) can the phrase 'God the Father' be interpreted in any way other than figuratively or symbolically? To affirm that the fatherhood of God is literally true is, so the philosopher observes, as absurd as the statement that it is 'literally raining cats and dogs'. For anyone to become a father in the literal sense requires that his sperm, at some stage, must have been shed. Since none of the Christian creeds, quite understandably, makes such an affirmation about God, it follows that the only conceivable interpretation of God's Fatherhood, like that of Jesus as 'the only-begotten Son of the Father', is symbolic. The same must also be the case with many other clauses in the Christian creeds, such as the Ascension (already mentioned), the resurrection, and the concept of a 'spiritual body' which is, literally, a contradiction in terms, even assuming that there can be any consensus as to the meaning of the word 'spiritual'.

A discussion of this nature illustrates an area of enquiry which has dominated western philosophy for half a century: the *philosophy of language* – sustained, if not pioneered, by a brooding genius, Ludwig Wittgenstein (1889–1951). What is the relationship between the words we use and the things, the feelings, the ideas, the values with which they are connected? How do groups of words – phrases or sentences – gain their meaning, and how can one arrive at a 'true' definition of a word? (How do you define the word 'red' to a sighted, let alone a blind, person?) In this field, under the influence of the so-called Logical Positivists in the early 1930s, an extreme stage was reached when it was affirmed that one could speak philosophically only of those aspects of life which could be tested and measured. Thus, effectively, it was deemed impossible to discuss such matters as ethics, religion, politics or aesthetics, since these involve the use of words like 'right', 'wrong', 'beauty', 'ugliness', 'spiritual', 'soul', 'democracy', 'progressive', and so on – all elusive terms which cannot be nailed down. 'Whereof we cannot speak,' wrote Wittgenstein in his earlier work, the *Tractatus Logico-Philosophicus*, (though he later modified this view) 'thereof let us be silent'. Since then, many philosophers have taken a less extreme stance, acknowledging that with a large number of the issues we discuss there must be a certain element of vagueness. (Try giving an accurate, comprehensive definition of the apparently straightforward word 'inhabitant'; then, if you can, consult the Hospers book already referred to and check whether you have recognised all the difficulties involved. Hospers discusses it under 'Vagueness' in his chapter on 'Philosophy of Language'.)

In all these, and other fields of enquiry, the philosophical approach is that of exploring unwritten assumptions, unquestioned values, and an uncritical acceptance of terms of reference. The philosopher works not to destroy but to bring about increased understanding and, if it is not too pretentious a term, enlightenment. Though this is never likely to be wholly achieved, and though in the process it will seem to some that he is being hyper-fastidious in his questions (illustrated in not a few music-hall sketches) he will be justifying his existence if he helps to keep others on their toes by challenging any glib generalisations.

THE PHILOSOPHER'S FIELD

Are there then no areas of enquiry which belong to philosophy *per se?* There are philosophers who contend that this is so, and that the concerns so far mentioned sum up the philosopher's role. It is certainly the case that when philosophy reached its first peak in the Western world around the fifth century BC – the time of Socrates, Plato, and Aristotle – the word embraced the entire known curriculum. Study of philosophy then included the sciences, mathematics, geometry, jurisprudence, astronomy, history, and so on. Since then, most of these subjects have, so to speak, fled the nest and become discrete areas of enquiry in their own right, so that our universities and colleges have faculties of science, mathematics, law, humanities, geography, and a host of others.

But to state that there are no fields remaining which the philosopher can properly call his own seems both pusillanimous and, in fact, wrong. There appear to me to be two groups of material which belong nowhere else but in the philosophical field and reflect what I believe to be two of the, if not the two, basic elements of the human being: every person is, on the one hand, a thinking, enquiring animal, asking the question 'why?', and, on the other, a social animal, involved with other people, needing to make decisions about behaviour, relationships, priorities in the use of time and energy, and therefore asking the question 'how?' or 'what?'.

Epistemology

The first of these elements, asking the question 'why?', is reflected in the study of epistemology, metaphysics, and (though this is often taught in faculties of mathematics) logic. Epistemology, or the theory of knowledge, concerns itself, as its name suggests, with the question of what it is to know something. To the non-philosophically-minded this may seem to be spending precious time on the pursuit of the obvious. Surely, it will be argued, I either know something or I don't. If I enter a general knowledge quiz, I can either answer the question or I cannot. (I may have forgotten the answer, but that is just a matter of recall.) So far as demonstrable matters of fact are concerned, this point of view is reasonable and undeniable; and the significant point about questions asked in a quiz is that their answers can be found in an encyclopaedia or dictionary. But there remain many issues about which people claim to have knowledge which cannot be verified in this way.

Consider the following two groups of statements.

(1) 'I know that California is on the west coast of the United States.'
  'I know that water at sea level boils at 100 degrees centigrade.'
  'I know that the speed of sound is 762 mph.'
  'I know that when a solid is weighed in air and in a liquid, the

apparent loss in weight is equal to the weight of the liquid displaced by the solid.'

(2) 'I know the sun will rise tomorrow.'
'I know that creatures exist in outer space.'
'I know my wife loves me.'
'I know that inanimate objects remain in a building when there is no human being around to perceive them.'
'I know my dead uncle still counsels me whenever I have problems.'
'I know that Jesus is alive today: he spoke to me in my car this morning.'

(Both the last two statements have been made to me personally.)

It is clear that there are two categories of statement here, and that the status of the verb 'to know' differs in each. The student here will be expected not only to identify the different statuses, but also to tackle more subtle issues, such as the 'truth' of the statement about creatures in outer space if this is not verified until many years after it was made. Think about it.

We thus return to the problem of verification. How, and on what basis, does one test the accuracy of one's assertions? The question of individual *perception* is important here, because it is far from clear how much credence can be put on data conveyed by the senses. I describe the pen with which I wrote the first draft of this book as maroon-coloured, and with this all but the colour-blind will no doubt agree. But it appears maroon only because I was using it in natural daylight; under certain lights used by one of my sons when he runs a disco it will appear quite different in colour; and at night time different again. Which is the 'true' colour of the pen? Further: even though people may agree about these apparent changes in colour, how can I be sure that the sense of maroonness, or whatever, which they get from looking at the pen is the same as that which my brain receives? How can I even be sure that your toothache feels like mine? I know that I am not a robot, but how can you, or anyone else, be certain of this, or I of the rest of the human race? We all of us take so much, physically and mentally, for granted which for normal purposes will suffice. But many issues sometimes need to be carefully analysed and explored, if only to remind ourselves that things are not always as they seem. If that were the case most of us would declare the earth to be flat.

Metaphysics

This debate leads to the vexed problem of the relationship between the mind and the brain, and links epistemology with metaphysics, the question of whether there is an entity in life besides the physical, or material. Is the mind simply the brain viewed from a different perspective, or is it, as Plato, for instance, believed, a distinct and separate entity? Have we sure grounds for accepting a dualistic view of the person: an indestructible self associated in some way with a decaying mortal body, the 'odd little traveller, fellow guest' as described in Hadrian's poem on the soul? Is the universe constituted of a single component, matter, or does it also contain a second component, loosely termed 'spirit'? Many people throughout history and in present times have believed and do believe in a God of some sort; is this belief, which has been highly influential in shaping many people's lives and decisions, defensible philosophically? The study of metaphysics will include a discussion of the three 'classical' arguments for God's existence: the cosmological, the ontological, and the teleological, or, otherwise expressed, the arguments from causality, by definition, and from design. (We look briefly at Kant's moral argument in Chapter Five.) The whole issue of whether life is teleological, that is, purposive or meaningful, falls into this area of study, and this is often linked with the idea of an afterlife – an idea as old as philosophy itself.

All these metaphysical questions link up with the theory of knowledge over the question of the difference between knowledge and firm belief. Many of the world's most praiseworthy deeds have been performed, not on the basis of sure knowledge, but on that of belief. This is true of the voyage of Columbus, the conquest of Everest, the discovery of radium, and Lincoln's attaining the American Presidency. It would therefore be short-sighted, if not absurd, for the philosopher to ignore any consideration of the nature of belief.

Logic

All these and many more enquiries will be given a firmer basis through the study of logic which, as mentioned earlier, is a discipline in its own right, though often taught in departments of philosophy. It is important that any student should develop consistency in argument and be able to structure his ideas so as to be able to recognise the difference between arguments which are both valid and sound, valid but not sound, and neither valid nor sound. He will learn the distinction between deductive and inductive reasoning, and in general should discover that the process of studying logic, whether symbolic or philosophical, will train the mind as exercise trains the body. In a world dominated by people who, if their bodies were as their minds, would be fat and flabby, a mind trained to distinguish between sound reasoning on the one hand and emotive arguments, special pleading, and downright deception on the other, should not be underestimated, even if the process of acquiring it may sometimes be painful.

So much, then, for some of the issues discussed by philosophers in answer to the question 'why?'. The rest of this book, however, is concerned with the other aspect of the human being mentioned earlier: the maker of decisions. People inevitably involve themselves with others, and the process often results in complexities within the relationships so created. Decisions have to be made about right and wrong behaviour, about which human characteristics are most worth encouraging and developing, and which moral and social priorities should be upheld. The study of all this is termed Ethics, or Moral Philosophy.

There is of course much more to philosophy than can even be hinted at in so short a summary as this. Enough, I hope, has been said to indicate why it still remains an area of study pursued by many, whether formally students or otherwise. It would be no exaggeration to state that anyone who asks questions which involve a closer analysis of ideas, attitudes, and behaviour than is undertaken in the general run of things is a philosopher of sorts. One doesn't need to be odd to be a philosopher. Some of the great philosophers of the past may have fitted that description, perhaps because they were a little divorced from the world around them. But Spinoza was a lens polisher, Locke a medical doctor, and J. S. Mill worked for the East India Company, was for a time an MP, and active in social reform. From this century we may contrast the eccentric and world-denying Wittgenstein with the extrovert Russell, involved throughout his long life in political action, first President of the Campaign for Nuclear Disarmament, and even in his eighties the bane of many policemen with their Black Marias.

It was Russell who wrote of philosophy:

> Philosophy is to be studied, not for the sake of any definite answers to its questions, since no definite answers can, as a rule, be known to be true, but rather for the sake of the questions themselves; because these questions enlarge our conception of what is possible, enrich our intellectual imagination, and diminish the dogmatic assurance which closes the mind against speculation; but above all because, through the greatness of the universe which philosophy contemplates, the mind also is rendered great, and becomes capable of that union with the universe which constitutes its highest good.

This is the last paragraph of his book *The Problems of Philosophy* which I was fortunate to find on my father's bookshelves when I was seventeen. Reading it meant giving my life a direction which it may not have otherwise taken. It is a direction I have been glad to follow, since the path has been well trodden by men of the calibre of Plato and Aristotle, Descartes and Kant, Wittgenstein and Russell. The writings of these men will not be studied directly in this book, but every sentence owes a debt to them and to their fellows. With their backs to stand on, one ought to be able to see at least a little way beyond the nearest molehill.

CASE STUDY 1: TOLERANCE: WHERE DO YOU DRAW THE LINE?

Following are a series of sets of statements, each set relating to one particular moral or social issue. Each statement is (it is hoped: you may disagree!) a little more adventurous/daring/liberal than the preceding. The purpose of the exercise is for you to test your tolerance threshold: where do you draw the line? You may, if you wish, award yourself a mark for every step you are prepared to take so that the higher your final total, the more tolerant you may consider yourself to be. (You may wish to switch the order of some of the statements: if so, ask yourself why you make this judgment.) Be as honest with yourself as you can, and then see how you compare with others willing to test themselves with the same statements.

1 (a) Parents teach their children political or religious views which are almost universally condemned in their society.
  (b) Parents tell their children that it's all right to go shop-lifting, travel without paying the fare, fiddle tax, and dodge the TV licence.
  (c) Parents 'discipline' their children by beating them.
  (d) Parents allow children of 12–13 to watch 'video nasties', drink, and go to places where they are likely to become promiscuous and take drugs.
  (e) Parents neglect to feed and clothe their children adequately.

2 (a) A public library has books by Marx, Lenin, and Trotsky.
  (b) A trade union leader tells his members: 'The time has come to sweep away the institutions of capitalist society'.
  (c) A socialist school teacher tells his class: 'As members of the working class you should fight against the oppressive rules of the bourgeoisie'.
  (d) A left-wing paper organises a fund to finance a revolution in the Persian Gulf.
  (e) A Marxist splinter group trains its members in the techniques of revolutionary violence.

3 (a) A religious sect which proclaims that the world will end next Saturday.
  (b) A religious sect which specialises in preaching to lonely old

women that their only chance of salvation is to give all their money to the sect's leader.

   (c) A religion which practises polygamy.

   (d) A religious sect which demands that its members separate from unbelieving relatives.

   (e) A religious sect which bans blood transfusions.

4 (a) Your local authority leases a school hall to a racist group.

   (b) A professor of psychology publicises evidence purporting to show that some races are by nature inferior to others in intelligence.

   (c) A newspaper article is headed: 'Why Race Killings Mount: the Case for Repatriation'.

   (d) A speaker urges his audience to 'take to the streets and protect yourselves against the menace of the black invasion'.

   (e) A prominent historian assures German audiences that descriptions of the holocaust have been grossly exaggerated.

5 (a) Someone calls you a fool.

   (b) Someone writes a letter to a newspaper accusing you of 'incompetence and near-criminal stupidity'.

   (c) Someone writes an anonymous letter to your employer telling him (truthfully) that you were once a mental patient.

   (d) A television news programme distorts your actions in such a way as to make you seem ridiculous and irresponsible.

   (e) A biographer tells your life story with a string of inaccuracies, insinuations, unfavourable judgments, and malicious fabrications.

6 (a) A baby, grossly handicapped physically and mentally, is allowed to die.

   (b) An elderly person, terminally ill with inoperable cancer, is allowed to die.

   (c) You kill an intruder who is about to violate the person you love.

   (d) The 'Mr Big' who runs the drug distribution in your area is shot dead by the police.

   (e) An internationally-feared dictator is killed by hired assassins.

7 (a) You are encouraged to use a virtually foolproof tax fiddle.

   (b) You find a purse containing £100 in cash and decide to keep it.

   (c) You keep excess change given you at a supermarket/local shop.

   (d) Without incurring any risk, you falsify your claims for expenses.

   (e) You use your firm's phone, stationery, pens, etc., for strictly private activities.

8 (a) Your local newsagent sells girlie magazines.
   (b) A local council-owned sauna allows mixed sessions.
   (c) A cinema club opens near you, showing uncensored sex films.
   (d) You are offered £1000 to pose for *Playboy/Playgirl* magazine.
   (e) The council proposes to legalise a brothel in your area.

9 (a) A film depicting horrific post-nuclear war scenes is shown on
        TV.
   (b) Bloody scenes of killing and mutilating in the Middle East
        conflict are shown on TV news.
   (c) Films depicting gang muggings, murder, and rape are shown
        on TV.
   (d) The same films are made available at your local video-hire
        shop.
   (e) The government proposes to introduce public executions for
        crimes of terrorism.

10 (a) Two 14-year-olds make love.
   (b) A 15-year-old boy makes love to a 13-year-old girl.
   (c) Two mentally subnormal 14-year-olds make love.
   (d) A 60-year-old man makes love to a 13-year-old girl.
   (e) A magazine carries an advert: '60-year-old man wants teenage
        girl for sex fun'.

CASE STUDY 2: THE BEST AND THE GOOD

There is a well-known dictum, or ditty, which must have been written by
a multitude of well-meaning uncles and aunts in a host of children's
autograph books: 'Good, better, best, Never let it rest, Till your good is
better, And your better, best.' Many people probably get through life
without ever challenging the truth of this saying. But it was challenged
by the philosopher Aristotle (384–322 BC) in his *Nichomachean Ethics*, in
which he stated, 'The best is the enemy of the good'. This may at first
sound a strange if not insidious, remark, but he had in mind those people
– perfectionists, as we'd call them today – for whom only the highest
standard in any area is acceptable: students who are almost suicidal if
their essays are marked lower than the top grade; people – both men and
women – who are ill at ease if there is a single item out of place in their
home. For such people, a situation which is really quite satisfactory is
viewed as little short of disastrous simply because it is capable of being
improved on. In order to counteract this attitude, one old lady (the
author's mother) stuck a card on her kitchen wall bearing the following
inscription: 'This house is clean enough to be healthy and dirty enough
to be comfortable.'

Discuss this as a general philosophy of life. Even if we don't go so far as to modify another well-known saying into 'If a job's worth doing, it's worth doing badly', would we, do you think, be happier as a species if we could find contentment in what is 'good enough' without always striving after perfection? What are the implications of this idea for those religions which present an ideal person as a central feature of their belief system? Would we be happier if we lived by the code: 'Never do today what can be left till tomorrow'?

'To know all makes one tolerant' – Mme de Stael
Would an equivalent of this statement be: 'If you haven't tried it, don't knock it'? How, then, do you react to that?

Chapter Two

The scope of ethics

Ethics is one of the central concerns of philosophy; but what exactly are we doing when studying it? What is its essential nature?

ETHICS AND MORALS

It is important at the outset to distinguish between ethics and morals. In common speech they are often used interchangeably, but in philosophy they have different connotations. Put briefly, ethics means the *theory* of right and wrong conduct; morals, its *practice*. It is more accurate to speak of ethical, rather than moral, principles; and of a moral, rather than ethical, way of behaviour. Ethics involves the values that a person seeks to express in a certain situation; morals, the way he sets about achieving this. Ethics takes the overall view; our morals bring us, so to speak, to the coal-face, where we are involved in the minutiae of behaviour.

It will not be difficult to think up many examples in daily usage which contradict this definition: people use the phrase 'moral principles', or 'ethical conduct'. But as a rule of thumb it should prove helpful when discussing the issues raised in this book, and I express the hope that consistency on this matter will be maintained. One can speak of medical ethics, but hardly of medical morals: here one would speak of a doctor's morals. Medical ethics concerns the general principles, such as the alleviation of suffering, which the profession tries, or should try, to observe; a doctor's morals refer to his own personal behaviour, and are more the concern of his friends and neighbours than of his patients. (A popular concept is that a person's morals mean primarily, if not exclusively, his sexual behaviour: while such behaviour is, of course, included in this area, it is only one of the countless number of issues which are relevantly involved.)

The use of the negatives of the two words may help to clarify the distinction. Industrial espionage may be described as 'unethical' because it destroys any trust between two companies: it is a matter of business ethics. On the other hand, a man who lets another person go to prison for a crime committed by himself would be adding a further act of immorality to that of the crime itself.

It may be noted in passing that there is a further opposite to the word moral: amoral. The difference between the two opposites is that while 'immoral' means 'not observing a particular known moral rule', 'amoral' means 'not relevant to, or concerned with, morals'. One would not call a dog immoral for fouling a pavement (though one might so describe its owner if no steps were taken to prevent this), nor an infant for throwing his food on the floor. Only when they understand the difference between right and wrong behaviour can people be judged immoral. Thus the psychopath who does not understand this difference must be described as amoral rather than immoral.

Ethics, then, could be said to relate to morals as aims to objectives. A youth leader may state that his objective with a group of young people is to get them up a particular mountain; but his aim is to develop autonomy and self-confidence in them. So ethics is concerned with the principles of human behaviour, morals with the application of these principles in a particular situation.

THE DISTINCTIVENESS OF ETHICAL AND MORAL QUESTIONS

We must now turn to a consideration of the distinctive nature, assuming there is such, of these issues. In what way are they different from those raised within other disciplines, such as literature, or science?

(a) The first difference is that *nobody can avoid them*. It is possible, however unlikely or undesirable, to get through life without making any kind of literary judgment: never to reflect on who is one's favourite author, or to consider the relative merits of, say, Agatha Christie and Edgar Allan Poe. Equally, one can proceed quite amicably along life's highway without worrying about the age of the solar system, the causes of cancer, or how a car engine or television set works. One can experience an apparently full and satisfying life while still being illiterate or innumerate, knowing nothing about history and (like a student of mine in California who had never even heard of the Atlantic Ocean but seemed nonetheless perpetually radiant) even less about geography.

All of these issues we can avoid, along with many others; but nobody can get through life without ethics, even if he doesn't know the meaning of the word. Consciously or unconsciously all of us are every day making moral decisions. Unless we are hermits (and even to become a hermit means making a moral decision) we meet other people: some we like, some we dislike, while about many we know little and so have no opinion. All of them, however, impose themselves on our lives to a greater or lesser extent, even if it is only by poking an elbow in our ribs on the underground. This means that we have to decide how to deal with them – whether to be friendly, or indifferent, or antipathetic towards them. How we speak to them will affect them; even a glance can mar or enhance another person's day. Whether we are aware of it or not, the fact is that we do have ethical attitudes and are taking moral stances every day of our lives. We can live without Shakespeare, or bacon, or the radio: we cannot live without other people. Even Robinson Crusoe on his desert island used tools made by others and knowledge received via others (see (e) below).

(b) This leads us to the second distinguishing factor about morals: *other people are, however remotely, involved in these decisions.* There is no such thing as private morality.

About most moral issues this is self-evident. The acts of lying, or stealing, or trafficking in drugs clearly involve others; so also does the attitude one takes towards the neighbours, donating to charity, or providing contraceptives to minors (see Case Study 5). But the same is true even about matters which, on the surface, seem to be of concern only to the individual agent. Let us take the example of smoking. Obviously, if I smoke in a public place I will affect others: they receive my tobacco smoke at second-hand and some are offended by this. But suppose I decide to smoke only in my shed, which serves as my study and into which nobody else is ever compelled to enter? Is this not then a totally private matter?

It is certainly more a private matter than is the habit of smoking in public; but I am still taking the risk of contracting lung cancer (or, in the case of my pipe, tongue or lip cancer); and this means that I am taking the risk of depriving others, for better or for worse, of my existence. Even if it could be proved that pipe-smoking is not injurious to health, this decision must still involve me – again, for better or for worse – in denying others of my company; in addition, I would still be paying out money on tobacco which could be spent in ways that would generally be considered more deserving. Even such apparently minor issues, morally speaking, as watching television instead of doing a chore, or buying a more expensive car than was originally planned, cannot be conducted in a vacuum. Whenever priorities have to be established regarding the use of one's time, abilities, or possessions, others, however remotely, will be affected.

(c) It follows from this that *moral decisions matter*: they affect the lives, the self-esteem, the happiness of others. This factor is shared by ethics with scientific, and, specifically, medical research. It matters to all of us that doctors and surgeons understand our ailments and can provide the remedies for them. Similarly, it matters that teachers understand the process in which they are engaged; few parents would be happy to discover that their children's teachers' chief aim was the dissemination of a certain religious or political viewpoint rather than the enhancement of learning. But in these other fields there are numerous factors which do not matter. It is, for example, of no concern to me whether my doctor prescribes one form of antibiotic rather than another, or that my children are taught French primarily in a language laboratory rather than through classroom interaction. In both these cases it is the end products – the recovery from illness, or the ability to speak a foreign language – which are the important issues. *The difference with ethics and morals is that everything we do matters because everything we do is capable of affecting other people's lives.*

Let us pursue this a little further. All of us are repelled, if not angered, by certain attitudes and qualities in other people. But what kind of attitudes or qualities? Can you imagine yourself refusing to speak again to a friend because he considered Hardy, rather than Dickens or Eliot, to be the greatest British nineteenth-century novelist? What sort of family would it be who divided over differences about the 'big bang' and 'steady state' theories concerning the origin of the universe? Have any life-long feuds been caused over disagreements about the strengths and weaknesses of action painting? Did any person ever refuse to speak again to another because one believed that St Paul's prison letters were written from Ephesus, the other, from Rome? Anyone who behaved like this would, quite literally, need his head examining.

Now switch the area of debate to moral issues and the difference becomes clear. I would not knowingly allow into my house either a drug pedlar or a supporter of apartheid in South Africa. Two sisters of my acquaintance ignored each other for twenty years – though they both lived in the same street – because of a difference of opinion over the character of their elder brother. There are people in a mining village in Wales today who do not speak to their next-door neighbours because they are grandchildren of 'scabs' in the miners' strike of 1926. These attitudes may be adjudged by some to be immature; but where ethical issues are involved, differences of opinion can cause divisions between people so deep that not even time can heal them.

(d) A fourth factor about these issues is one which helps to explain the intensity with which they are often discussed: *there can never be a final solution in this field.* We may debate the merits of capital punishment, nuclear disarmament or euthanasia until doomsday, but we shall never reach a definitive conclusion. Perhaps this is one reason why the philosopher is suspect to many members of the general public, who expect answers to their deepest, most searching questions. They look to ministers of religion for comfort in the presence of death, to doctors for the cure of disease, to lawyers when in legal trouble, and to social workers when facing family disorders. All these specialists make positive affirmations, even if they are sometimes wrong. What affirmations does the moral philosopher make? After all, he too faces searching questions. Is abortion morally acceptable? Should the smoking of pot be legalised?

Should animals be bred for slaughter? Is adultery always wrong? Questions like these could fill a book, but the philosopher's reply to them must be equivocal: perhaps yes, perhaps no, yes and no, neither yes nor no, maybe . . .. His training will lead him not to make an *ex cathedra* adjudication on these issues, but to outline the principles involved where there is a moral dilemma, and to emphasise the need to be sure of the relevant facts of the situation: without facts there can be only prejudice. The individual concerned must then act in the way he thinks right. (If moral philosophers were called out on strike, the cause would be settled long before they had concluded their debate on the ethics of striking.)

All this may (and, in fact, does) cause many people to be irritated with philosophers. For learned people to discuss the day-to-day issues which create human problems, yet apparently remain aloof, may well exasperate those seeking an answer. What we must accept is that this is how it is in philosophy. Speaking as a human being, as my friends know to their cost, I have opinions about almost every subject under the sun, and argue the case for them whenever the opportunity arises. Speaking as a philosopher, however, I can indicate only the rights and wrongs of both sides of an issue; and this remains the case even when discussing such apparently cut-and-dried matters as the Ku Klux Klan, the morality of war, the standpoint of the neo-fascists, or the use of assassination as a political weapon. None of these can be simply graded 'right' or 'wrong', as though one were marking a piece of French prose translation, or assessing a project on the circulation of blood.

Any criticisms of the moral philosopher on the grounds of his apparent pusillanimity, or lack of the courage of his convictions, should, however, be tempered by the realisation that he is not alone in his unwillingness or inability to come off the fence. The same is true in other fields: no literary expert can prove that Milton was a better poet than Donne; no historian that the Marxist interpretation of history is right; no physicist that the lineal view of time is wrong; no theologian that God exists. When you think about it, would it really be preferable that the situation were otherwise? In a world in which every one of its four billion inhabitants has a different experience of life, do we really desire a 'final solution' to any of these matters? Some of history's most dangerous people have been those appearing to have no shadow of a doubt about what is good or bad, right or wrong. (See Case Study 10, What is 'truth'?, p. 63.)

(e) The fifth distinctive feature of moral questions relates to the issue of choice: *without choice*, as we shall see further in Chapters 9 and 10, *morality cannot be involved*. Here the main contrast to moral theory is that of science, where choice of opinion exists only in those areas where fuller knowledge has not yet been attained. (This is not to state that any law, however long established, will ever be held by the scientist to be beyond modification, but there are laws which have been tested so often that, for all practical purposes, their viability is not challenged. No scientist experiments merely on the 'probability' that gravity still operates, or that hydrochloric acid can still be attained from a mixture of salt and sulphuric acid.)

Choice, then, is an element in any situation which the scientist must always be seeking to eliminate. In morals, choice is both essential and unavoidable; *where no choice exists, no moral judgment can be made, and where it does exist, it cannot be escaped from.*

Examples abound of people who, under extreme duress, behaved in ways which would normally have been condemned by society, but were exonerated because of the compulsion involved in their situations. The mother who smothered her baby rather than let it be tortured to death by the Gestapo was not afterwards charged with infanticide. The survivors of an air crash at high altitude who ate their dead companions in order to remain alive were not accused of cannibalism. The total abstainer from alcohol who is dying of thirst would not be held morally blameworthy if he broke his vow because the only liquid available to him was alcoholic. Nobody who is given no choice as to how he behaves can be criticised on moral grounds.

But here we must pause, and I ask you to look again at the three examples just given. All the events, whether actual or hypothetical, took place under 'compulsion': there was, allegedly, no choice. But was this really the case? The mother *could* have chosen to take her own life rather than her baby's, the crash survivors to die rather than eat their dead companions, the abstainer to maintain his abstinence to the death. After all, devout Jehovah's Witnesses refuse, on religious grounds, to accept blood transfusions either for themselves or for their children, even when this is the only way of saving their lives. Is there not still a choice, even under duress? How compelling is compulsion? Adolf Eichmann, Commandant of an extermination camp for Jews, made the defence at his trial that what he did was under Hitler's orders, and that he would have been shot for refusing to act as he did. His judges decided that that was a choice which had remained for him; and Eichmann was hanged.

Of course, it is, fortunately, not every day that we face such grave issues as these (no pun intended). The question remains, however, as to how far 'compulsion' is a legitimate excuse for behaviour which would otherwise be condemned. The 'professional foul' at football is defended on the grounds that the perpetrator 'has no choice'; but he does have a choice: he can accept the fact that his opponent has won the ball and is likely to score a goal. The workman who joins a union because otherwise he will be cold-shouldered by his colleagues, or doesn't join a union because otherwise his boss will sack him, may argue that he, too, has no choice; but he could choose to work in discomfort, or to be unemployed, rather than do what he, for the sake of the argument, feels to be wrong. The point here is not whether or not he is justified in his behaviour: that is a matter for his own conscience, and he must live with that. What is manifestly the case is that it is simply untrue to state that in this situation no choice is possible. 'Ought,' said Kant, 'implies can.' There must be few situations in life where the element of compulsion is so overwhelming that choice of any kind is impossible.

There is a fact about moral dilemmas which relates to this: *choice is not only essential, but unavoidable.* It may be argued that many people seem able to ignore such choices. This is certainly the case; but to ignore an issue is not to avoid it, as will be confirmed by many a broken-down motorist who has done nothing over a period of time about the unusual grating sound in his engine. (Hitler rose to power on the backs of people who looked away as Nazism grew in Germany.) By not getting involved in a moral issue we are still making a choice: non-commitment can, probably will, affect the outcome, in however small a way. I may argue that few people are likely to be affected by my views on a proposed new highway through a natural beauty spot, or the introduction of sex education or peace studies in my local school, or violence on television: but because these issues exist, I cannot avoid them. By choosing not to attend a public meeting, or write to my MP or the TV authorities, I affect the ultimate outcome, whether I like it or not. To live at all is to take a moral stance: and that involves choice. Nobody can be neutral: many an election has been won or lost by the neutrals, or 'don't knows'. The priest who passed by on the other side was making his choice.

(f) This brings us to the sixth significant factor about moral issues, which concerns the nature of moral reasoning. While scientific reasoning (to take an example already used) aims to discover the truth, *moral reasoning aims to discover the right forms of action*; like the reasoning involved in say, political or educational theorising, it relates directly to the way people behave, or should behave. It is, in brief, an example of practical reasoning or, to use the title of a journal relating to this field, of applied philosophy.

When a scientist observes certain phenomena hitherto unexplained, his basic question is, why does this occur? Thenceforward, every experiment he conducts in this area will have as its objective the attempt to answer that question. He will feel satisfied only when he can declare 'this is true': and only then is he likely to divulge to others the results of his research. For him, as for the engineer, the physician, or the lawyer, there can be no acceptance of grey areas or ambiguities; every statement must ultimately be verifiable in accordance with accepted standards. The truth, however laboriously discovered, must out.

The problem in the field of morals is, as we have seen, that, because there is no agreed plan, or chart, or table, by reference to which a decision can be reached, no moral statement can be declared unequivocally to be 'true or 'false'. (As we shall see in Chapter Six, Jeremy Bentham produced a paradigm which he believed would enable people to make moral decisions on utilitarian lines, but few people take his proposals seriously.) Yet the irony of the situation, so far as the student of moral philosophy is concerned, is that, while no definitive statement on moral issues can be made, action of some sort is demanded. In the debate on abortion, for instance, it can be readily acknowledged that on both sides deep-seated principles are held; and whatever is allowed in this field by law must offend one of the groups of protagonists. But action of some kind is absolutely necessary: the law, as we have seen, must either make provision for abortion, or disallow it. It cannot just do nothing about the matter.

What, then, can the moral philosopher say about this? He cannot, like the scientist, stand up (either in his bath or at a press conference) and cry: 'Eureka!' All he can do is to urge, if not insist, that the debate be conducted with logical consistency, intellectual honesty, and a catholic comprehension of the relevant facts. This may not sound earth-shattering, but in a world in which many crucial debates, such as on capital punishment, the treatment of football hooligans or inner-city rioters, or experiments on animals, are conducted in an atmosphere of heat rather than light, this contribution must be necessary, even if not sufficient, for the achievement of a wise conclusion, rather than one based on prejudice, emotion, or fear.

However much philosophy generally can be conducted from the ivory tower, the study of moral philosophy brings the student into the market-place, even if he doesn't always dirty his shoes. This should be illustrated throughout this book, not least in the case studies after each chapter.

MOTIVES

A major concern of ethics is the question of what is, or should be, (and these are two different issues, as we shall see in Chapter Four) the prime motivation for human behaviour. Independently of what we do, why do we do it? And, assuming that we can find the answer to this question, is there any way in which our motives can or should be changed?

Altruism

The main question is the extent to which our motives are, or should be, altruistic, or how far they are inescapably selfish; whether we should be other-considering as opposed to self-considering, self-denying or other-denying. Most philosophers and religious teachers have throughout the ages declared themselves in favour of altruism. Forms of the Jewish command 'Thou shalt love thy neighbour as thyself' (Leviticus 19, 18) can be found in a score of moral codes. Some hermits and other ascetics have taken the way of self-denial to extreme lengths, depriving them-selves not only of luxuries but also of what to most of us are basic necessities of life, such as being reasonably clothed, fed, and housed. The problem with this excessiveness is whether practitioners of such a life style can love others as they might wish to be loved. 'Do as you would be done by', as expressed by a hermit dressed in a sack, eating a handful of beans a day, and living in a cave is unlikely to create much enthusiasm in the mind of a pauper compelled to wear rags, eat only crusts, and live in an abandoned shack. The commandment does not state, 'Love thy neighbour and hate thyself', or 'Love thy neighbour and harm thyself': it tells us 'Love thy neighbour *as* thyself', which is a quite different matter. I am unlikely to make much of a contribution to my neighbour's well-being if I am indifferent to my own. (It is, incidentally, doubly absurd that 'loving one's neighbour' is assumed to be of Christian origin. First, as we have noted, it originates not in the New Testament but in the Old, centuries before the time of Christ. Second, it is a thoroughly *human* statement, acceptable by all people of any religious belief or none.)

Extreme ascetics belong in the minority: but society has never lacked its share of those who dedicate themselves to the cause of altruism. They engage themselves in 'good works', in charitable activity for the poor, the oppressed, the unfairly treated. Such people are often described as 'do-gooders', which is hardly an affectionate term (and perhaps somewhat harsh). George Bernard Shaw said of one lady, 'She lived for others; you could tell the others by their haunted expression.' Disraeli criticised Gladstone as 'a man without a single redeeming defect': being straightlaced often seems to go hand-in-hand with pomposity, never an appealing quality. Perhaps the most charitable actions are those which don't leave the recipient with a sense of being beholden to the agent. Equally, while the 'golden rule', quoted above, may serve as a general rule of thumb when considering others, it is worth bearing in mind that, because of individual differences, how one person may wish to be 'done by' may not be the case for another. One needs only to experience the embarrassment of being presented with too much food by an over-enthusiastic hostess to be aware of this.

Hobbes

Is it realistic to expect people generally to behave in an altruistic way? Altruism may be desirable, but is it natural? The view that it is not so was forcefully presented by the English philosopher, Thomas Hobbes (1588–1679). He argued that human nature is unalterably selfish, aimed at personal satisfaction and pleasure, at whoever else's expense. 'The condition of man,' he wrote, 'is a condition of war, of everyone against everyone.' We may easily recognise this quality in those who are at the beginning and end of life; infants howling for food or comfort, querulous old people demanding attention; and visitors to mental hospitals may confirm Ibsen's view, expressed in *Peer Gynt*, that the patients 'live in a cask of self, controlled by a bung of self'.

Selfishness as Hobbes describes it can certainly be seen around us: but is it the norm for the average 'mature' adult? Don't most people realise, most of the time at least, that they can't go through life claiming total satisfaction of all their wants? Don't most people accept that they must modify their demands if they are to live harmoniously with their neighbours? Of course they do, said Hobbes: but we must not deceive ourselves that such behaviour represents altruism. It is simply the appreciation that if everybody demanded total satisfaction for himself all the time, life would be unbearable for all: so compromises are made in our personal demands: but made not out of altruism but by the same desire for satisfaction. Better to accept three-quarters and live in comfort, than go for the lot in discomfort.

This viewpoint Hobbes expounded in his theory of politics which will be discussed in Chapter Eleven. It is reflected in the – usually disparaging – use of the phrase 'human nature'. Hobbes himself described life as 'solitary, poor, nasty, brutish, and short' (this despite his ninety years); it sounds a harsh description, but it must be asked how far removed it is from the view of human nature held by many close observers of life. ' – you, Jack, I'm all right' seems to be a common attitude of human beings, as in other species. This is especially true when commodities are scarce: it needs only a rumour, much less an official pronouncement, to send people out grabbing what they can. (I know one person who, in such a situation, filled a pram with toilet rolls; and another who filled her car – front, back, and boot (trunk) – with bread.)

Even those actions which on the surface appear altruistic can be (and often are) interpreted as acts of selfishness, performed for personal gratification. The missionary in a leper colony may be motivated by a desire for inner satisfaction and outward appreciation; the man risking his life for another may simply be preferring that risk to the sense of shame he might afterwards bear for life if he did nothing; the martyr may prefer death to a lifetime of dishonour as a traitor to his cause. Examples are endless.

Clearly, nobody can 'prove' this issue one way or the other. Maybe altruistic behaviour gives us pleasure: but does that diminish the worth of such behaviour? Hobbes himself, a notorious unbeliever, was once seen by the Dean of St Paul's giving alms to a beggar. The Dean suggested that, whether Hobbes believed it or not, it was ultimately the example of Jesus which inspired such behaviour. Hobbes replied that he gave as he did because it brought pleasure both to the beggar who received the money and to him, the giver. (Thomas Hobbes 3; Dean of St Paul's 0.) In Chapter Five we shall consider Kant's criticism of this, in his defence of duty as the ultimate motive for behaviour. For the moment, two final points seem worth making.

Firstly, if it could be proved that all our actions were motivated by self-interest, would this be too much to live with? Having accepted, and come to terms with, this viewpoint, might not people find that they could live together amicably enough, never expecting too much from others, but enough so as to avoid unnecessary bruisings? We could even expect aid in time of need, either because others would know that some time they might need the same themselves, or because they feared the community's rebuke if they were known to have done nothing at such a time.

Secondly, it is worth asking whether human motives have to be polarised in the way suggested in this section. Can we not simply say that most people have mixed motives, and that the mixture varies from person to person? We may agree that even behaviour which has all the hallmarks of being altruistic cannot be proved to be so; but, as we have seen, this is true of most of our cherished beliefs. Personally, I feel it would be a distortion of the facts to interpret the self-sacrifice of Captain Oates at the South Pole as not primarily motivated by altruism towards his companions; and the same goes for the soldier in a tank, during the war in the Middle East, who threw himself upon a hand grenade thrown inside in order to lessen the impact of the explosion on his comrades. It may have been a reflex action brought about by his training; he may have had a death wish (because he'd just heard that his wife was leaving him, for example); he may have been overwhelmed with the desire for glory. I doubt if the survivors make such comments.

ETHICAL PRINCIPLES

In the first section of this chapter, it was suggested that the basic distinction between ethical principles and moral rules is that the former are concerned with the overriding aims of human behaviour, the latter with the application of these aims in day-to-day situations. The question which now presents itself is: where do these principles originate? Why are we so sure that the principles of, for instance, equality, justice, benevolence, or freedom should be preserved?

We certainly seem to be aware of these principles at an early age. If I had ever returned from a week's conference and brought one of my sons a cricket bat as a coming-home present, the second a packet of stamp hinges, and the third nothing at all, I should not have been surprised to hear a good deal of sound and fury, with the statement 'that's not fair' predominant – at least from two of them. It seems that there is, even in young minds, an elementary sense of justice at work: and the fact that on my departure I had promised none of them anything would not in any way have affected their conviction that justice, by whatever name they termed it, had not been done.

Again, if in a school I were to punish one student out of all proportion to his misdeeds, while totally overlooking those of another, I could be accused of acting unjustly, of not treating them equally. In a wide range of life's activities it is possible, without having studied philosophy, moral or otherwise, to identify injustice at work. A professor can very easily give a higher grade for an essay to a student whom he likes than to one whom he dislikes; in the United States, it is estimated that a negro charged with theft has almost twice as much chance of being found guilty than has his white counterpart; and even in these days of increased sexual equality, many women know to their cost that their career prospects at work fall far behind those of males, even though both have similar qualifications and experience.

All these situations arouse in most of us the sense that, if they are factual, justice is not being done. This sense can stir deep emotions, and cause people to become enmeshed in polemics, and even to engage themselves in social and political activity which may divide them from their neighbours. But where does this sense originate? Why, in an unequal world, does the sense of equality between people persist? Why, amid so much malevolence, does the sense of benevolence exist? Why, when life is so manifestly unfair (in the distribution of talents and possessions, the possibilities of personal fulfilment, the occurrence of physical ailments and disease, and so on) does the idea of justice constantly present itself?

Plato

The answer of Plato two-and-a-half millennia ago was straightforward. He believed in the immortality of the soul, and in reincarnation. In between incarnations, he believed, the soul inhabited the 'ideal' world, to which all human ideas aspire, and which is the unseen inspiration of all human virtue. All the noble principles he viewed as the prevailing qualities in this ideal world, where everyone was treated justly, benevolently, equally. So, when returning to our present world of experience in a new incarnation, we bring with us dim, but nonetheless actual, memories of that ideal state. In Wordsworth's phrase in his 'Ode on the Intimations of Immortality' we come 'trailing clouds of glory'. Our sense of justice, and of all the other ethical principles, is, said Plato, a memory of the 'Form' of these encountered in that ideal world; and, however confusedly, we recall our existence during that blissful interregnum. So the two-year-old who says 'that's not fair' is unconsciously reflecting his heavenly experience of fairness, and judging his present experience by that former one.

If this view of the basis of our awareness of ethical principles were to be universally accepted, a difficult problem in moral philosophy would have been solved. Principles could then be treated as objective values, existing independently of human judgment or experience. The problem is that the theory of reincarnation is just that: a theory, not open to any acceptable process of verification. It certainly accounts for a number of apparently inexplicable experiences; but the theory itself then becomes the problem, since there is no generally acknowledged way of demonstrating its truth. It is like answering the problem of the origin of the universe by positing the idea of a Creator God without appreciating that all that has happened is that the problem has been pushed one stage further back, since the question of God's origin still remains. (Kant's belief in an afterlife, as we shall see in Chapter Five, was similarly based on what may be termed logical necessity: since life in this world is manifestly unfair to many people, there must be an afterlife where these injustices can be evened out. The same question mark hangs over Kant's theory as over Plato's.)

There are however those who accept the objectivity of ethical principles without agreeing with Plato's incarnation theory. Most of these would probably take the Kantian line that these principles reflect in our midst the nature of God, who is a moral God (or who *is* morality). Others hold that these principles are part of the 'nature of things', and are as independent of human discovery and assessment as are the principles of mathematics, or of logic. On the face of it, there are grounds for accepting this objective view of ethical principles. When I say, 'Benevolence ought to be pursued,' I don't seem to be saying that on the whole benevolence ought to be pursued (but there could be exceptions); or that, while *I* consider benevolence to be desirable, you are entitled to differ; I am not advocating it just on Mondays, Wednesdays, and Fridays and leaving the matter open on other days of the week. What I am affirming is that, in all human encounters, benevolence should be pursued, and this remains the case even if you, along with most of the human race, disagree. It remains the case, or so I deeply feel, even if I have a run of experiences which suggest the reverse. R. L. Stevenson, dying in his prime of tuberculosis, could still write: 'I believe in the ultimate goodness of things; and if I awoke in hell I should still believe it.' So the principle of benevolence seems to remain with us, despite the vast amount of malevolence, violence, cruelty, indifference, in the world.

The origin of principles

The independence, or objectivity, of ethical principles – the fact that they seem not to depend on human assessment in order to be viable – seems to be confirmed when one reflects on the question of when a principle first became a principle. Is it when it was first given utterance? A comparison with the principles of science will reveal the absurdity of this idea. Newton first enunciated the principle of gravity in the seventeenth century. He was the first actually to write words to the effect that bodies tend to attract each other (quite a nice principle, when you reflect on it). Nobody before him, so far as we are aware, had actually stated this: but that is not to infer that the principle of gravity did not obtain, or gravity itself operate, prior to Newton. (The point remains valid even if the principle was first enunciated earlier by, say, an Arab, or Indian, or Russian: nobody changed a zero gravity situation into the one that we know; apples have always fallen down, not up, from trees.)

So, it is argued, is the situation with ethical principles. 'Love thy neighbour as thyself' was first written, say, around 1000 BC. Nobody who has read or heard that statement, except, perhaps, a psychopath, will disagree with it (which is not to say that everybody acts upon it). But did its validity commence only at the time when it was first given verbal expression? Of course not. If the principle was universally valid after 1000 BC, it was universally valid before 1000 BC. It was universal from the moment when homo sapiens first appeared on this planet and began to interact with other members of his species. One may dare to state that it is and has been valid in all communities on any sphere where life as we know it has come into being; and one cannot imagine any future community's existing where this is not the case.

How is this phenomenon to be explained? As stated earlier, it can be explained either by reference to Plato's theory of the immortal soul, or by the existence of God. Both these theories account for the phenomenon, but both, satisfying though they may be to those who hold them, involve taking on trust ideas which remain open to question. To explain is not to justify. A notorious English mass-murderer, the so-called Yorkshire Ripper, explained his hideous murders as the consequence of divine commands heard in a graveyard. He may have sincerely believed this, but it made no difference either to the public's opinion of him or to the trial court's verdict against him.

There are in fact many people who, while accepting the forcefulness with which ethical principles seem to confront them, deny both the existence of God and the immortality of the soul. After all, mathematical and logical principles exist, but few people present the hypothesis of God, or of heaven, in order to explain them. We don't say 'two times two make four because God has so decreed it': we say that this, along with all mathematical principles, lies in the nature of numeracy. I don't state that the reason why my pipe cannot both exist and not exist at the same time is that this is how it is in heaven: I state that this is logically inevitable. In the universe that we know, both mathematical and logical principles are necessarily true. If they were not, we should be in another, unimaginable universe, and all human thought as we know it would be meaningless.

Can we not say the same of ethical principles? I used the phrase earlier that they were part of 'the nature of things', and with this I'll stick. But we must be clear as to how they became so important, even in a world which often ignores them. The fact is that, without these principles as guides to behaviour, human beings could never have learned how to live and – more important – survive together. This is, of course, the view of Charles Darwin, which will receive further consideration in Chapter

Four. Over the millennia, on this view, the human race has survived because, however inadequately and with whatever lapses, these principles have remained fixed at the back of people's minds. Would we have continued to exist as a race if the principles had been otherwise? We should hardly have survived a day, let alone millennia, if all human beings shared a deeply ingrained sense of malevolence towards others. Who would ever turn his back on another, what two people would ever sleep together, if this were the situation?

To act justly, then, is not so to act because justice exists independently of man (in heaven, or in the nature of God) but because justice works: it has an inbuilt survivability factor. Injustice, like malevolence or human bondage, contains within itself the seeds of its own destruction. This we human beings have discovered through experience – by trial and error, if you like. To ask for the 'concept' of justice, like that of any of the other principles mentioned, is to seek the impossible: there is no such animal. (See Chapter Ten for a criticism of the concept of 'concept'.) Like all such words, it cannot even be defined except by reference to examples of it in practice, which is known as an ostensive definition. (If you disagree about this, try writing a definition of 'justice' without giving either examples, or cognate words like 'fairness': then try doing the same with other words outside the area of moral principles, such as 'beauty', 'courage', or even 'small' or 'green'.)

All this was expressed succinctly, two thousand years before the theory of evolution was expounded, by Plato's pupil, Aristotle (384–322 BC). One paragraph from his *Nichomachean Ethics* epitomises his viewpoint:

But the virtues we get by first exercising them, as also happens in the case of the arts as well. For the things we have to learn before we can do them, we learn by doing them, e.g. men become builders by building and lyre players by playing the lyre; so do we become just by doing just acts, temperate by doing temperate acts, brave by doing brave acts. This is confirmed by what happens in the State; for legislators make the citizens good by forming habits in them . . .. By doing the acts that we do in our transactions with other men we become just or unjust, and by doing the things that we do in the presence of danger, and by habituating ourselves to feel fear or confidence, we become brave or cowardly.[1]

The role of the State in instilling virtue in its citizens will be discussed in Chapter Eleven. Meanwhile we may end this section by offering a variation on a famous joke.

[1] Bk II, chs 3, 4

Famous joke:
A: Can you play the violin?
B: I don't know – I've never tried.

Variation:
A: Are you a brave person?
B: I don't know – I've never been frightened.

MORAL RULES: ABSOLUTE OR RELATIVE?

It is no difficult matter to state ethical principles, since as principles they are generally unchallengeable. To declare oneself in favour of tolerance, or justice, or kindness (especially to animals and children) will cause few eyebrows to be raised; few people openly advocate bigotry, hatred, or tyranny as guiding principles of life. The problem with principles lies not in reaching agreement as to their validity, but in establishing some kind of hierarchy or pecking order when they clash, as they occasionally do. We have already seen that on the question of abortion the principle 'Thou shalt not kill' (affirmed by the anti-abortionist) competes with that of the woman's freedom and right to choose (held by the pro-abortionist). Another major division among people is brought about by the clash of two other principles: being one's 'brother's keeper' and accepting universal individual responsibility. What responsibility does the successful, possibly hard-working and self-sacrificial member of the community bear towards the less fortunate, possibly feckless members of the same community? Should the one group leave the other to 'stew in their own juice', or should they acknowledge, and express in a practical form, a certain responsibility towards them? Should the wise virgins have given the foolish virgins some of their oil (Matthew, 25)? The extent of any nation's budget allocated to the social services hinges on this issue.

Fortunately, disagreements on fundamentals like these are relatively rare, (and when they do occur there is normally a generation of heat rather than of light, simply because, as we have seen, there exist no facts which can be used to verify a principle one way or the other.) Where we usually find debates occurring is when principles have to be translated into action – the establishing of a law, or the treatment of another person. We may well all agree that benevolence ought to be pursued: but how does one best act benevolently towards a cretin, a bomber, a hijacker, a person dying painfully from cancer, a totally paralysed geriatric, or even the club bore?

In such situations it is quite possible to receive diametrically opposing answers from two people observing the same principle. Let us take the example of treatment of a severely subnormal baby. Two people may both agree that, on principle, they should act in the baby's best interests.

So far, so good: but one of them may reach the conclusion that this means letting it die quickly and painlessly, while the other may affirm that its life should be maintained at whatever cost. Agreement on a principle by no means guarantees agreement on action. Yet action there must be, and often, as in the above example, there can be no ready compromise between divergent proposals. Either capital punishment exists as part of a nation's penal policy, or it does not. Schools either allow corporal punishment for certain offences, or they do not. Something has to be done about the bully, the terrorist, the thief, the cheat, the liar. There has to be a policy on the treatment of animals, the admission of juveniles into pubs and bars, football hooliganism, violence on television. In short, there have to be rules; the alternative would be anarchy, which could mean only one thing: the survival and dominance of the physically strongest, the rule of the bully and the lout.

Since not many anarchists are likely to be reading this, I assume that there is general agreement so far. Where there is likely to be division of opinion is over the status of moral rules: are they representative of an ideal universal order, whether human or divine, and therefore fixed and unchangeable, or are they a reflection only of the attitudes and values of a limited group at a certain time and in a certain place, and therefore flexible and infinitely variable? Are they hewn, like the Ten Commandments, in the rock which may break others but cannot itself be broken, or are they, like the laws of cricket, susceptible to modification or total reversal on a majority vote of the TCCB? Are moral rules absolute or relative?

(a) Absolutism

The strength of absolutism lies in its being a clear-cut position: there are no grey areas. Whether we are discussing homosexuality, vivisection, making war, or making love before or outside marriage, there is a straightforward answer: yes, or no. The absolutist can denounce, without fear or qualm, foxhunting, strike-breaking, closed shops, open shops on Sundays, betting, blood-letting, smoking pot, smoking, drinking alcohol, drinking tea, eating pork, eating lamb, eating beef (if you're a Jew married to a Muslim and living in India you're likely to have to do without all three), playing games on the Sabbath, playing snooker any day, dancing, swearing, long hair, short hair, fur coats, leather shoes, exposing a cleavage or exposing anything, pornography, hagiography, Catholicism, Protestantism, socialism, Conservatism, public brothels and private medicine. I may seem to be sending absolutism up with these examples, but I have met people who will defend any one of the viewpoints vehemently and with total conviction.

In this conviction lies its appeal. Because absolute rules are, by definition, applied absolutely, or without exception, there is no need for discussion or agonising debate on any issue. It is certain that for some people this removes a potential source of perplexity, anxiety, and insecurity. One group of people for whom such an approach may be considered highly desirable is young children. A person not yet old enough to work out rights and wrongs in his own mind is likely to feel much more at ease knowing precisely what the rules of behaviour are, how far he may go in a particular direction, what is permitted and what is disallowed. The word 'forbidden' can be the foundation of a child's sense of security.

Similarly, people who are naturally observant of rules are likely to find the absolutist approach congenial. Faced with a complex moral dilemma, they can work out their individual response according to 'the book': Is it ever right to kill, to cheat, to steal, to lie? The Commandments forbid these, so there's an end to the matter. Should I use contraceptives or In Vitro Fertilisation? The Church says no, so that's that. In a world of blacks and whites, there is no need to agonise over alleged grey areas.

The absolutist may claim, with a fair amount of justice, that the greatest leaders of the human race, the most dynamic instigators of change in society, the people to whom others have most frequently turned for strength and guidance have, for better or for worse, generally been absolutists. What communist or capitalist leader ever declared (or would have become leader if he had declared) that there was 'something to be said' for the other side's point of view? What nationalist, black or otherwise, who opposes his nation's rulers would stand a chance of influencing his fellows if he openly acknowledged the complexities of the government's problems? What anti-smoking enthusiast would enhance his cause by conceding that pipe-smoking, by encouraging relaxation, may prolong life? The world has been moulded by absolutists, seeing only one clearly defined point of view, not by relativists, recognising that viewpoints must vary because there is no definitive right or wrong in morals. This statement calls for a fuller analysis of relativism, before proceeding to a critique of absolutism.

(b) Relativism

In his book *Human Conduct*, Chapter Ten, John Hospers delineates several different schools of relativism, which means that any generalisations must be treated with care (very apposite for a philosophical view which in any case discourages generalising).

(i) Sceptical relativism The argument here is that we just cannot know what forms of behaviour are right and what wrong; it reflects the true/false dilemma already referred to (Chapter One). Unquestionably this approach is reasonable; I cannot possibly know – however certain I may be within myself – that my decision on any moral issue is the right

one: I can believe it firmly, but, in the sense that I know the truth of the Pythagoras theorem, my so-called knowledge in the moral field must be treated as no more than a hunch, inspired or otherwise.

The problem for anyone taking this stance is, as we have seen, that he is regularly faced with situations in which moral decisions can't be avoided. Even though we may never know how best (whatever that word may mean in this context) to treat convicted criminals, something must be done with them; even letting them go free is doing something. Problems don't evaporate just because people can't solve them.

(ii) Nihilistic relativism   This is the belief that there is no such thing as moral judgment, that the words 'right' and 'wrong' are meaningless. When I say that racial bigotry, or male chauvinism, or nudity on the stage are wrong, I don't mean that there is anything inherently immoral in any of these attitudes or activities, only that I don't happen to like the idea of any of them. All so-called moral judgments I may make must consequently be recognised as being no more than an expression of my own feelings.

One obvious example of this is the way people's emotions can easily be roused against the slaughtering of, or experimentation on, animals by a display of carefully-chosen photographs. Most of us are repelled by the sight of large quantities of blood; few of us can bear with equanimity the appearance of a friend or relative in hospital with tubes of various kinds protruding from his body. Many of the pictures we see published by animal activists simply capitalise on this revulsion, and persuade people to make a moral issue out of a physiological reaction. (This is not to say that there isn't a case to be made for animal rights, which we shall explore in Case Study 43; but the cause is not advanced – at least among those looking for cogent arguments – by this flagrant appeal to the emotions.) Generally speaking, this immediate revulsion is only a temporary reaction to what seems unsightly because it hardly, if at all, comes the way of most people. But the slaughterhouse worker becomes accustomed to the gore as the undertaker to human corpses, or the fastidious medical student to surgical operations.

The nihilistic relativist would argue that the overtly emotional factors illustrated in this example epitomise, even if more obviously than is often the case, the processes behind all so-called moral decisions; and there is at least an element of truth in this. It would be absurd to deny that emotional reactions to certain forms of behaviour play some part in helping us to arrive at a conclusion as to the desirability or otherwise of that behaviour. After every shooting of a public figure in the United States in recent years there has been a massive upsurge of feeling against the gun lobby in that country, and the call to make the obtaining of arms much more difficult; this suggests that emotion has been at work among the citizens.

The trouble is that, in a world in which constancy of resolve is required for moral attitudes to change or be changed, feelings remain fickle. They wane as quickly as they are aroused, as is illustrated by the speed at which anti-gun lobby fever has always evaporated in America. It seems that feelings are not enough to sustain a cause for any great length of time: yet causes such as those against slavery or capital punishment have persisted over long periods of time, right through to their successful outcome.

However, there seems to me to be a weakness in nihilistic relativism more basic than this. When I declare that it is wrong to torture a small child, or commit rape, or shoot innocent hostages in a hijack, I'm not saying this merely because I'm sickened by such behaviour (though of course I am). I'm saying this behaviour is wrong, whatever people may feel.

Where this sense of wrongness originates will be discussed in Chapter Four, but the fact is that it does exist, and not just because of emotional revulsion. I have no strong feelings about the existence of the Masonic Order; I cannot get worked up about dirty dealings on the Stock Exchange or the expenditure of millions of pounds on an airstrip in the Falklands: but I believe all these to be morally wrong, and am prepared to argue my case even though I have no emotional reaction to any of the issues.

(iii) Sociological relativism   This is a more general description of relativism, and is what most people probably have in mind when they discuss the issue in relation to absolutism. It may be viewed both from the geographical and the historical perspectives.

Geographical perspective   One doesn't need to be a professional anthropologist to be aware that there are throughout the world many conflicting ideas about how to behave. One of the problems for Western nations when trying to find a modus vivendi with other nations is the clash of moral codes. To the Westerner it seems obscene to chop off a man's hand as a punishment for theft; to many Muslims this is simply the prescribed punishment, as is flogging for drinking alcohol and, perhaps, stoning for adultery. The Westerner may condemn what he deems to be inhuman practices, reflecting a cruel society, in the Middle East; the Middle Easterner however will, for his part, condemn the excessive liberalism of the West, leading inevitably, he may well believe, to a high incidence of crime and immorality.

Other examples of this clash of culture can easily be found. Some societies practise polygamy or polyandry, others, monogamy; paedophilic sex is encouraged by some, debarred by others; nomadic Eskimos leave their old behind when they are too feeble for the trek; others would view this grim necessity as tantamount to, if not actual, murder. For the relativist, such differences create no problem: different tribes, different customs. But for the absolutist they create a major dilemma. Absolutism implies that forms of behaviour are universally right or wrong: how then is such a judgment to be made geographically? The answer of nineteenth-century British missionaries to Africa and Asia was that western absolutes were more absolute than those of other parts of the world. Hence, for example, female converts to Christianity were made to cover their breasts as a sign of their new-found faith – surely more an indication of Victorian prudery than of a universal moral code (and perhaps also a lack of appreciation that a country's climate may be the determinative factor on such matters: one cannot imagine the missionaries having the same problem with Eskimo converts). It is an interesting question whether there is *any* form of behaviour practised by an indigenous community which would be indefensible anywhere else (has the cannibal a point of view, assuming, of course, that the meal had died naturally?)

Historical perspective Viewed from the historical perspective, this sociological approach to the issue provides stronger support for the relativist viewpoint, and further problems for the absolutist. It is not a matter of contention but simply a statement of fact that – to take only the English-speaking world – forms of behaviour which were in the past condemned for one reason or another are now more or less acceptable. We may grumble about the horrors of the twentieth century, but we no longer allow acts of cruelty for public pleasure as in the Roman games; homosexuals can socialise more openly together; unmarried mothers are no longer treated as a social embarrassment; couples can openly live together without first going through the marriage ceremony; four-letter words can be used in the media, and sex education taught in schools. Animal rights activists may condemn the way society still ill-treats animals, but we no longer sacrifice them in religious ceremonies (I often reflect on the views of the fatted calf on the return of the prodigal son in the parable). The mentally handicapped are no longer penned in like wild animals; lesbians, gypsies, and epileptics are no-longer stigmatised; children are no longer instructed to be 'seen but not heard'. All these are generalisations, of course, but they illustrate the changing attitudes of society on many issues. (Not all agree with change, of course, as these words illustrate: 'It is a general complaint that this nation of late years is grown more numerously and excessively vicious than heretofor; pride, luxury, drunkenness, whoredom, cursing, swearing, bold and open atheism everywhere abounding.' Mary Whitehouse? or a member of the Moral Majority? John Milton in the seventeenth century!) (See Case Study 6, p. 45.)

(iv) Ethical relativism, or situation ethics This school affirms that the rightness or wrongness of behaviour are relative to the circumstances –

the time, the place, the particular people involved, and so on. The treatment of offspring, for example, which may be right for one set of parents may be wrong for another. What is acceptable in one set of circumstances, (such as swearing in male company) may be unacceptable in others (such as mixed company: there are men who can switch from using swearwords almost as punctuation marks, to the total elimination of such words, simply by the arrival of a woman).

The absolutist would reply that, granted these variations occur, there remains one set of standards which must ultimately be deemed superior to all others; and that deep down most people would agree. This may be a valid point in circumstances where a choice of options is available. The weakness of absolutism, and the strength of relativism, is that this affirmation is often made in circumstances where the ideal option is not on offer. In these circumstances the affirmation of an ideal rule appears as no more than a theoretical but impracticable exercise.

Let us take, for example, the problem facing a mother who discovers that her fourteen-year-old daughter is having a full-blown sexual relationship with her seventeen-year-old boyfriend. The mother disapproves of such relationships at so early an age: what is she to do? She may remonstrate with her daughter, arguing that she is too young to be so committed; but the daughter may disagree. Does the mother then prevent the two lovers from meeting (by locking her in her room, for instance)? She might then incur the charge of cruelty. In fact, if the mother is an absolutist, believing that having sex before a certain age (such as 16, the age of consent, or later) is morally wrong, she faces an impossible situation: so long as her daughter persists in her behaviour, the option of sexual abstinence for a further number of years, while still, of course, open to the daughter, is not one that the mother can apply. The relativist in this situation, even if agreeing with the mother's beliefs about a minimum age for sexual commitment, would be likely to look for the *best possible* (not necessarily the ideal) way of coping with the problem. This may well be to ensure that at least the young couple are using contraceptives, so that no unwanted pregnancy is likely to occur. This circumstance illustrates how easily the rigidity of absolutism becomes irrelevant when moral decisions have to be made. It exemplifies Aristotle's adage: 'The best is the enemy of the good'. (See Case Study 2, p. 16).

Situation ethics, then, means that the moral agent does not engage in debate on moral issues with his options already determined; it may be that these options are not available. He will instead approach these issues pragmatically, looking for the best option on the table. Faced with the same problem in different circumstances, he may well reach a different conclusion. To conclude that the girl in the above example should go on the pill should not be interpreted as a recommendation that all girls at puberty should do the same. This would be to switch from a relativist to an absolutist position.

Can we adjudicate between the two positions? The main problem for the absolutist, it seems, is that he is often demanding the impossible. He is inclined to assume that options are available which do not in fact exist. A pacifist during the Rhodesian crisis of 1965, when a full-scale rebellion, an act of treason, was committed by the servants of the British government in a colonial territory, told me that he would support any action on the part of the government, so long as violence was not involved. But, given the circumstances, this was no longer an option. Whether by immediate police action, or through an indefinitely long policy of economic restraints on the country (sanctions), violence in some form was inevitable. A non-violent solution might have been possible had the circumstances been different. But the circumstances were what they were: an illegal take-over bid for the country had successfully occurred, with 95 per cent of its citizens disenfranchised. The pacifist, an absolutist against violence, was in effect entering the conference chamber armed with Plan C when only Plans A and B were on offer. (See Case Study 35, p. 265.)

Relativism too is not without its problems. A major question which it raises is whether the average citizen (assuming such a person exists: I've never known anybody admit to being one) is capable of judging every situation on its merits. This means being willing to sit down and mull over the pros and cons of any issue, rather than defer to precedents and accepted norms of behaviour: a procedure likely to involve the expenditure of time and energy, which may not be available to everybody. For many people it is more straightforward simply to state the code of behaviour observed by their group, and to abide by that. But this attitude, too, raises problems, which will be pursued in later chapters.

It may be that the supreme contribution to morals made by the absolutist is that of compelling their fellows never to lose sight of ideals. The pacifist, for example, while apparently making unrealistic demands, presents a viewpoint that society must surely reject at its peril: the belief that violence, in all its aspects, is evil, injurious both to homo sapiens and to the environment in which he is placed. At a time when people seem to be increasingly accepting violence as an inevitable aspect of living, even as a means of pursuing national policies, how can one write such people off? Has not the idealist a continuing role to play in society? Whether or not we actually make any progress in any direction, he will at least give us an aim, a goal. If this is true, it follows that society would be profoundly handicapped without its prophets, its seers, its visionaries. Their picture of the future seems preferable to one based on cynicism and despair. The Don Quixote of today may be tomorrow's realist.

It seems reasonable to conclude, therefore, that we need both absolutists and relativists, and that any one of us may move from one side to the other according to the issue. Most of us, most of the time, oppose killing, or lying, or stealing; and it would be difficult to imagine a situation where rape or torture could be condoned. Most of us would prefer that people be generous rather than miserly, good-humoured rather than cantankerous, broad- rather than narrow-minded. We deplore prejudice, bigotry, hypocrisy; we applaud sincerity, courtesy, tolerance. But on the other, relativist, hand, those of us who live in a monogamous society are unlikely to lose any sleep over the existence of polygamous or polyandrous societies elsewhere; those who won't indulge in alcohol can coexist with those who do; the communist and the capitalist can be friends. Maybe in the end we are relative absolutists some of the time and absolute relativists for the rest.

CASE STUDY 3: LOVE THY NEIGHBOUR

In the foregoing chapter it was assumed that the principle of benevolence, frequently expressed in such commands as 'Love thy neighbour as thyself', must be universally accepted. But is this really the case? The following dialogue between protagonists A and B suggests that all may not be quite as clear-cut as was supposed. Follow the debate through, and see how you would continue it.

A	**B**
1 It's common teaching in different religions – the Golden Rule, and so on.	Yes, but it usually means the in-group only, like 'neighbour' in Judaism.
2 Anyway, benevolence to others, as opposed to malevolence, is taught in all religious and non-religious moralities.	Not true: malevolence is taught as a way of life in some pre-literate societies, and malevolence towards a despised group is central to Marxism (capitalists), Nazism (Jews), Black Muslims (whites), to name but three.
3 Well, there is evolution of religions towards an ethical and benevolent teaching – primitive religions are way down the evolutionary ladder, and Nazism, etc., are regressions, so don't count.	Very dubious. Anthropologists don't accept that 'primitive' societies are less evolved – only *differently* evolved. Several twentieth-century moralities are less benevolent than Taoism, Confucianism, Buddhism.
4 To hell with religion: philosophers at least teach altruism, despite their differences on other matters.	Rubbish: there's nothing altruistic about the existentialists – Nietzsche, Sartre, Camus. And

41

what about Hobbes, or
Machiavelli?

5 It's the anti-rational philosophers
who reject altruism. Benevolence is
right because it's reasonable.

Not so: reason tells you how to
get what you want, not what you
want in the first place. Self-
interest is neither more nor less
rational than altruism.

6 Benevolence must be right because
it's natural to be compassionate and
rejoice in other people's joy.

No more natural than the
opposite. The 'man slips on a
banana-skin' joke is very basic.
And what about delight in
violence?

7 Loving one's neighbour must be
the strongest instinct in society,
otherwise people couldn't cooperate
at all.

An exaggeration. People need
one another, but cooperation and
using others can be entirely self-
centred.

8 The herd instinct is essential – even
animals show this.

Men and animals equally show
that individual survival often
overrides the herd instinct.

Your move! (The discussion on the meaning of 'love' (pp. 306–9) may
help.)

CASE STUDY 4: A TOTAL ABSTAINER'S DILEMMA

What follows is a description of an incident which actually happened to a
former colleague of mine. He had been raised in the total abstinence
tradition, and only a person who has experienced this can appreciate with
what venom alcohol is condemned in such circles. It is King Alcohol, the
seducer, the destroyer, the underlying cause of all crime and all evil. It
should be abjured even if recommended for medicinal purposes; the
wine at Holy Communion must be grape juice. Alcohol is the devil
incarnate.

My colleague had reached his mid-twenties without alcohol's ever
having passed his lips. Unusually for a total abstainer, he was a rugby
player. In one game he faced an opponent who continually played
unfairly, cheated, committed foul after foul, and, on several occasions,
bit him (not allowed by the rules, apparently). In the changing room after
the game, my colleague was beginning to wonder, in the light of his
opponent's behaviour, whether he should turn to a gentler sport, such as
chess or darts. He was suddenly astonished to see his opposite number
entering the changing room bearing two pints of beer. Haltingly, the
other party apologised for his behaviour on the field and, clearly under

his captain's instructions, offered one of the glasses of beer as a token of peace, or, in more philosophical words, a symbol of reconciliation. What was my colleague to do? If he accepted and drank the beer he would be breaking a life-long rule. (It could be put more strongly: by drinking, he would be destroying an edifice which he had built for himself, and overriding the principles which his parents had devotedly instilled into him.) But if he refused on the grounds that his abstinence rule was absolute, he might leave his opponent convinced that the peace offer had been rejected, and the human relationship which, in his embarrassed way, he was trying to establish, had been nipped in the bud.

My colleague decided that a gesture of reconciliation was more important than maintaining a rule: he drank the beer.

Was he right? It could be argued that he might have been able to explain the situation to the other man, and that this would have been understood. But would it – or, more to the point, could he be sure that it would?

Jesus is quoted as saying: 'The sabbath was made for man, not man for the sabbath.' (Mark 2, 27) Does that mean that all rules are relative in human relationships? Or are there some rules which must not be broken, no matter how painful it may be to oneself and others if they are strictly maintained?

Winston Churchill's physician, Lord Moran, once remarked of the French President, General De Gaulle: 'He's so stuffed with principles that he has no room for Christian charity.'

How relevant is this comment to the discussion?

CASE STUDY 5: THE PARENT'S RIGHT TO KNOW

In the autumn of 1985, the Law Lords, the highest court of appeal in Britain, decided by a majority of two to one that under-age girls (that is, girls under 16, the legal age of consent) should be allowed access to contraceptives on the advice of their doctors without necessarily obtaining the permission of their parents. It was ruled that, where the doctor thought this to be in his/her patient's best interests, parents need not be informed at all.

This decision confirmed an original decision in the lower court which had itself been reversed in the court of appeal.

A Mrs Victoria Gillick, a member of the Life Organisation, a mainly, but not exclusively, Roman Catholic Group, had originally brought the case to make parental involvement compulsory, on the following grounds:

1 On such a matter, the consent of parents was both natural – they were still the legal guardians of the girls – and desirable – such issues

should not be matters of secrecy within a family.

2 Because parents must understand their children more than anyone else could – including family doctors – they are ideally situated to counsel their children against rash adventures which they might later regret.

3 Allowing the use of contraceptives only on the doctor's agreement means that doctor and patient become co-conspirators against parents.

4 The free use of contraceptives could encourage a girl to become promiscuous. In turn this would increase the risk of cervical cancer, and a number of sexually-transmitted diseases. In particular, it threatens her with the risk of catching AIDS.

Underlying these arguments was the belief, openly expressed by Mrs Gillick and her supporters, that girls in their early teens were too young to enter into a full physical sexual commitment.

The Law Lords' decision, which was supported by the British Medical Association, the Royal College of Nursing, the Mothers' Union, and the Family Practitioners Association, among other interested bodies, was based on the following arguments:

1 Many girls could not discuss these matters with their parents.

2 Parents were not necessarily ideal confidants. Many were indifferent to their children's behaviour, and many more out of sympathy with their children on this, as on a whole host of issues.

3 Doctors would not allow their young patients automatic access to contraceptive devices, but only after careful counselling and if it were seen to be in the girls' best interests.

4 There was the risk – in some cases, as proved to be the case during the period between the judgment of the appeal court and its reversal by the Law Lords – a high chance that some girls would begin or continue to have sexual intercourse even if contraceptives were denied to them. The risk of pregnancies among these girls would (and did) therefore increase. This in turn would lead to an increase in the number seeking abortion.

Recognising that the law can never remain static on issues like this, and that the British scene may be irrelevant in other countries, what do you think should be the law? Consider in particular the following questions:

1 If a girl is going to have sexual intercourse anyway, with or without her parents' acquiescence, isn't it wiser that she should at least be protected from any unwanted pregnancy through the use of contraceptives?

2 If a girl cannot discuss such matters with her parents, isn't this a sign of something deeply wrong within that family, whether the fault be on the side of the parents, the girl, or both? If so, what would be the value, or force, of the parents' expressed wishes in any case?

3 Is it right that anyone – whether a doctor or anyone else – should in effect encourage a person to break the law relating to the age of consent?

4 Is there a need for an age of consent? Or at least, since children are maturing more quickly than in the past, should it not be lowered? (Romeo and Juliet were both in their early teens.)

5 How far did the Life Organisation express an absolutist attitude – no sex before sixteen – which could not possibly be applied in many cases? How far is the relativist position of the Law Lords and their supporters the only realistic, if not ideal, position? In other words, even though it be generally agreed that under-age sex is not to be encouraged, since abstinence cannot be enforced on others, the best policy, if only for the sake of potentially unwanted babies in the future, is to ensure that at least conception is controlled?

How far do you view the whole contentious issue as a clash between deep conviction, usually based on religious beliefs, and practical reality?

CASE STUDY 6: CHANGES IN MORAL ATTITUDES

There are suggestions (on p. 38) of areas of human behaviour about which, over the years, there has been a change of attitude on the part of the general public. See if you can add to this list (e.g. on Sabbath observance, hire purchase, credit-buying, cockfighting and other uses of animals for sport; and – perhaps supremely – the role of women in society). Discuss whether the changes have, in your view, been for the better or for the worse. Then – and perhaps more interestingly – see if you can do a bit of prophesying. Are there any accepted practices or forms of behaviour today which you think future generations will look back on in disgust, asking themselves, 'How could they have done such things?' You may think that the list will include the breeding and slaughter of animals for food, the pollution of the atmosphere by the internal combustion engine, the use of nuclear power for energy – or even the institution of marriage. What do you do now without undue anxiety for which you think your grandchildren may criticise if not condemn you?

How far do you think your answers will bring about any change in your life-style?

CASE STUDY 7: IS MORAL NEUTRALITY POSSIBLE?

It was suggested (on p. 19) that one of the distinctive features of moral issues is that one cannot avoid them: not to get involved in them is itself a moral decision, and non-participation on anybody's part will affect the situation in however small a way. As Francis Bacon wrote: 'Evil men prosper while good men do nothing.' Discuss this with reference to the following situations:

1 The Government proposes to close down an industry, which will bring about the wholesale destruction of many communities.
2 You are presented with a petition to urge the local highways department to reroute traffic away from an area where children and old people are in constant danger.
3 Your local council has given permission for a new supermarket to be built on ground which has for centuries been common land.
4 You witness a road accident and know who was at fault. You are asked to be prepared to give evidence in court.
5 You hear that an American missile base/a hostel for ex-prisoners/a safe house for alcoholics is to be set up in your area.
6 You know that your neighbours are violently abusing their children.

See how large a list you can compile of other situations in which non-action on your part could influence the outcome. Can you think of *any* circumstances where moral issues are involved and it is possible to be neutral?

Chapter Three

Facts and values

We saw in Chapter One how important it is, in philosophy and in general, to distinguish between statements which are open to verification and those which are not. Examples of both types of statements were given in that brief mention of the issue, but it is now necessary to take a closer look at the problems raised by the distinction. In particular, we need to delineate carefully the different types of words and statements which fall under the general category of 'evaluative'.

Take a look, first of all, at the following statements:

Three feet make one yard.
Franklin D. Roosevelt was four times elected President of the USA.
Wednesday is named after the god Thor.
Paris is the capital of France.
Los Angeles is north of San Francisco.
The practice of having only one spouse is called monotony.
The Trumpet Voluntary was not composed by Purcell, as was once thought, but by Jeremiah Clarke.

What do these statements have in common? Not, it will be immediately noted, that they are all true: some are, some are not. The common factor in all of them is that they are verifiable: their truth or falsehood can be demonstrated by reference to a dictionary, or atlas, or encyclopedia.

Now consider the following:

Jogging is a healthy exercise.
The early bird catches the worm.
Many hands make light work.
Women are worse drivers than men.
Negroes are less intelligent than caucasians.
The country needs firm government.
Our God is marching on.

It will be immediately obvious that here we have a different category of statement from the first group: though often dogmatically affirmed, each of these is a value judgment, not capable of being verified, as a simple analysis will show. Jogging may be healthy for some, but it certainly wasn't for an acquaintance of mine who died of a heart attack immediately afterwards. (Assurances to his widow that he 'looked well' did nothing for her equanimity.) Late risers who resent the holier-than-thou attitude invariably assumed by early birds can comfort themselves with the consideration that it's the early worm that gets caught. And if many hands make light work, it is also the case that too many cooks spoil the broth, as I remind my wife from time to time.

The fourth sentence would require a good deal of analysis of the word 'worse': much begging of questions occurs when generalisations are made about the sexes, illustrated in the following true conversation:

> Passenger in car (to driver): Look at that idiot in front; I bet it's a woman.
> Driver: No it's not; it's a man.
> Passenger: Well, it's a man driving like a woman.

Statements like this, and the fifth one in the list, reflect a prejudice on the part of the speaker which is unlikely to be modified by an examination of relevant facts, such as the cost, on average, for car insurance for women *vis-à-vis* men (it is lower), and the achievements of negroes when presented with the same opportunities as caucasians, assuming that 'the same opportunities' could ever occur in this context.

With the sixth statement many people would presumably agree, and their apparent accord would no doubt continue until asked to spell out in detail what is meant by the word 'firm'. Supporters of the left and of the right in politics would then no doubt have to disentangle themselves in order to produce their different recipes for government. This statement is an example of 'pre-digested thinking': using words which are in common speech and therefore apparently unambiguous when in fact their meaning is open to a wide range of interpretations. The world of advertising uses such words continuously and deliberately: 'new' usually means that the commodity's price has been raised; 'lifelong' means 'until the next model comes out'; and 'exclusive' (watch this one) invariably means 'expensive'. We may condemn advertisers for a gross misuse of language, but at least there is no hypocrisy in this field: their aim is to sell their commodity – nothing more, nothing less. In politics, the situation is much more insidious, because although, as with advertising, words are used simply to create an impression, or to charge an atmosphere – words like progressive, imperialist, fascist, reactionary, Marxist, democratic, liberal, wet, or red – matters in this field are different because no politician will ever admit to anything less than total sincerity. Sad and regrettable though it may be, the meaning of all these words will vary according to the context in which they are spoken, and the attitudes and values of the speaker. What is firm government to one group will be obstinacy to another and pure pig-headedness to a third. It is a fascinating and instructive exercise to devise irregular verbs on this basis, such as 'I am a freedom fighter; you are a violent rebel; he is a murdering psychopath.' Do we speak of a teenage gang or a group of adolescents? of an abattoir or a slaughterhouse? of young criminals or problem children? of corporal punishment or flogging? Is your neighbour a Jew or is he Jewish? The words we use in these contexts have taken over a force of their own, independent of their meaning; they have been described as 'purr' words and 'snarl' words and, cleverly used in the press, on the public platform, from the pulpit, or on TV, can mould people's opinions.

It is necessary therefore, when undertaking any examination of values, to be conscious that words are often loaded and ambiguous and used by their perpetrators as a lamp-post to a drunken man: more for support than illumination. Look at these two reports of the same event (used in P. McGeeney's *Life and Literacy*):

(i) 'Peter Speldon, that Bible-punching do-gooder, sneaked into the meeting late to give a rabble-rousing speech in favour of mongrelisation of the races.'

(ii) 'Peter Speldon, the well-known supporter of anti-apartheid, entered the hall almost unnoticed after the meeting began, and afterwards gave an impassioned speech in favour of inter-racial marriage.'

The first report clearly says more about the prejudices of the writer than of what was said in the hall; the second is a more objective account of what occurred, though not uninfluenced by the writer's evident sympathy with the speaker: I particularly like the phrase 'after the meeting began' in place of 'late', and have used it on numerous occasions.

The second list on p. 47, then, is a series of unverifiable value judgments, matters of debate, not of fact, and reaching their climax, perhaps, in the final statement, where the word 'cause' is replaced by 'God', presumably to give an added dimension to that cause. As it stands, the sentence is meaningless; in fact it would still be meaningless with the suggested alteration, since it is difficult to see how a cause can march: but there is no doubt that the hymn from which this is taken played its part in winning the American Civil War for the Union.

That wars are not won by philosophical analysis should surprise nobody. What is – or should be – more surprising is that the category of words and phrases which we have been describing is not unknown among people who have, presumably, been trained in critical analysis. I have heard two schoolteachers reach apparent agreement about what is the overriding aim of education: that it is to produce 'mature' citizens (an issue discussed in Case Study 39). It was only when they were pushed a little harder by their colleagues, who had never known them previously to have agreed about anything, that they found themselves to be in reality poles apart: for one, 'mature' meant 'law-abiding, rule-governed, authority-accepting', while for the other to be mature meant to challenge authority, and to accept rules and laws only if and when validified through experience. The same problem arises over interpretations of the word 'creative'. Parents who wish to encourage this quality in their offspring are likely to disagree radically as to what this implies. Some, probably most, will agree that there are limits to the behaviour that can be allowed when expressing the creative urge; others – and I have lived alongside one such couple in California – believe that any kind of restriction on their child's behaviour will erode his creativity and therefore must not be imposed upon him, even if this means allowing him to hurl the china around the house or daub his bedroom walls with his own faeces. (Even this liberated couple felt compelled, at one o'clock one morning when their two-year-old was understandably howling his head off through fatigue, to suggest that he 'be mature'.)

Words of this nature are used daily as though there is a consensus as to their meaning, when in fact that meaning depends entirely on the values of the person using them. One further example should make this plain. In recent years in the UK there has been a call for more efficient teachers in the nation's schools, and for inefficient teachers to be removed from their jobs or at least passed over when promotion is on hand. Few people have objected to this call. We all want to see efficiency encouraged and inefficiency discouraged. But what makes an efficient teacher? What are his trademarks? Is it punctuality, politeness to superiors, tidiness in dress (whatever that may mean)? Is it enthusiasm, ability to motivate others? Is it expertise in his chosen field, being up to date on the latest developments? Is it, as some cynics have suggested, ability to survive? Until there is universal agreement on the criteria of teaching efficiency, it would seem pointless to characterise this as the sole criterion of promotion in that field.

The catholicity of values

Having established that the basic difference between the two lists of statements quoted earlier in the chapter is that those in the first list can be verified, while those in the second can not, we must now take note of a further factor relating to the second group. While some of the statements in this group have implications for human behaviour, several of them have no such implication. Axiology, the study, or understanding, of values, is certainly concerned with moral issues; but values are also significant in a wide range of fields where morals are not relevant, or only tangentially so. (The word 'axiology' is not one that springs daily to most people's lips, but it is a crisp epitomisation of the general theme under discussion. It is derived from two Greek words: 'axios', meaning 'worthy' in the sense of what is of value, and 'logos', which, as we have seen, can be translated variously, such as 'word' or 'discourse'.) The value of a painting, for instance, will depend to a great extent on the esteem in which the artist is held, and the authenticity of the painting. A copy, however indistinguishable from the original, is unlikely to have anything like the value of the original (though the situation might be reversed if it were the case that a great painter had copied an original by a less-renowned person). Similarly, it would be quite natural to speak of a hierarchy of values in the medical and scientific fields. Research into the causes of cancer would generally be viewed as being of more value than into those of baldness; the development of labour-saving devices would rank in most people's minds more highly than that of toxic gases for use in war (though in time of war, or when war is threatened, these might change position in public esteem, as does the value of works of art from generation to generation). One can also speak of religious, such as Islamic, values. In this latter case, one may be speaking of desired, and required, codes of behaviour; but one will also be bearing in mind the place of the Islamic holy book, the Koran, as the basic container of truth; of Mohammed as the unique prophet of this truth; and of Allah as the Creator of all truth.

'Ought'

Typically, statements of value contain the words of approval, disapproval, and obligation: good, bad, and ought (or ought not), and their cognates; but even these words, which on the surface seem to possess a strong moral connotation, can be, and often are, employed in fields other than the ethical. The word 'ought', for example, can be used in a purely prudential sense, such as in telling a person that he ought to get his shoes mended, or that he ought to visit the dentist. No moral obligation is involved in either of these situations: just that it would be in the person's interests to do as advised. He ought to follow this advice if he wishes to avoid getting his feet wet, or suffering toothache. With some ought-sentences it is not easy to be sure whether the prudential or the moral consideration is uppermost. 'You ought to obey the law' could be based on either (otherwise you might be found out and punished, or because the law is established for our own good). Ought a person to obey the legal speed limit if he is rushing a sick person to hospital? (Some people think that all ought statements are reducible to expressions of self-interest, as we saw when considering the views of Hobbes.)

Another use of ought is in the sense of what may be expected. I ought to have finished typing out this chapter by the time I go to bed tonight. The books I have taken off my shelves to sell to my students ought to bring me in about £20; and none of these books ought to be beyond their range of understanding. Here the idea of obligation, prudential or moral, is totally absent.

'Good'

Let's take a look at a variety of uses of the word 'good'. Here are a few examples, which must have been uttered on a host of occasions, some having moral implications, others, not:

This is a good knife.
You are sitting on a good chair.
The Mayor of Casterbridge is a good book.
Geoff Boycott is a good cricketer.
Joe Bloggs is a good burglar.
Sergeant Kluger is a good killer.
I want to be a good parent.
Mother Teresa is a good person.
God is good.

Let us examine each of these in turn.

What exactly is a good knife? Clearly, the answer to this question depends on the knife's purpose. If its main use, like the scouts' knife of old, is for taking stones out of horses' hooves, then it will need to be small and manipulable. If I'm looking for a knife with which to carve the Sunday joint, then size, sharpness, and comfort to the hand will be top considerations. Nevertheless, even though we may have varying views about the qualities required in a good knife, there will probably in the end be certain common features in all answers.

But what about a good chair? Having suffered for years from back trouble of various sorts, a good chair for me is one which supports my back without allowing it to droop into the debilitating shape of a question mark. It may not be comfortable to others but, like the hard bed recommended by orthopaedic surgeons, it does my back good. It would, however, present no overwhelming difficulty to a group of adjudicants to agree on what constitutes a good chair: it must be one which is firm, comfortable, fitting the curvature of the spine of the person using it.

We turn now to a good book. Here again, as with the earlier uses of the word, 'good' carries the stamp of approval. If I tell a friend that this book of Hardy's is good, by implication it must be one which I have enjoyed (I am hardly likely to recommend it otherwise.) It may be because of the author's narrative skills, or his characterisation, his philosophy, or whatever. But the fact that *I* have enjoyed it does not mean, as any recommender of books must know from experience, that a third party will also enjoy it. Some people find Hardy simply exasperating, as some find the thrillers of John Le Carré, which I enjoy, verbose and obscure. The so-called goodness or badness of any book will depend on the predilections of the reader, and these will vary from person to person. After all, most published books are not bestsellers, but appeal to only a minority of the reading public.

The same kind of considerations apply to the next statement (which non-cricketers may skip). The assessment of Boycott in the hierarchy of cricketers' batsmen will depend largely on how highly the assessor ranks technique and the refusal to take risks, compared with a more cavalier approach to the game which is more exciting to the spectator but may not always feature in the cricketing records. For some, one hour of Botham is worth a day of Boycott: but that is a value judgment, understandable only to cricketing aficionados.

The next two are included in order simply to illustrate how odd the contexts can be in which the word 'good' can be validly used. Neither of the men would rank very highly in most people's league of desirable citizens, but the word 'good', when applied to them, is not intended as an indication of moral approbation, rather a recognition of the skill and expertise with which they accomplish their respective tasks. I suppose there might be a situation when, for purely altruistic reasons, I needed a spot of burgling to be done: Joe Bloggs would obviously be the man for this; and if there were a homicidal maniac on the prowl in my neighbourhood I might be glad that the sergeant lived next door.

It is with the next two statements that deeper problems arise. To state that one wishes to be a good parent will no doubt be viewed by most people as a laudable aim; but what exactly has been said? Few people with children are likely to affirm that they wish to be bad parents, so the aim to be a good parent must be common to all of them. Since there are as many different approaches to parenthood as there are sets of parents, we are left with nothing in particular to analyse. One pair may believe that parenthood involves careful cossetting of offspring, another that it involves the imposition of a strict code of behaviour, another the instillation of a particular set of beliefs, yet another that it means standing back, so to speak, and allowing their children to think, explore, develop for themselves. It is impossible to state, as though the issue were clear-cut like a mathematical theorem, that one approach is good and another bad; or that there are universal rules for good parenthood. How children are raised will depend on the values, the priorities in life, held by the parents: and these, as we have seen, are varied, with no possibility of external, objective verification. All that an observer can do is to assess how far parents act consistently with their own declared criteria. If retrospective action could be taken when children had reached the age of, say, fourteen, and a different method of raising them tried out, some comparison might then be possible. But, as the existentialist Kierkegaard remarked, while we may assess life's challenges retrospectively, life itself has to be lived prospectively. We may learn from our mistakes and successes, or even change our minds about our modus vivendi or life-style, but we cannot undo what has been done.

When we turn to the concept of a good person, matters become even more complex. I, like most people, have a range of friends whom I might describe as 'good fellows' or 'good sorts'. But what is meant by such a designation? Everything depends on the qualities which I consider most admirable in a human being, which in turn will depend on a number of intangible factors, such as my character and temperament. A list of people whom I like and admire would differ from any similar list that you or anyone else might produce. To take the example chosen earlier: Mother Teresa of Calcutta has been described by many people as a good person, not to say a saint. This is because those observers have been impressed by her asceticism, her lifetime of devotion to the dispossessed of the earth, her total neglect of personal comforts and physical rewards. No doubt all this is true; I personally find it impossible, however, to describe as good a person who has affirmed that the poverty-stricken millions of Ethiopia and other African countries are 'blessed of God' because they are His instruments for awakening the consciences of the affluent, thus inspiring the rich of the world to give to the poor. Such a facile acceptance of human suffering seems to me shallow, and even cynical.

For me, then, the epithet 'good' cannot be applied to Mother Teresa; does that mean that she is therefore not a good person? It is impossible to answer this in the way anticipated by anyone who may put such a question. Whatever the answer given, it will reveal more about the values of the speaker than it does about the person assessed. From my list of people whom I hold in esteem you could write a reasonably accurate pen-portrait of me.

What are we to make of the statement 'God is good'? This is too complex an issue to be analysed here, so all we need to establish at this stage is that the sentence is a tautology. Since, for most believers, 'God' means the sum total of benevolence as they conceive it, and since 'good' means those values in life of which they approve, we are left only with the statement, after logical analysis of the original, 'The good is benevolence as people generally conceive it', which is saying even less than the politician who declares himself in favour of a better way of life for all.

Omission of 'code' words

It was stated earlier that most value judgments typically contain words like 'good' and 'ought' which have a moral ring to them, but can be used in contexts other than a discussion of morals. It must also now be stated that these words are not essential in the expression of value judgments, though their presence will normally be implied. 'This is stealing', for example, does not contain any evaluative word, but the implication in what is said must be that (a) stealing is not a good activity and therefore (b) the person addressed ought not to do it. This may appear to be merely a matter of linguistics, but in fact the omission of the 'code' words is often the cause of much confusion and contention. Many injustices throughout the world have occurred because value judgments have been stated as though they were matters of fact. Here are a few which I have heard over the years, all having unspoken moral implications. I have put some of these implications in brackets: see if you can identify what lies behind the other remarks:

Liberals live in Cloud-cuckoo-land (they ought not to be taken seriously).
Opponents of capital punishment encourage violent crime.
Abortion is murder (it should be made illegal).
Prison sentences in this country are too short.
Corporal punishment will reduce crime.
Rugby is a man's game.
Homosexuality is unnatural (homosexuals should be banned/imprisoned/wiped out).
Where would we be but for the police?
The community needs people like me; philosophers are parasites (an accountant).
Pity we didn't kill more of the bastards (after the Falklands War).
South Africa is the only country that knows how to deal with the blacks.
Seducing women sorts out the men from the boys.
The Germans are krauts.
Communism is a disease.
Students are immature and irresponsible.
How can you understand about life, in your ivory tower? (An estate agent/realtor.)
The Welsh bring down the tone of the place.
Catholics don't belong in Northern Ireland.
Nobody needs to be out of work: the unemployed are all spongers on the state. (Or, as the mayor of a large city is reported to have said: 'There is no housing shortage in this city: this is just a malicious rumour being spread by people with nowhere to live.')

These represent a fair cross-section of the attitudes expressed in one particular meeting place. Perhaps a picture of the type of people who hold such views will have formed itself in your mind. As with all value judgments, the statements are more autobiographical than illuminative of any issue. You may assert that the opinions expressed are biased, bigoted, and prejudiced: and you would be right. But whatever set of opinions quoted would suffer from these characteristics. If I were to quote from a different group, I would make an alternative list, beginning with 'All policemen are pigs', and continuing from there. It is vital to bear in mind, when discussing moral values, that there is no such creature as an unbiased person. We all have our prejudices; the real danger, in terms of discussing matters with the hope of achieving some form of illumination, lies in not realising this. So (to reiterate a point already twice stated) if I were to describe an acquaintance as one who 'knows the cost of everything and the value of nothing', you would need to learn a good deal more about me and my prejudices than has been revealed so far, if you were to reach an assessment of either the meaning or the truth of my assertion.

Empirical and normative

In accordance with the title of this chapter, we have considered, with a fair number of examples, the difference between facts and values, between what is demonstrably the case and what ought to be the case. These two types of statement are often described by philosophers as empirical and normative. Empirical statements are those made as the result of observation and the use of reason; they describe matters of fact. Normative statements are concerned with rules (in ethics, rules of behaviour) and the recommendations or proposals which follow from these. The central feature of these latter statements is that they cannot be presented as facts. I may scream 'Genocide is wrong' until I'm hoarse, and you may well agree with me: but this does not make the affirmation a fact, and this is the case even if the whole of the human race affirm it. All that can be said is that I am expressing a point of view about a form of behaviour which I deem to be abhorrent – a point of view with which, as it happens, few people openly disagree.

This is not to say that facts have no place in discussion based on normative statements, or value judgments. These statements or judgments are not made in a vacuum, but on the basis of something read, discussed, or experienced. If another person disagrees with the judgment, it will therefore be pointless for me simply to react by shouting my own views even more loudly. What we need to do if we consider that someone is expressing a wrong – perhaps dangerously wrong – opinion is to encourage him to take a closer, or broader, look at the facts of the situation. A.J. Ayer pointed this out half a century ago in his *Language,Truth and Logic*[1]:

> When someone disagrees with us about the moral value of a certain action . . . what we attempt to show is that he is mistaken about the facts of the case. We argue that he has misconceived the agent's motive: or that he has misjudged the effects of the action . . . or that he has failed to take into account the special circumstances in which the agent was placed. Or else we employ more general arguments about the effects which actions of a certain type tend to produce, or the qualities which are usually manifested in their performance.

Even after all this, there can be no guarantee of success: the person I am arguing with may belong to a moral and cultural tradition so different from mine that he may doubt the evidence of his own eyes if I am the one who presents it. There seems little to be gained from my debating any moral or political issue with, for instance, a person who sincerely thinks the *Guardian* newspaper is a 'communist rag'. As was written in the Book of Ecclesiastes: 'There is a time for speech, and a time for silence.'

In the world of facts – of proven hypotheses and chemical formulae, of prices and products and technical knowhow – we are in a state of security. We know where we are and, probably, where we're going. There is no such security in the world of values. Here we are in a state of perpetual change, where no one person's sense of what is of worth can automatically be judged as being more significant than another's. In the world of values there are no experts, no professionals, no authorities: a toddler's point of view, if not heard as often as that of a successful columnist or author, remains nonetheless a point of view which must be taken into consideration when decisions are made which involve him. When you think about it, it is these matters of value which are the subject of most of our interesting discussions, and the source of most of our enjoyable experiences. If you prefer to discuss the distinctive features of your car when you meet your friends, you will be free to do so; but if that, and similar matters, is all you can find to talk about, you will be missing out on those issues which give life its tang.

CASE STUDY 8: CENSORSHIP

Censorship is an issue over which value judgments are constantly being made. On the one hand, it is argued that certain restrictions should be placed on what people are allowed to read or see, whether on TV, in the

---

[1] Pelican edition, pp. 146 f.

cinema, or on the stage. On the other, it is contended that such restrictions would, and do, represent a curtailment of any individual's right to decide. We shall pursue this matter in dialogue form, concentrating exclusively on the issue as it arises from the portrayal of sex and violence in the media and the arts, and leaving till Chapter Eleven the related, but different, problem of political censorship.

1 Something must be done about all the sex and violence that's being shown these days. You can't go to the cinema without seeing people hacked to pieces, and half the TV programmes bring in nudity at some point. There was even one about yoga the other day where the women all showed the body postures naked. It's just an excuse for lechery.

I agree that there are too many violent films around these days – and it's even worse in the States – but I don't think there's as much gratuitous sex (assuming nudity always implies sex, which I'm not so sure about) as there was in the 1970s. Anyway, you can't ban them altogether if you're trying to show life as it really is. I reckon they're both here to stay – sex in particular.

2 But the world isn't full of homicidal maniacs or police who shoot first and ask questions afterwards. And most of the sex you see is either adulterous or involves prostitutes. How often do you get a sex scene between a husband and wife? I reckon these kinds of programmes are having an appalling effect on moral standards, especially among the young. They're being brought up to believe that it's normal to go around beating up people you don't like, or popping into bed with anyone you fancy.

Half the trouble is that people seem to enjoy seeing this sort of thing, or reading about it. If half a dozen students throw an egg at a visiting politician it'll be in all the papers; but when twenty thousand students demonstrate peacefully at the Ministry of Education not a word is reported. People just don't want to know about life on the straight and narrow, probably because they have too much of that themselves. They get their kicks by watching others breaking loose, and if that's what they want I can't see that they're harming anyone.

3 They're harming themselves – they're being corrupted, and they copy what they see. Look at the way the incidence of muggings went up after *The Clockwork Orange* went the rounds; and look at the way divorce and rapes are on

I don't know how you'd go about proving any connection here. The word 'mugging' came to be used after that film for crimes previously described differently. But they've always happened, just as sex crimes the increase: you can't tell me this has no connection with what's being shown on the media day in, day out.

4   It stands to reason there's a connection. The cinema and TV people are cashing in on the worst elements of human nature and bringing out the animal in us. Look at the way people went wild about *Rambo* – a mass killer commended even by the US President. And I saw a film last week that was full of explicit acts of copulation – close-ups, oral sex, the lot. Nothing left to the imagination. Absolutely disgusting.

5   Well I'd have them banned. We don't need this sort of thing in a civilised society. We're going the way of the Roman empire – orgies, murders, filth. We need a watchdog, and one with teeth. I'd appoint a board of censors with absolute power to ban anything that's likely to corrupt.

have always happened. If there's been an increase in these – and I'm not granting you that there has – you could just as well say that the media are reflecting what's going on around them, rather than causing it.

I agree about *Rambo* and films like it, and it doesn't surprise me one bit that it was Reagan's cup of tea: what do you expect from a man with the brains and sensitivity of a wild west cowboy? But why are you so upset about the sex film? For a start, you must have known what it was about before you paid to go in: you can't have thought it was a Disney film, or been frogmarched inside. And what's so disgusting about showing sexual intimacy? I can't see that there's anything disgusting that happens between a man and a woman. Actually, I've learned a few things from films like that.

Would that include the *Sun* newspaper? I notice one chief constable had all copies confiscated in his area a while ago because he disapproved of the page three picture. Most people thought this was absurd, but you're likely to have the same reaction whatever you ban. What one person finds dirty another finds perfectly normal or even artistic. You can't legislate for all people's tastes. Are you going to ban nude paintings like *The Rape of the Sabine Women*, or any picture that shows massacres? And why stop there? The Bible is full of sex and violence – Solomon and his concubines, Saul slaying the Amalekites, David playing Peeping Tom with Bathsheba, everyone smiting and being smitten. And what are you going to do with Shakespeare?

6 If it's great art, it can be kept. But what I'm talking about isn't art but exploitation – exploitation of the subjects and of the readers and viewers. These people need to be protected against themselves. That's why we need a body of good, sensible people who know what's best for us – like bishops, doctors, lawyers.

How can anyone else know what's best for me? I'm the sole judge of that. And if you must have control, why bring in all these middle-class professionals? Why should their attitude be more sensible, as you call it, than bookies' or football managers'? At least you haven't brought in MPs: the sort of bills they've tried to introduce on the subject make one wonder if they ever get further than the local bar.

7 But you agree that something has to be done?

Not by censorship. I admit I'm very disturbed by the way people throughout the world seem to be accepting violence as a part of life, and even as a means of achieving political ends. But you won't change this by banning films, just as you won't stop men enjoying looking at nude women by banning girlie magazines. My concern is for freedom to choose; I don't want any Big Brother up there telling me what I can and cannot look at. There are enough restrictions on our freedom already without imposing another major one. It may mean we have to risk things happening occasionally that we'd be better off without – like child porn, or scenes of gore like *The Chainsaw Massacres*. We must hope that the public themselves will ban such things by having nothing to do with them. But that risk is preferable, I think, to the certainty of intolerance, narrow-mindedness, and injustice which will happen if you appoint censors. And, incidentally, it wouldn't be *you* who appointed them, but the Prime Minister. And if some of them had their way we'd spend the rest of our viewing lives watching *Dallas* or *Neighbours*. Surely any situation is preferable to that?

8 I reckon that any form of censorship will be preferable to the present *Laissez-faire* attitude. There are plenty of people around to deal with the matter sensibly. If this means that some films have to be cut, and some books and magazines have to be taken off the shelves, that seems to me a small price to pay for improving the moral tone of the nation. You've got to learn the difference between freedom and license.

Where, if anywhere, would *you* draw the line, and what measures would you encourage to establish it?

CASE STUDY 9: PORNOGRAPHY

Which, if any, of the following would you call 'pornographic'?
   Which, if any, would you like to have banned?

1 A picture of a naked body in a medical textbook.
2 The same picture shown on television on a medical programme.
3 The same picture shown on television on a comedy programme.
4 A picture of a couple having intercourse in a book called *The Married Couple's Guide to a Happy Love Life*.
5 The same picture in a children's comic book.
6 A picture of a woman in a swimming costume in a newspaper report of a swimming competition.

7 A similar picture in a newspaper report of a 'Miss World' competition.

8 A similar picture in a men's 'girlie' magazine.

9 A book of Indian art showing pictures of temple sculptures in which gods and goddesses in human and animal form engage in a variety of sex acts.

10 A TV documentary showing the same sculptures.

11 A school textbook showing the same sculptures.

12 Page 3 of the *Sun*.

13 A video cassette showing sexual intercourse between men and women.

14 A video cassette showing sex between adults and young children.

15 A video cassette showing sex between people and animals.

16 An advert for women's underwear showing a semi-naked woman.

17 An advert for motorbikes showing a semi-naked woman.

18 An advert for vodka showing a semi-naked woman.

19 Adverts with implicit sexual overtones advertising anything from bananas to washing-up liquid.

20 Television adverts for contraceptives.

21 A television documentary on rape designed to elicit sympathy for rape victims.

22 A film showing scenes of rape in which the rapist is the hero.

23 Television adverts for a homosexual dating agency.

24 A film portraying bondage and sadistic sex.

25 Teenage magazines advocating promiscuity.

26 Teenage magazines advocating homosexuality.

27 A play in which masturbation takes place on the stage.

28 A parliamentary bill to legalise magazines on paedophilia (sex with children).

29 A prostitute's advert in a shop window offering 'private massage – hotels visited at any hour of day or night'.

30 A detailed newspaper report of a brutal sex crime.

31 A television film depicting women solely as objects for the sexual gratification of men.

32 A television film depicting a woman who gets to the top by having sex with influential men.

33 A television series depicting beautiful but selfish and inane women who live luxuriously off their millionaire husbands' earnings.

Why do you judge something to be pornographic?

(a) Because it makes you feel –
    angry?
    disgusted?
    ashamed?
    insecure?

(b) Because it portrays nudity?
(c) Because it portrays sexual intercourse?
(d) Because it portrays sexual perversion?
(e) Because it degrades women?
(f) Because it 'offends public decency'?
(g) Because it has a 'tendency to deprave or corrupt'?
(h) For some other reason?

'Pornography: treatment of obscene subjects'
'Obscene: repulsive, filthy, loathsome, indecent, lewd'

– Oxford English Dictionary

Note, however, 'Erotica: literature dealing with sexual love'
Do you think there is a difference between erotica and pornography?
If so, how would you describe it?

CASE STUDY 10: WHAT IS TRUTH?

In this chapter, we have seen that the truth or falsehood of factual statements can be verified: this is not so for statements in the field of art or politics, or morals, or religion, which are value judgments and therefore unverifiable. So can we ever justifiably claim that anything in these areas is 'true'? Try this out with the following questions, then reflect over the final, crucial, question.

Can one fairly state 'It is (not) true that . . .' regarding the following:

A Art
(i) Beethoven was a greater composer than Paul McCartney.
(ii) All literature is of equal value; so long as a piece of writing evokes some response in some reader it has literary merit to compare with works of the most famous.
(iii) I know what I like, and if I like it, it's art.
(iv) Real art evokes depth of feeling in people: much of what passes as art fails this test because of its triteness.

B Politics
(i) Governments should ensure that the poor in the community are adequately provided for by the wealthy.
(ii) In politics, half a loaf is better than no bread. Better to govern by compromising some of one's principles than not to govern at all.
(iii) All government information – whether about contracts, defence, the secret services, or high-ranking public officials – should be fully available to the general public.
(iv) If a government minister is found to have lied to his/her peers and to the people (s)he should, as a matter of course, resign.

C Morals

(i) If a terminally ill patient/a paraplegic wishes to die, (s)he should be legally enabled to do so.
(ii) Capital punishment is barbaric.
(iii) Eating animal flesh/human flesh is wrong.
(iv) Thou shalt not commit adultery.

D Religion

(i) God exists/God does not exist.
(ii) There is a spiritual dimension in life, to which atheists are blind.
(iii) God counsels/directs/sustains/comforts us in our innermost being.
(iv) Jesus is Lord.

Whenever a value judgment is claimed to be 'true' there is (is there not?) a recipe for conflict: others will claim that the opposite is 'true' and the first assertion 'false'. So how dangerous is it to use the word 'true' in relation to anything other than factual statements? *Is there an ultimate 'Truth'?*

Chapter Four

Our knowledge of right and wrong

We have seen that the word 'ought', which, on the face of it, has a moral connotation, has, among other characteristics, a prudential implication: 'ought' in the sense that it would be in the person's interests to act in a certain way. Some people believe, perhaps rather cynically, that all 'ought' statements fall into this category, with the exception of those which imply 'living up to expectation' which we noted in Chapter Three ('At your age you ought to be able to run a mile in five minutes', etc.).

It is certainly the case that over many ought statements there hangs an element of ambiguity. If I tell my son that he ought to go and dig a sick neighbour's garden because she's ill, I am not necessarily suggesting that he make a gratuitous altruistic gesture: she may well pay him for his trouble. Similarly, if I say that I ought to visit a sick (but not very likeable) relative from time to time, it could be argued that I do this only in the hope of being remembered in his will, or of obtaining kudos with my wife. If I advise a friend that he ought to give up alcohol, I may be bearing in mind only the state of his health, or his pocket, rather than any moral considerations, such as that one ought not to cloud one's mind or alter one's metabolism through use of drugs – though even if this is the prime intention, it could be argued that prudential factors underlie the matter: he might fall down (metaphorically or literally) on his job, or get himself involved in a road accident.

However, while it is clear that many of our forms of behaviour about which people are inclined to make a moral song and dance are undoubtedly motivated primarily by prudential considerations, it seems obvious that there are situations where this is not the case. Suppose, for instance, the above-mentioned relative lives in a council house with a few worthless pieces of furniture, and has nothing to leave in his will except his overdraft. And suppose that my wife, far from approving of my visiting him, does her best to discourage me from doing so, on the grounds that I could be spending my time more profitably (in more than one sense) elsewhere. What then is the relevance of prudential considerations? Or suppose that my son is a proud person who would not dream of accepting money from a sick neighbour for work done out of the goodness of his heart (none my sons reading this will identify with such a description, but such people do exist): have we not then a situation with a purely moral motive, even if it could be shown that the altruistic deed was performed primarily in order to gain an inner feeling of satisfaction through giving up time and energy on another person's behalf?

A host of examples spring to mind – and you can make your own list if you reflect for a few minutes – of non-prudentially-motivated behaviour springing from a sense of obligation. Why did the elderly lady who found an expensive camera in a bag which had fallen off a friend's motorbike walk over a mile with this to the nearest police station, where the loss had been reported, then, at the request of the police officer, walk a further mile-and-a-half to my friend's house in order to return it, and then indignantly refuse any reward? We shall take a closer look at this question in Chapters Five and Six, but at this stage it seems reasonable to conclude that, whatever her motive, it had no prudential component. What consideration other than moral lay behind the action of the person who anonymously returned a wallet to its owner with all its contents, including cash, untouched, and actually paid for its return by registered mail? What was prudential about the behaviour of the IRA officer, captured by the Black and Tans in County Cork in 1919 and about to be shot, who spent his last minutes pleading for the life of the young man (my father-in-law) who had been with him in his vehicle at the time of the capture?

It seems absurd to deny that much of our behaviour is motivated by ethical considerations. Why this is so is not the question here; at this stage our concern is not with the why but with the how. Where do we get our knowledge of right and wrong? What is the origin of our sense of 'ought'? We shall look at some of the most prominent answers to this question which have been offered by philosophers and others from time to time.

(a) **Our parents**

There must be few people who can truthfully deny that, at least in their earliest years, their parents' attitudes, admonitions, and examples, played a major part in formulating their own awareness of right and wrong. Until a child begins to form associations with others outside the home, parental attitudes on virtually any issue that may arise are all that he is likely to experience. 'Show me the child, and I'll give you the man' – so runs the old saying: and this is illustrated by the frequency with which children's moral views in later life, probably after an intermission for a period of rebellion, reflect most of their parents' sense of values. (It is perhaps because of this obvious association that we are disturbed to read of political régimes which openly encourage children to report to local officers details of their parents' views and behaviour.) Speaking personally, I know how deeply embedded in me for many years were my parents' firm sabbatarian views; I still recall the Sunday morning when I spent on an icecream the money given me for the church collection: the sense of impending doom which descended on me as I ate it remains a powerful childhood memory. There are, however, obvious problems if we assert that this answer tells the whole story. In the first place, there are numerous parents who, in the eyes of most people around them, are wrong on certain moral matters; they may be Jehovah's Witnesses who, if allowed to act according to their own convictions, would refuse their children a blood transfusion, even in the most critical of circumstances; they may be members of a fascist group who instil in their children a hatred of all races other than their own; they may belong to a radical political group and teach their children the virtues of bloody revolution. Less tangibly, but equally insidiously, they may bring up their children to believe in some class-based superiority to others in the neighbourhood and beyond; or they may threaten their later chances of a happy sex life by teaching them that this activity is in some way 'dirty'; or, potentially most damaging of all, they may impose themselves on their children in so strongly authoritarian a way that for the remainder of their lives their offspring find it virtually impossible to enter confidently into relationships with others. 'Like father, like son': but what if father is a lying, thieving, bullying braggart who treats women like dirt? Are we to view with equanimity the continuing survival of such a macho male attitude because of some undefined sense of the divine right of families to bestow on successive generations whatever prejudices they will?

The second difficulty with this answer can perhaps ease our minds on the question just raised. Views of what forms of behaviour are right or wrong may vary from generation to generation. The phrase 'the generation gap' became popular in the 1960s and 70s, and perhaps at that time the force of this alleged divide was exaggerated. But it hardly needs arguing that, while some offspring faithfully reflect most of their parents' moral views and behaviour throughout their lives, others, even on the most major of issues, knowingly move in divergent directions. Many people will, if they are honest with themselves, acknowledge that on a range of moral issues they are no longer in step with their parents, even though they still hold them in love and respect. It would seem difficult to establish any causal link between parental attitudes and such departures.

Added to this is the fact that many parents themselves modify their views, perhaps as a result of their children's alternative emphases. Sometimes, the direction is from an 'anything goes' view of morality towards one with more rigour, from one where lines of distinction have tended to be blurred to one where 'right' and 'wrong' are clearly defined: yesterday's teddy boys have become today's upholders of strict standards. My own experience has been the reverse of this: the Victorian, moral-majority views of my parents were modified over the years (without being entirely dissipated), partly, I think, because on some issues none of their four children went along with them. (It will be interesting to discover whether this more liberal approach is pursued by the next generation with their children, or whether there is a pendulum-like swing back to greater rigour.) Whatever the answer to that mystery, the fact remains that by designating parents as the possessors of a good deal of authority *vis-à-vis* their children's earliest appreciation of moral issues, we have been discussing the *means* by which this comes about, not the ultimate *source* of this awareness. Parents certainly constitute for most people the initial pipeline by which norms and attitudes are conveyed; but the same happened to them under their own parents' influence, and to them from theirs, and so on back through the generations. We are no nearer to solving the problem of the basic source of our knowledge of right and wrong.

(b) The conscience

'Always let your conscience be your guide': how sound is that advice? Much depends on one's understanding of what precisely the conscience is. The assumption behind the quotation is that it constitutes some kind of inner self, pure and untainted by selfishness and all the vices of the person seen by others and with whom they must deal. It has been described as 'another man within me that's angry with me';[1] more cynically as 'the inner voice that warns us that someone may be looking'.[2] Either way, it is being described as an entity in its own right, inexorably linked with, but capable of judgment on, its owner.

Many people have spent their lives following the dictates of their consciences; some, by the same measure, have risked, and even surrendered, their lives. George Washington's conscience would not let him tell a lie; Martin Luther's led him to denounce the authorities whom he had been brought up to accept as of God, culminating in his speech at the Diet of Worms when he faced the possibility of death with the words 'Here I stand; I can do no other'; Dietrich Bonhoeffer's brought him back from the safety of North America to the menace of Nazi Germany where he was eventually executed because of his opposition to Hitler and all that he stood for. The pacifist in wartime may be described as a 'conscientious objector'; we speak today of 'prisoners of conscience'; on a more universal level, men have found themselves physically incapable of the act of adultery, despite intense sexual desire, because of a deep conscientious objection to marital infidelity.

Most of us could probably make our own list of behaviour we could not indulge in, acts we could not perform, because of the dictates of our consciences, and we could perhaps give a nod of approval to Mark Twain who wrote: 'I have noticed my conscience for many years, and I know it

[1] Sir Thomas Browne, *Religio Medici*, pt 2
[2] H.L. Mencken, *Crestomathy*

is more trouble and bother to me than anything else I started with.' But in that last phrase an important question is begged. The implication is that the conscience is something we inherit at birth, remaining a fellow traveller with us throughout our lives. Experience assures us that this cannot, however, be the case: there are similar objections to this view as to that of parents as the source of moral awareness. In a word, the conscience lacks consistency, either between people in general or in any individual in particular.

Just think for a moment of what appalling acts of behaviour have been, and still are, performed with a clear conscience (and sometimes in the name of the conscience). At the time of the reformation, Catholics and Protestants cheerfully cut off each other's parts and burnt each other at the stake in the (not always insincere) belief that thereby they were giving the others' souls a last chance of redemption. In the name of the conscience, women have been executed as witches, nuns walled up in their convents because of indications of attraction to men, opponents of political regimes have been tortured to the point of insanity, and a whole race faced extermination: as any reader of *Mein Kampf* will be aware, there was no more conscientious man in history than Adolf Hitler. That this kind of behaviour is not just an unfortunate historical transitionary phase is indicated by the fact that in scores of countries today men and women are being imprisoned without trial, tortured to the point of insanity, and brutally executed, solely because of conscientious differences of opinion.

Leaving aside these momentous examples, it is obvious that in all kinds of humble, everyday matters, people's consciences vary as to the issues they feel conscientious about. For some it is the eating of flesh; for others the purchasing of goods from a particular country; for others using condoms. Some people could not conscientiously enter a public house (I know of one man, an able trades union shop steward, who gave up his position because that was where his union meetings took place); some people could not live with themselves if they did not give part of their income to the Third World; a man in my area went to prison because he persistently deducted from his income tax payments that proportion allocated for defence, and others risk the same penalty by protesting outside military establishments; while people whose consciences guide them differently sincerely believe that the one is insane and the others are traitors.

Even within one individual this so-called fellow traveller is inconsistent. Matters about which I had conscientious feelings years ago (such as Sabbath observance) no longer affect me; other matters have taken the place of these earlier ones, and I have already indicated enough of these without boring you with more. It appears that this conscience that travels with us is as changeable as an April day: how then can we possibly say that it is the final guide to moral behaviour? The question is whether we

69

should personalise it in this way at all, since this process gives it an air of authority which, on close analysis, it cannot possibly possess. Need we say any more than that the conscience is the arrival in our conscious minds of the conclusion of debates which have occurred subconsciously over matters about which there are conflicting viewpoints and pressures? It represents our view on moral matters as we perceive them at any given moment. Pending the arrival of new viewpoints and new pressures, we may well let our conscience be our guide, to be confirmed every time we face a similar problem; but new experiences will require us, so to speak, to reopen any investigation; and the conscience may well change. Sometimes, as we saw, discussing in Case Study 4 my colleague's first pint of beer, it may wrong.

The conscience may, then, be the means whereby we know, or are fairly sure of, what is right for us at any particular moment; but, again, we have done no more than establish a *means* whereby this knowledge is conveyed to us; we are still no nearer the *source* of this knowledge.

(c) The law of the land

At one level this is the obvious answer to our dilemma. Our country's laws exist independently of us: they preceded our arrival and will proceed after our departure. Many facets of our behaviour – more, perhaps, than most people realise – reflect our acceptance of certain procedures on the grounds that they are legal, and the rejection of others because they are illegal. Most people, for instance, will do all they can to avoid paying income tax, even if this means hiring an expensive accountant: this is a perfectly legal activity; on the other hand, only those prepared to risk severe punishment will engage themselves in tax evasion, which is illegal. It seems that there is a strong element of truth in Aristotle's claim that the purpose and process of the law is to make citizens good (or make good citizens).

It would be fascinating and self-revealing to reflect on which laws of our country we would continue to observe if there were no longer any law enforcement; we should in effect be asking ourselves how far we behave as we do from a general conviction that such behaviour is 'right', and how far because of the fear of being found out and punished. How many shops, especially supermarkets, would be able to stay open? How many libraries would survive? What kind of order would there be on the roads, in the streets? Who would feel safe from the thug, the bully, the rapist? Locksmiths could well become millionaires and security guards the first essential in banks, museums, stores – probably in all public places: and what would then prevent them from assuming total control of the state? Without laws, what is there to prevent anyone from becoming an outlaw? (I will refrain from making any pun on in-laws.) It looks as if Aristotle is right, as far as he goes, and that we need the law to keep us on the right track; the alternative, a state of no law, or anarchy, would seem to be a recipe for chaos. This situation, if it is the case, also seems to confirm Hobbes's view that, human nature being inherently selfish, we need the agreed norms and sanctions of the law in order to keep everyone from turning against his neighbour. Some smaller communities throughout the world, possessed with an overriding ideal, have apparently managed to live together harmoniously without any formal laws: various pacifist communities have been noteworthy examples of this. But there seems no hope of establishing this ideal in a world of massive populations and conflicting interests.

The issue we are dealing with, however, is that of the origin of our awareness of right and wrong, good and bad. The law no doubt instils into us certain habits of behaviour; but there are many obvious problems to be faced if it is presented as the source, as well as the definer and upholder, of morals. What, after all, is the law? It is not an independent impersonal entity; it is not a form of holy writ handed down from who-knows-where. It is a series of rules, regulations, which successive generations have concocted in their own interests. It expresses, or should express, the needs (as opposed to the wants, which are not necessarily fulfilled) of the people for whom it is made. In particular circumstances (such as in a state of war) particular and temporary laws must be made (such as blackouts and rationing); over the years, certain laws become irrelevant, and new laws become necessary because of new situations. The laws about Sunday trading in Great Britain have become, over the centuries, irrelevant to the point of absurdity: *Playboy* can be bought legally, but not a Bible; fresh vegetables, but not tinned. And in the State of Connecticut it used to be the case (and may still be so) that it was illegal for a man to kiss his wife in public on a Sunday. These laws were originally devised in order to facilitate obedience to the Commandment to keep the Sabbath Day holy; those who have striven to change the laws have not denied the value of one day's break in seven, but rather have questioned whether the law as it has stood for centuries necessarily embodies the only, or even the ideal, means of achieving this.

Other new laws have become necessary because of changes in society; sometimes these have been no more than developments in technology, such as the invention of the internal combustion engine. The arrival of the motor car and its equivalents resulted in the making of new laws relating to its speed, noise, direction, place of parking, roadworthiness, safety, and the alertness of the driver; in Finland it is illegal to smoke and drive. Other new laws reflect society's more liberal outlook compared with that of, say, the Victorian age; the Lord Chamberlain, for instance, no longer censors manuscripts of plays before they are produced on stage.

These examples reinforce the objection to the idea of the law as an eternal entity, providing us with our sense of right and wrong. The clearer picture that emerges is that of the law as – and I don't use this word in a pejorative sense – a time-server. It reflects – or, at least, it ideally reflects – the attitudes, the priorities, even the values maintained by the majority of the community (few laws are likely to please everybody) in which it is observed or enforced. Thus the bill to allow abortion in certain circumstances, passed by the House of Commons in 1967, would hardly have been given a hearing much before that date; and future generations may modify it, either restrictively or liberally, or even abolish it altogether according to the extent and direction of society's changing views on the issue. The law cannot be static, which it would be by definition if it were an 'eternal entity'. It must change in order to reflect changing values, and if it ever appears to be inconsistent, then this perhaps typifies human values. It is inconsistent (not to say hypocritical) to condemn and illegalise bull-fighting but to allow fox-, deer-, or hare-hunting; it seems a grave distortion of values to sentence a man to thirty years in jail for stealing banknotes (in the great train robbery) and another to ten years for grievous bodily harm. If these, and the legion of examples of misplaced priorities which you could no doubt cite, cause you to affirm with Dickens's Mr Bumble that 'the law is a' ass', then you may as well blame a parrot for using obscene language. If the above expressions of the law are wrong, they are wrong because people have revered property more than they have revered living creatures, human or animal. The law is no better, and certainly no worse, than its makers.

The eternal verity which the law should at all times be trying to enshrine, preserve, and enforce, is that of justice. But this, as we have seen, is one of those supremely evaluative words which render themselves incapable of definition (if you don't believe me, try, as I suggested in Chapter One, to define the word). How far any law reflects justice, when this is itself indefinable in terms acceptable to any legal expert, and how far justice can ever be said to have been done, let alone seen to have been done, is a matter for speculation. The Midwest judge, Roy Bean, who habitually called out in his court 'Bring the guilty bastard in and let's give him a fair trial' may be an extreme example of human foibles clouding the idea of justice, but to this observer (as to certain legal experts with whom I've discussed the matter) the connection between justice and the administration of the law is at best tenuous. Luck seems to play a major part in the proceedings – the quality of one's lawyer, the mood of the judge and/or the jury, the demeanour of the accused, the 'current mood' nationally so far as the alleged offence is concerned: with all these to contend with, justice often appears like Keats's knight at arms: 'Alone, and palely loitering'. (See Case Study 15, p. 103.)

A final objection to the idea of the law as the source of our knowledge of right and wrong springs from the fact that our sense of what is morally right or wrong, and what the law declares to be right or wrong, may not coincide. It is illegal, but hardly immoral, for me to drive my car over a nearby bridge which is being preserved as part of a beauty spot, or to drive through a red traffic light late at night, or to dump garden rubbish on some nearby disused land. It is not illegal, but some would view it as immoral, to commit adultery, to engage in homosexual activities, to traffic in women's bodies, or to exploit other people for financial gain. (A fellow student of mine in Bonn, Germany, once described as 'immoral' the fact that the then British prime minister and the leader of the opposition used regularly, after a vituperative debate in the House of Commons, to have a cordial meal together.)

The first set of examples – activities which are illegal but not necessarily immoral – would lead a rule utilitarian to ask: what if everybody did the same? We shall discuss this issue in Chapter Six. The second set gives rise to a much more important question: how far is any citizen justified in deliberately and consciously breaking the law where he feels this to be immoral? We shall return to this issue in Chapter Eleven.

It appears that we are still no further forward in our quest for the source of moral awareness in people. It has been suggested that perhaps we should acknowledge the primacy of the 'spirit of the law' in this connection, and recognise that the law itself is inevitably an inadequate and incomplete embodiment of this. The trouble then is like that which we have with the idea of justice: it is impossible to define. Few people are sent to prison for breaking the spirit, as opposed to the letter, of the law.

(d) Society, or one's peers

Those who hold the view that a man is known by the company he keeps may well go on to maintain that it is in this same context that his views of acceptable and non-acceptable behaviour are established. It is certainly the case that in many respects our behaviour reflects the attitudes of the peer group in which we happen to find ourselves. Many a parent will testify to this, after they have experienced radical changes in their children when they begin to develop relationships outside the home. 'He's got in with the wrong set' is the excuse commonly made by such parents to friends and relatives who note how the child seems to be setting aside the moral standards accepted in the home. Even when we are older, after, presumably, becoming more set both in our ways and in our values, it is difficult and perhaps pointless to avoid being influenced by the moral attitudes of those with whom we mix: even our choice of leisure pursuits is likely to be so influenced. The same process occurs, inevitably, in areas of moral concern. The racialist who is thrown, for a period of time, among people with more liberal views runs the risk, if so it may be termed, of being forced to modify his views, as happened to a fellow climber on a week-long expedition in which I, with a number of other friends, was once involved. And the person who lives for a time within an enclosed community must be very thick-skinned indeed to be untouched by the ethos of that community – whether this be a communal home, a monastery, or a boarding-school. Most of us, if we examine our moral attitudes with honesty, will be able to pinpoint a particular group who either enforced or reinforced one or more of them.

It would therefore be foolish, and in many cases demonstrably wrong, to deny the fact of the influence of the values held by people around us on those which we express as our own. We may not go as far as a certain lady of my acquaintance whose every expression of opinion on moral matters – from the case for capital punishment to that against gambling – began with the phrase 'like x says' (x being her husband) but it's a reasonable supposition that most of our expressions of opinion were either heard or read elsewhere. That we have not, however, solved the problem raised in this chapter is indicated by two facts, the first being a simple acknowledgment of most people's experience, the second rather subtler.

It is a fact that the majority of people divide their time among a number of groups. To begin with, they have their home and their school, college, or place of work. In addition, they have their friends, who may belong to any of these, but may be found in neither. They could be members of a club, or political organisation, of a pressure group or evening class or church, or a combination of some of these. And while this is not inevitable, it is eminently possible that some conflict of values will exist between groups of this sort. The secretary who engages in anti-nuclear activities may find that her work colleagues are, for political reasons, out of sympathy with such activities, her fellow church members on religious grounds, and her family for domestic reasons. Which group is doing the influencing in this situation? Her fellow activists all came together independently of the other groups, not encouraged by any of them: even her daily newspaper expresses a different line. Are we to take it that people are like chameleons, changing their values as they move from group to group? If this is universally the case (as it admittedly is in certain instances) then our quest is as pointless as that for the end of the rainbow, and as impossible to locate as the nucleus of an atom when studying its velocity. Yet, somewhere along the line, the jumble which constitutes most people's minds occasionally straightens itself out, and an idea becomes crystal clear, so that the person can state boldly 'this is right' or 'that is bad'.

This brings us to the second problem concerning the social explanation for human behaviour. How, if all our moral views are taken from our peers – whichever section of acquaintances and friends these happen to be – has any change in moral attitudes over the centuries come about? That changes in this field have occurred over the centuries has already been illustrated several times in this and earlier chapters. But for any change to occur, someone must have said for the first time, or, antecedently to any discussion, someone must have thought along the lines of, 'we can do better than this'. If this had never happened, no group would or could have ever revised its views; without the innovator, it must have remained static. Bees have organised their lives efficiently for millions of years, and are a fascinating object of study; but there is no evidence that bees have changed in any appreciable way over this period. The bee of today is not greatly dissimilar to that of ancient Egypt; modern human societies differ in many respects from those of our ancestors, and these changes have taken place because someone, somewhere, objected to the accepted norms. Whether the resultant changes can always be characterised under the generic term 'progress' is a moot point, and not relevant here. The fact is that, for better or for worse, movement has occurred throughout history because of the stand taken by the rebel, the pioneer, the critic, the prophet. Where the group comes to accept the proposals of such individuals, radical changes in that group's attitudes can occur, as we have seen, for instance, in the attitude to single-parent families, and the status of marriage, over one generation in the West. What, then, is the source of the reformer's insights and zeal, and where does society's willingness to accept proposed changes originate?

(e) God

Throughout history, few societies have lacked among their members those who have believed that the ultimate inspiration for all human appreciation of right and wrong lies not in man himself but in his creator – the almighty, all-powerful, all-knowing Being whom he calls God. Today, in the Western world at any rate, there are probably fewer people who would be prepared to make such an affirmation, but the point of view persists, and, in the United States is vociferously, not to say belligerently, expressed in the media and by politicians. (It is doubtful whether any person would be nominated for the US presidency, much less be elected, if he professed himself an atheist. It is significant that all presidents in recent years have made a point of emphasising their religious affiliation and of publicly socialising with well-known religious leaders.) Many less exalted people, faced with the question posed at the end of the previous section, are quite likely to state that, in the absence of any more satisfactory explanation, God must be the source of our moral awareness.

For those who do not wish to examine this explanation in greater depth, this conviction can remain with them throughout their lives, giving them confidence in defending their life-styles in general, and directing them amid situations fraught with moral dilemmas in particular. Maybe as you read this you are agreeing with this point of view; certainly we must all be acquainted with people for whom God is both the instigator and guardian of their moral standards, and who evince a serenity, as a result of the confidence which this belief often gives, not expressed by those who are more aware of the pitfalls in this theory.

75

We shall be considering in Chapter Eight the logical problems associated with the attempt to link one's sense of moral obligation with the commands of God. All that is necessary at this stage is the adumbration of some of the more obvious problems which arise with this viewpoint.

The first question relates to the receiver of God's commands: why should it be this person rather than another, or perhaps a number of others? The answer given by an upholder of the God theory may well be that this matter constitutes no problem at all. Since God is all-wise, He knows best whom to choose, as the wise foreman, or military officer, or politician knows whom to appoint as his second-in-command.

Very well: granted that God's method of correcting false ideas of what is right and wrong is to select a worthy person to be the mouthpiece of any necessary change and the instigator of progress in the moral field, it seems fair to ask why this laborious process has been needed at all. Assuming that God is unchanging, immutable, it follows that His assessment of certain forms of behaviour as good, and others as bad, of certain actions as virtuous and others as vicious, has been for ever the same. (To believe in a fickle God, inconstant in opinion and irresponsible in behaviour, would make philosophical discussion of the matter quite futile. If it is the case, as Gloucester lamented in *King Lear*, that 'as flies to wanton boys are we to the gods; They kill us for their sport', then such a being or beings is/are unworthy of our consideration, since human beings rise, morally, higher than this.) Why didn't this eternally-wise God bestow this wisdom upon homo sapiens from the very beginning, and thus reduce the risk of human misery consequent on human wickedness?

Again, the defender of the God theory is likely to counter with the argument that this is to prejudge, and therefore misjudge, God's intentions. It was, so they argue, not His will that human beings should possess all knowledge of good and evil from the very beginning. This would be like surrounding a child from his earliest years with every conceivable object of desire, with the result that he never really appreciates them. Only by experiencing the rewards of goodness, and enduring those of wickedness, has the real value of following the path of virtue, or the straight-and-narrow – call it what you will – been not only read, marked, and learned by man, but also, more to the point, inwardly digested: and this is a continuing process.

This sounds reasonable enough but for three major problems. The first is simply a fact of life – sad or otherwise. If there is any degree of fairness and consistency in God's nature (and, as was mentioned above, there seems little point in continuing the discussion if the case is otherwise) then one seems to be justified in looking for some kind of correlation between virtue and reward, between vice and punishment. Any study of human societies will indicate that no such correlation exists. It may happen, but just as likely it may not. The experience of suffering, whether through material loss, tragic bereavement, disabling disease, or foreshortening of life is shared by good and bad – however these people may be defined – alike. There is in my morning newspaper an article about a man who has treated his employees with venom, his colleagues with contempt, and his rivals with derision: he is a multi-millionaire, and one of the most powerful men in the world. He will probably die lauded with honour and effusive obituary notices. In the same issue of the newspaper is a short note about the death of a man in another country who spent the final third of his life enduring imprisonment and torture at the hands of a political régime condemned by most of the world. These are, of course, extreme examples, and in any case no argument should be based solely on individual samples: others could tell a different story. But they are typical enough of a good deal of human experience to make it impossible to substantiate the case for correlating virtue with happiness, vice with misery. Virtue may be its own reward, but, if the general argument of this section is sound, it should normally be expected to have desirable bi-products: and this is manifestly not the case. (We shall return to the problem of evil in Case Study 26, p. 196.)

The second problem concerns the inconsistency of God as found in those writings and pronouncements through which He has made known the nature of good and bad. He has allegedly spoken through such holy books as the Old and New Testaments and the Koran and, throughout succeeding centuries, through the minds of those claiming to interpret these writings. To state this is to expose the problem. Throughout these writings and affirmations there is a range of moral views so varied that virtually any action or attitude can have its precedent quoted from one authoritative source or another. Shall we give up alcohol? Turn to Jeremiah 35. Shall we drink wine? Turn to St John 8, and drink it instead of water. How many wives should we have? Solomon numbered his in three figures, though his additional mistresses nearly reached the four-figure total; Mohammed settled for four; St Paul preferred to recommend celibacy. Should one kill one's enemies? Saul was commanded by the prophet Samuel (the former temple boy) to slaughter the Amalekites, and was removed from the kingship because he spared one of them; Jesus said, 'Love your enemies', but he also condemned them as 'snakes . . . vipers' brood . . . condemned to hell' (Matthew 23, 33); Mohammed preached the virtues of Holy War.

It may be argued that, throughout the scriptures, there is a progression in the appreciation of right and wrong: maybe, but this has not happened chronologically (the book of Hosea in the Old Testament, for instance, seems more morally advanced than that of Revelation in the New, and more advanced still than much of the Koran), and it is in any case a subjective judgment when a certain form of behaviour is deemed 'higher' than another. (An incredible amount of pure unalloyed hatred towards those who beg to differ can show itself through a careful selection of passages in any of these three holy books, and this hatred is seen nightly on the religious channel on American TV.)

The third problem with the theory of progression in morals linked with a growing appreciation of the divine will is, quite simply, that it does not accord with historical facts as we read them. It would be comforting for us, living as we do at the end of the twentieth century, to feel that we have now attained certain moral heights from which we can both look back on the foibles of our ancestors, and forward to nobler things to come. Experience teaches us that this is a fond illusion. Some of the civilisations of the past – in India, China, Greece, and Rome, for example – displayed, during certain phases, forms of behaviour, especially in their treatment of the less fortunate members of the community, which compare favourably with any we may put forward today.

> After two thousand years of Mass
> We've got as far as poison gas

wrote Hardy in 1924. One dare not contemplate the extent to which man's ability to inflict untold agony on his fellows – all in the name of God, according to numerous national leaders – has multiplied since then. In a world of environmental destruction, mass starvation, and wars in the name of religion, all overshadowed by man's capacity to destroy every living entity a hundred times over, how can anyone rationally speak of moral progress under the influence of a belief in God?

While, then, for some people the idea of God as the source of moral awareness gives an answer to the dilemma discussed in this chapter, it is an answer as intangible as that of the conscience: on analysis, it moves further away, leaving us none the wiser. The equation of God with certain forms of behaviour may, for some people, give those forms a sanction they would not otherwise possess; but this whole procedure seems artificial, an unfair exploitation of human irrationality.

(f) Reason

We have already seen, in Chapter Three, that, where two people disagree on a moral issue – about how convicted murderers should be treated, for instance, or whether censorship is necessary in the media – the modus operandi which seems to offer most hope of reaching a consensus is that of seeking out and examining the facts of the situation; to put aside, as far as possible, the emotions, prejudices, and habitual ways of looking at the issue as pursued by both the individuals and their peer groups. In other words, it was suggested that the only way forward lay in the application of *reason* to the problem. Thus the supporter of capital punishment may argue that, because the criminal has taken a life, it's 'only reasonable' that he should lose his. Similarly, if a connection could be established scientifically between violence depicted on the screen and violent behaviour in real life, it would be reasonable to pass a law which banned such scenes from public viewing; and the deprivation of freedom to choose, on the part of those viewers who are unlikely to be thus affected by them, would be, reasonably speaking, a small price to pay. The whole gamut of moral dilemmas could be similarly considered, with the same conclusion following: in the end, altruism, by whatever forms of behaviour it is expressed, is more reasonable than its alternatives – greed, selfishness, lust, malevolence. It is therefore human reason, the factor of life which, supremely, exalts us among the various species, which should be acknowledged as the major, if not sole, source of our knowledge of right and wrong: the very word 'knowledge' in that phrase implies this.

At first sight this seems an acceptable argument. It *must* be reasonable to treat everyone equally and to act logically and consistently; irrational behaviour *must* be judged to be bad. Surely, anyone who disagrees with this requires only to be shown the error of his ideas and ways: he *ought* to agree, even if he doesn't. Those who are impressed by analogies between human and animal behaviour can support altruism on the grounds that it is the herd instinct become conscious in a rational animal, and that to reject this idea in favour of any other is to abandon our birthright; those who view man as the creature of God can support it on the grounds that it accords with the wisdom of God – and so on, through all the theories of human nature.

Reason and altruism   Now all this may be true; but the question is, is it an argument for altruism? It may be the case that individuals tend to pay some regard to the interests of groups, but this does not prove that they *should* do so. Much less does it prove that a human being should pay as much regard to the interests of every other human group as to his own; it could just as plausibly be argued that man shares with animals an overwhelming preoccupation with individual survival, even at the expense of others. Even the argument that the world would be a better place for everyone if everyone behaved altruistically is not as certain as it may appear at first glance. A wife might not find the world a better place if a husband started to count everyone else's welfare as of equal importance to her own; and a world where spontaneity – even spontaneous selfishness – was replaced by rational calculation could sound too much like some of the nightmares depicted in science fiction and certain horror films. The contention that altruism is reasonable because it would make the world a better place for everyone is a vicious circle, because the point at issue is precisely whether it *is* reasonable to aim at making the world a better place for everyone.

It may be argued that we know this intuitively, but this is both factually wrong and logically irrelevant. The comparative study of civilisations reveals that the ideal of counting all human beings as having equal rights is an 'erratic boulder rather than a dominant mountain range' in the geography of human thought. Even if the facts were quite otherwise, and it could plausibly be held that everyone really knew that altruism was right, an intuition, however universal, is not a rational argument. The advocate of altruism can in theory appeal to intuition or to reason or to both. What he cannot do is to count intuition as proof that altruism is reasonable.

The argument that moral issues can be resolved in the court of reason and rationality seems, therefore, to be falsified by the realities of the human situation. Some of the noblest acts in the history of human behaviour have been quite irrational. I have spoken to a man who won the highest award for gallantry which Britain can give – the Victoria Cross – who can recall nothing of the events leading up to his award because his mind had ceased to function at the time, owing to the incredible amount of adrenalin pumping through his system. Reason would no doubt have told him that what he was attempting to do was wrong because it couldn't be done. Still in the sphere of war, reason surely shows that the best way to treat prisoners is to kill them: that way, you don't have to waste human and material resources in looking after them. The American Indians, in earlier times, followed this path of reason: when one tribe conquered another they simply wiped out all their males: not very altruistic, perhaps, but a reasonable way of ensuring that they weren't troubled by them again.

Reason suggests to me that if I've made my packet through hard work and self-sacrifice I shouldn't be expected to squander it on the feckless who've done neither of these: the ant must outlive the grasshopper. If, as reason suggests, everyone has the same rights as everyone else, then we should acknowledge this not only for bankers, bishops, and bricklayers, but also for persistent rapists, necrophiliacs, potential suicides, and homicidal maniacs. And if the idea of equality of rights is established only by reason, we must exclude from consideration the subnormal, the senile, and babies.

Unless some argument can be put forward which has not been considered above, it does not seem that the thesis that reason tells us what is good and bad can be substantiated. Reason may tell us how to proceed when we decide what our behaviour in a certain situation should be: it will not provide us with the decision itself. It may provide us with supporting evidence for a moral viewpoint, but that will not prove that that viewpoint is 'right'. In other words, while reason can be used in evaluating the correctness of arguments, it does not seem to have a place in other types of discourse. One can, obviously, reason about poetry, or love, or commands, but the language of poetry, of love, and of commands is not itself subject to rational criticism. To treat phrases like 'truth is beauty', or 'with my body I thee worship', or 'Thou shalt not commit adultery' as propositions, even when they have the same verbal form as propositions, is to misunderstand the language.

If one looks at the kind of contexts in which reasoning is commonly acknowledged to be appropriate it seems undeniable that reason is a tool, useful for certain purposes, but that it cannot stand alone or claim to judge all causes. The formal validity of a syllogism is no guarantee of its factual accuracy. ('All people have the right to freedom; murderers are people; therefore . . .', etc, is formally valid, but is it right?) Thus it is appropriate to discuss whether a man who loves a girl should make love to her, or marry her first, or leave her; it is ludicrously inappropriate to seek a rational justification for loving her in the first place. As Molière remarked in *Le Misanthrope*: 'Ce n'est pas la raison qui règle l'amour.' There is no need for and no prospect of finding rational justification for fearing pain, for struggling to survive, for laughing at jokes, for sympathising with suffering or for any of the fundamental human activities which anybody but a psychologist would call instinctive. A mother loves her child because she loves it; the hungry man's problem is not to know if he is rationally justified in eating, but to find food.

It may be that the most important use of reason is to help individuals to realise the extent to which their wellbeing is inextricably tied up with the wellbeing not only of their immediate family and friends or groups with which they identify themselves but of the whole human race. If a meeting of Arab oil sheiks in Cairo can put 50,000 British immediately out of work, insularity, whether interpreted figuratively or literally, does not seem very sensible. That much can be conceded: but it does not seem justifiable to proceed from there and affirm that reason demands altruistic morality. If this were the case, it would be reasonable to expect to find some kind of consensus on moral issues, particularly among those, such as philosophers or clergymen, who have a high regard for the powers of reason and who wish to persuade people to be less selfish. The absence of any such consensus suggests, though of course it does not prove, that an agreed rational basis for morality has not been found because there is no such basis.

(g) Feelings

If reason is to be judged as no more than a tool of morality, a means of getting us along the road, so to speak, the question still remains as to how we come to know which road to take in the first place. An alternative answer is that this assurance is provided by our feelings or emotions. It is feelings, so the argument goes, which regulate the lives of people, and, at least in ideal circumstances, lead them to the making of their most important decisions. It is feelings which direct us towards our job in life: a feeling of warmth, perhaps, towards one vocation compared with that of boredom about other possibilities; our feelings play a major part in choosing whom we shall live with and, given the choice, where we shall live. Feelings determine who our friends shall be and, with them, what activities will rank high in our estimation. When moral issues confront us, we know what is right or wrong because we can feel the answer deep within ourselves. We may provide others with reasons why we consider certain forms of behaviour to be wrong, but basically our decisions are arrived at through a 'gut' reaction, just as our assessment of other people – whether to trust them, or whether we like or dislike them, for instance – generally comes about through what we feel when we meet them.

Obviously, there is a good deal of truth in this. Those forms of behaviour about which we speak most ardently, whether in support of or against them, are quite likely to be those to which our emotional reactions are strongest. Some people denounce single-sex relationships not because they have anxieties about the relationship itself, nor because their holy book does so, but because they are repelled by the way love is expressed in such relationships. Racial attitudes develop in some people because they feel the same about people with a different pigmentation from themselves; others oppose any form of torture because they are literally sickened by such – to them – bestial activity. Empathy for animals makes many people vegetarians or anti-vivisectionists, or opponents of blood sports; the feeling of horror brought about by contemplating both the effect and after-effects of nuclear war makes a public demonstrator out of many an otherwise retiring citizen. Few people make moral pronouncements on matters about which they don't *feel* strongly.

It is therefore valid to state that feelings play a part in the process of making a moral decision, in some people more than in others. There are however several problems facing anyone who concludes from this that he has answered the problem posed in this chapter. In the first place, he will have committed himself to a facet of life which is at best changeable, at worst capricious or fickle. Just as one can modify one's first impression of another person, so feelings, or moods, can change – and much more rapidly and dramatically. Some people are more volatile than others, of course, but few people's feelings remain constant for any great length of time: people change their moods with the hour of the day. Consequently, a person whose moral stance is founded entirely on what he feels at the time is likely to be an unreliable supporter of any cause which demands continuous commitment. Few books would be written, scientific discoveries made, battles won, or injustices removed if writers, researchers, soldiers, or reformers operated only when they felt like it.

Leading from this is the fact that feelings can harden into prejudices, by a process of inductive reasoning. Just as one can assess another person on the basis of what is felt at the first encounter and allow that assessment – quite possibly, in the long term, a completely false one – to control all later dealings with that person, so people can reach life-long conclusions about issues with grave significance for human behaviour based solely on the circumstances of the first encounter with them. People have prejudices against whole nations simply because of a single unfortunate meeting with one of their representatives; attitudes to people of a different colour from their own are similarly formed; causes are supported or neglected on the basis solely of a happy or unhappy first meeting with other protagonists of these causes. Some people even seem to take pride in this way of judging issues. 'I know I'm prejudiced,' one will say, 'but I just don't like/trust the French.' A multiplication of those who reach conclusions in this way can and does cause untold misery in the long term.

Following on from this is the fact of the danger involved if feelings are allowed to be the sole, or even just the dominant, guide when making moral decisions. No doubt the relative of a murderer's victim would be likely to feel passionately that the criminal should suffer the same fate as the victim. Some people, looking at the matter dispassionately, may well agree with this: but the victim's relatives are the last people who should have the authority to declare what should be done with the guilty party; if the penal system of the land were settled by people's immediate emotional reactions to crime, many injustices would be committed, and the penal system replaced by a process not far different from mob law.

The behaviour of a mob when roused is itself a fitting condemnation of the belief that feelings should govern issues of right and wrong. In these situations, as Shakespeare showed in *Julius Caesar* when the mob was moved one way and another by the speakers' oratory, feelings expand and intensify to the point where reason ceases to function, and acts of great wickedness are performed, often by people who, recollecting events in the privacy of their homes – or their cells – can scarcely believe that they acted as they did. There are in all people feelings which have no place in a civilised community: feelings of lust, and cruelty, and the urge to destroy. It were better, surely, that these feelings be kept under control; but the case for this is weakened if it is accepted that feelings and emotion are the sole arbiters of moral conduct.

So far as moral philosophy is concerned, the prime difficulty experienced when a person proclaims something to be right or wrong simply because he feels this to be the case is that communication and discussion with that person is consequently wellnigh impossible. It is as pointless to discuss the rights and wrongs of abortion with a person who beats his heart and declares that it must be wrong because he feels so 'deep in here' as it was for me to debate the truth of Christianity on a BBC programme with the man quoted in Chapter One who said, 'I know Jesus is alive today: he was speaking to me in my car this morning.' There is, quite simply, no answer to that.

Emotion, left to itself, will declare reason redundant; yet while, as we have seen, reason will not on its own reveal the good and the bad, it has its part to play in the human process of reaching moral conclusions, even if not so central a part as has been claimed for it by certain philosophers and others. We may perhaps say that reason often tells us what needs to be done; emotion gives the motivation. 'Passion,' the American philosopher, Emerson, wrote, 'though a bad regulator, is a powerful spring.' To make moral decisions irrationally would be subhuman; to make them unfeelingly would be inhuman. Without reason, morality is blind; without emotion, it is lame.

It would be a gross misunderstanding of human nature, whatever interpretation of this we adopt, if we excluded the place of emotion in the moral decision-making process. But the fact that we do judge certain emotions to be more desirable than others, and some emotions, perhaps, not desirable at all, indicates that we engage ourselves in a process of continuous assessment of the emotions. So where does the knowledge originate on which such assessments are based? The problem remains unsolved.

(h) Evolution: morality as a process of natural selection[1]

The word evolution is commonplace today, but a century ago it was not to be used in polite society. Even today in many parts of the United States – not least in so-called enlightened California – it is treated as a dirty word used, like the words communist, or liberal, only by degenerates. It may seem odd to a modern student in the West that a theory which seems to explain so much scientifically should be treated with such animosity, yet the fact is that your chance of getting a teaching job in many American states would be minimal, if not non-existent, if you didn't at least prevaricate on the issue.

Charles Darwin's book, *The Origin of Species*, which lifted the theory out of the scientific journals and into the public eye, was published in 1859, and the first edition sold out in a single day. In it, Darwin denied the soundness of the 'immutability' theory – the belief that there occurred a single act of creation – and offered instead the idea of continuous creation over the billions of years of life on our planet. The central feature of this theory is the influence of the environment on the evolution of species. Those species which, sometimes over many generations, adjusted themselves to their environment – such as the ants – survived; those that did not or could not do so – such as, perhaps, the dinosaurs – became extinct. Homo sapiens evolved and survived because of his ability to use the environment to his advantage.

The major element in this process is the obtaining of an adequate supply of food; this each creature achieves by consuming lower, or

[1] This must not be confused with the idea of 'natural law' as expounded by the medieval philosopher, Thomas Aquinas.

smaller, or less agile forms of life than its own: the preying mantis devours a fly, is itself consumed by a lizard, which is eaten by a stoat, which is then carried off by a hawk. This chain continues unbroken until an environmental change occurs – such as an alteration of atmospheric conditions – which decreases, or entirely removes, one of the links; this occurrence could then bring about an 'unnatural' multiplication of the species immediately lower in the chain, and threaten the survival of those further up. The picture that Darwin depicts is therefore very different from the view of nature presented, for instance, in the story of the Garden of Eden, and illustrated in the hymn 'All things bright and beautiful . . . the Lord God made them all': hence the animosity of the Church. Darwin argued that if it were not for this endless process of predator and prey, any single species could multiply until it covered the earth. The cohabitation of species on the planet is possible only because of this constant warfare, in which even the cooperation which can be observed among creatures of the same species must be acknowledged as just one form the competition takes.

Darwin summed up the central theme of his theory in these words:

Can it, then, be thought improbable, seeing that variations useful to man have undoubtedly occurred, that other variations useful in some way to each being in the great and complex battle of life, should occur in the course of many successive generations? If such do occur, can we doubt (remembering that many more individuals are born than can possibly survive) that individuals having any advantage, however slight, over others, would have the best chance of surviving and procreating their kind? On the other hand, we may feel sure that any variation in the least degree injurious would be rigidly destroyed. This preservation of favourable individual differences and variations, and the destruction of those which are injurious, I have called Natural Selection, or the Survival of the Fittest. (Chapter Four)

You may feel that the use of capital letters in that last sentence is somewhat pretentious, but for over a century those phrases have been slogans or rallying calls for an entire view of life, comparable to 'Allah be Praised', 'Up the Workers', or even 'Beer is Best'.

In his next and, so far as his contemporaries were concerned, even more controversial book *The Descent of Man* (1871), Darwin related his theory specifically to homo sapiens – our evolution from the ape, and the development of the features which, on the whole, distinguish us from all other species. He discussed the development of language, of musical and other artistic skills, of reason and religion, and illustrated the role these played in human survival. Our concern is with the development of our sense of right and wrong. Darwin's theory is that, just as we learned skills, like tool-making, by a process of trial and error, so we learned which forms of behaviour had what may be described as an inbuilt survivability factor, and which did not. Forms of behaviour which threatened a group's existence, such as murder, robbery, treachery, and the like, were forbidden, often on penalty of death, for no group which condoned such crimes could long endure. In general, however, the same offences, when committed against another group or tribe, were permitted and even approved. The more scalps a Plains Indian collected from other tribes, the greater his reputation. (The continuance of tribalism, by whatever name it may be called, throughout human history presents a problem for moral theorists, which will be taken up later, specifically in Chapter Six.)

This evolutionary theory of ethics seems to accord with a good deal of human moral awareness if we examine carefully how we came to experience this. Just as we learn not to put a finger into a naked flame, so we discover that certain forms of behaviour meet with approval from those around us while others are treated with antagonism. Life is a good deal more comfortable, in consequence, if we follow the former rather than the latter. Anybody who has experienced, say, an outbreak of theft in a community knows how painful this can be for all its members: where mutual trust and co-operation had been the norm, doubt and suspicion take over. In extreme instances an attitude of mutual hatred can develop in such a community, putting at risk the survival of that community in its original form, with its ethos of goodwill. We could well be described as like Pavlov's dogs, discovering how to behave by this process of trial and error. It may explain why, with the increasing speed of communication between peoples, our sense of tribal affiliation has had to change from a sense of belonging only to an extremely localised group to one that is considerably larger and broader. It may explain why soldiers take prisoners of war and don't exterminate the vanquished: all soldiers hope to survive into a post-war period, and fewer would do so if no prisoners were taken. It explains the greed of people in times of shortages in particular commodities; the cooperation between people in times of natural hazard; and changes in social attitudes, such as towards male and female roles in communities which no longer depend on male brawn for survival.

The evolutionary theory of ethics will explain much; the question is whether it is the correct explanation. For any of the examples used, one or more of the earlier theories could be substituted. More significant are certain facts of life which don't seem to fit into the evolutionary pattern at all. Darwin speaks of the survival of the fittest: we accept that by this he did not mean (as it is popularly misinterpreted) the joggers and slimmers and early-to-bed-early-to-rise brigade (though these are not necessarily excluded!) but those people (as, in earlier millennia, those species) who most successfully adapted to or fitted in with their environment. For the human species, this has meant the use of particular skills, such as manual dexterity, and over the centuries this has increasingly meant the development and application of intellectual skills. One would expect, therefore, if the theory is sound, to see some correlation between the possession of such skills and fertility, even though this is no guarantee of the handing-down of such skills (bright parents have dim-witted children and vice versa). Ironically, the present situation in the West is the reverse of this. The intelligent tend to take safeguards and strictly control the size of their families, while the feckless have the large broods. The 'dumb blonde' is a good deal more likely to get pregnant than the career-minded woman, and the male whose main attributes lie elsewhere than between his ears more likely to make her so. If it is the case that the whole planet is threatened by over-population, then the breeding of large numbers of offspring must be viewed as anti-social, creating an ever-increasing demand on limited resources: yet the majority of the current representatives of the human species don't seem to have got this message. Is the evolutionary process engaging itself in some comprehensive form of hara-kiri? In the past, offspring were important for their economic value: with the increasing mechanisation and computerisation throughout the world, this is generally no longer the case, yet the urge to reproduce one's kind continues virtually unabated. Only a policy of compulsory sterilisation on the part of government is likely to halt the trend: but that very policy would be judged by most observers to be immoral because it is unnatural. Evolution has landed us in a catch-22 situation. (See Case Study 44, p. 321.)

For our present purposes, the significance of this situation is that we seem to be making a moral judgment independently of the evolutionary process. This process seems to be sadly lacking in its ability to preserve moral qualities we admire above those we hold in contempt. In time of war, it is the hero who stands his ground who faces annihilation more surely than the coward who flees, while back at home is the wealthy character with connections who thereby avoided being enlisted in the first place. In the increasingly ruthless war of the business jungle, it is the bully and the exploiter of others who tends to come out on top of the gentle, compassionate soul who takes seriously the commandment not to covet his neighbour's customers. There are even those who make this into a definable policy, or philosophy, under the title 'social Darwinism'. In both the United States and Great Britain (to look no further) this has been exalted to the status of a national virtue, with honours showered on the victors while the losers are left to cope as best they can. Darwin would have rejected any association with such an outlook, but there is a cruel logical link between the ideas of that gentle seeker after truth and the rapaciousness of monetarist policies, supported philosophically in our time by Ayn Rand, who called selfishness a virtue and commended aggressive competition as the law of life. (See her novels *The*

Fountainhead, and *Atlas Shrugged*, where her philosophy of objectivism is characterised.)

It may be argued that the goal of evolution is not the survival of the individual, as just described, but of the group, or species; and the key to progress is the struggle for power between groups. The implication of this is that the value of a person lies not in any quality he may possess *per se* but in his contribution to the success of the class, the state, or the race. For a philosophical backing for this theory, you may choose between the dialectical materialism of Marx and Engels, with its modifications by Lenin and Trotsky, and the doctrines of a master race and emerging superman deriving, however unjustifiably (see Chapter Seven) from Nietzsche's existentialism. In each case there remains the problem, mentioned earlier, of the ability of the individual to step back and make a moral assessment of the theories, based on an independent perception of their worth or otherwise. It is hardly likely that evolution will lead a person to criticise, and possibly reject, that same evolutionary process.

Even if we study the development of cultures chronologically, it is not possible to prove that there is any ascending order of moral merit. We may be tempted to arrange them like this:

Twentieth century top people
(morally mature)
|
The Roman Empire
(civilised, but not very)
|
Cave men (and women)
(unspeakable)

But what if you choose different examples?

Nazi Germany
|
The Renaissance
|
Classical Athens

It is really not very plausible to rate the conquistadores higher than the Incas on the moral evolutionary scale, nor to put the Vandals and Goths above the Romans whom they overcame, or to admire the China of Mao more than that of Confucius. The fact is that, if evolution is to be traced in history, the time-scale must be quite different from the time-scale biologists talk about. If, on the other hand, human evolution is believed to be as slow as the evolution of other species (for which, as Darwin remarked, nature has 'all the time in the world') then it is not possible to draw any conclusions about the development of morality, because we can know nothing at all about the morality of people living hundreds of thousands of years ago.

A more mystical doctrine, linking evolution with religion, is found in the writings of Father Teilhard de Chardin, particularly in *The Phenomenon of Man*. He stresses the critical importance of discontinuous leaps in evolution, and looks forward to the transformation of human consciousness, and ultimately of the whole cosmos, in initiatives which will create a new harmony and synthesis of values. If man is at the start of a stage of what Teilhard called 'ultra-hominisation', it may be that the significance of evolution for morality will emerge clearly only from some future vantage point; if this is so, speculation at this stage as to what the outcome will be would be futile (though, admittedly, fascinating: after all, it may appear that evolutionary theory is no more than an incidental aberration, rooted in a misapprehension of the true significance of time; but that is another matter).

Whatever version of the evolutionary theory is held (and there are many to choose from) it seems that, however much biologists may depend upon it, those seeking the ultimate basis of our moral sense must look elsewhere. One further theory must be discussed, if only because it has found a good deal of acceptance in the past, not least by some of the moral philosophers.

(i) A natural progression from the facts of the case: 'ought' derives from 'is'

On the face of it, this answer appears to be, as its designation suggests, the most natural of all. Is it not the common experience of people that, faced with a moral issue, they know, apparently instinctively, what they ought to do? Are not all the agonisings involved in the alternatives presented in this chapter really quite superfluous? Why not just behave in the way that comes naturally?

Consider, for instance, the following syllogisms:

(a) It is not desirable to surrender control of one's mental faculties.
    Alcohol causes a lowering of control in this area.
    The drinking of alcohol should be avoided.
(b) Everyone naturally wants to be as healthy as possible.
    Cigarette smoking can be injurious to one's health.
    One should refrain from smoking cigarettes.
(c) The world needs to eliminate deaths by violent means.
    The sale of arms internationally means that such deaths will go on happening.
    Trafficking in arms should be made illegal.

In all of these arguments we appear to be deriving a statement of moral obligation from statements of fact. (It may be argued that, in each of the above examples, the first statement is more a value judgment than a statement of fact, but this is a quibble, because, so far as the vast majority of people are concerned, those statements are held to be self-evidently true). And it is through thought processes like this that most people reach conclusions about what is good or bad, and how they should behave in various circumstances. If your child isn't vaccinated it could get whooping cough; naturally, you don't want it to get whooping cough, so you ought to get it vaccinated; if you don't revise you might fail your exam; obviously, you wouldn't want to fail, so you ought to revise.

Straightforward enough though these examples appear, illustrating the link between what is the case and what ought to be done about it, none of the final judgments can be defined as moral in the sense discussed in Chapter Three. They are all examples of the prudential use of 'ought': it would be in one's best interests to act in a certain way (for one's health's, or safety's, or pocket's sake). If it is true that x is 'good' for you (physical exercise, a non-fat diet, a daily bath/vitamin pill/orgasm) then, for your own good, you should be doing what you can to ensure that these are part of your daily routine; but the reasons for doing so are founded on expediency rather than morality (unless you assert that, because all these things help to keep you healthy, you are thereby taking steps to avoid being ill and becoming a burden to others – not the reason usually given for these forms of behaviour).

It may seem that the distinction I am here making between the prudential and moral use of 'ought' is one that is so fine that one cannot possibly determine the category into which any particular statement can be slotted. This is indeed often the case: many a person has made a moral issue, and gained kudos with his fellows, from basically self-interested behaviour. Firms gain a name for possessing a social conscience by donating to charity money that would in any case be otherwise grabbed by the Inland Revenue; nephews and nieces are kind and generous to detestable uncle George because he's loaded, he can't have long to go, and they're his next of kin. But fine though this distinction may often be, so that the observer cannot be absolutely sure of the basic motive, there is a distinction between action motivated by prudence and behaviour based on a purely moral sense of what is right or wrong.

I'll illustrate this by first giving the same kind of syllogism as earlier in this section:

It is a fact that hanging is (not) a deterrent to murder.
We all want to deter potential murderers.
So, we ought (not) to bring back hanging.

We can leave aside the vexed issue, long debated by penologists, as to whether capital punishment is or is not a deterrent in these circumstances: we will assume that the matter has been incontrovertibly resolved one way or the other. Is the matter then settled once and for all? Can we say that we have finally resolved whether hanging is morally right or morally wrong? We most certainly have not, as can be shown by two possible reactions to such conclusive evidence. On the one hand, a person could argue that the taking of another person's life is so obscene a crime that the murderer has forfeited the right to go on living. Whether his execution will deter other would-be murderers from behaving as he did is irrelevant: he did a grave wrong and must suffer the consequences. On the other hand, a person may argue that the cold-blooded execution of a man by state decree is nothing more than official murder, as obscene as the crime for which it is being administered. Two wrongs don't make a right, therefore the criminal should not be hanged, whatever the statistics may 'prove' about the deterrent effect of this. In the first case, hanging is supported even if the statistics indicate that such punishment in fact encourages others to commit murder; in the second case it is opposed even if the statistics prove the opposite. In both cases, the decision is reached despite, not as a result of, the facts: an appeal is made, tacitly at least, to a sense of right and wrong which is quite independent of the factual situation. The 'ought' is simply not derived from the 'is': considerations other than prudential take precedence.

One more example may clarify this issue further. It derives from a situation where the facts are clear but the judgment about what ought consequently to be done varies according to the values of the people making the decision. It is a fact that some children and some adults learn more slowly than others; in this respect, at least, it is not the case that we are all equal, and nobody in his right mind will dispute it. The question which arises in this situation is, what is the imperative which follows from this fact? What should be done educationally about the slow learner? A range of divergent answers can be given to this, each claiming to follow from the facts of the situation. One person may argue that, since the education system cannot possibly adjust to the speed of every individual learner, the same length of education should be given to all, and the slower take their chances with the quicker. Another may say that, since everyone is entitled to the same post-education opportunities as everyone else, the slow learner should be given more years of formal education than the rest, since otherwise he will suffer throughout his life from a handicap not of his choosing. A third person, on the basis of precisely the same facts, may argue the case that, since the slow learner will always be left behind in any learning group of which he is a member, it is pointless, and even unkind to the individual concerned, to attempt to give him more than the basic skills in literacy and numeracy: he should therefore receive less education than the others.

It is of no significance to the present discussion which of the above proposals seems 'right'; the point is that each proponent can defend his point of view as following naturally from the facts: each can claim to be deriving an ought from an is. What is clear, however, is that, however vociferously the claim may be made that a logical connection has been established between the two, this claim is fallacious. The whole theory is in fact known in philosophy as the *naturalistic fallacy*. Some philosophical writers have attempted to prove it otherwise and you can follow up the whole debate in a symposium entitled The *Is-Ought Question*[1] if you feel so inclined. It is not denied that people do often, as a matter of fact, make the connection in their own minds and to their own satisfaction. What is demonstrably the case, however, is that, obvious though the connection may seem to be, the moral agent is actually taking his moral cue, so to speak, from another, quite independent, source.

What this source is remains an enigma. We can list and discuss the multifarious answers which have been presented over the centuries, and some may seem to you more realistic than others. But no final solution is possible, even though many people find it convenient to proceed as though this were not the case. Perhaps some people need the security they feel when committing themselves to a particular theory as to the source of their awareness of right and wrong. The philosopher can offer no such security.

CASE STUDY 11: WHY BE MORAL?

In this chapter we have discussed possible sources of moral awareness without reaching any conclusion except that there is no definitive conclusion. A question which may occur to you as a result is, if I don't know where my moral sense comes from, why be moral at all? Why bother myself with a problem that will, as far as anyone can tell, remain for ever elusive? This case study allows you to think through this question – or debate it with colleagues – in a systematic way. It includes examples of issues already discussed, and of answers which will be presented in the next section of this book.

1 The answer depends on what you think 'being moral' means. It could mean doing what promotes the greatest good of the greatest number (utilitarianism); obeying your conscience; keeping God's law; acting in line with the *mores* of your society; striving for the victory of the working class; or living a life of deliberate self-denial, particularly in the sexual field. Anyway, there are difficulties.
2 If you mean choosing the greatest good of the greatest number, the reason for being moral could be that it is 'natural' to work for the survival of the species and its welfare.
But – is it? What counts as 'welfare'?

[1] W. D. Hudson (ed.), Macmillan, 1969

How do we measure competing claims (e.g., Jews or Palestinian Arabs)?

3 If you mean obeying conscience, the reason could be that, if you don't, you feel remorse and unhappiness.

But – are you sure you can distinguish conscience from subconscious wishes, repressed fantasies, internalised parental commands *pace* Freud?

And – is conscience more reliable than reason, emotion, tradition, or habit?

4 If you mean keeping God's law, the reason could be (a) God is almighty, or (b) what God commands is what is good for us.

But – how do you choose between the 57 varieties of God's law (Koran, Talmud, Zend Avesta, Vedas, Bible, etc.), and, if you pick the Bible, which of the thousands of interpretations do you accept?

and – if (a), is might right?

if (b), how do you know? And if you do know, why do you need God?

5 If you mean going along with the ways of your society, the reason could be that if you don't (more or less) you get clobbered.

But – what if you can get away with breaking social conventions? Why not?

And – which society: your ethnic group, nation, class, occupational group, peer group, family, church, voluntary association? What if they conflict?

6 If you mean serving a political cause (e.g., socialism, patriotism) the reason could be that you are serving the destiny of humanity.

But – why care about the oppressed masses, or national honour, or future generations?

7 If you mean what the puritans on both sides of the Atlantic (the moral majority in America, Mary Whitehouse and her followers in Britain) mean, your reason for being moral could be prudential (you could get VD, or AIDS, and in any case what would the neighbours say?)

But – sexual morals vary: how do you choose?

8 One answer is that people make moral (or any other) decisions to try and fulfil their own purposes (being happy, doing their own thing).

If this is so, what most of us need is better information about ourselves and the world, not sermons and regulations.

Dare one say: forget being moral – be sensible?

CASE STUDY 12: AUTHORITY AND AUTONOMY

One issue which arises from the discussion in this chapter is that of the extent to which our knowledge/awareness of right and wrong in morals depends on the strength or wisdom of others outside ourselves, and how far moral awareness is a faculty which we build in and for ourselves. Are moral convictions based on external authority or on internal autonomy, and, whatever the answer, *should they be*? In the first category are included: parents, the law, society, and God; and in the second, conscience, feelings, reason, and (to the extent that all people are dominated by the will to survive), evolution. (The Is-ought question on pp. 89–92 is neutral on this issue.) How far do you think it is enough for individuals to base their moral perspective on received authority? How far is it essential, in your view, for individuals to work through issues for themselves autonomously? (Note: that last word literally means 'having one's own name', i.e. speaking for oneself on the basis of one's own experience, rather than unquestioningly following guidelines laid down by others.)

Reflect on this dilemma with the following three examples of external authority in mind (there is a separate case study on the law on pp. 103–5.)

1 Autonomy *vis-à-vis* one's parents

(a) How essential is it that, in order to achieve autonomy, any child must eventually challenge the expression of moral values received from its parents? If you agree with this, how would you answer a person who said that they had never felt the need to rebel in this way because they were in total sympathy with their parents' outlook?

(b) The psychologists Laing and Janov argued that most people are restricted by compulsions which result from their early upbringing. Those who follow the teachings of this school (see *Psychological Libertarianism*, p. 240) believe that the most healthy procedure is to undergo so-called 'insight' or 'primal' therapy by which, over a long period of time, the client/patient can rid him/herself of parental influences. Is this a desirable procedure? And does your answer depend on whether the influence of the parents concerned was regarded as good, or bad? How do you react to the middle-aged woman who, after years of primal therapy, wrote to her elderly parents criticising the way she had been brought up, and asking them never to communicate with her again, thereafter returning all correspondence and presents, and refusing to attend their eventual funerals?

2 Society

How far is it (a) desirable and (b) possible to be totally autonomous in any Western society, short of disappearing into a hermitage? Consider this apropos of some of the following situations:

(i) Believing the wearing of suits to be insidious ('power dressing') one decides always to wear casual gear. (Why would this be less of a problem in California, say, than in an English provincial city?)

(ii) You live in an area whose inhabitants hold covert, if not overt, racialist views ('blacks lower the tone of the place', etc.). You deliberately take on a black couple as lodgers.

(iii) A neighbour lives as though he is a law unto himself. He holds noisy late-night parties, revs up his motorbike at all times of the day or night, and laughs at any suggestion that he should conform to the life-styles of his neighbours.

(iv) The tree in one person's garden overshadows the people next door so that they can seldom sit in the sun. They request that the tree be removed, even offering to share the expense of this, but their neighbour likes the tree and rejects their request.

(v) Two females sunbathe topless in their garden whenever possible. Their neighbours argue that this is not done, what with impressionable children on either side, and ask them to show more respect.

(vi) Two men openly live together as lovers.

3 God

(a) A Jesuit priest remarked: 'Give me a child till he's seven and I'll keep him for life.' Having experienced the strength of this early teaching, an ex-Catholic campaigns to have religious instruction banned in schools, on the grounds that it is wicked to indoctrinate children with religious dogmas.

(b) Should blasphemy – taking God's name in vain (e.g. by denouncing or belittling religious convictions arising from belief in Him) cease to be a punishable offence? Does the fourth of President Roosevelt's freedoms – freedom of worship – mean freedom to be overtly (and perhaps outrageously) irreligious?

(c) Should the use of God's name be removed from public places and events, e.g. swearing an oath in court by 'Almighty God'?

(d) Should the Church of England be disestablished, and Britain declared to be a secular, rather than a Christian, nation?

Would these last four proposals be more, or less, acceptable in the United States than the United Kingdom?

Having reflected on these issues, can you begin to make some sort of assessment of you own 'autonomy quotient'? To what extent, and over what issues, do you think you would be prepared to raise your head over the parapet, so to speak, and speak out against any opinion which is (apparently) currently held and expressed by the majority of your family, neighbours, and peers?

CASE STUDY 13: VIOLENCE IN THE INNER CITIES: INNATE OR SOCIALLY CAUSED?

Most of the world's large cities have experienced, over recent years, violent confrontations among those who live in them. In Britain and the US in particular, there have been notorious trouble spots which have resulted in mayhem and murder, causing deep concern to authorities and public alike. It would be no exaggeration to describe this as the greatest single problem facing the human race today: greater than that of disease, or famine, or even of war. The causes which have been suggested for this problem, together with the proposed cures, may be divided into the two categories mentioned above. A list of both (which is by no means comprehensive: you may be able to add to it) is offered below. See if you can place them in some order of importance and priority, so that you discover whether your emphasis is on innate or social conditioning. Bear in mind, if the problem appears to you to lend itself to a straightforward solution, that a host of experts – sociologists, psychologists, penologists, biologists, and politicians, to name but a few – have grappled with the problem for decades but appear to be no nearer to finding that solution.

A The cause(s)

(a) Innate

   (i) *Colour prejudice* (racialism). But not all riots have been inter-racial.
  (ii) *Adolescent aggression.* But not all adolescents behave in this way; and people older than adolescents have been involved. Can one generalise biologically?
 (iii) *Natural hatred of authority* – represented in these cases by the police. But many riots break out before the police arrive.
  (iv) *The male desire for dominance* (biology again). But most males don't behave in this way; and females are not uninvolved in these incidents. Can we blame it all on the sex drive?
   (v) *Lack of a firm religious belief as a control mechanism.* How true? Many groups belong to some religious sect, and behave as they do partly in accordance with their beliefs.
  (vi) *Low intellect and poor teaching in schools.* Some followers may not be very bright, but can we say this about the leaders? And are schools to be blamed for social conditions of their pupils, and parental attitudes?
 (vii) *Some people are born wicked.* Maybe: but never in wealthy suburbs?
(viii) *The police:* the profession attracts violently-disposed people who

take it out on others. Maybe some, but can one generalise truthfully?

(b) Socially caused

(i) *Deprivation* – unemployment, bad housing, poor education, etc. But not all unemployed riot, and many citizens who would never engage in violence have received the minimum of formal education and live in below-standard accommodation.

(ii) *The have-nots attacking the haves* (class divisions). Why then did those who rioted in Handsworth in inner Birmingham do so among themselves, and not go on the rampage against the wealthier citizens of Handsworth Wood, half-a-mile down the road?

(iii) *Deliberate provocation* (political – embarrassing to the government). Difficult to prove, and doesn't explain why the incidents have occurred in a particular type of area (e.g. Handsworth, not Handsworth Wood), usually classified as 'deprived'.

(iv) *Crowding people together in a small area* (high-rise flats, etc.) – thus threatening their territorial instinct. But Hong Kong is the most crowded city in the world: what is its statistics for rioting?

(v) *Violent activity the only way to express adulthood* (links with (i) above). But many in similar circumstances gain this self-confidence without such behaviour, while others don't seem to need to show so blatantly that they have 'arrived'.

(vi) *Mob fever*. Perhaps in the later stages, but at the beginning?

(vii) *Influence of the media*. Would the violence cease if cameras were banned? In 1985 the South African government took such a step. Violence thereafter, if anything, increased.

B Resolutions to the problem

Proposals of ways of dealing with the situation vary, generally speaking, between those who accept the cause as innate and those who look for social explanation. Their suggestions may loosely be divided into the use of the stick, and the carrot.

(a) The stick

(i) *Repatriate all coloured immigrants and/or their children*. Would any of the suggestions under (a) and (b) above, with the exception of (a) (i), cease to have any validity if this were to happen?

(ii) *Stiffen the penalties for violent behaviour*. If the grounds for this behaviour are innate, will the introduction of longer prison sentences, or corporal punishment, change things?

97

(iii) *Increase police numbers and give them more power* (arm them, as in the USA?) Might this not be counter-productive (see (a) (iii))? And suppose there is some truth in (a) (viii)?

(iv) *Accept that there is a pecking order in life* and thank the Lord if you live outside riot-prone areas.(!)

(b) The carrot

(i) *Knock down the bad housing and rehouse the tenants.* But can we afford the billions that this would cost? And may we not then be simply removing the problem geographically but not existentially?

(ii) *Create jobs for the unemployed* by massive investment of public money. But can jobs be created on a permanent basis in an artificial way? And which part of public funds should be sacrificed to make this possible? (Beware the easy answer, 'Defence'. In this field, isn't it difficult, even impossible, for any nation to act unilaterally?) Whose money is it anyway?

(iii) *Increase opportunities for education and training.* Again – the problem of cost; and there are many well-educated and highly-skilled people who are unemployed.

(iv) *Create new types of community* on a smaller basis. How realistic are such proposals, admirable though they may be, when millions are unemployed and millions more living in the inner cities? Is not such a proposal equivalent to, and as realistic as, declaring oneself in favour of a better and more fulfilling life for all?

Can you think up a policy for dealing with this situation that you would dare to present, say, at a public meeting?

CASE STUDY 14: MALE AND FEMALE ROLES

According to ethologists, one of the innate elements in homo sapiens, inherited from his/her animal forebears, is the sexual role. This implies, if it is true, that men and women have each a distinctive part to play in life, so that any attempt (for example, by extreme feminists) to blur or destroy this distinction will cause trouble because it is unnatural. The following dialogue on the subject, between a male and a female, was overheard on the top of Helvellyn in the Lake District, in north England.

M	F
1 I don't know why you had to insist on coming on this climb. You've held us up all the way since Stryding Edge. Why can't you	I've made it haven't I? Why do you men always have to spoil things by making them competitive? Can't you just

women accept that there are some things better left to men?

enjoy climbing for its own sake?

2 Climbing's just one example. There are plenty of activities which should be left to men because they need physical strength beyond the capacities of most women. That's how it's always been in nature: the male is the hunter, the protector, or the provider; the female looks after domestic matters.

Women are weaker than men physically only because they haven't been encouraged to develop in this way – they're taught to play with dolls, not to join the males at football. And not all species leave the tough jobs to the male. Lionesses do as much hunting – probably more – as their mates. And what about the bees: how much protecting and hard work do the drones do?

3 Well, primitive man certainly did see this as his role, and primitive women accepted this: they seem to have been happy enough staying at home looking after the kids.

To hell with primitive man – and primitive women as well. Without birth control they were bound physiologically to a domestic routine. Today, childbirth represents a very small percentage of the lives of most Western women – very few have more than two or three kids at most.

4 But caring for children isn't just for the period around childbirth: it goes on for years. Look at what the sociologists say about the harm it can do to children if they come home from school to an empty house.

I agree: even older children get a sense of security by finding someone at home after school. But this can as well be the father as the mother; it could even be a childminder who gets to be liked and trusted.

5 The central biological fact still remains: the human race has survived only because the male has been the aggressor, the dominant one, while the female has been domesticated. In time of war it's still the men who do the fighting.

Maybe they do; but don't forget that it was because women were able to run the munitions factories as capably as men in the first world war that the whole idea of woman's role in society was changed. Anyway, that aggressive instinct is no longer needed in an ordered society where people don't have to protect their bit of land. Men don't seem to have realised this –

99

look at the huge percentage of people imprisoned for violent crimes who are men. Women can be aggressive enough in a different way when it's necessary: just watch female shoppers on the first day of a sale. They'll beat the men hands down.

6 And boots up, I suppose. OK, I agree that the macho-type male is a bit of an anachronism today; but it's still obvious that some jobs need men more than women, and vice versa. I can't imagine many women being much use as navvies, or garbage collectors, or furniture removers. And other jobs, like nursing, or secretarial work, or pre-school or infant teaching, seem more natural to women. Perhaps because they've got more patience. How many men work on assembly lines in chocolate factories? Even today, farmers will call on local female labour when hoeing has to be done. They don't seem to get as distracted by the boredom as men.

Well, they may get distracted by the men, but I take your point. Most women aren't strong enough to do some of the more physically demanding jobs – but neither are most men. The introduction of labour-saving devices has made us all weaker. That's evolution. And women don't 'take to' boring jobs more naturally than men; it's just that in the past they've had to do them because men wouldn't. Now things are changing, and you'll be seeing a lot more male secretaries along with the male nurses and teachers of the young, of which there are already plenty.

7 Male dominance will still show itself in their role as creators and decision makers. It is simply a fact that there have been no great female musicians, or philosophers, or mathematicians. And when it comes to making decisions, in politics or any other organisation, it's the men who take the lead.

Men dominated in these fields in the past, but that's all changing, for reasons we've already gone into. And even in a male-dominated world, we still managed to produce some of the greatest novelists in the English language, like the Brontës, Jane Austen, George Eliot. She even had to take a male pseudonym to get her work published, but she made it.

8 So why didn't some other females make it as musicians?

Perhaps because women have been more concerned with the human factors in life; so –

literature rather than music, psychology rather than mathematics.

9 So you are accepting that there are differences between the two roles? That men are more natural leaders, and women followers? How many *women* would like to have a female boss? The word 'bitch' is still feminine, even when applied to a man.

I'm accepting that in the past few women had the chance to become prominent – though we still produced our Boadiceas and Queen Elizabeths. But look at the world today and you'll find plenty of women leaders, in the world of science and business as well as in politics. And I think the male form of 'bitch' is 'bastard'. I don't like either of them.

10 All your examples are of educated, middle-class women. There's not so much of this among the less educated, or the working classes. Most of these women vote as their husbands tell them, and half of them never utter an opinion unless they've got it from their husbands. I have a relative who begins any answer to any question I may put to her about her opinions with 'Well, like Charlie says . . .' If Charlie hasn't spoken, she has no opinion.

The sort of women you're talking about represent a dying breed which, I agree, is still a secondary role. But Rome wasn't built in a day, and when you think how attitudes have changed in this country about the role of women over a mere twenty years, you'll have to admit it's pretty remarkable. Just wait for another twenty years and you won't know what's hit you.

11 I honestly think you're wrong about this, because I think that, deep down, women don't want the isolation that comes with leadership. Even today, most women want nothing more than to marry and settle down with a family. From what I hear, Arab women, despite what seem to us awful restrictions, are basically happy. What I know for sure is that the unhappiest women I've met are the Americans. Most of them have to see their psychiatrists twice a week.

There's still a lot of pressure on girls to assume the role of domesticity, and some of them take the way of least resistance. And as for American women and their psychiatrists, don't you think it's more to do with the country itself, with all its violence, than with the women themselves? There are more murders every year in the city of Houston than in the whole of the British Isles. And how come you're an expert on Arab women

101

all of a sudden? I'd say it's more a case of what you've never had you never miss.

12 Well, personally I can't understand why women don't want to go on being kept by men. It must be preferable to work. Most work is a routine chore, not making executive decisions or producing TV programmes – which is what you women seem to want.

The same goes for men. I know lots of husbands who are more domesticated than their wives. And if there is a choice, and the family doesn't need two incomes, where the woman can earn more than the man it seems common sense to let her be the breadwinner.

13 It still seems to me that, even at work, some roles are much more suited to men than to women. In the university where I study, some departments are predominantly full of women – like Humanities, Nursing, Fashion, Education, and Biology – while others are predominantly male, like Engineering, Maths, Computing, Chemistry, and Surveying.

People are still influenced by their early schooling, and in this country certain jobs are earmarked for men or women early on. But this is changing, and will continue to do so as more and more women demand not only equal rights with men, but equal opportunities. Not all women will get exactly the job they want – but neither do all men. We can't all be Margaret Thatchers.

14 Thank God for that! But this brings us to the central point: by demanding an equal role with men, women lose their femininity. Look at those Russian female construction workers: they might as well be sexless. And a lot of the women I've seen holding down jobs in this country seem very unappealing as women.

It depends what you're looking for in women. If all you want is a simpering sycophant, you've had it mate. From now on we're our own mistresses, not just sex objects for ogling males.

15 So you want to destroy the male sex drive, do you?

Not at all: women enjoy sex just as much as men, but we understand a bit more than men about how to control it. I'm still the same woman beneath all this climbing gear.

16 Prove it.

102

CASE STUDY 15: ETHICS AND THE LAW

Of all the possible sources of our knowledge of right and wrong debated in this chapter, it is possible that 'the law of the land' is the answer that reflects most accurately the viewpoint of most of us. But to what are we then really committing ourselves? Discuss this with the following three issues in mind:

A 'The Law is a' ass'

Those who agree with Mr Bumble have an attitude to the law which is not far short of contempt. In the light of the following considerations, see if you agree that the cynical are justified in their opinion.

1 'Even if a few innocent people are punished unfairly, it is better for the health of the nation as a whole that they should suffer than that the representatives of the law, by reversing an earlier decision made in court, should suggest that the law is fallible.' – Lord Denning, senior British judge, 1989.
   Do you agree with this, or do you hold the reverse view that it is preferable that a score of guilty men go free than that one innocent person is judged guilty? How far would your viewpoint be modified if capital punishment were restored in the UK, as in numerous states of the USA?

2 It sometimes occurs that a crime increases in prevalence in a particular community, with the consequence that the punishment relating to this crime begins to be more severe: this has, for example, been the case with 'joy-riding' in the UK. Is the law strengthened or weakened by the concept of 'the state of play' apropos of a particular crime?

3 The same crime, before different judges, will possibly carry a widely different penalty. This has occurred with the crime of rape, which some judges treat as little more than a schoolboy prank (and sentence accordingly) while others treat it as little short of murder, with corresponding lengthy sentences. What does this divergence say about the law?

4 Very often, crimes against the person (violent assaults, etc.) bring a lighter sentence than those against property: steal a man's car and you will be facing the direst of consequences, batter him until he is comatose and you may well be looking at no more than a probationary sentence. (This is no exaggeration: the 'Great train robbers' of 1963 faced jail sentences of up to 30 years: many a murderer has served a sentence of under a third of that before being released.) Can you detect some sort of logic behind this, or does it bring you to the conclusion that the law is crazy?

5 'If you get Judge X, you'll win your case; if you get Y or Z you've

no chance': the words of a solicitor to a client in a civil case in 1993. He was basing this statement on his knowledge of the prejudices of the three judges concerned: how does it affect your view of 'the law'?

6 Look again at the examples of the law in the UK regarding Sunday trading (p. 71). How seriously can you treat a legal system which compels the manager of a cathedral shop not to sell Bibles on a Sunday, but allows the sale of chess sets, beer mugs, and other 'worldly' paraphernalia?

7 In the UK, it is illegal to sell alcohol to young people under the age of 18. In the Netherlands, it is illegal to trade in cannabis. Yet in both these countries these laws are broken openly and regularly while the police turn a blind eye. Does it encourage people to respect the law if it is so flagrantly flouted? Do you think that a country should either revise laws of this nature, or else enforce them in all circumstances? Would it, for example, be preferable that the law should act as in the state of California in the USA: the carrying of identity cards should be required if people are to enter into bars or any place where age is a significant (i.e. legal) factor?

B Is it ever morally right to break the law?

See if you can decide on situations where this apparent impossibility, or absurdity, becomes a fair response to a situation. You may well have examples of your own, but here are a few suggestions to get the discussion under way:

(i)   The pacifist in wartime who refuses to support his country's military machine.

(ii) The husband who is driving his wife, heavily into labour, to the nearest maternity ward, saves precious minutes by driving straight over a roundabout, and then parks the car in a no-parking zone near the entrance to the ward.

(iii) The enlisted soldier who, at the outbreak of the Gulf War in 1991, toured the UK, denouncing Britain's involvement in this operation.

(iv) Jean-Paul Sartre visiting French troops in Algeria during the battle for that country's independence, seeking to persuade them to lay down their arms in the cause of a 'greater justice'.

(v)   Jean Valjean, in Victor Hugo's *Les Miserables*, stealing a loaf of bread to feed his starving family.

C Changes in the law

What changes, if any, would you like to see in the law of your country? Again, here are a few suggestions which may spark you off:

(i)   The legalisation of marriages between lesbians or homosexuals.
(ii) The legalisation of cannabis (and other drugs?)

(iii) The 'demystifying' of court procedure by, e.g., the non-wearing of wigs or formal gowns, greater informality in the style of speech, holding trials in less imposing buildings.

(iv) A stronger emphasis, with greater penalties for law-breakers, on ecological or environmental misdemeanours: banning leaded petrol, outlawing the tipping of toxic wastes, enforcing painless killing in abattoirs; i.e. multiply the powers of Environmental Health Officers.

Section Two

Approaches to ethical theory

Chapter Five

Ends and means I: Kant

For the middle phase of the book, we turn from general issues to a consideration of four major approaches to ethics. These approaches are by no means comprehensive in the field, as a reading of, for instance, Alasdair MacIntyre's *A Short History of Ethics* will indicate: but they represent the highest peaks of ethical theory, and are diverse enough to cover the range, without necessarily including every intermediate slope. Furthermore, they are all theories of right and wrong behaviour which remain attractive to a host of students even today. Any comparative study of ethics will need more than is included here if no nuance is to be neglected; what is equally certain is that nobody can be said to have studied the subject at all comprehensively if any of these is ignored.

One of the central questions facing any human being is: does the end justify the means? Some would say that this is the most important issue that will confront anyone throughout his life. Some of the forms of behaviour which we applaud or condemn most strongly are categorised as right or wrong on the basis of our answer to this question. It has been discussed by a large number of philosophers, but two in particular have presented the case for the negative and affirmative answers respectively; they are the subjects of this chapter and the next.

Immanuel Kant (1724–1804)

If a football team were to be selected from among the great philosophers, Kant would be among the handful under consideration for the position of centre forward. In philosophy generally he stands out as one of the giants, and in moral philosophy in particular he has been described as one of the great dividing points in the history of ethics. All this is, perhaps, surprising since, though extraordinary as a philosopher, he lived a very ordinary life. The German poet, Heinrich Heine, wrote of him:

He had neither life nor history, for he lived a melancholy ordered and abstract old bachelor life in a quiet retired street in Koenigsberg, an old town on the northeast border of Germany. I do not believe that the great clock of the cathedral there did its daily work more dispassionately and regularly than its compatriot Immanuel Kant. Rising, coffee drinking, writing, reading college lectures, eating, walking, all had their fixed time, and the neighbours knew that it was exactly half-past three when Immanuel Kant . . . left his house door and went to the Lime Tree Avenue, which is still called, in memory of him, the Philosopher's Walk.

Though an intellectual giant, physically Kant was little over five feet tall. His body was misshapen; he was for most of his life a hypochondriac; and throughout his long life he abstained from the pleasures of wine, women, and song. He seldom left his native Koenigsberg, and never went more than a hundred kilometres from it. His personal life was in some respects similar to that of his English contemporary, John Wesley, after whose methodical life-style the Methodist branch of the Christian Church was named. Kant's parents belonged to a similar kind of pietistic tradition.

His entire life revolved around the local university, first as a student, then as a tutor, finally as professor. For most of his academic career he studied and taught the physical sciences; his first philosophical work, *The Critique of Pure Reason* was not published until he was fifty-seven, and all the work for which he is famous was written in the last part of his life.Two intellectual experiences changed the course of his life. The first was his reading of the French philosopher Rousseau, through whom, as he wrote, 'I learned to respect human nature, and I should consider myself far more useless than the ordinary working man if I did not believe that this view could give worth to all others to establish the rights of man.' (The only piece of art in Kant's study was a picture of Rousseau.)

The second experience, which finally changed the course of his thinking, was that of reading the Scottish philosopher, Hume. Kant described him as the man who 'awakened me from my dogmatic slumbers'. It seems that it is never too late in life for this to happen. His philosophical investigations were to reflect, in their underlying assumptions, the age in which he lived: the so-called Age of Enlightenment. It was the age when reason was placed above all other faculties, the age following Descartes's 'cogito, ergo sum', of Newton's physicism and Hume's empiricism (see Chapter Thirteen). Kant pursued this theme, arguing that man is no empty slate, a *tabula rasa*; he is a combination of both experience and a priori intuitions and concepts, and it is the mind's role to organise the complexities and conflicts which the combination of these often brings about. It acts, so to speak, as an umpire in this situation. 'Concepts,'

Kant wrote, 'without perception are empty; perceptions without concepts are blind.'

Goodwill Kant's moral theory arises from the belief that man is free, and that his moral conviction is brought about by inner reasoning rather than by external forces. He viewed morals as, consequently, independent of the world around us, the world that we experience, which he viewed as morally neutral. What is it, then, which makes any precept moral? What, if anything, distinguishes such precepts from others that we may state: what can we unreservedly describe as 'good'? His answer was that the only good is the good will – what our motives and intentions are when we decide to behave in a particular way in our dealings with other people. Whether our behaviour is in itself 'good' it is not possible to say until we decide how far it has been motivated in this way. Actions which may appear as meritorious to the casual observer – or even, perhaps, to their recipients – may well merit condemnation if judged by this norm. Thus a companion in a bar may buy me a drink, and appear to be acting generously, which would be commendable; but if he precedes the act by saying sarcastically 'I suppose *you* won't say no' he in fact belittles me by his financial outlay; and even if he doesn't use such words, his apparent generosity evaporates if it is known that he buys other people drinks only because he expects to be treated in return.

This absolute emphasis on the good will as the sole determinant of moral goodness places Kant firmly among those who stress principles rather than consequences: he was a *deontologist*, not a *teleologist*. For him, the consequences were irrelevant in the assessing of the goodness or otherwise of moral behaviour. In other words, to recall the issue which is central to this chapter, the end did not justify the means. The actual outcome in the pub scene was that I received a free drink; but this outcome, desirable though it may in a sense be, cannot be the criterion by which the worth of the action should be tested. If this were so, then human beings would ultimately have to be viewed as no more than means to an end, the end in this case being the donor's gaining a reputation for generosity, or being 'one-up' on the recipient. Kant was emphatic in refusing to tolerate such an abuse of other people:

Every man is to be respected as an absolute end in himself; and it is a crime against the dignity that belongs to him as a human being to use him as a mere means for some external purpose.

Thus any form of exploitation of people, of treating them as anything less than autonomous beings, must be condemned. To use people for one's own gratification, whether this be through such universally condemned means as rape or physical assault, or through the more subtle means of conning the gullible or capitalising on another person's sexual attraction to you, is to treat others as no more than cogs in machines, and to refuse to let them be free agents.

By putting such an emphasis on the good will, Kant relegates in his list of human priorities many qualities in life which people, then and since, have valued highly: qualities such as health, wealth, or the intellect. None of these are unimportant: Kant himself spent more time than most in worrying about his health, he was certainly not poverty-stricken, and his intellect was among the greatest the world has seen. But all of them, in his view, must be ranked, in any moral hierarchy, lower than the good will. It, uniquely, can face up to opposition and controversy. The good will can conquer the world.

It is unlikely that anyone will dispute the main argument so far. Any person motivated entirely by goodwill towards others is likely to be applauded; equally, anyone who takes malevolence as the spring of his behaviour should not be surprised if he lives a lonely existence. Judging from the case presented so far, the end cannot possibly justify the means, since this must cause people to be treated as objects, things, rather than as self-conscious beings. We cannot but be in favour of the good will. The question that follows is, how can I be sure that this is in fact the motive of my behaviour? It is perfectly simple for me to persuade myself and – though sometimes with more difficulty – others that this is why I behave as I do. But the examination of one's motives is intensely difficult because they often seem to be mixed up. I may fool myself that I have performed a supererogatory act of charity by doing an unaccustomed bit of kindness, when my real intention is to get someone in a good mood for the moment when I make a particular demanding request of him. Fundamental selfishness can parade itself in the guise of altruism, without my even being aware of this myself. How can such self-deception, not to say the misleading of others, be avoided?

Duty Kant's answer to this very difficult question was simple and direct. We learn what goodwill is when we learn the meaning of *duty*. Actions performed out of a sense of duty are those which we can confidently say are motivated by goodwill. A person who acts out of this sense cannot be found guilty (though he may be accused) of ulterior motives, evil intentions, or treating people as less than human. He will be honest with himself and just towards others. He will be able to overcome the demands of self interest, and to avoid having favourites, or their opposite, in his moral dealings with other human beings. 'Duty for duty's sake' must be the concept to bear in mind if we wish to be sure of the real nature of our motives. Whatever be the consequences of doing one's duty, whether it results in acclamation or condemnation, that is the right way to behave. It will help us to avoid the temptation of acting only so as to please ourselves, or to find favour with others. It will give us a clear line amid all our conflicting feelings, and a consistency in the face of a mixture of motives. (Bear in mind, 'deon' = 'duty', hence 'deontology'.)

Kant argued that, so far as the moral worth of any action is concerned, personal inclination is irrelevant. How we *feel* about the way we behave is a matter over which we have no choice: feelings are morally neutral. Where we do have a choice is between inclination and duty. President Lincoln was once visited by a delegation of commissioners from South Carolina. Sympathetic though he was to their request, he said to them: 'As President, I have no eyes but constitutional eyes; I cannot see you.' Thus he expressed his sense of duty; and such sentiments have been reflected in the behaviour of frightened men who have yet volunteered to fight for their countries, of people who overcome the temptation to steal even when they know they could not possibly be found out, of mothers who have sacrificed their jobs for their children, even when they have felt no particular fondness for them. Kant even went so far as to affirm that actions are worthier if done only out of obedience to our sense of duty, with our inclinations being disregarded. So the soldier who enjoys fighting, the citizen who gains inner satisfaction from keeping the law, the mother who prefers rearing children to going to work, rank lower in the moral ratings than those who do these things reluctantly. If we are given excessive change, it is commendable to return this because it is our duty to do so; it is not so commendable if we get pleasure from the process.

Problems with duty   Before proceeding to the central theme of Kant's moral philosophy, we may acknowledge that his eulogising of duty has not met with universal approval. There is, for a start, the problem of the *clash of duties*: to one's family, one's employer, one's country, even to God (Wordsworth's 'Ode to Duty' begins with the words 'Stern daughter of the voice of God . . .'). In response to duty's call men have felt compelled to sacrifice one for the other – family for job or vice versa, job for country, and so on: Buddha even sacrificed his family for his new-found revelation. Kant no doubt satisfied himself on the dilemmas thus raised, but for many the problem still remains. Perhaps his – to some people – simplistic approach on this matter reflects his own life-style: his life and his work were one; not for him the conflicting claims of home and study, of time spent with books, and involvement in political or social reform. His life followed a fixed routine; on the one day when he missed his afternoon walk (for reasons that will be revealed in Chapter Twelve) many of his neighbours fled to the local church in the (mistaken, as it turned out) belief that the end of the world was nigh. The call of duty presented no problem to him.

The second criticism perhaps reflects a more positive response to Hobbes than is to be found in Kant: is our moral behaviour really to be accounted less worthy if it gives us satisfaction than it would be if we gained no sense of pleasure from it whatsoever? Admitted that it's *harder* to be kind to one we dislike than one we like: is it basically *better*? As Kant himself said, we cannot choose our inclinations: why then should my kindness to the former rank as worthier than to the latter just because of a factor over which I have not the least control? After all, it's not my fault if I happen to like someone. Bertrand Russell expressed this grievance in his usual pithy way: 'If he (Kant) really believed what he thinks he believes, he would not regard heaven as a place where the good are happy, but as a place where they have never-ending opportunities of doing kindnesses to people whom they dislike.'[1]

The third criticism of the concept of duty is that *it tends to lead to an acceptance of, and obedience to, authority*, which normally means those set in authority over us. This was probably less of a problem in Kant's day than in our more autonomous (at least for the West) twentieth century. Patriotism, respect for the police as upholders of the law, and indeed deference to people in high places generally are, for better or for worse, less frequent than they were before 'the age of the common man'. There is today considerably more emphasis on personal fulfilment than existed two hundred years ago, so that the command to do one's duty does not have the same imposing ring to it as to our forefathers. With courses on personal assertiveness springing up everywhere it is no wonder that the notion of duty seems to have been shelved. (This may be only a temporary phenomenon, of course, and future generations may well come to assess us as a generation without ideals; if people get tired of living in a society where few can be relied on, perhaps there will be a hankering after the Kantian approach to living, where people's word is more likely to be their bond, but the problem remains.)

A person who gives his sense of duty top priority can sometimes be troublesome to others. A former colleague of mine always felt it his duty to give up one pleasure for Lent; one year he resolved to do without his weekly visit to a local restaurant for afternoon tea and cakes – a worthy action, no doubt, but I was the person who had taken great pleasure in accompanying him on those occasions. No doubt Kant sometimes caused irritation to others if his adherence to his routine inconvenienced them; and his rigorous approach to the learning process caused him to be merciless with students whose work he considered lacking in academic rigour. But Kant is not alone among philosophers in these respects: Wittgenstein, by all accounts, was stricter still; in my own experience, Heidegger and even Russell had nothing to learn from Kant; and, if we

---

[1] *Human Society in Ethics and Politics*

can believe contemporary comments, his students viewed him with warmth as well as trepidation.

The categorical imperative

We turn now to Kant's most important contribution to moral thinking, and a statement which ranks among the most famous in the world. Granted that the only thing which makes behaviour truly good is the good will; and granted that our perception of this is brought about by our awareness of duty: how can we be sure where our duty lies? In particular, considering how easily any of us can deceive ourselves about our own motives, how can we prove to ourselves that the behaviour we propose to engage in is in reality based on a sense of duty, and not on the desire to satisfy our feelings or inclinations? It is no problem to disguise a selfish desire as an expression of duty: 'For the sake of our children's health we put them to bed early.' 'The Government are increasing the tax on tobacco because of our duty to the public's health.' 'I'm giving this student an A because I ought to reward hard work.' These statements could be rewritten much more briefly: 'We like to do our own thing in the evenings.' 'We need more revenue.' 'I'm too lazy to analyse the essay carefully.' So: how can we be sure that we aren't constantly making such rationalisations of our behaviour?

Kant's answer was that we must universalise what we propose to do; the principle is known by the ugly, but nonetheless clarifying, word, *universalisability*. What he meant was that we shall know where our duty lies if we ask ourselves the simple but fundamental question: would I wish everyone to behave as I am now proposing to do in these circumstances? His expression of this principle is known as Kant's *categorical imperative*. In it, he states:

Act only on that maxim whereby thou canst at the same time will that it should become a universal law.

It is worth pausing at this point and thinking over for yourself the implications of this.

It should be helpful if we begin by clearing up some of the language problems. The principle is described as 'categorical', which contrasts with 'hypothetical'; and within the sentence are the two words, which seem similar but have a different meaning, 'maxim' and 'law'.

A hypothetical imperative is one which suggests what should be done under certain conditions, or if certain consequences are desired. Typically, such sentences would start with the word 'if', and many of them fall under the umbrella of prudential advice, which we have already discussed. 'If you want something to be done about your backache, spend a little money on an osteopath.' 'If you wish to lose weight, you should watch your diet.' Or, on a purely mechanical basis, 'If you want your torch to work you should change the battery.' To all these admonitions and those like them a straightforward reason can be given in answer to the question, why? – 'because food is the main factor determining a person's weight' – and so on.

A categorical imperative is not like this, because it stands unconditionally. When I say categorically 'You ought to do so-and-so' and you ask me why you should do it, the answer I give – indeed, the only answer I am able to give – is 'because you ought, that's why'. No other reason is necessary, because we are not dealing in the world of prudential advice which may need reasoned argument before it is accepted, but with issues which are right or wrong *per se*. What is true *prima facie* is true without needing further rationalisation: such imperatives must be accepted, according to Kant, as self-evidently true, so that to ask for the reason why they are true would be as absurd as to ask why two twos are four, or why an object cannot both exist and not exist at the same time. The genocide practised by the Nazi regime in Germany was wrong simply because it could not possibly accord with the categorical imperative.

In the categorical imperative, as elsewhere, Kant uses the word maxim to mean 'a subjective principle of action'. By this he meant the rule or policy of life adopted by any particular person, but not necessarily required of anyone else. Thus maxims may, and do, vary between people: some may choose to marry, while others follow a life of celibacy; some may give a percentage of their income to charity, while others put it into a trust fund for their children. Nobody need be upset because another person's maxims are different from his own (though in fact people do sometimes get upset over such matters, as many children trying to find their own norms will admit regarding their parents).

A law, in contrast, applies to everybody. By making a law of his personal maxim an individual is deciding that he will always and in all situations act in that way; what Kant is saying is that the way to determine the laws in our lives is by the process of deciding whether we can will that everyone else should follow them. They are forms of behaviour to which there can be no exceptions, no individual cases, no special pleading. Such laws, in Kant's mind, assumed a metaphysical quality, to be regarded with an almost, if not actual, religious fervour. He wrote:

Two things fill the mind with ever-increasing wonder and awe, the more often and the more intensely the mind is drawn to them: the starry heavens above me and the moral law within me.[1]

[1] *Critique of Pure Reason* – conclusion

Kant pursues this theme at great length and with a wide range of examples, dividing the laws into duties owed to oneself and those owed to others. Both of these are further subdivided into perfect and imperfect duties, by which he seems to distinguish those forms of behaviour which require some specific act, such as telling the truth, from those which don't indicate precisely the required act in any situation, such as being kind to one's neighbour. At the risk of over-simplifying the whole discussion, which could easily continue for the remainder of this book, we shall look at the central issue of Kant's philosophy by considering the example of a perfect duty to others which he himself used: *keeping a promise*.

Promise-keeping   His argument was that this must be a universal law. Promise-keeping is the basis of trust between people; if promises are treated only as maxims of individuals, but not universal, then the essence of promise-keeping evaporates into thin air, and the words which express the promise become meaningless. If a local handyman promises to mend a door in my house on a particular day and then doesn't appear, I am unlikely to take seriously either his word or that of any other handyman on later occasions. If, on the other hand, he says no more than 'I will come on such-and-such a date unless something else (inclement weather, for example, or a more lucrative contract) turns up,' then his words, in terms of any sure consequences, are virtually meaningless. Phrases like 'as soon as possible' or 'when I get round to it' in this context usually carry the same note of assurance as 'Don't ring us: we'll ring you.'

Clearly, life would run more smoothly for us if all promises made to us were fulfilled: if we knew that, come what may, the word of a particular person could be relied on. The trouble is that life for the promise-maker is not always as uncomplicated as this situation would require. Supposing I promise to visit a sick friend, but on the way am witness to a road accident in which a person is injured. Do I, like the Pharisee in the parable of the Good Samaritan, pass by 'on the other side' because I have a prior engagement? Obviously not; and Kant acknowledged that promises must be stated in terms which indicate that they will be kept unless a more demanding need confronts me; but then we are back to a hypothetical imperative, since any two people may well disagree about what constitutes a 'more demanding need' in this context. We may universalise the situation by stating that 'we will always act in response to the greatest need in others which confronts us at a particular time': but since this imperative contains no specific course of action to follow, it falls into Kant's category of imperfect duties.

The impasse we seem to arrive at when trying to apply the categorical imperative is that either the particular law is stated in such specific terms that it is difficult not to find grounds for making exceptions, or in such non-specific terms as to take us no further forward in knowing what, precisely, will be done at any time. The injunction 'Always tell the truth, whatever the consequences' may sound worthy enough, but the world would be devastated if it were universally applied. In certain situations (among diplomats, or businessmen perhaps) such devastation may be deemed by others to be highly desirable; but what would be the reaction of an escapee from an extermination camp whom I had hidden in my loft when I truthfully answered his pursuers' question as to whether he were in my house or not? If we make the law 'Always tell the truth unless it will cause people pain' we are back to an imperfect duty. Equally, such high-sounding laws as 'Always act in another's best interests' leaves the field open for a wide-ranging variety of actions, depending on the agent's understanding of what another's best interests are.

It seems, therefore, that the categorical imperative, which in theory may well have looked straightforward enough, is somewhat difficult to apply in practice. 'Never speak unless you are spoken to', 'always let a companion go through a door first', 'don't start eating until someone else does' are all recipes for frustrating situations; while the golden rule, which finds a strong echo in this imperative – 'do unto others as you would they should do unto you' – overlooks the basic fact that we all have differing needs, and what I want is not necessarily what others want. Should I, for instance, go around handing out Condor long-cut pipe tobacco to all and sundry, as this is what I'd like them to do to me?

Nevertheless, a fair number of people have found the idea of universalisability a useful rule of thumb when facing a moral dilemma. My guess is that a high proportion of those who stop to help somebody in some form of distress do so because they think, consciously or unconsciously, that they themselves might one day be similarly in need of help, and they would like to feel that this would be forthcoming; they may even take the matter further and reflect on what the world would be like if nobody ever went out of their way, or inconvenienced themselves, to aid someone else in distress. Is it not with a similar kind of thinking in mind that people give back excess change, return a lost wallet, with its cash contents, to its owner, and even throw away an envelope with an unfranked stamp? (My father, who would have made a loyal disciple of Kant, used to do this on the grounds that 'it's done its job'.)

Kantian ethics allows each individual to be his own moral authority, and it was this emphasis which was taken up by the existentialists two centuries later (see Chapter Seven). Man is looked upon as an autonomous creature, capable of expressing this quality through a continuous process of rational judgments. Kant thus lifts the moral decision-making process above that of the gratification solely of personal desire (I'm going to do this because I feel like it') or the pursuit of pleasure. His own lifestyle, which was a living expression of his philosophy – not always the case with philosophers – may express a rigidness and rigour which are not fashionable today, but, at least under some lights, presents a more commendable, even desirable, image of the human species than is to be found in excessive libertarianism (in the popular sense of the word: Kant was a libertarian in the philosophical sense).

Furthermore, Kant's emphasis on man's rational autonomy led to his refusal to accept any external authority for morality, in particular, any divine authority. Man chooses freely how he shall behave; he is not under holy orders (even if he's in holy orders), since this would imply that he was subject to laws outside himself and so prevented from becoming a mature moral agent. Again, this emphasis was later to be reiterated by the existentialists (the issue is in fact so important that it will also be considered in Chapters Eight and Ten.) Kant therefore refused to go along with those who would decline either to commend a person for good conduct, on the grounds that, since he was merely obeying orders, only the law-giver should be commended ('I, yet not I, but Christ . . .' said St Paul), or to condemn him for bad conduct, on the grounds that his instructions may have been wrong, or he may simply have misunderstood them.

The main weakness of Kant's theory, apart from any that may have been already discussed in passing, is that its emphasis lies primarily in telling us what we ought not, rather than what we ought, to do. As MacIntyre writes[1] 'Morality (as presented by the categorical imperative) sets limits to the ways in which and the means by which we conduct our lives; it does not give them direction.' It tells us that we should not cheat at cards, crib in exams, or kick a man when he's down; it is considerably less helpful in telling us what is desirable, what ends we should have in mind, what kind of behaviour we should wish to see universalised. We can hardly take Kant's own life-style to guide us on this matter: apart from the obvious fact that one aspect of this, his celibacy, would bring about the extinction of the human race, this would be to deny the central truth of Kant's teaching that, because each of us is an autonomous, rational human being, we must apply the categorical imperative to our own lives, not simply try to imitate the way another person has done this.

One further question follows from this: can we ever be sure that we are right to universalise any maxim on the basis that the kind of world which would emerge, if this, or any other, maxim were observed universally, would be the best of all possible worlds? This may be the case so far as *I* am able to judge: but how can I be sure that I'm right and my friend round the corner, whose response to the categorical imperative is radically different from mine, is wrong? Why should I insist that my desire to see a caring society, in which the rich and successful are taxed in order to look after the poor and unsuccessful, is a preferable piece of universalisation to that of a person who prefers the ideal of a society in which it is openly conceded that some – whether through hard work or good luck –

---

[1]Op. cit., p. 197

succeed and others fail, and that as long as you are prepared to accept the situation if you happen to be among the failures there is no need to worry about the unfairness of life? Or, looked at another way, why not follow the way of Tao and let all such worldly considerations pass by; or, as Kant himself affirmed, come to terms with the unfairness underlying much human experience in this world (which, even with Kant's longevity, is fleeting) and look to another life afterwards where such inequalities will be evened out? We are back to the problem raised in Chapter Two: where two different absolutes are in conflict, how can we be sure which, if either, is right?

Kant's influence in the field of moral philosophy, notwithstanding the questions he left unanswered, has continued unabated since his death: one can disagree with him, but one cannot discount him. At the age of seventy, his most recent work, 'Religion Within the Bounds of Mere Reason', was banned by the Prussian King, Friedrich Wilhelm II, and all discussion of it forbidden. But it was published after the king's death, and that abortive act of censorship illustrates the futility of resisting the force of an idea. Right to the end, the categorical imperative was strong in Kant. Ten days before he died, plagued with mental unrest and sleeplessness, he was visited by his doctor and struggled to his feet. When the doctor protested against this act of courtesy, Kant replied: 'The sense of humanity has not yet left me.' It is not to be wondered at that Kant's neighbours described him as 'the beloved philosopher'.

CASE STUDY 16: WHO SHALL LIVE?

Here is a dilemma facing the medical world today: establishing priorities amid a scarcity of resources, in this case a scarcity of kidney machines in a particular hospital. Some years ago, this scarcity resulted in four people applying (without realising this, of course) for what was at the time the sole available dialysis machine in the renal unit. Obviously, only one of the four could be admitted. The others might be able to have their houses made suitable for the installation of a home dialysis machine, and the possibility of a kidney transplant existed for most, if not all, of them: but both these procedures would require time, during which any one of them could die. The only way to be sure that this did not occur for one of them was to put him or her *immediately* (and regularly thereafter) on the available machine.

How would you set about making the decision? Imagine that you are one of the hospital team who has to decide between the four sick people. The script which follows contains the verbatim reports on all four written by the medical social worker. Only the names have been changed. Also available to the team will be the patient's medical records. These will show whether any of the four has any other serious ailment: if so, that patient would be excluded from the dialysis machine because, harsh though it may sound, it would be unfair to any of those refused access, and to their relatives, if he/she were to die soon after of renal failure, while the person selected died at the same time, not of renal failure, but of something else such as heart or lung failure. We can take it, since these records are naturally not available to us, that there was nothing else seriously wrong with the patients. Besides the medical social worker (MSW), the team would be likely to include the surgeons, registrar, doctor(s), sister, senior nurses, and any others working in or attached to the renal unit, such as the home dialysis administrator, whose job is to assess the suitability of patients' homes for the installation of a machine.

So your task is straightforward: who shall live – or, put less dramatically, which of the four will you choose to ensure does not die of renal failure because of lack of access to a dialysis machine? More importantly, on what basis, by the application of what criteria, do you reach your decision? How far do you consider the categorical imperative to be relevant and applicable? Can you establish a universal law or principle that may ease the burden of those involved in the making of such grim, but humanly necessary (as matters are) decisions?

The most rewarding use of this study would be to do it with a group of friends or colleagues. You might proceed as follows:

1 Read the records carefully.
2 Without any discussion whatsoever, take a straw poll on which person you would choose.
3 Discuss the grounds on which each person's choice was made, and see if you can agree on any kind of priority of criteria (age, family responsibility and support, usefulness to the community, etc.)
4 Take a final vote, and see if there has been a switch since the second stage. You may find it necessary to take a series of votes, each time eliminating the last on the list, in order to reach a decision with the maximum amount of agreement possible.

Case No. 1	John White
Age	26 years
Employment	Part-time university lecturer, part-time researcher working for Ph.D in psychology.
Family circumstances	Family immigrated when John, only child, was of school age. Father now dead, mother has returned to Barbados.
Housing	Rented bedsitter in cosmopolitan street. Poor amenities, stove on landing, etc.; lavatory shared with eight other tenants; no bathroom.

After another year, Mr White will become entitled to accommodation within the university.

Medical social worker's report

I visited Mr White in his bedsitter. Although he is obviously a very fastidious young man and has done his best to make his room habitable, the condition of the house is so bad that his efforts are largely wasted. Apparently, the landlord owns several houses in the street and lets rooms to tenants, his sole means of income. He has repeatedly refused to do anything to repair the state of these houses. The roof leaks, the plumbing is inefficient, and there is dry rot on the stairs. Despite his depressing surroundings, Mr White is a cheerful young man. It appears that he considers himself lucky to have found anywhere to live at all. I spoke to him about his mother; she returned home after his father's death three years ago due to homesickness. Mr White sends her part of his salary each month. Mr White has adjusted to the fact of his serious illness very quickly. Through his contacts at the university he has gained a good deal of information about the routine use of a kidney machine and assured me that he would be able to adjust his working hours to fit in with the hospital schedule. As he is young, he may be suitable for a transplant operation later on. One of the problems is his lack of a permanent home. Judging by his general attitude towards his tenants, the landlord would hardly tolerate the alterations that would be required for a home kidney machine to be installed – in any case, it would mean that the whole house would have to be rewired and have new plumbing. Unfortunately, Mr White is not in a financial position to gain a mortgage in order to buy his own property, though the university may help here – I gather that he is highly thought of there and, until his illness, was expected to achieve a senior post within a fairly short time.

Signed - Amy Collins

Case No. 2	William Johnston
Age	52 years
Employment	Crane driver, shift work 6 am – 2 pm, 2 pm – 10 pm alternate weeks.
Family circumstances	Wife, 49, works as cleaner, mornings only. Four children; two married daughters, one lives near the family home; two sons, 13 and 15 years – the elder plans to leave school in the summer, the younger is academically inclined, has prospects of going to college. Also grandmother (Mr Johnston's mother),

	83, arthritic, recently had cataract operation.
Housing	Rented house in decaying terrace. Very shabby outside, plaster falling off walls, etc. Family have been on housing list for 15 years.

Medical social worker's report

Mrs Johnston is a plump, homely woman, devoted to her family. The house shows signs of do-it-yourself activities, for example, Mr Johnston laid new boards on the living-room floor, and, at the time when he was taken ill, was about to redecorate the kitchen. Mrs Johnston told me that he has to do this at least once a year as damp comes through the outside wall continuously – she showed me a corner where mould was forming on the paintwork. The boys were at school when I called, but I got the impression that this is a happy family. Mrs Johnston is a placid personality and shows a wonderful sense of humour. Mr Johnston's mother can be very difficult at times but I got the impression that Mrs Johnston does not let this get her down. She reacted vehemently against my asking whether she had considered placing the old lady in a home, so that she would not find the additional strain of tending her sick husband so great. Money is a problem at the moment; Mr Johnston's firm are not supplementing his sick pay and the weekly income is reduced by a third. But Mrs Johnston is more worried about what job her husband will be fit to do when he comes out of hospital than about money itself; she says that her husband will never settle for early retirement and she cannot see the firm giving him a less physically demanding job. I promised to look into this. She also enquired about the possibility of a transplant operation. I told her as gently as I could that her husband is rather too old to be considered for this, though of course he is basically a strong man.

Signed – Amy Collins

Case No. 3	Sue Gibson
Age	37 years
Employment	Civil Servant; senior position in department of economic statistics.
Family circumstances	Unmarried. Lives with and supports aged mother (79) and sister with Down's Syndrome (30).
Housing	A rather dark two-bedroom flat; the sisters share a bedroom. Flat owned by Miss Gibson and her mother. Apart from a married brother who lives and works abroad, there are no other relatives.

123

Medical social worker's report

I visited Mrs Gibson and her younger daughter quite early in the morning. Mrs Gibson is obviously at a loss without Sue; the Down's Syndrome daughter is difficult to handle and is too strong for Mrs Gibson to control. I witnessed a struggle between the two as Mrs Gibson tried to persuade her daughter to dress. Mrs Gibson is a thin, wiry little woman, very shy by nature, she whispered answers to my questions. I think she feels that she has had an unlucky deal in life. Her husband was killed when the children were quite young, the younger daughter has always been a problem and would have been placed in an institution long ago had not Sue rebelled against the idea. Now that Sue too has ill health Mrs Gibson feels that her world is falling about her. Sue has been a strong emotional prop as well as the breadwinner for the last 20 years. I spoke to Mrs Gibson about the feasibility of installing a home kidney unit – this would mean Sue having a room to herself and a water tank with a larger capacity would be an essential. Mrs Gibson said that she would be prepared to share her bedroom with her younger daughter but I sensed that she felt misgivings on the subject – after all, she is now an old lady and finds her younger daughter's noisy ways very wearing. It seems to me that the only hope is for Sue to be persuaded that her sister should be removed from the family home – on the grounds of her mother's health if not her own.

Signed – Amy Collins

Case No. 4	Jim Spencer
Age	17 years
Employment	Assistant baker 6 am – 2 pm
Family circumstances	Lives with parents. Father (47) is an insurance agent. Mother used to work part-time in a children's nursery but gave up due to nervous troubles – she is still receiving out-patient treatment. There was a daughter, two years younger than Jim, she was killed 18 months ago in a road accident.
Housing	A three-bedroom bungalow with garden on outskirts of town. Mortgage almost paid off. Garden and house well cared for.

Medical social worker's report

I visited the Spencers in the early evening. Mr Spencer is a friendly man and offered me a drink as soon as I was inside the door. Mrs Spencer struck me as full of tension, making quick, bird-like movements and talking in a breathless tone, not waiting for a response. Mr Spencer seems fairly philosophical about Jim's illness but Mrs Spencer makes no attempt to hide her strong feelings of bitterness and resentment – it is almost as if she feels that Jim has become ill to spite her. The home is comfortably furnished, Mrs Spencer has a washing machine and a huge range of kitchen gadgets – money is obviously not a problem. I broached the subject of adapting Jim's bedroom for a home kidney unit and I must confess that I was shocked by Mrs Spencer's hostility to the idea. She is a woman who attaches great importance to routine. Since the beginning of her nervous troubles, dating from the death of her daughter, she has not liked to receive visitors of any kind, even her own relations. Mr Spencer confided to me when she left the room for a moment that he always arranges for people such as the old man who does the garden to come while his wife is at the hospital. I am at a loss as to what to suggest here. In every way this home is ideal to receive a kidney unit apart from the mother's neuroses. I think this young man should receive the earliest consideration for a transplant operation.

Signed – Amy Collins

It has been suggested that decisions of this sort should be taken by a lay panel, rather than by the hospital professionals. How do you react to that idea? What kind of people would you wish to see included on such a panel, and who would select, or elect, them?

A consultant's comment on this proposal, together with the criteria practised by his team when making the agonising decision illustrated in the dilemma outlined in this case study, can be found at the end of the book. You may disagree with his criteria, but if they were applied it makes clear which of the four must have been chosen; so don't turn to that page until you and your colleagues have given the problem a lengthy airing. (Appendix 1.)

CASE STUDY 17: HOMICIDE

On the face of it, one obvious area of behaviour to which the categorical imperative could be applied is that of killing a fellow human being. It seems difficult to imagine that the deliberate taking of another person's life could ever be universalised. Yet killing in one way or another is occurring continuously throughout the world, and it may well be that with much of it you are in sympathy. The full extent of the types of killing, or alleged killing, to which many people raise no moral objections – for instance, in war, as a punishment, to avoid a painful and lingering death, and so on – has, along with the ethical implications involved, been comprehensively discussed in Jonathon Glover's admirable book *Causing Death and Saving Lives*. The exercise which follows is intended to allow you to reflect on the circumstances, if any, in which the deliberate ending of a life, or allowing a life to end, regrettable though it may be, is preferable to – and so more desirable than – any alternative form of behaviour. If you agree with any of the examples suggested, you should ask yourself what principle or value you would thereby be ranking more highly than 'thou shalt not kill'. (It may be worth knowing that Kant himself, for reasons that we shall return to in Case Study 33 (pp. 242–4), believed in capital punishment for convicted murderers.)

Which of the following would you approve of, and why?

1 Killing a blackmailer/hijacker/kidnapper.
2 Killing one who has blasphemed against or transgressed religious laws.
3 Assassinating a dictator (Hitler, Amin).
4 Preventive murder (killing a man about to kill others).
5 Killing combatants in war.
6 Killing non-combatants in war (Hiroshima, Vietnam).
7 Revolutionary executions.
8 Capital punishment for gangsters/multiple murderers.
9 Capital punishment for terrorists.
10 Capital punishment for 'special category' murders (the Yorkshire Ripper, the Moors murderers, the Boston Strangler).
11 Capital punishment for the murder of a policeman.
12 Capital punishment for traitors/deserters.
13 Capital punishment for murder of a spouse/partner.
14 Capital punishment for child murderers.
15 Capital punishment for child abusers/molesters.
16 Capital punishment for other offences (e.g., rape, economic sabotage, spying, assisting in armed robbery, physical assault causing grievous bodily and/or mental harm).
17 Voluntary euthanasia.
18 Euthanasia for those dying in pain/the senile/the permanently unconscious.
19 Turning off the life-support machine when there is no hope of recovery.
20 Allowing severely malformed babies to die.
21 Allowing severely brain-damaged babies to die (see Case Study 15 for a separate study on 20 and 21).
22 Extermination of the mentally defective.
23 Extermination of dangerous and incurable psychopaths.
24 Abortion of deformed foetuses.
25 Abortion when the mother's life is in danger.
26 Abortion for rape victims.
27 Abortion for social or medical reasons.
28 Abortion on demand.
29 Allowing people to die after suicide attempts (e.g., drug overdose).

30 Allowing people to take risks likely to lead to their death (e.g., dangerous sports, dangerous drugs, riding motorbikes without crash helmets).
31 Allowing children to take grave risks.
32 Suicide in exceptional circumstances.
33 Suicide on impulse.
34 Suicide pacts.
35 Allowing people to refuse medical treatment which might save their lives
36 Allowing people to refuse medical treatment which might save their children's lives.
37 Allowing people in the Third World to die of hunger and preventable disease.
38 Nuclear energy programmes.
39 Nuclear weapon installations.
40 Killing animals for food.
41 Experimenting on animals to the point of death for medical purposes.
42 Killing animals for sport.
43 Killing insects (to avoid this as much as possible the Jainites in India brush the ground in front of them as they walked).
44 Killing a sick animal, e.g., a racehorse with a broken leg – Jainites tend even the most feeble and decrepit of animals until they die naturally.

THREE CASE STUDIES WHICH TEST KANT'S MORAL THEORIES

CASE STUDY 18: DO YOUR DUTY?

Kant is recognised as both the apostle and high priest of duty as the surest guide to moral behaviour. Yet, as was suggested on p. 113, it is difficult to feel whole-hearted about his particular application of the idea in the light of his monolithic life-style: his duty was entirely to his work, and nothing else in his life (except, possibly, his hypochondria) was allowed to interfere with this. Most of us, however, are committed to a variety of activities and social groups, all of which make demands on us from the duty angle. Kant in his writings seems to suggest that if we face a clash of duties we shall know what takes precedence, simply by following the categorical imperative (p. 115). But does this really work? Talk (or think) this through with some of the following dilemmas in mind:

(a) You are on your way to address a meeting of people who have

127

travelled considerable distances to hear you. On the way you witness a road accident where a pedestrian is seriously injured by a car driver who does not stop (the dilemma, perhaps, of the Pharisee in the parable of the Good Samaritan).

(b) All the people in your office fiddle their expenses, and for one not to do the same would mean exposing this practice to those in higher authority. Yet your conscience tells you not to involve yourself in this activity.

(c) You have some important work to catch up on urgently, but a close friend whom you now see only rarely since she moved away, turns up unexpectedly with a couple of hours to spare on her way elsewhere.

(d) 'If I had to choose between betraying my country and betraying my friend I hope I should have the guts to betray my country.' – E.M. Forster. Do you agree?

(e) A married couple wish to separate, but have children at an impressionable age.

(f) You have run up debts which you can't repay without sacrificing your student career and returning to a boring, non-demanding job. (In days gone by, men in this predicament were expected to commit suicide, but you may think that to be taking the idea of duty somewhat too seriously.)

(g) You are a nurse who believes strongly in the sanctity of life. You are instructed to give 'nursing care only' to a newborn, profoundly handicapped infant (meaning that you are to allow it to die as comfortably as possible).

(h) Similarly, you are told by relatives of a dying patient not to tell him that his illness is terminal: but he constantly asks you for his prognosis.

(i) You share a sexual attraction with someone other than your partner, whom you are sure will not find out if you are unfaithful.

(j) See example (c), p. 175.

CASE STUDY 19: THE CASE OF THE LYING CHANCELLOR

In September, 1949, the pound sterling was devalued against the US dollar. In those days, the pound did not 'float' or 'find its market level' as it does today: the rate of exchange was fixed, and could be altered (and this happened rarely) only by the decision of the Chancellor of the Exchequer. In 1949 the Chancellor was Sir Stafford Cripps, one of the towering figures of the Labour Party, and among the most brilliant intellectuals ever to have entered the House of Commons. He was in addition a deeply religious man, austere, puritanical, even remote. (Winston Churchill is said to have remarked bitingly about him: 'There, but for the Grace of God, goes God.')

For weeks before the devaluation was announced there had been speculation that this was due to happen. Consistently throughout this period Cripps denied that there were any such plans. To press and public alike his reply was invariably the same: 'There will be no devaluation.' He maintained this stance right up to the moment when he went to the Despatch Box in the House of Commons and made his historic announcement. The debate to which this led was one of the most memorable in the history of Parliament, but the political aspects of the issue are not our concern. (If you are interested you can read a full account of the event in Michael Foot's biography of Aneurin Bevin, Vol. II, pp. 266–73.)

For many people at the time (and there are plenty who still affirm this) the main cause of sorrow at the announcement was not the fall in value of the pound in their pockets but the devaluation of a respected man's reputation. Cripps was known internationally as a man of honour and integrity; he was accepted generally as being in the George Washington league of those who 'could not tell a lie'. Yet with one brief speech he revealed that for weeks he had been lying openly, deliberately, and consistently; and not just to his friends and colleagues but to the nation and the world. It was a bitter blow for any idealists who held that such matters as truth-telling should (and therefore could: it was Kant who is said to have remarked, 'Ought implies can') always occur – in fact, be taken for granted – in every feature of human intercourse. To be let down by one of the most respected standard bearers of this approach made the blow so much more deadly. It was as if Immanuel Kant had begun not only to throw refuse into his neighbours' gardens but had then accused them of stealing it.

By others at the time, however, this reaction was looked upon as totally unrealistic, taking no account of the desperate dilemma that faced the Chancellor. What, it was asked, could Cripps realistically have done instead? If he had said, in reply to press questions, 'Yes, on such-and-such a date I shall be devaluing the pound by x percent', everyone in the country would have been changing their pounds into dollars (or, since that suggests the kind of magical gifts which not even the most dedicated capitalist possesses, exchanging the one for the other); the economic consequences for the country would have been disastrous. If he had said 'No comment', people would have jumped to their own conclusions, with the same consequences. If he had said 'I don't know', he would still, at least in the later stages, have been telling a lie, nobody would have believed him, and speculation of almost the same proportions would have occurred. He could have resigned rather than lie, but again people would have drawn their own conclusions from such an act; after all, there had been talk of devaluation throughout the whole summer, and a resignation of that magnitude would not have been interpreted at that time as a purely accidental coincidence. The choice, therefore, before the Chancellor was either economic disaster for the nation, or a lie on his conscience. The only way out of this dilemma was not to have been there in the first place!

What is your opinion? Do you think that sometimes people have to compromise with even the most high-sounding and universally accepted principles? If so, on what basis would you make the decision that such a compromise is right or desirable in one set of circumstances, but not in another? If not – that is, if you believe that people should tell the truth in all circumstances, whatever the consequences – have you thought what this might imply concerning people's daily communication with each other? Supposing an old lady of whom you are very fond bakes you a cake which you find excruciating and then, desperately anxious to have pleased you, she asks you later whether you enjoyed it: what do you say? Is a doctor acting wrongly if (s)he untruthfully answers a dying patient's question about his prospects, out of fear that the patient could not cope mentally with the truth? If your partner buys an expensive new garment which you dislike intensely, do you tell him/her the truth – the whole truth – when asked your opinion of it?

See if you can universalise truth-telling in such terms that nobody should be caused unnecessary pain – something like, Always tell the truth unless by so doing you will needlessly hurt another person. If this were a categorical imperative, would you ever be sure that others were not lying in order to spare your feelings? Could you ever believe anything that anybody ever told you about yourself unless this caused you pain? (And how do you qualify, or quantify, 'needlessly' in this context?)

Can you express any categorical imperative other than in the form of 'Do not do x except when . . .'? ('Do not steal except when this will save a life', etc.) How categorical is the resultant so-called imperative? Is Kant logically wrong?

CASE STUDY 20: A PERSONAL INVENTORY

The following exercise may sound simple, but it is not. Ask yourself the questions, Is there anything which, in all conceivable circumstances, I would rather die than do? You may think of obvious examples: you'd rather die than kill another person, for instance. But supposing the other person is a homicidal maniac who has already killed several times? You'd rather die than kill your own child? But supposing – which is unlikely but not inconceivable – that you are in the hands of a sadist who gives you the choice: either kill your child quickly yourself or he will kill him slowly and agonisingly? You could not torture another person? What then do you do if you have in your hands a bomber who won't tell you where and when he has set the bomb to explode? You are a male who would rather die than commit rape? Would you stick firmly to that decision if you knew that only by raping the unsuspecting girl in the next flat could you deter a maniac from torturing her to death?

These examples are all obviously extreme – extreme enough to be irrelevant for all practical purposes. But they cannot be ruled out altogether because occasionally some unfortunate person has been placed in one or other of these diabolical situations, and the original question deliberately included the words 'in all conceivable circumstances'. I have had it suggested to me that universal genocide must be in the category of acts that anyone would rather die than commit. But suppose you have in your possession a tin containing a chemical so lethal that, released into the atmosphere, it would exterminate all life on earth within 24 hours; and suppose you knew that the planet was about to be overrun by millions of aliens whose intention was to use every human being for grotesque scientific experiments? . . . But perhaps this is allowing fantasy to run too wild.

Chapter Six

Ends and means II: Mill and utilitarianism

We have already seen that one way of expressing in words the difference between those who hold that the end never justifies the means, and those who think otherwise, is to designate the first group as deontologists (from the Greek words 'deon' and 'logos' meaning 'understanding of duty') and the second as teleologists (from 'telos' meaning 'end' or 'purpose'). Another way of expressing this distinction is that for the first group certain forms of behaviour are *intrinsically* right or wrong, while for the second group they are so only *extrinsically*, or *instrumentally*. Kant is firmly in the first camp (some would say that he played a large part in pitching it). For him, moral behaviour contains its own imperative: it is right or wrong *per se*, and any attempt to criticise or defend it on the basis of consequences, or likely consequences, to which it may lead, is superfluous. Good behaviour is self-justifying, bad behaviour is self-condemning: no other supporting evidence is required.

The instrumentalist in morals takes the diametrically opposed view on this matter. For him the principle, or motive, which underlies any form of behaviour is not the key to the merits or flaws in that behaviour. Behaviour must be assessed independently of the moral agent concerned; what drives him to behave as he does may be a matter of interest to a psychologist: it is irrelevant to anyone attempting to judge the moral worth of his behaviour. This can be achieved only by considering the consequences of that behaviour. In technical language, this means making an empirical, as opposed to a normative, judgment; and while there have been several schools of philosophy which have advocated this 'consequentialist' approach (such as hedonism, the view that pleasure ought to be pursued) the most famous expression of it was made by the group of philosophers known, by choice, as the utilitarians.

Utilitarianism is an ugly word but expresses accurately the doctrine of which it is the name. The utility of anything is its usefulness in practice; this school of philosophy applies this idea to moral behaviour, and is commonly known as 'the greatest happiness principle' or the principle of 'the greatest happiness of the greatest number'. One of the great utilitarians, Jeremy Bentham (1748–1832) defined it in these terms:

Utilitarianism is what tends to produce, benefit, or advance pleasure, good or happiness, either for the individual or for the community. The good of the greatest number is the criterion of right or wrong.

Bentham's godson, who wrote the book *Utilitarianism* which will form the basis of our delineation of the theory, John Stuart Mill (1806–73), put it in similar terms:

The creed which accepts as the foundation of morals, Utilitarianism, or the Greatest Happiness principle, holds that actions are right in proportion as they tend to promote happiness, wrong as they tend to produce the reverse of happiness. By happiness is intended pleasure and the absence of pain; by unhappiness pain and the privation of pleasure.

Mill himself disclaimed any entitlement to being called a pioneer in philosophical thought just because the word was new. He argued that utilitarianism was a new name for an old way of thinking, going back as far as Socrates and Aristotle, both of whom argued that the rightness or wrongness of human conduct was determined by its good or bad consequences. There was however a major difference between the doctrine as outlined by these ancient Greeks and by the nineteenth-century Englishman. The Greek view had a metaphysical element which was totally lacking in Mill or, earlier, in Bentham. 'The good' and 'the bad' were concepts of what should be pursued, or shunned; and the process of doing one or the other of these was necessary for all people, not for any pragmatic reasons, but because this was part of 'the nature of things': this is how things are. For Mill, it was essential to show the truth of the theory in practice, in (for example) social and political reform.

The first utilitarian view of ethics by an important modern figure was offered a century before Mill's book by David Hume (1711–76) in his *Essay concerning the Principles of Morals*. In this, he argued that our judgments of good and bad are reflections of our emotions of approval or disapproval concerning actions and events. We approve of what we feel to be pleasurable and useful, either to ourselves or to others. Our basic moral sentiments are guided by what Hume termed the 'social virtues' of benevolence and justice, virtues which lead to the general wellbeing of the human race, or 'public utility'. Public utility, or the happiness of others, is pleasurable and agreeable to the individual moral agent; and pleasure is the ultimate end of human action.

Hume applied his theory in what we could call today an elitist direction: the pleasure he wrote about was not that of the common horde, but of the cultivated, civilised man of affairs. Bentham developed the principle of utilitarianism as a tool of radical social and political reform (he and his followers were known as radicals); for him, far from being elitist, it was a theory with universal, egalitarian application. Words like 'happiness', 'pleasure', 'enjoyment', 'satisfaction', 'contentment' all really mean the same, indicating a clear sort of 'feeling' which, said Bentham, is always comparable whenever it is experienced. 'The child's game of push-pin is as good as poetry', he wrote. He added that it was possible, in his opinion, to measure happiness or pleasure according, among other things, to its intensity, duration, being sure of getting it, its nearness or remoteness. In making the assessment as to the behaviour which should follow from this detailed analysis, there should be no favourites and nobody underestimated; it should be a totally impartial process with, in Bentham's words, 'everybody to count as one; nobody to count as more than one.' He devised as a guide to those facing the crucial question of how much pleasure and how much pain were consequent on particular courses of action what he termed his 'felicific calculus', and to help people remember what this contained he devised a mnemonic jingle:

Intense, long, certain, speedy, fruitful, pure –
Such marks in *pleasures* and in *pains* endure.
Such pleasures seek if *private* be thy end:
If it be *public*, wide let them *extend*.
Such *pains* avoid, whichever be thy view:
If pains *must* come, let them *extend* to few.

Bentham's dominant passion was for social reform; and this passion he shared with his lifelong friend, James Mill (Mill senior, for the unwary), who himself made his mark as a philosopher of some standing, particularly with a treatise *On Government* which he wrote originally as an article for *Encyclopaedia Britannica*, but which was used as a primary source of inspiration by the political reformers of the time, who believed that representative government was the cure for all human ills. When John Stuart was born, his father, along with Bentham, decided that he should be trained as a 'thinker of integrity', so that he could become the leader of those whose aim was to rid the nation of these ills. Consequently, it was decided that the boy should be educated privately and intensely; Mill (meaning now J.S.) relates the remarkable story of his incredible childhood – if so it may be called – in his *Autobiography*. From the age of three he was allowed neither play nor playmates: his days were to be occupied solely with study, interrupted only by walks with his father, when he could summarise what he had learned that day.

Mill's progress according to this life pattern can be briefly summarised, with, perhaps, a feeling of awe. He began to study Greek at the age of three and Latin at eight; by the age of twelve he had read almost all the major classical authors in the original, and was a master of history, mathematics and science; between twelve and fourteen he studied economics and philosophy. When he reached the age for university, his father decided that neither Oxford nor Cambridge had anything to teach him (and, being under ecclesiastical control, they were in any case viewed with suspicion). At eighteen he was editing Bentham's works; but soon after, he experienced what he termed 'a crisis in my mental life', which was probably – and unremarkably – what we should call a nervous breakdown. He recovered from this, partly through reading the poetry of Wordsworth, partly through the care of Harriet Taylor, whom he later married. He thus developed the life of feeling alongside that of the intellect, and became one of the most 'complete' men of his, or any other, times. The philosopher A. N. Whitehead wrote of his upbringing and its outcome:

His education might have produced a neurotic, a monster, or a mere 'intellectual machine set to grind certain tunes'. Instead, by some miracle of recovered balance, it helped to produce one of the most brilliant men of his generation.

His life was full and many-faceted: there can hardly have been a greater contrast to the life of Immanuel Kant. He became nationally and internationally known as a social reformer, writer, philosopher, and parliamentarian. He was the first man ever to advocate in the House of Commons the cause of women's suffrage, and, more than any other human being, male or female, pioneered for the rights of women generally. His masterpiece *On Liberty* remains compulsory reading for anyone in the least concerned about the establishment and preservation of human freedom. (See Chapter Eleven.)

Mill's defence of the utilitarian theory of morals was written primarily as a reply to critics of the theory, many of them in the church establishment. The idea that happiness should be the aim of human behaviour presented, so they believed, a challenge to a faith founded on the concept of victory through vicarious suffering. His book is entitled *Utilitarianism*, and is brief enough (my edition has 60 pages) to read at a sitting – though it will take more than that to digest it thoroughly. Before debating the pros and cons of the theory, let's take a look at what Mill himself said.

Mill's utilitarianism

In the opening chapter, Mill simply affirms that utilitarianism is the ultimate standard of right and wrong conduct, and that the pursuit of happiness has formed the basis of all sound moral philosophies. He then proceeds to remove some of the current misconceptions – as he believed them to be – about the theory. It had been condemned particularly on the ground that it encouraged the satisfaction of base sensual desires. Bentham had laid himself open to this charge by allowing that no distinction could or should be made between forms of happiness: bingo or Bach, soap opera or grand opera – whatever gave people pleasure should be treated as of equal worth. Mill disagreed with Bentham about this, arguing that pleasures could be graded according to their quality, and that the 'higher' levels of pleasure – intellectual, aesthetic, imaginative, and so on – were to be preferred to the satisfaction of mere animal instincts. It may well be the case that these 'lower' pleasures are more certain of fulfilment than are the so-called higher pleasures; but the uncertain fulfilment of the intellectual man is preferable to the secure bliss of a moron. No human happiness is truly possible, Mill argued, without a 'sense of dignity'. He then stated what has become a famous aphorism:

It is better to be a human being dissatisfied than a pig satisfied; better to be Socrates dissatisfied than a fool satisfied.

How can one be sure about this? Because, answers Mill, a wise and good man, having experienced both, can judge, because he knows: the pig or fool, having experienced only the lower pleasures, doesn't know.

But, continued the critics, isn't the pursuit of happiness a selfish activity, and therefore not worthy to rank among other laudable aims? Mill's answer to this was to reiterate that the utilitarian was concerned not just with the moral agent's own personal happiness, but with the greatest amount altogether. Even if the price of possessing a noble character is to experience unhappiness or discontent, this nobility is likely to increase the happiness of others. Utilitarianism is impartial about those whom it makes happier.

To the objection that perfect happiness is not attainable – at least in this world – Mill's reply was that, granted this is the case, we should take whatever happiness is possible. He was not suggesting that one should aim to achieve constant euphoria, but simply the predominance of happiness over unhappiness. Certain ills do in fact prevent happiness – 'disease, poverty, unkindness, loss of affections' – but most external evils are removable by individual effort and social progress. 'All the grand sources of human suffering', he wrote, 'are in a great degree, many of them almost entirely, conquerable by human care and effort.'

The critics of utilitarianism (and on this matter church leaders were especially prominent) had argued that renunciation was a worthier ideal than happiness, and that we should be looking for joy in heaven rather than engage ourselves in the lesser pursuit of seeking this on earth. (It was this kind of preaching which caused Mill's contemporary, Marx, to describe religion as 'the opium of the masses'.) Mill's reply was that, with 95 percent of the population underprivileged, *involuntary* renunciation was occurring universally. Voluntary self-sacrifice was desirable if, and only if, such action actually led to an increase in the amount of happiness in the world; otherwise it must be adjudged as no more than pathological masochistic asceticism; in other words the argument was humbug.

Critics who tackled the problem on a more philosophical basis took the Kantian line that utilitarianism was an inadequate guide to good and bad behaviour because it took no account of a person's motives when weighing up the consequences of his behaviour: wasn't it desirable that individual actions should always be motivated by the general good? If a man 'means well' in what he does, must this not count as a plus when assessing the merits of his deed, however undesirable the outcome may be? Mill disagreed with this: for him the test was not personal motivation but objective results: saving a drowning man is always good, whatever the motivation of the rescuer. Naturally, there would normally be a discernible parallel between the motive and consequences of a person's behaviour; but this was not always so, and, in any case, 'the motive has nothing to do with the morality of the action, though much with the worth of the agent'. The motive 'the general good' is, anyway, open to objection because, in most instances, this does not mean the good of the whole human race – with which utilitarianism is concerned – but only the limited circle of people who are involved in that situation.

Very well, said the critics: we are concerned with the happiness of the whole of mankind. How can any individual moral agent possibly bear all in mind every time he makes a moral decision? Has he the time or imagination to think through the vast range of ramifications that this would involve, stretching limitlessly ahead in time, and outwards geographically? Mill is not so unrealistic as to deny that this is a problem; but he contends that the moral agent doesn't start afresh with every moral decision he makes. He has the experience of the ages to help him decide what is good or useful; as a result of this he does not need to spend time and energy debating general principles every time any of these relate to a particular situation. While there may be exceptions, such forms of behaviour as lying, stealing or killing are unlikely to be condoned. The real issue was that objections to these and similar undesirable forms of behaviour should be based on utilitarianism rather than on some imaginary panacea such as the concept of duty; but Mill agreed that behaviour yielding consequences desirable in the immediate future may well have to be modified because of the long-term implications. He was concerned to stress that utilitarianism was not, as critics suggested, a form of expediency; he could be just as critical as they were of, for instance, a politician who put his own personal gratification ahead of the needs of those whom he represented, or of any person who told a lie for immediate gain. Such behaviour, he agreed, destroyed any sense of loyalty, honour, or truthfulness which sustain the social bond, all human communication, and ultimately human happiness itself.

This emphasis on impartiality was the underlying theme of the remainder of the book, in which Mill applied utilitarianism to the idea and practice of justice. He suggested that the legal formulation of justice as 'rendering unto each his due' is akin to the impartiality expressed in utilitarianism, which calls us to 'treat all equally well who have deserved equally well of us'. This final part of the book indicates how paramount was Mill's concern for social reform, as a result of which more people might be expected to achieve a greater degree of happiness than was possible in the conditions which then obtained. It was the straightforward application of utilitarian principles in the field of public morality that brought A. N. Whitehead to assert of their exponents:

Most of what has been practically effective in morals, in religion, or in political theory, from their day to this has derived strength from one or other of these men. Their doctrines have been largely repudiated as theoretical foundations, but as practical working principles they dominate the world.[1]

This is a bold assessment, both positively and negatively: we must see for ourselves whether it is sound or otherwise.

Critique of utilitarianism

We can, I think, readily understand why many people have found the theory both obvious and attractive, and why it has been, and still is, extremely influential. It seems (to many people, anyway) uncontroversial that morality should have a lot to do with people's happiness. Furthermore, 'happiness' isn't meaningless; we're not usually totally puzzled by what someone means when they say they're happy, and we do – sometimes, at least – know what courses of action will, or are likely to, make us or other people happy, and act on this basis. We say things like 'doing action A will make Y so happy that it's worth the inconvenience to

[1] *Adventures of Ideas*, p. 46

X'; and we may well say of ourselves, 'I'm happier now than I was then' – or vice versa.

In addition, the utilitarian view of the guidelines by which happiness may most confidently be assured seems entirely praiseworthy. The stress laid on impartiality, unselfishness, altruism seems to transcend self-interest and take into account the interests of all concerned. It is not too difficult for most of us to give such guidelines our backing. The basic criterion by which we test everything we do – 'the greatest happiness of the greatest number' – seems, for once, clear and rational, and having what is rare in philosophy: the virtue of simplicity. We have only one criterion to bother about: what could be more straightforward than that?

Utilitarianism also seems to be flexible; no law, or principle, or institution is sacrosanct or unchallengeable. We can't defend things or ideas merely on the basis of authority or tradition: we have to justify them on the 'principle of utility'. So, if you criticise utilitarianism, you don't have to do so on the basis that happiness and morality have nothing to do with each other, so that we never do or never should take happiness into account when making moral decisions. The question is not whether happiness ever is or should be a factor in this process, but whether it is the only thing we should ever take into account, or whether we should always take it into account.

Meaning of happiness At this point the problems start. To begin with (and this is a problem even if happiness is accepted as only one of several factors to be considered when making moral judgments) *what exactly do we mean by happiness*, and how do we know for certain when we've achieved it? If we substitute words like 'fulfilment' or 'satisfaction' we still leave their meanings unspecified. We may define happiness as 'a state of achieving one's desire'; we should then have to face the question, how do we know what it is that we desire? The answer to this may be: because it (the object of desire) is desirable. We have thus reached the profoundly self-evident statement (a truism) that we desire the desirable, a statement hardly likely to cause any philosopher to join Archimedes naked from his bath, crying 'Eureka'; and we are no further forward if we replace desirable' with 'capable of being desired'.

Suppose we stay put with the 'state of achieving one's desire', without pursuing in too great depth what the phrase means. We are still left with the twin problems of the content of what we desire and the constancy of our desires. What is it that makes us happy? In what state are we happy? I said above that we sometimes say 'I'm happier than I was': but can we be sure of this? There are certain obvious situations – such as being freed from a concentration camp, or finding the job you've been seeking for years, or having a member of your family survive a crisis in a serious illness – when this can be unequivocally stated; but can one otherwise make such affirmative statements? Just as I cannot say 'I would have been happier if . . .' because I simply don't know how I would have felt under the conditions of 'if . . .', so it is impossible to compare my current consciousness of happiness or contentment with that of any earlier period in my life. In fact one can completely delude oneself in making such comparisons. Many years ago I worked for a time in Scotland, and I look back with warmth on that period: I would say now that I was happy then. Recently, however, I have been rereading my (fairly lengthy) diaries of the period, and have found them full of expressions of misery and disconsolation. 'What am I doing here?' 'Why did I accept this job? are typical entries. This seems to confirm what Mill himself said: 'Ask yourself whether you are happy and you cease to be so.'

The second problem must be even more worrying to those whose aim is happiness and define this as the achievement of desire: *desires change* or, even worse, can be altered or manipulated. Mill, when discussing the higher and lower pleasures (to which we shall return), stated that society should be, by a process of education and example, directing its members to desire the higher pleasures, which is not far short of the paternalistic attitude that people should be made to want what is good for them – the definition of that last phrase being, of course, determined by the directors rather than the directed. Lord Reith applied this philosophy in his role as first Director-General of the BBC: hence that institution's nickname of 'Aunty'. More immediately, and infinitely less subtly, the world of advertising is daily trying to change our desires by suggesting that if we do not possess the commodity which they are attempting to sell us, we cannot possibly be as happy as we thought we were. The whole aim of the capitalist world is to cause people to desire what they do not need and so grow discontented (and therefore unhappy) with what they have; but this is a never-ending process, since such happiness can last only until the advent of the next model, or a new commodity. (A wealthy acquaintance of mine in California was made utterly miserable by my remark – intended as a joke – that his house had every gadget except a musical toilet roll. His lack of this was his constant lament for the remainder of the evening.)

Is happiness the sole end? This leads to the fundamental issue of *whether happiness ought always to be pursued*, even when it is virtually certain what action will increase the sum total of this. At first sight it must seem obvious that this is the case, unless we happen to be possessed with a martyr complex; but there are circumstances in which this is by no means obvious, as may be illustrated by a situation I faced when teaching at California State University. Students there are under enormous pressure – from society in general and their parents in particular – to achieve the highest grades in their examinations. Anything lower than a B is unacceptable, and for most students it has to be an A if they are to avoid parental wrath (and perhaps withdrawal of financial support). There is the further factor that no work is double-marked: grades are entered into the university's central computer, and are known only to the professor and student concerned. Many students will therefore do everything in their power to have C and D grades raised to A and B: this can mean long discussions and an even longer formal appeals procedure. What could be more straightforward, from the utilitarian point of view, than that the professor should simply hand out these higher grades ad lib? He will save himself time and energy; the students will be happy, their parents happier still; no other credit to be taken by the students during later semesters depends on the level of success in this course, so the university, if not happier, is certainly no less happy. All concerned can cheerfully pack their bags and take an earlier holiday than was planned. Why then did I, and colleagues like me, insist on giving some students, however vociferous their complaints, the lower grades? Was there not some value more important than happiness underlying this encounter?

Mill himself remains quite adamant on this issue:

No reason can be given why the general happiness is desirable except that each person, so far as he believes it to be attainable, desires his own happiness. This, however, being a fact, we have not only all the proof which the case admits of, but all which it is possible to require, that happiness is a good: that each person's happiness is a good to that person and the general happiness a good to the aggregate of all persons.

This raises an interesting issue of logistics. Does it follow logically from the fact (assuming this to be the case) that people desire individual happiness that the general happiness will thereby be increased? Is it legitimate to infer the one from the other? If you think about this carefully you will see that, even though part of the whole (whatever that may constitute) is desired by someone, it does not follow that the whole is itself necessarily desired by anyone. It is to be expected that, in Abraham Lincoln's phrase, any government will please all the people some of the time (though Robert Kennedy averred that there were some people who couldn't be pleased any of the time): what is not so certain is whether the second half of Lincoln's utterance is true, that some of the people may be pleased all of the time. This may accidentally be true in politics, but it doesn't follow from the first half of the statement.

Higher and lower pleasures We turn now to that element in Mill's writings which has received the most consistent criticism: his distinction between higher and lower pleasures. We may grant that some kind of distinction between people's ways of finding pleasure may be made: this is obviously the case. If we must, we will designate some pleasures as 'higher' and others as 'lower', though it would seem preferable to avoid these question-begging words and keep to terms which are more open to verification, such as pleasures of the mind, aesthetic pleasures, physical pleasures, and so on. The question is not whether these distinctions exist, nor whether any of them should be more highly esteemed than others, but *whether it is legitimate to state that the happiness derived from one is greater than that from the others.* It is difficult to know how one might set about proving this. My neighbour enjoys bingo; I enjoy Brecht; she would hate to have to watch *Mother Courage*, while I would find an 'eyes-down' session painful. Who is to judge which of us derives the greater amount of happiness from our respective activities? This whole area is full of pit-holes; many geniuses (Beethoven, for one) seem to have lived unhappy lives: many 'simple' people have apparently been idyllically happy, gaining pleasure from keeping their homes homely and caring for their children and grandchildren. I can think of no way of demonstrating that the genius, simply because of his superior intellect, is happier than the man in the street (whoever he may be – I've always wondered what the female equivalent of this absurd phrase is), that the artist, because of his aesthetic awareness, is more fulfilled than the person who reaches his artistic heights by placing plastic ducks on his living-room wall. We may make an artistic distinction between Michelangelo's *David* and a set of garden gnomes: we cannot say or, if we do, we cannot prove it, that the one gives greater happiness than the other.

Impartiality   A further cause for concern lies in the *egalitarian view of people* which utilitarians insist on. On the face of it, this sounds fine: 'Everybody to count for one, nobody for more than one,' wrote Bentham. Mill modified this slightly, though the effect is the same: 'every person has an equal claim to happiness.' So far as issues that affect the public are concerned, this is a laudable aim (and to be fair to Bentham and Mill, we should remember that their main concern lay in the field of social and political reform). The law of the land should be administered impartially: the owner of a Rolls-Royce as likely to get a parking ticket as the owner of a clapped-out Mini; finance ministers should have the whole nation in mind when preparing their budgets, not just a favoured minority; access to medical and surgical treatment should be as open to the poor as to the rich. The issue is not whether this utilitarian principle is viable in public life, but whether it accurately reflects the way people view and treat each other as individuals. Manifestly, it does not. The fact is that in all our lives there are some people whom we count more highly than others, particularly members of our family and close friends. Blood is thicker than water: ask any parents to choose between saving their child from some disaster or saving a genius and, of course, they would save the child: any set of parents who did otherwise would be judged by others to be behaving like monsters:

and, if such forms of behaviour were universally followed, the sum total of human happiness would fall. The same is true in reverse: some people count in our estimation as less than one because by their behaviour they have forfeited their claim to happiness. If I had to choose between saving the life of a mass murderer of women and that of the robin sitting outside my window as I write (obviously a man-spotting bird, since he spends hours watching me at the desk) I should unhesitatingly choose the latter. I have heard it suggested that the utilitarians were expressing an ideal for the human race, and that ultimately we ought to be as concerned for the happiness of poor peasants at the other end of the globe as for our own kith and kin; maybe: but as human beings are at the present time, such idealism is clearly unrealistic.

How certain are consequences? There remain some inter-connected problems. The fundamental test of the rightness or wrongness of human behaviour is, according to utilitarianism, the consequences of that behaviour rather than its motives or intentions. Clearly, then, the person who 'means well' but whose behaviour leads to unfortunate consequences will not rank highly in any utilitarian league of laudable moral agents. The question to be asked, however, is how far any person, at the time when he makes his moral decision, can do any more than 'mean well'. *Is it ever possible to state with absolute certainty what the outcome of our behaviour will be?* Mill admitted that there may be some doubt about this, but argued that people learn from their own experience, and from that of others, what kind of reactions are likely to various forms of behaviour. But 'likely' is not 'certain', and we all know how wrong we can be when assessing the effects of our decisions. Human beings are so infinitely varied in their characters and temperaments that it is impossible, as the utilitarians attempt to do, to generalise about their responses to others' behaviour. Mill writes as though one can usually work out rationally how people will react in different circumstances, and in this he probably reflects his own highly intellectual upbringing. But people are more unpredictable than the laws of science or the rules of logic, as many a distressed lover will acknowledge.

This leads to the related problem of how far, and how widely, the web woven by a moral decision may spread. Immediate consequences may often be accurately foreseen, and it may often be possible to know with a fair degree of assurance how the individual most closely affected by the decision will react. But just as a move in a game of chess multiplies the possibilities for the next move, and so on throughout the game, so one set of consequences spreads out into a variety of further consequences, and one person's reaction will then affect others not immediately involved. How far ahead, how widely, should we or can we be looking? The word of advice given to a friend may not show any outcome for a generation or

143

more; the affair which was intended as a brief fling between two people may have ramifications which affect scores of others, for better or worse, over the years and in different places.

Once we begin to reflect on the incredible complications associated with human behaviour, it becomes easier to understand why some people, despairing of ever being able to work out the variations with any degree of accuracy, fall back on some idea like the categorical imperative, or the will of God. At least they then can have something definite, however intangible, to hold on to, rather than relying on their own limited experience and inadequate powers of reasoning. The utilitarian approach, like that of existentialism which we shall consider next, seems to require more of human beings than many are capable of providing. Yet how can one completely turn one's back on words like these from Mill's *Utilitarianism*?

'Ought' and 'should' grow into 'must', and recognised indispensability becomes a moral necessity, analogous to the physical and often not inferior to it in binding force . . .

Justice is a name for certain classes of moral rules which concern the essentials of human wellbeing, leading to a sense of absolute obligation. They are 'the rules which forbid mankind to hurt one another', fundamental for social harmony. All need assurance of not being harmed by others: this common interest obliges evil for evil, good for good, to retaliate against those who violate the primary moralities.

If utilitarianism teaches us no more than respect for persons it will have justified its existence as a school of moral philosophy.

Rule utilitarianism

What we have described above is known as act utilitarianism: each act is to be judged by its own individual consequences. Successors to Bentham and Mill suggested a modification of this theory in what has become known as rule utilitarianism. The question asked by followers of this code is not whether any particular act in isolation can be justified on the grounds that it is likely to increase the sum total of human happiness, but whether the total would increase if the act became a general practice - a rule. On this basis, many forms of behaviour which might gain general approbation on the principles of act utilitarianism could well be rejected. On those principles, for instance, there might be occasions when stealing could be justified: the story of Jean Valjean in *Les Misérables* springs to mind as a possible example of this. The rule utilitarian would broaden out the whole issue. While not denying that sound arguments may be presented for that individual act of theft, the question he would put would be along the lines of 'supposing everyone in need felt morally justified in stealing from those not in need?', or 'supposing society as a whole were to condone theft as a legitimate means of evening out its spoils: would we as a whole be any happier?' You may wish to reflect on this, as on a series of similar dilemmas which will be presented in the first of the case studies which follow.

There are obvious similarities between rule utilitarianism and Kant's theory of universalisability. The difference between them lies in their respective aims: Kant is concerned to universalise the principle on which people act; rule utilitarianism, like act utilitarianism, is concerned with the increase in happiness. For utilitarians the end may sometimes justify the means, however unpleasant these may be in themselves; for Kant this can never be the case, however unpleasant the consequences. A simple illustration may help to delineate the emphasis made by each of the schools. Is it justifiable for a person living in a dingy apartment to take a handful of daffodils from a public park? The act utilitarian may well say yes, on the grounds that the individual would be happier, and none of the public would miss a few flowers from the many growing there. Kant would say no, on the grounds that this would constitute an act of stealing, and stealing is wrong. The rule utilitarian would also say no, but on the grounds that, if everyone did as this individual proposed, the park would be denuded of daffodils, and the happiness of those walking past would be reduced.

In debating the eternal question of ends versus means we have again reached an impasse; while the protagonists on both sides expressed themselves with a conviction which would appear to bar any objections as invalid, these objections cannot be brushed aside. Perhaps we can simply take a matter-of-fact line (which may sound suspiciously like that of Hobbes). Most actions seem to be straightforward attempts to get what one wants or avoid what one does not want. If this means that people are egocentric, then we must come to terms with this: it does not necessarily mean that they (we) are indifferent to others. Man is (amongst other things) a social animal, so one person's happiness involves the happiness of (at least some) others. I *cannot* be happy if my wife or child is ill or if a man is bleeding to death before my eyes – this is not unselfishness, but an expression of biological nature. It may well be the case that *all* human action is directed to the individual's own happiness, even paradoxical cases like self-sacrifice or suicide, but 'happiness' here is obviously not pleasure. It seems, therefore, to be unnecessary and conducive to misery all round for people to encourage children to 'put others first' or to feel guilty about being selfish. It seems preferable to teach that to try to be happy *at the expense of others* is almost certain to be self-frustrating. (In one sense of 'happy' it is always self-frustrating.)

145

CASE STUDY 21: DEALING WITH DILEMMAS (REAL OR IMAGINARY/FANTASY)

Here are a number of situations for you to consider. Ask yourself what would be the responses of Kant and the act/rule utilitarians, and see if you find yourself agreeing with one school in preference to the others. Don't be afraid to rule out any answer as absurd.

(a) A plane with 200 passengers on board has been hijacked by terrorists. The plane is grounded in a country in which a number of the hijackers' associates have been imprisoned for acts of murder committed ruthlessly in that country and in others. The hijackers demand the release of all these prisoners, and state that they will exterminate all the passengers if this is not done. To show they mean business, they shoot the youngest passenger, a child of six, in the head, and drop her body on to the concrete. What should the authorities do? The hijackers are known to have enough weapons to blow up the plane: 200 innocent people could die; but by acceding to these demands, the authorities could be giving the all-clear to similar potential hijackers throughout the world. On what principle should the solution be determined?

(b) A country is overrun by an enemy power. The citizens of that country are told by their new rulers that they will be well treated if they cooperate. Most agree to this, and life continues as before except for a few restrictions. These restrictions are intensified, however, because of the activities of a minority of the citizens who engage in 'underground' assaults on their illegal rulers, risking thereby both their own lives and the lives of any who help them. How far, and in what respects, does the 'greatest happiness principle' relate to this situation? Does any other principle emerge as of greater importance?

(c) Refer back to the text (pp. 140–1) and ask yourself what is the desirable outcome in the American scene described. Does the question of happiness arise? If so, how is it or should it be realised? If not, what should be the overriding considerations in that situation? From what course, or on what basis, do these considerations originate?

(d) In July 1944 an attempt was made by a number of high-ranking Germans to assassinate the Fuehrer, Adolf Hitler. This was done because, following the Normandy landings by the Allies, it seemed clear to the would-be assassins that the defeat of Germany was inevitable. Better, therefore, to surrender immediately rather than continue fighting, since this would only delay the inevitable and mean the loss of many more lives on both sides. Hitler refused to accept defeat, arguing that he would fight until the last German was dead. Only his death would prevent what seemed to be many unnecessary deaths on the battlefield; but this meant a cold-blooded act of murder. On this question, how, in particular, do you think Kant would have reacted?

(e) Three men are dying in the same hospital, one of heart disease, the second of kidney disease, the third of liver disease. A fourth man visits the hospital's blood transfusion unit to give a pint of blood. He is known to be healthy in all respects; he has no relatives, and no close friends. The haematologist knows about the circumstances of all four men, and when giving the fourth his initial blood test injects him with a fatal drug. The man's healthy organs are then used to replace the diseased organs of the other three men, all of whom have dependent families. The haematologist's defence at his trial was that he was a philanthropist who, by getting rid of one man whom few would miss, had saved the lives of three who were much wanted. The net gain of lives was therefore two, and the increase of happiness all around incalculable.

(f) A drug has been developed which could cure a hitherto incurable disease. But it may have side-effects worse than the disease it is intended to cure. The only way to be sure is to test it on a living human being, and preferably two or three. If the drug is then found to have no side-effects, it will save hundreds of lives. In the prisons are men who have committed crimes so appalling that they will have to be kept in isolation for the rest of their lives simply to protect them from the murderous intents of their fellow prisoners. The doctor who has developed the drug wants to use three of these men for the tests.

(g) At a children's party a plate of cakes is passed round. With the child of the house and his mother (who is serving) left to be served, there remain two cakes, one a cream cake, the other a rock cake. The child is offered the plate, and grabs the cream cake. His mother reprimands him, stating that he should have left the better cake for someone else. The child asks which cake she would have taken if she had served herself before him. 'The rock cake, of course,' she replies. 'Well, that's what you've got,' he says.

(h) A masochist and a sadist spend a convivial evening together. Who does what to whom?

(i) (An example from an Open University Course.) The chief of police in a large American city has for years been trying to nail the man whom he knows to be the head of the local mafia, responsible for killings, acts of violence, protection rackets and a cause of deep misery to many of the citizens. For years this man has been able to elude the police because he has always had henchmen to do his dirty work, while he parades himself as a pillar of the local business community. A murder is eventually committed in which all the evidence leads to this man. The police chief arrests him, confident of getting a guilty verdict at the trial, and feeling that by putting such a person out of circulation for life he will have achieved his life's ambition, and rid the community of an open wound. Before the trial begins, however, he receives a letter from another man, confessing to the murder for which the mafia chief is awaiting trial. The details of this confession are so accurate that it is clear that he is speaking the truth. At the end he writes that, since he can no longer live with his conscience, he intends to commit suicide after posting the letter. Only the police chief knows what he has written. The chief makes enquiries, and discovers that the man has in fact been found dead, in circumstances which can be only suicide. The man in gaol is obviously not guilty of the crime for which he will almost certainly be found guilty. On the other hand, he has been effectively guilty of a score of other vicious crimes for which the law has been unable to touch him. What should the police chief do with the letter?

(j) You are a member of the resources sub-committee of the management board of a regional hospital. A month before the end of the financial year, the finance officer announces that there are several thousand pounds which must be spent in that time if it is not to be lost, and possibly bring about a cut in the following year's budget. The committee has received a number of requests for the money from different units in the hospital. Your task is to choose between the rival claimants, and you agree as a group to act on utilitarian lines and select the one which relates most directly to the needs of the community served by the hospital. Which do you select? The list before you contains the following proposals:

1 An extra dialysis machine for the renal unit, which is overstretched.
2 An extra bed to be placed in every ward, to speed up all admissions.
3 New furnishings for the psychiatric wing, including curtains and carpets, and the total redecoration of this wing, which is run-down and depressing for all who enter it.
4 A rehabilitation unit for drug addicts, who are not catered for at present.
5 A brain scanner which will discover diseases of the brain earlier than is possible with existing equipment.
6 The money to be used to fund research into preventative medicine, and an intensive advertising campaign on ways to keep healthy.

(k) In August 1945, the US Air Force made history by dropping atomic bombs on the Japanese cities of Hiroshima and Nagasaki. These two bombs between them killed an estimated 100,000 civilians and reduced both cities to rubble. The effect of the radiation, over an enormous area, continued for decades afterwards. The Allied defence of their action was (and remains) that nothing less than this would have brought about the surrender of Japan, whose High Command had announced its intention to continue the war until the last Allied or Japanese soldier was dead. This could have meant that many times more than the 100,000 would have been killed. As it was, Japan surrendered immediately on seeing the incredible devastation caused by these bombs, with, *inter alia*, the release from a living hell of thousands of Allied prisoners of war. Did the end (the immediate cessation of hostilities in Asia) justify the means, not only in terms of the megadeaths but also the introduction of a new dimension into warfare which has dominated international relations (and the human psyche) ever since: the threat of nuclear war?

CASE STUDY 22: TREATMENT OF SEVERELY HANDICAPPED INFANTS

In most of the Western World, there is an extremely thin divide between obeying and breaking the law so far as the treatment of 'severely handi-capped' infants is concerned. The condition itself is not easily categor-ised, but can be generally taken to mean malfunctioning of vital organs – brain, heart, liver, lungs, kidneys, and so on – so intense that the infant, even if recognisably human, will never be able to engage itself in human activity – such as communication with other persons.

There are three possible ways of treating these creatures:

1 They should be kept alive regardless of cost.
2 They should be allowed to die by natural causes.
3 They should be put out of their misery speedily.

The law at present rests around the second option, though supporters of both the first and third options frequently protest openly about this. In fact, it was an organisation which supports option 1, the Life organisation (mainly, but not exclusively, represented by Roman Catholics) which in 1981 in England brought a charge of murder against a paediatrician, Dr Leonard Arthur, because he had prescribed 'nursing care only' for one such infant, rejected by its parents. The child died after 36 hours. Dr Arthur was found not guilty, but the organisation, through its chairperson Mrs Nuala Scarisbrick, vowed to continue with its campaign against doctors who did not openly and avowedly pursue option 1 in their work.

On the other hand, supporters of option 3 felt that the delay in letting the child die was unnecessarily cruel. The comedian Spike Milligan, for instance, reminded readers of the *Guardian* of the symptoms of extreme pain and distress shown by the infant, and commented: 'I find the intention human but the execution horrendous. A vet puts a dog to sleep in a few seconds. Why the long agony of this baby?' Against this, a retired journalist, Malcolm Muggeridge, stated in another newspaper that by his instructions Dr Arthur had put himself in the same league as those doctors who made such infamous experiments on human beings in

149

the Nazi German concentration camps. There is clearly a strong feeling among many people that, one way or another, the vagueness inherent in the law as it stands ('letting die' rather than 'killing') should be cleared up. In the hope that you never have to face this dilemma as a parent, you may wish to reflect over the following questions.

1 To what extent do you think that anyone can decide that a severely subnormal baby, however malformed, cannot achieve happiness, with the result that death is seen as a more acceptable alternative for it?
2 The phrase 'quality of life' is often introduced in this context. Do you think this is relevant? How would you go about assessing another person's quality of life?
3 If the law were changed, and all such infants were kept alive, even though (as would normally be the case) they were rejected by their parents, do you think it society's duty to care for them in perpetuity? Would *you* help with the caring?
4 Can you distinguish between actively killing and passively letting die? ('Thou shalt not kill, but needst not strive Officiously to keep alive'.) If you cannot, does this lead you to the Milligan line, based perhaps on utilitarian principles, or to the Scarisbrick line, based on the Kantian view that all killing is wrong?
5 Whose interests should be paramount in this situation: the child's, the parents', the doctors' and nurses' (assuming these coincide, which is not inevitable), or society's? Since members of society disagree about what is right and what is wrong in these and related circumstances, how should agreement be reached about what ought to be done?

150

Chapter Seven

Existentialism and ethics

We turn now, in the phrase of a satirical BBC TV series, to something completely different. If you were to read Bertrand Russell's still-popular *History of Western Philosophy*, written before the Second World War, you will find no mention of the branch of philosophy known as existentialism. This is because while, as we shall see, it had its exponents in the nineteenth century, it came to the fore in mainland Europe only in the 1940s, and later still in the English-speaking world. In this chapter we shall look at the ideas of people whose lives overlapped ours (Sartre died as recently as 1980, and I have personally met – at a respectful distance in most cases – several of the others who will be mentioned.) This is therefore a philosophy of our own era, though that criterion is not in itself sufficient to place it higher than earlier schools of thought in any philosophical league table, as one might with scientists.

In fact, a considerable number of British philosophers hold the opinion that existentialism has no place at all in the philosophy league, for the simple reason that it is not a philosophy. It has been described as more a mood than a philosophy; a developmental stage – meaning, presumably a phase of development out of which mature people may be expected to grow. One eminent Oxford philosopher has described the writings of the existentialists as like a blown-up balloon which, in its inflated state, may look impressive but when pricked is mere shrivelled-up rubber. Courses are taught in British universities and elsewhere, purporting to introduce students to the problems of philosophy, which dispense with existentialism with little more than a passing reference: philosophy even as taught by the Open University, which by its title suggests comprehensiveness, is conspicuous by this neglect.

Whether the assessment made by these people is sound or otherwise is a judgment you must make for yourself on the basis of any reading in this field that you are prepared to undertake. It will in fact be a considerable undertaking, since much of the literature of the subject, whether primary or secondary sources, is written in turgid prose and displays a degree of verbosity which at times gives the reader sympathy for the tree that was made into paper for the books; and this is brought about not simply because most of them were written originally in the native (to English readers, foreign) tongues of the authors, and seem to lose in translation whatever sparkle they had in the original. Hell may, as Sartre suggested, be other people but sometimes one is tempted to say that it is other people's books.

One thing is certain of existentialism (and it may be this feature which some academic philosophers find threatening): as much as any school of philosophy and a good deal more than most, it is of the marketplace, and not a retreat for recluses. It compels its exponents to take account of their relationships with others, their sense of priorities, their personal responsibilities; in other words, it is a philosophy (and I hope at least to illustrate that this designation is not inapposite) born of, and involved in, real-life situations and conflicts and so, as a simple matter of fact, has influenced a large number of people in recent years who may have never considered themselves to be philosophically-minded.

Kierkegaard

One book *about* the existentialists which can be unreservedly recommended is by William Barrett, entitled *Irrational Man*. The author goes back as far as the Old Testament to find the earliest expressions of existentialist thought, but we can content ourselves by starting with the nineteenth century, and the Danish theologian and philosopher, *Søren Kierkegaard* (1813–55), often described as the 'father of existentialism'. Those who read Sartre will recognise in Kierkegaard the origin of certain phrases that were to become central in existentialist thought. He wrote of man's existence as a free-willed personality, not the slave of a mechanistic universe, but capable of determining his own future, and consequently his 'essence', by the decisions he made. He strongly opposed the views of the German philosopher Hegel, who had declared that 'the real is the rational and the rational is the real'. In his book *Either/Or*, Kierkegaard affirmed that existence is not just an abstract thing, quiescently occupying the sphere of pure thought, but is something which reaches to the very 'ground of our being', is rediscovered and re-expressed daily by the either/or decisions which we make. These decisions may well cause the agent fear and distress, but it is through them, because they mean taking a leap into the unknown, that we create our 'selves'.

Though Kierkegaard believed in God, and was in fact a minister of the Presbyterian Church in Denmark, his belief was no trite acceptance of a God 'out there', always available to strengthen, counsel, and sustain those who affirm their belief in Him: faith for Kierkegaard was a leap in the dark without any certainty that the right decision had been made. There was for him no blinding light, no miraculous revelation: he had to proceed according to the strength provided him by his own courage, without falling back on institutionalised creeds or ecclesiastical structures. He rejected the complacency and comfort which were brought about by what he termed a 'being' person in favour of the dynamic, but painful and sometimes fearful, striving of a 'becoming' person (and those two words with their underlying significance were to be taken up and explored by Sartre a century later). He therefore advocated individual acceptance of responsibility and the refusal to pass through life blindly and unaware, like contented sheep. We must grasp our freedom and express it continuously, however terrifying the ordeal such responsibility brings.

It was this concern for people's commitment to life with all its many-sided facets rather than engaging themselves merely in the escapism of abstract thought, that stamps Kierkegaard as a pioneer of a new approach to philosophy. In his last book, *Concluding Unscientific Postscript*, he wrote:

It is easier to indulge in abstract thought than it is to exist, unless we understand by this latter term what is loosely called existing, in analogy with what is loosely called being a subject. Existing is ordinarily regarded as no very complex thing, much less an art, since we all exist, but abstract thinking takes rank as an accomplishment. But really to exist, so as to interpenetrate one's existence with consciousness, at one and the same time eternal as if far removed from existence, and yet also present in existence and the process of becoming: that is truly difficult.

Nowadays a thinker is a curious creature who during certain hours of the day exhibits a very remarkable ingenuity, but has nothing otherwise in common with a human being.

After that last remark, we should perhaps not be surprised that numerous philosophers today refuse to include existentialism in the philosophical curriculum!

Nietzsche

Kierkegaard's religious form of existentialism was to be pursued in the twentieth century by a number of eminent theologians such as Karl Barth, Reinhold Niebuhr, Paul Tillich, and Martin Buber. His most famous successors, however, expounded existentialist ideas within an atheistic framework, and this is how they have mainly (though not entirely) been interpreted. One successor whose name is familiar to many quite independently of existentialist philosophy is *Friedrich Nietzsche* (1844–1900). He shared Kierkegaard's views about the anguish of living, but stressed that the human situation was starker than even the Dane had been willing to acknowledge. Surrounded by 'encircling gloom', Kierkegaard had committed himself to a life of faith; he had rejected all the conventional áids to the sustaining of faith which were provided by the church, but had still held on to the belief that at the ground of his being was God; he could consequently step forward blindly in faith, even if only one step at a time. Nietzsche dispensed even with this lifeline, and expounded a theory of the 'death of God'. In his most famous work, *Thus Spake Zarathustra*, he tells of a madman who cries out in the marketplace:

Where is God gone? I mean to tell you! We have killed Him – you and I! We are all His murderers! . . . God is dead! God remains dead! And we have killed Him! . . . Is not the magnitude of this deed too great for us? Shall we not ourselves have to become Gods, merely to seem worthy of it? There never was a greater event – and on account of it, all who are born after us belong to a higher history than any history hitherto!

Nietzsche is here using the word 'God' in a way which philosophers of religion must question, since the idea is not one of which death can logically be predicated. But the meaning behind the phrase is clear, and simply takes Kierkegaard's thinking one stage further: man must dispense altogether with the theistic belief that there exists an almighty, all-caring Being to whom he can turn for guidance, comfort, and strength. In particular, he must reject the idea of God as the source and embodiment of values. These he must find within the essence of his own life by sublimating the raw will to power, which Nietzsche believed exists in all people, and, left to itself, can become animalistic and destructive, to a will to create. He must overcome himself, and so become a creative being, the *Übermensch*. This word has normally been translated into English as 'superman', and Nietzsche has often been condemned as the *éminence grise* behind Hitler, with his interpretation of the superman within the context of racialist views. Nietzsche certainly despised egalitarian theories of human nature: he poured scorn on democracy, socialism, and any kind of belief in equal rights for all; but his ideas were directed not to the founding of any kind of 'master race' but towards the development of the 'overman', which is how *Übermensch* should be translated.

The chief way in which man must overcome himself is by ceasing to look outside and beyond himself for his morals. He saw Zarathustra, the ancient Persian philosopher (often known as Zoroaster), as the first moralist because he had rejected any belief in the metaphysical nature of morals – the idea that these exist as a concept independently of the decisions which human beings have to make. Nietzsche dubbed those whose aim in life is towards an afterlife 'after-worldsmen'; their values he described as 'life-denying', and their morality stemming from 'a poor ignorant weakness, which no longer wants to want'. The crucial need, he believed, was for man to find new values before being overcome by despair and nihilism. Like Kierkegaard, he was aware of the fearfulness this must bring about in the minds of those accustomed to a comfortable, herd-like existence. He wrote, 'One must have chaos within oneself to give birth to a dancing star. I ask you: do you still have this chaos?' This theme he developed in later books, particularly in *Toward the Geneaology of Morals* and *Beyond Good and Evil*. In his final years he went insane, and a strongly egotistical note entered his writings; but he had already written enough to prepare the way for his twentieth-century successors: and these were to be found, not among the Nazis, who distorted his views for their own ulterior purposes, but among liberal humanists like the Frenchman Albert Camus. He and other existentialist philosophers were his real heirs.

Heidegger

The greatest scholar of the existentialist school (though he denied that he belonged to it) was the German professor, Martin Heidegger (1889–1976). Though not an atheist, in his writings he considered the consequences for the human situation of 'man without God.' In his incredibly difficult book *Sein und Zeit* (*Being and Time*), he continued along the path trodden by his predecessors by indicating a major change brought about in our understanding of ourselves as a result of losing the 'divine dimension' in life. With God it was possible to believe that life had a plan, a purpose, an overriding goal; that we are all part of 'that one far-off divine event to which the whole creation moves' (quoted in Chapter One). Everyone, no matter how lowly his state, or how unlucky he may be in his share of life's blessings – health, intelligence, happiness, and so on – could take heart from the conviction that he was put into the world for a purpose which would continue to unfold in a future existence. This perspective, said Heidegger, has now gone: so what are we left with?

Thrownness Fundamentally, there is the tragedy of what Heidegger termed '*Geworfenheit*' or 'thrown-ness' (a word not known to most Germans, since Heidegger devised it himself, so don't worry if you've never heard it before.) He is here referring to the accident of birth. We are 'thrown' into the world haphazardly, so that in no way can we begin to rationalise why we were born where we were, when we were, and, above all, to whom we were. We don't choose any of these; and yet between them they can make or break any person's life, so that we may either proceed to experience a life of fulfilment and joy, or be surrounded by barriers so durable that these rewards seem cut off from us as though by prison walls. Heidegger does not suggest that everything is absolutely determined by this *Geworfenheit*, but realistically indicates how far-reaching its effects are on the majority of lives.

The field of being The second consequence, he suggests, is that we are *limited to the world of our individual consciousness*: our field is the one that we perceive around us – the people we meet, the ideas we encounter, the paths we follow, the opportunities accidentally presented to us. This limitation is, according to Heidegger, the supreme tragedy of our existence. Through (often) no fault of our own, and unless we experience a little bit of luck, we may well undergo a life of littleness, of insubstantiation, often experienced through others rather than at first hand. (How many people enjoy soap operas because of the vicarious sense of achievement, of fulfilling relationships and encounters with people thus obtained?) 'Set out to face the long littleness of life,' wrote one contemporary existentialist; or, as the film star, Kirk Douglas said even after a life of apparent excitement on the screen, 'Life's like a B-movie – it's that corny.' Nevertheless, what meaning I attach to life remains *my* decision: it is not that of my parents, or of my priest, or of my political leaders. It rests on my shoulders to make sense of what may be, on the face of it, senseless. My world of perception is mine, and nobody else's; and nobody can take it away from me: isn't that a bonus?

Images in the mind Against the optimism that this thought may engender, Heidegger presents a further stark fact of life. Our own perception of the world, our own field, is certainly ours; but this includes our perception of other people: everyone with whom we are in some form of communication, at whatever level, is an image in each of our minds; but the image I hold of another person will be different from the image you hold of him, and different again from the image he holds of himself. *And the same is true of the image he and others hold of me.* Their perception of me may change from time to time, but at any moment, during any particular act of communication, the image they have formed of me is fixed in their minds: *I am an object in their field*, and however different this may be from the me that I myself perceive, it is on the basis of their perception of me that they will proceed in their relationship with me.

This may seem complex, but the simple result is that we are all objects in the minds of other people, and they react to us according to what they perceive this object to be. If you don't believe this, think how you react when you accidentally meet a great sports star or entertainer. The image you hold of them as a result of reading about or watching them dominates such an encounter; you may be amazed that they do such mundane things as travel on a train, or talk about the weather, or go to the lavatory. John McEnroe, the tennis star, described being a celebrity as like being raped: he wanted to be himself as he perceived himself, but the reporters and the public at large would not treat him in this way. In their minds he was the superstar, or superbrat, or whatever; and from that he could not escape.

This is clearly an extreme example of the state that Heidegger described; but we must all have people in our lives whom we consider to have the wrong image about us, and experience the frustration of knowing that there is little we can do about this. I have colleagues who, in my belief, have the wrong end of the stick about me; and I know that, whatever attempts I may make to change this, with some, at least, I shall never be successful (and anyway, maybe their image is a more valid representation of me than I like to think). I suspect that, however high you climb in life, to your parents you will always be the child they nurtured and fostered. (When Harry Truman became US President on the death of Franklin Roosevelt, we are told that his aged mother's only comment was 'Behave yourself, Harry'.) This image-making is of course at its most deadly when it relates to whole sections of people – to members of a particular nation, or colour, or class. We may make jokes about this – good jokes, such as the question of whether the world's shortest book is the Italian Book of War Heroes, the German Book of Humour, the Australian Book of Culture, or the American Book of Self-Denial: but it is no joke when we speak of the number of megadeaths after a nuclear war, or describe another person as just a black, or a 'yob', and therefore not worth consideration; it is certainly no joke to be thought of in that way by others.

The only way out of this dilemma, this tragic situation as Heidegger considered it, is to be an 'authentic' person, to live as far as possible without labels and without masks, and to reveal to others, as consistently as possible, the self that we conceive ourselves to be. We shall return to this idea when considering the ideas of Sartre (who, in any case, expressed authenticity in his life more apparently than Heidegger: he, as I recall, donned the professorial mask without any apparent reluctance).

Death   Is there then no hope, no meaning to life? Yes, replies Heidegger: there is the *absolute fact of death*, and it is this fact which has been and remains the sole inspiration of what is most worthwhile in life, and the supreme motivation for attaining it. To many people this statement will appear totally paradoxical. How can there be any meaning in life, when all we can look forward to is oblivion? Why, if that is the case, should anyone concern himself with the needs of others, act self-sacrificially, or indeed try to be 'moral' at all? If 'death closes all' (Tennyson again) then let us eat, drink, and be merry, if we can, for we have committed ourselves to the absurdity of existence: a world in which there is no fairness, no justice, no equality of ability or opportunity. If, in Russell's words, 'all the noonday brightness of human genius is destined to extinction in the vast death of the solar system', what is the point of that genius's existing in the first place? If all the creative and intellectual achievement of the whole human race is eventually to cease, totally, to exist, why make any effort now? If 'the rest is silence', why the preliminary sounds? It seems, as Kant suggested, that without some kind of belief in a form of continuing consciousness after the death of the body – whether this is proved ultimately to be a true belief or not – we must simply accept that any so-called 'moral life' is pointless, since experience indicates that, in this world, goodness and happiness, or fulfilment, by no means always coincide. Without the hope of a future world in which all will be rectified, we must simply accept that life, which began by chance and will end by chance, is absurd; and since we had no choice over the former event and, short of suicide, none over our end, we remain deluded creatures, seeing visions and dreaming dreams, which must forever taunt us because they are insubstantial, and haunt us because they can never be preserved.

I suspect that, whether actually articulated, or unconsciously, this is the conviction of the majority of the human race, and has been so throughout history. I believe it to be the supreme motivation of all forms of religious belief. Heidegger, however, presents us with a thesis about death which is the reverse of the attitude just outlined. He viewed death, and the anxiety brought about in our minds because of its inevitability, as the basic motivating factor of all that we do, creative or otherwise. 'Without anxiety,' he wrote, 'there can be no creativity'. It is only the knowledge that our time of existence is short that makes us put any effort into anything; without this awareness, our existence would be an unending process of continuous postponement. If you doubt this, ask yourself this question: if we knew for certain that we were to live for ever, that there was no such thing as death, would we ever stretch ourselves to achieve *anything*? Suppose you and I had eternity stretching before us: would I write this book *now*? Would you take the trouble to read it *now*? Surely, with infinite time ahead of us, we can leave such chores until tomorrow, or next year, or for a million years. We could rewrite a well-known motto: 'Never do today what can possibly be left till tomorrow' – except that this would include everything, so there would be no point in coining such advice. With eternity at our disposal, nothing, absolutely nothing, matters. Only the absolute fact of death and the relative brevity of life bring any sense of urgency, of significance, into any of our activities, or ideas, or relationships. If life were to go on for ever, there would be no achievements, no growth: Everest would be left unscaled, and the Unfinished Symphony never started. Men and women would no longer be human as we understand that term; we should be no more than objects, things, as vital as suet pudding, and as alive as a grain of sand.

The tragedy that we must live with, Heidegger reminds us, is that, while death is the most important fact in the life of every single human being, nobody will ever experience his own death. Others will share this experience, but not the deceased: he is no longer involved. The sorrows of death are the sorrows of the living, not of the dead. The child learns this when he contemplates dying in order to teach his unjust parents a lesson – and then has to remind himself that this revenge is pointless, since he won't be around to enjoy their discomfiture. The *Geworfenheit* operates at the end, as at the beginning; the two most important events in life – our coming into existence and our going out of existence – do not belong to us in any way at all. (For further reflections on this theme, see the author's *East of Existentialism*, Ch. 5.)

Sartre

We turn now to the man who, simply because he expressed his views through more popular channels than philosophical tomes (though he wrote these too, of course) put existentialism on the English-speaking map: the Frenchman, *Jean-Paul Sartre* (1905–80). His major philosophical work was *L'Etre et le néant* ('Being and Nothingness'); but this, like Heidegger's *Being and Time*, makes difficult reading, and you would be wiser to start with his shorter and much more comprehensible *Existentialism and Humanism*. You may already be familiar with some of his novels and plays, such as his trilogy under the title of *Roads to Freedom* and his play *No Exit*, which has been produced on stage and television throughout the world.

Like his English contemporary, Bertrand Russell, Sartre was a man of action as well as of the intellect. Throughout the German occupation of France of 1940–5, he was active in the Resistance, and was imprisoned for nine months by the Germans on account of this. His commitment to the events taking place around him continued after the war. During the Algerian crisis he supported the cause of Algerian independence, and his apartment was twice bombed by right-wing terrorists because he encouraged French youths not to serve in the militia against the Algerian rebels; only General De Gaulle, the French President, kept Sartre out of jail at the time, arguing 'Sartre is also France'. He refused to accept a speaking engagement in the United States in 1965 because of the American people's acceptance of their government's military action in Vietnam: no worthwhile dialogue could take place under those circumstances, he said; and in 1968 he was at the head of the students and trade unionists who were demonstrating in thousands on the streets of Paris in favour of democratic rights – demonstrations which had major repercussions in both Britain and America, and in the Western world generally.

Existence and essence   Sartre's thesis begins with the statement, 'Existence precedes essence'. This may sound an obscure notion, but Sartre made its meaning quite plain. He began by contrasting human beings with inanimate objects. He used the example of a paperknife, but I prefer to use my favourite visual aid – my pipe. The pipe I have in my mouth as

I write has a certain shape (curved) and size (large); it is made from a certain type of wood (briar) with a plastic stem. The point of all these details is that all these dimensions and constituent elements were known to the maker of the pipe before it was made. While it was still on the drawing-board, he knew exactly what it would be made of, be used for, look like, and feel like. (It looks large enough to be used for growing household plants, as a matter of fact, but I've never heard of anyone abusing such a precious object in that way.) In other words, the *essence* of the pipe – what it *is*, what it's *for*, what is to *become* of it – predated its actual coming into existence. Its essence preceded its existence, throughout which it remains static, unchanged and unchanging. A pipe is a pipe, and there's an end to the matter; over the years I may grow fonder of it until it becomes my favourite pipe, so that I am encouraged, like Jerome K. Jerome in *Three Men on the Bummel*, to dedicate a book to it; but this simply illustrates my subjective appreciation of it: the pipe remains, and will forever remain, a piece of dead wood.

What then, asks Sartre, is the essence of a human being? The religious person will answer that this essence is in the mind of God before a person's birth or creation. That answer may be satisfactory for those religious people – like Muslims or Predestinarians in Christianity – who believe that Allah, or God, has foreordained the eternal destiny of every human being; but it certainly won't satisfy those religious people who believe in the freedom of the will and the ability to choose, which this allows – and, of course, to atheists like Sartre God was a superfluous concept. The answer, Sartre suggests, is that there is no such thing as a fixed, or established, human essence; this would be to suggest that what we are for is determined before our birth and is unavoidable. His thesis was that at birth we come into existence and from that point proceed to create our own essences. We bring this about by the choices we make: by the work we do, the people we associate with, the priorities we establish in the use of our time, the relationships we develop, the commitments we enter into, the moral decisions we make, the rules we follow. The essence of each one of us is what we make of ourselves through our free choices, made rationally and without constraint. We make of ourselves what we will. Some will have a greater advantage, a better start, than others; but nobody, argues Sartre, should go through life making whining excuses for his frustrations or failures: not everyone can, by objective standards, achieve as much as everybody else (Sartre is not arguing that we all have equal abilities); but everyone is capable of creating his essence if he is willing to make the kind of choices just mentioned. Not everybody can be president or prime minister, TV producer or university professor: but nobody need get himself into a rut (which, in all respects but depth, is indistinguishable from a grave). By taking thought, by using will-power, and by expressing his freedom, any person, Sartre believed, was capable of self-development and so creating his own essence; the limits are those which each individual imposes on himself when he says, 'That's enough of that'. In the words of the German playwright and existentialist, Bertold Brecht: 'Man is what he has done'.

Pour-soi and en-soi   We are thus presented with the portrayal of man as a subjective, self-conscious being, surrounded by an objective world – the world of biology, of politics, of economics, of culture; to all these man can relate himself as, more importantly for the theme of this book, he can relate on a social level to those whom Heidegger had described as belonging in each person's 'field': the implications of this kind of re- lationship forming, as we shall see, the basis of Sartre's view of ethics and personal morality. Sartre characterises human consciousness as *être-pour- soi* (being-for-itself), and the object of consciousness as *être-en-soi* (being- in-itself.) This has been described as a dualistic view of human beings, but that word is confusing, since it is redolent of Platonic and certain religious theories of human nature. It would be preferable to describe the situation as a dichotomy, or simply two modes of being; and for Sartre man's aim must be to overcome this dichotomy. By reflecting on the objective world he makes it, quite naturally, part of his consciousness: the *en-soi* becomes *pour-soi*; and by universalising this process so as to include all such reflections in a unified whole, he will achieve the essential man. (There is more than a hint of Taoist thought here, as we shall see in Chapter Thirteen.) By refusing to engage in this reflective activity, by choosing not to commit himself to the world of his awareness, man is in danger of making himself into an object only of other people's awareness, fixed, unchanging, an *être-en-soi*. Sartre made no attempt to disguise his contempt for such people.

Thus, Sartre suggested in a famous phrase, man is his own project. If you have ever embarked on such an exercise you will understand why he said this. You begin by listing potential areas of research and exploration; but in the process you are almost certain to find that certain areas which initially looked important, and likely therefore to be fruitful areas of study, no longer appear so; while others which you had originally considered to be minor issues, or totally unimportant, assume a larger significance as the research proceeds through its developmental pro- cesses, through modification and adaptation. Consequently the finished product looks far different from the original plan: if it doesn't, then you've either been incredibly lucky, or, more likely, indolent in pursuing new areas of exploration as you have discovered them. So, argued Sartre, is the being-for-itself: forever growing, committing itself to new situ- ations and challenges as they arise, changing direction where necessary, and being prepared at all times to take a risk.

There is, then, for Sartre no such thing as human nature. The phrase suggests that there is some kind of overriding pattern to which we all more or less conform – an example of one of Plato's 'Forms', an ideal, with reality as a copy. Not so, says Sartre: we all have our own natures which we are ourselves in the process of creating. To affirm, then, that human beings are by nature selfish is as absurd as to state that we are fundamentally altruistic. Some people take one direction, others, another: the choice in either case is theirs. There is not, nor ever can be, such a person as a 'born leader' or a 'born loser'. Nobody is 'born' anything. A person acquires what are termed 'leadership qualities' by being willing and choosing to act first, to take a risk, in tricky, difficult, or dangerous circumstances and situations. A loser loses out because he makes unwise or pusillanimous choices, or perhaps because he holds back when critical demands are made upon him.

Free will   The word 'choice' in that last paragraph introduces one of the central ideas of existentialism: man is free to choose, free to be; anything which smacks of determinism, whether from the psychological, socio-logical, environmental, or religious point of view, is firmly rejected. Existentialism is a libertarian philosophy. The general discussion of free will is in Chapter Ten, but it is important to emphasise at this stage the implications for moral theory brought about by a commitment to a belief in the freedom of the will. In the first place it means 'freedom from': when making moral decisions, the agent is his own agent, not acting on behalf of an institution. He does not need to commit himself to any set of a priori values; there is no ideal Form setting him in certain directions; he is not answerable to any divine commands, whether these be hewn in the rock on Sinai or howled at him from every pulpit in the land. He can treat with derision the descriptions of his fate on the Day of Wrath and Judgment, whether made by the Pope in his ecclesia, the religious fundamentalists on their TV stations, or the Mullahs of Islam from their mosques. He is totally uninterested in either the furniture of heaven or the temperature of hell.

In existentialist ethics there is no *super*natural or *supra*natural code of behaviour to which the individual must conform. Our rules for living are those that we decide on for ourselves; and if in the end we decide that on certain matters codifiers of morality centuries ago were right, they still remain *our* rules because they will have been tried and tested for our-selves, and found acceptable on the basis of personal experience. We are free, therefore, from pretence, from pretentiousness, from the 'tyranny of convention'; above all, we are free from the necessity of wearing some sort of mask in order to make ourselves presentable, or acceptable, to our fellow human beings. They must take us as they find us, or not at all.

This may sound appealing: but Sartre suggests that this may not be the case. It was G.B. Shaw, the Irish playwright, who said, 'People fear freedom; that's why they avoid it.' It is because this freedom, and the choices to which it leads, brings responsibility. There may be no a priori values, but there are values – the values that any individual determines for himself by the choices he makes and the actions he performs. The only good is the good which man himself creates; and this is true, not only for the individual character, but also for the whole of society. 'In reality, things will be such as men have decided they shall be.' Thus – and here we home in again on the agony of Kierkegaard's 'either/or', and the terror of Nietzsche's madman in the marketplace – the individual moral agent is responsible not only for himself, but for all men; 'for in effect, of all the actions a man may take in order to create himself as he wills to be, there is not one which is not creative, at the same time, of an image of man such as he believes he ought to be. To choose between this and that is at the same time to affirm the value of that which is chosen.'

It must be clear that this conclusion follows logically from the premises. If it is the case that man is capable at all times of making free choices; that these choices are thus rational; that there is no compulsion, from any source, on the decision-maker; that there is therefore no element of prejudice, bigotry, or ignorance: then the choices must be indicative of what is right for all men. The view of existentialism, widely held in the English-speaking world of the 1960s, that it meant 'doing your own thing', was therefore a gross misrepresentation of the philosophy, even if some of Sartre's language lent credence to this view. He is in fact much closer to the universalisability approach of Kant, whom he held in high regard. After all, if there is no element of consistency in the rational processes of human beings, it must be doubted if there can ever be any agreement between those who employ their powers of reason in any field – scientific as much as philosophical.

Anguish, abandonment, despair   The burden of responsibility which freedom of choice brings in its wake is described by Sartre as the cause of anguish. Man is 'condemned' to be free; he is alone, with nobody else to turn to, in the process of determining his own essence. The anguish is the anguish of total, inescapable responsibility. He carries his own can: he must say, in the famous phrase of US President Harry Truman: 'The buck stops here.' Sartre wrote what might have been a commentary on that remark:

Each and every individual man must commit himself and act upon his commitment. Man cannot know what is to be; he only knows what is in his power to make things so. Beyond that, he can count on nothing.

The act of choice is much more than just that of choosing a commitment and then acting on it. As was suggested in Chapter Two, even the refusal to make a choice is itself a choice – in this case, the choice of abstention. Evil men prosper when good men do nothing; history is full of examples of men burying their heads in the sand and then pleading that they were blameless for the havoc brought about while they so chose to be uncommitted. Sartre suggested that the greatest expression of freedom lay in man's ability to say 'no', and he has wrongly been accused of being negative because of this. But there was nothing negative in Sartre's refusal to cooperate with the Germans during their occupation of his country; and – to move away from the existentialists for a moment – whatever criticisms may be made on political grounds of Bertrand Russell's activities in the Campaign for Nuclear Disarmament, it would be absurd to describe his opposition to Britain's possession of nuclear weapons as 'negative'. There is nothing negative in saying 'no' to an alcoholic drink at a party; those Americans who said no to the nation's involvement in the Vietnam war were not being negative, any more than the Germans who risked their lives by opposing Hitler were being negative. The word 'no' can signal a change of state for an individual, a community, or an entire nation. But it may well cause anguish as a consequence.

This anguish is intensified because of the sense of what Sartre described as *abandonment*. Primarily, this means abandonment by God who, as men have conceived Him, has provided strength and comfort to millions of people throughout the ages. 'When I walk through the waters, thou shalt be with me; And through the fire, it shall not consume', wrote the prophet of old. That support, says Sartre, is no more. 'God is love', proclaim religious posters; but for Sartre 'there is no love apart from the deeds of love; no potentiality of love other than that which is manifested in loving.'

This state of abandonment means not only that we are denied any divine counsel, but human counsel too. This is not to say that we do not, or ought not to, seek advice from our friends from time to time: for most of us this is a natural and desirable course to take when we are in a quandary. The significant point here, however, is that it is still *our* choice which friends or other counsellors we consult. Even if we turn to a priest, or a psychiatrist, a Samaritan, or a marriage guidance counsellor, that act is one of choice on our part: *which* priest, *which* specialist – that is for us to decide. And having listened to their advice (assuming they give any at all – we may simply be using them as a means of thinking aloud and sorting out a particular dilemma for ourselves) it is our choice whether or not to follow it. So we remain abandoned, responsible for our own destinies; we are no longer in a position to say 'Let *them* do something about it', whether by 'them' we mean our political leaders, the clergy, doctors, teachers, or whoever. The responses required in any situation are responses that we must be prepared to make as the result of our own free choices; and this can create a tremendous sense of loneliness.

The word that Sartre uses to express this feeling is *despair*. He means by this the despair felt by any individual at the realisation that he has no other resources than those he contains within himself; he is limited to the strength of his own will. Only the willpower that we have been able to create within ourselves through our way of facing up to (or avoiding) life's challenges and complexities will enable us, at any moment, to get through. This is not to say (as has been suggested of existentialism, perhaps with the example of Sartre himself in mind) that we must be constantly acting aggressively towards others: one can assert oneself without being aggressive, maintain a stance without becoming a bully. What is required is that we show enough courage to express whatever we feel to be right, even when those around us disagree; to go meekly and unwillingly along with the majority because of fear of exposing oneself by expressing opposition: that, says Sartre, shows how the despair which he is describing can overwhelm a person's inner desire to act. But we must learn to live with this despair, and act 'authentically' despite it.

Authenticity   The word 'authentic' echoes one of Heidegger's emphases, and sums up the aims of existentialism as comprehensively as any we may choose. An authentic person, as described by Sartre, is one who acknowledges responsibility for himself and, in particular, his moral decisions. He avoids, or tries to avoid, becoming merely the object of other people's awareness, *être-en-soi*, recognising that whatever his 'nature' is to be, it will be as the result of his own choice: he will make of himself what he wills, *être-pour-soi*. If this means abandoning, or refusing to accept, the easy contentment of the farmyard animal, fed, watered, and cleaned at appropriate intervals, oblivious to crises and barred from decision-making, so be it: to be an authentic person, with all the traumas this involves, is infinitely to be preferred to a life of 'bad faith'. By this phrase, Sartre was referring to all who remained silent when a particular point of view needed to be expressed, all who held back when a step in a particular direction was called for, all who allowed themselves to be categorised according to one label or another, all who took refuge from reality, and thereby increased unreality, by wearing some kind of mask. Sartre wrote critically of the waiter who, away from work, behaved like a self-governing human being, but in the restaurant changed into a fawning sycophant, governed by those around him. The obsequious attitude invariably fostered by those whose interests lead them to take the view that 'the customer is always right' – whether adopted by shopkeepers, insurance salesmen, real estate agents, or commercial travellers (or reps as they are sometimes called) – was viewed by Sartre with the utmost contempt. To define oneself, and so behave, according to one's *function* was the worst possible expression of 'bad faith', by which he meant being untrue to oneself, or inauthentic.

Sartre himself declined, in 1965, the prestigious and lucrative Nobel Prize for Literature. His letter of refusal was typical of the man, illustrating how consistently he himself practised what he preached. 'A writer must refuse to allow himself to be transformed into an institution,' he wrote, 'even if it takes place in the most honourable form. . . . It is not the same thing if I sign Jean-Paul Sartre or if I sign Jean-Paul Sartre, Nobel Prize winner.' For the same reason he had refused the French Légion d'Honneur in 1945, offered him in recognition of his years of activity in the French Resistance. To an admiring student who averred that he would follow Sartre anywhere, he referred to Nietzsche: 'Be a man and do not follow me – but yourself.' He was thus directly in line with Nietzsche, in effect imparting to man the deity traditionally attributed to a transcendent almighty and omniscient Being. 'Even if God existed,' he wrote in *Existentialism and Humanism*, 'that would make no difference.' If we are to find fulfilment on earth, whether in individual or social terms, then it rests with man to bring this about: if he fails, it simply shall not be.

Critique of Existentialism

One wonders, on reflection, how far it is possible to universalise this ideal of authenticity. Wasn't he a little unfair to the waiter, who had to behave as he did for the basic reason that he was beholden to his customers as Sartre, writer, broadcaster, professor, had never had to be? He seems, moreover, to share some of John Stuart Mill's unrealistic awareness of people from a less academic and cultured background than his own. He acknowledged that some people had a more fortunate start than others in life, but never seems totally to have appreciated how dense can be the blinkers strapped to a socially handicapped person. How does one discuss authenticity with an Ethiopian refugee, a homeless Palestinian, or an unemployed school-leaver, devoid of even the most elementary of qualifications? It was clearly Sartre's appreciation that millions of people throughout the world are condemned to a narrow existence by circumstances beyond their control that led him to join the Communist Party later in life. He explained, to those who were puzzled by his behaviour, that this was his commitment; but his choice of party was surely made because its particular commitment was to social revolution and the levelling out of the wide variations in opportunities for fulfilment brought about by class distinctions. It still seems odd that a man so opposed to overriding rules should commit himself to such a strongly rule-governed organisation, with its prejudged interpretation of historical inevitability. If the Bible is to be rejected as a controlling factor in people's lives, so is the *Communist Manifesto* and Mao Tse Tung's *Little Red Book*.

A further criticism of existentialism is that it seems to be a philosophy primarily for situations of crisis and catastrophe, with which only heroic types of people are able to cope. So far as Heidegger and Sartre were concerned, this is explained by the fact that they wrote in such times, and they both had the intellect and strength of character to respond positively to the challenges involved. All of us can find similar challenges today if we care to look for them; and we can choose to involve ourselves in the process of overcoming them; but few of us, for simple economic reasons, can commit ourselves to this process as wholeheartedly as Sartre was able to do. It is an evaluative judgment how far everyone should feel obliged to be involved in activities concerned with political and social upheaval; it is impossible to be committed to every worthy cause, and for many people the commitment to, and sustaining of, a particular relationship is energy-draining and time-consuming enough. And while Sartre is surely right, that the act of saying 'No' can be a supreme expression of human freedom, it does not have to be expressed in the public arena in order to constitute a praiseworthy act of courage and endurance. The battle fought by many a smoker, or alcoholic, or drug-addict when he decides to say 'No' to his particular addiction can be as traumatic and as long-lasting as Luther's 'No' to Roman Catholicism or Sartre's 'No' to Nazism.

This 'Athanasius contra mundum' attitude of existentialism (and, perhaps, its occasional suggestion that 'après moi, le déluge') lends an air of individualism to the philosophy which does not seem always either attractive or desirable. D. H. Lawrence expressed this individualism vividly and succinctly in his *Studies in Classical American Literature*:

Each soul is alone and the aloneness of each soul is a double barrier to perfect relationships between two beings. Each soul should be alone. And in the end the desire for a perfect relationship is just a vicious, humanly craving. . . . Every relationship should have its absolute limits, its absolute reserves, essential to the singleness of the soul in each person.

Lawrence may well be right; but the question is whether we should allow this to commit ourselves to an *être-pour-soi* which either ignores or seeks to make superfluous our need for others, and our dependence on them in various ways and at various levels. I need my wife, my family, my colleagues, and my friends: all of these help me to explore different avenues in myself and fulfil different aspects of myself. My essence is, therefore, partly in their hands. I feel I have sacrificed no part of my authenticity as a person by acknowledging this.

The influence of existentialism has been far-reaching, and its exponents have varied widely in their emphases. It has evoked reactions in men of letters as well as men of ideas, in painters and poets besides theologians and philosophers, as some of the quotations which follow will illustrate. The result is that it is difficult to generalise about the existentialists: they have not formed themselves into a school, or circle, like the

Vienna Circle of logical positivists, or the Ayn Rand school of Objectivism; there is no existentialist broadsheet. One way of thinking which is common to all who may, however loosely, be embraced under the existentialist umbrella is that of rejecting any kind of metaphysical world view which unifies all thought and experience within a single overriding concept, or vision. There is no light at the end of the road, no omniscient Being who will eventually explain all the mysteries of life. All is not to be revealed: even the religious existentialists advocate a life motivated by faith and hope rather than knowledge or assurance. There is no answer to the question 'What is the meaning of life?' since the question is itself question-begging. Life, as reiterated by a famous comedian of the sixties, Al Read, is what you make it. If this seems absurd, then we have grasped one of the central themes of existentialism; rejecting all concepts of 'ultimate reality', the task of every person thrown willy-nilly into the world is to make what he can of the freedom he possesses and create his own nature according to his own perception of values, of right and wrong conduct, and of the priorities required in human relationships. William Barrett (op. cit., p. 80) expresses this view in these words:

This conception of human finitude places in question the supremacy that reason has traditionally been given over all other human functions in the history of Western philosophy. Theoretical knowledge may indeed be pursued as a personal passion, or its findings may have practical application; but its value above that of all other human enterprises (such as art or religion) cannot be enhanced by any claim that it will reach the Absolute. Suppose, for example, that there were a road and we were told we ought to walk it; in response to our question 'Why?', we might be told that we ought to do so because the walking itself would be pleasant or useful (good for our health); but if we were told that there is a priceless treasure at the end of the road, then the imperative to walk would carry overwhelming weight with us. It is this treasure at the end of the road that has disappeared from the modern horizon, for the simple reason that the end of the road has itself disappeared.

APPENDIX: EXPRESSIONS OF EXISTENTIALIST IDEAS

'We must change our fellow men from contented animals to suffering Gods conscious of a suffering world.'

– *L. Mumford*

'The essence of being human is that . . . one is prepared in the end to be defeated and broken up by life, which is the inevitable price of fastening one's love upon other individuals.'

– *G. Orwell*

'Indifference is paralysis of the soul, premature death.'

– *Chekhov*

'So it is that we can be terrors to each other, and people in lonely rooms suffer humiliation and even damage because of others in whose consciousness perhaps they scarcely figure at all. Eidola projected from the mind take on a life of their own, wandering to find their victims and maddening them with miseries and fears which the original source of these wanderings could not be justly charged with inflicting and might indeed be very puzzled to hear of.'
(Eidola: Phantoms)

– *Iris Murdoch*

'In our society, any man who does not weep at his mother's funeral runs the risk of being sentenced to death. . . . He is foreign to the society in which he lives, he wanders on the fringe, in the suburbs of private, solitary, sensual life. And this is why readers have been tempted to look upon him as a piece of social wreckage.'

– *A. Camus*

'The greatest intellectual economy is to accept the non-intelligibility of the world – and concern oneself with man.'

– *A. Camus*

'If this world had no meaning, totalitarianism is right. I cannot accept its being right.'

– *A. Camus*

'Are we going to accept despair without doing anything about it?'

– *A. Camus*

169

'Nothing, nothing has the least importance, and I knew quite why. . . .
From the dark horizon of my future, a sort of slow persistent breeze
had been blowing towards me . . . and on its way, that breeze had
levelled out all the ideas people had tried to foist on me in the equally
unreal years I was then living through . . . all alike would be
condemned to die one day; his turn too would come like the others.
And what difference did it make if, after being charged with murder,
he were executed because he didn't weep at his mother's funeral since
it all came to the same in the end.'

– A. Camus

'Life is terrible, thank God!'

– Dylan Thomas

'Suffering is the substance of life and the root of personality, and
suffering is universal. Suffering is that which unites all us living beings
together; it is the universal or divine blood that flows through us all.
That which we call Will, what is it but suffering?'

– Unamuno

'Loving all of it even while he had to hate some of it because he knows
now that you don't love because: you love despite; not for the virtues
but despite the faults.'

– William Faulkner

'To battle against princes and popes is easy compared with struggling
against the masses, the tyranny of equality, against the grin of
shallowness, nonsense, baseness and bestiality.'

– Kierkegaard

'. . . being man signifies precisely being always on the point of not
being man, being a living problem, an absolute and hazardous
adventure . . . being, in essence, drama! Because there is drama only
when we do not know what is going to happen, so that every instant is
pure peril and shuddering risk. While the tiger cannot cease being a
tiger, cannot be detigered, man lives in the perpetual risk of being
dehumanised.'

– José Ortega y Gasset

'Today, the first and perhaps the only duty of the philosopher is to defend man against himself: to defend man against the extraordinary temptation towards inhumanity to which – almost always without being aware of it – so many human beings today have yielded.'

– Gabriel Marcel

'The Hopi . . . working on the land does not set himself in opposition to it. He works *with* the elements, not against them. . . . He is in harmony with the elements, not in conflict, and he does not set out to conquer an opponent. He depends on the corn, but this is part of a mutual interdependence, it is not exploitation.'

– H. & H. A. Frankfort

'When I consider the short duration of my life, swallowed up in the eternity before and after the little space which I fill, and even can see, engulfed in the infinite immensity of space of which I am ignorant, and which knows me not, I am frightened. I am astonished at being here rather than there. Why now rather than then?'

– Pascal

'The individual cannot become human by himself. Self-being is only real in communication with another self-being. Alone, I sink into gloomy isolation – only in communication with others can I be revealed.'

– Karl Jaspers

'Suicide is the ultimate absurdity of human existence, like a millionaire killing himself because he is afraid of starving to death.'

– Sartre

'Man's experience of the world is basically an experience of limitation.'

– Sartre

'The act of suicide is a protest against limitation; the suicide regards life as a suicide.'

– Sartre

'For the first time in history, men are beginning to feel stifled by their own humanity.'

– Sartre

171

'. . . existing in a desert of freedom. You can observe the same thing when a schoolboy has a long holiday: he loses all sense of purpose after a while. The freedom bores him. He has no use for so much freedom. It makes him aware of his limitations, of his worthlessness.'

– Sartre

'The ultimate evil is the ability to make abstract that which is concrete.'

– Sartre

CASE STUDY 23: PASSING THE BUCK OR CARRYING THE CAN?

President Truman's famous dictum 'The buck stops here' (see p.163) is a classic expression of personal responsibility: others may refuse to act in a crucial situation but this person will do so, however painful the consequences. (His two most famous decisions were the dropping of the atom bombs on Hiroshima and Nagasaki (about which see exercise (k), pp.148–9) and the forcing of the UN to send (mostly American) troops to the defence of South Korea in 1949 when the communist North invaded it (see the TV series *MASH* for a variety of views about this).) This case study is designed to test whether you are, on the whole, a buck-passer or a can-carrier; one who risks a head over the parapet, or one who lies low.

(a) You notice some broken glass in a road heavy with traffic.
(b) A close friend has, unknown to her, suffered a grievous loss. You are one of a group who know about this, and discuss who should tell her.
(c) You have indisputable evidence that homosexuals and lesbians are being denied advancement in your workplace because of their sexual orientation. To speak out may bring a black mark against your promotion prospects.
(d) You discover that your boss is engaged in illegal trading.
(e) You see someone quietly pocketing an item from a shelf in a supermarket.
(f) A colleague whom you can't avoid has halitosis.
(g) The phone rings in the main hall in your college/block of flats. The chances are 20–1 against its being for you.
(h) You profoundly disagree with a proposed Government bill. A public demonstration against it is called for.

Be honest in your answers and give yourself a buck/can rating.

CASE STUDY 24: WHO'S TO BLAME?

The following extract is from Arnold Wesker's *Roots*, Act Three. The Bryant family are sitting down for tea, and the discussion ensues. The dilemma Beatie presents is, at one level, obviously unrealistic; at another, it raises some basic issues relating to moral choice and responsibility. See if, preferably in discussion with a group of people, you can answer Beatie's final question. You may well feel that none of the characters emerges from the story with any great credit, but Wesker himself, or Beatie, anyway, was quite convinced that one of the five was in a class apart in terms of personal responsibility, for reasons to do with the greatest moral dilemma of all. See if your conclusion is the same as emerges in the play; for those without a copy, a short note appears at the end of the book – but you would find it interesting to get hold of a copy and read the ensuing conversation for yourself. (See Appendix 2 – after you've argued the question through.)

Beatie: While we're waiting for him I'll set you a moral problem. You know what a moral problem is? It's a problem about right and wrong. I'll get you buggers thinking if it's the last thing I do. Now listen. There are four huts –

Frank: What?

Beatie: Huts. You know – them little things you live in. Now there are two huts on one side of a stream and two huts on the other side. On one side lives a girl in one hut and a wise man in the other. On the other side lives Tom in one hut and Archie in the other. Also there's a ferryman who runs a boat across the river. Now – listen, concentrate – the girl loves Archie but Archie doesn't love the girl. And Tom loves the girl but the girl doesn't go much on Tom.

Jimmy: Poor bugger.

Beatie: One day, the girl hears that Archie – who doesn't love her, remember- is going to America, so she decides to try once more to persuade him to take her with him. So listen what she does. She goes to the ferryman and asks him to take her across. The ferryman says, I will, but you must take off all your clothes.

Mrs Bryant: Well, whatever does he want to ask that for?

Beatie: It doesn't matter why – he does! Now the girl doesn't know what to do so she asks the wise man for advice, and he says, you must do what you think best.

Frank: Well, that wasn't much advice was it?

Beatie: No matter – he gives it. So the girl thinks about it and being so in love she decides to strip.

173

Pearl: Oh, I say!

Mr Bryant: Well, this is a rum old story, isn't it?

Beatie: Shut up, Father, and listen. Now, er– where was I?

Mr Bryant: She was stripping.

Beatie: Oh yes! So, the girl strips and the ferryman takes her over – he doesn't touch her or nothing – just takes her over and she rushes to Archie's hut to implore him to take her with him and to declare her love again. Now Archie promises to take her with him and so she sleeps with him the night. But when she wakes up in the morning he's gone. She's left alone. So she goes across to Tom and explains her plight and asks for help. But soon as ever he knows what she's done, he chucks her out, see? Poor little girl. Left alone, with no clothes and no friends and no hope of staying alive. Now – this is the question, think about it, don't answer quick – who is the person most responsible for her plight?

Jimmy: Well, can't she get back?

Beatie: No, she can't do anything. She's finished. She's had it. Now, *who's to blame?*

(*There is a general air of thought for a moment and Beatie looks triumphant and pleased with herself.*)

Mrs Bryant: Be you drinking your tea, look. Don't you worry about no naked girls. The girls won't get cold but the tea will.

Would the answer to Beatie's question be different if tackled, say, from an existentialist, a utilitarian, or a Kantian point of view?

CASE STUDY 25: EXISTENTIALIST DILEMMAS

In the case studies following the ends–means debate (Chapters Five and Six) the answers to each dilemma depended, in the main, on whether the moral agent judged principles or consequences as paramount in the making of moral decisions. Thus while a choice of procedures was always present, the answer, however unpalatable, was clear-cut once the procedure had been selected. But what is one to do if, having decided that consequences must be the main factor when making moral choices, a variety of possible consequences present themselves? If we settle for duty as our guide, what is to be done when duties clash? Here are some of the types of situations which admit neither of a ready answer nor a clear procedure. They are what may be termed existentialist dilemmas. How would you cope with them?

(a) Father is an executive of his firm in a town in northern England, mother teaches at the local primary school. Two children, 11 and 13, happy at school and in their neighbourhood. Father's next step up the ladder is to move to London: he is offered the post, with the clear warning that if he declines he will go no further in the promotion stakes. Commuting is out of the question if the family unit is to be preserved as it has been. Should they move? On what basis should they reach a decision? Would the matter be any different if the roles of father and mother were reversed?

(b) Long-awaited and carefully planned wedding is due. On the night before the event, bride's (or groom's) much-loved father dies. Should the wedding proceed as planned?

(c) (Sartre's own example.) In German-occupied Paris, a Frenchman feels he should escape to London in order to fight with De Gaulle and the Free French. At home is his elderly ailing mother: father is a Quisling, working for the Germans and treated as dead by the mother; the only other sibling, a brother, had died during the German invasion. The surviving son is all that the old lady has to live for; his leaving her could be the death of her. Should he go?

(d) A counsellor/social worker has little spare time with his/her children, but promises them to set aside a particular evening just for them. Just as the evening is beginning, a person knocks on the door obviously in need of careful counselling which will take the whole evening. What should the parent do?

(e) A close personal friend (not a sexual partner) confides in you that he/she is, as indicated by medical tests, an AIDS carrier. What should you do?

(f) You are falsely charged with a crime. You have an alibi, but giving this will implicate a third party in a distressing way (it could mean the possible break-up of his/her marriage).

(g) You have grown to hold in utter contempt the person you work for, yet to keep the job you have to be excessively subservient towards him/her at every encounter. You could resign, but this would mean no reference, and jobs like yours are hard to find. You have two dependants, but you feel that you are increasingly humiliating yourself by remaining under this person's thumb.

(h) A 17-year-old girl is anorexic. Her weight has fallen to 70 pounds and she is admitted to hospital. Doctors inform her and her parents that if she does not eat she will certainly die. She still refuses to eat, stating that she prefers to die. Her parents agree that the medical authorities shall be permitted to feed her compulsorily. Despite her violent and vituperative opposition to the treatment, this takes place. From that point on, she refuses to speak with or even see her parents again, stating that they have denied her her autonomous right to die. Whatever your view of the treatment, do you think that the parents were right to allow this action? Would you feel the same about any potential suicide, whatever the circumstances?

(i) A young businessman decides to live by the Objectivist principles of Ayn Rand (p. 87). He uses his skills and energies entirely for his own financial benefit; he ruthlessly exerts himself against weaker or less able business rivals, even (or especially) if this means bankrupting them. Inspired by the monetarism of Prime Minister Margaret Thatcher, he steels himself to feel no concern about the human consequences of his transactions. He opposes all forms of state aid to the needy on the grounds that the weak go naturally to the wall. He marries a wealthy woman whom he does not love, and becomes one of the most powerful men in the country. Comment on this scenario in the light of existentialist thought.

Chapter Eight

Morality and religion

It is difficult to recall a civilisation amongst whose citizens religion has not had a major part to play. Any student of social anthropology knows that when studying the lives and values of even the most localised of tribes, one is almost sure to be involved, among other things, in an examination of some form of religious beliefs. These have varied enormously from tribe to tribe and from one civilisation to the next: but in some form they have persisted. Even the socio-economic revolutions of the past century, which have seen a third of the world's population fall under Marxist regimes, have come nowhere near to making religion redundant. Persecuted, religious people have gone underground, only to reappear after the period of persecution. Religion has persevered in the face of opposition, defamation, and execution of its adherents; indeed, in some perverse way, such forms of persecution seem often to have served only to strengthen the steadfastness of believers. As one apologist wrote of the early Christian martyrs: 'The blood of the martyrs was the seed of the church.'

What is it about religion that gives it such durability? There are numerous answers that could be given to this question, depending on what interpretation is adopted for the word 'religion', which is wide-ranging, to put it mildly, in its emphases. Here is one list of characteristics associated with the word. (It is taken from W. P. Alston's *Philosophy of Language*, p. 88, and quoted in John Hospers's *Introduction to Philosophical Analysis*, p. 76f.)

1 Beliefs in supernatural beings (gods).
2 A distinction between sacred and profane objects.
3 Ritual acts focused around sacred objects.
4 A moral code believed to be sanctioned by the gods.
5 Characteristically religious feelings (awe, sense of mystery, sense of guilt, adoration, etc.) which tend to be aroused in the presence of sacred objects, and during the practice of ritual, and which are associated with the gods.
6 Prayer and other forms of communication with gods.
7 A world view, that is, a general picture of the world as a whole and of

the place of the individual in it, including a specification of its overall significance.

8 A more or less total organisation of one's life based on the world view.

9 A social organisation bound together by the preceding characteristics.

From this list one can make some general statements about what it is that makes people 'religious' or attracts them to religion. Some find comfort in the idea of an almighty being who is both aware of their existence and preparing a place for them hereafter. The fear of death, and the desire for a continuing existence after death, must be a major factor in drawing people to believe in one who, being eternal, bridges the great divide between life as it is experienced at present and the life to come and assures believers that they will participate in some way in this eternal experience.

For some people, religion unifies their will-power and gives them a purpose for living: to fulfil the edicts of their faith and, perhaps, encourage, and perhaps compel, others to do likewise. For some, religion codifies and satisfies their intellectual needs: it answers their most searching questions, such as 'why am I here?', 'what is the purpose of life?', 'has man a soul?', 'is there an ultimate reality?' To the lonely, religion can offer a community and the consolation that they are not forgotten; to the rejected, the sense of being accepted; to the dejected, the hope of better things to come. In the name of religion some of the world's most memorable deeds have been performed – both deeds of honour and deeds of depravity. The power of religion over people's lives throughout history has been immeasurable.

The item on the list just quoted which most concerns us is the fourth – the acceptance of morality as in some way sanctioned by the gods. Those who believe this affirm that questions of right and wrong conduct are not just a matter of personal opinion (though this is not to be totally discounted), not just accepting the mores of the community in which they live (though, again, these are not excluded from the decision-making process): what is judged to be right or wrong arises from the belief that (a) God exists, (b) God is moral, in the sense that He is concerned about how His followers behave, and (c) by various methods, God has conveyed His will to those who believe in (a) and (b). 'Not my will, but thine, be done' is the desired response of the faithful.

Anyone who has undertaken any study in the field of religion is likely to be complaining at this stage that this is a one-sided account, since there are religions in the world, such as Buddhism, which don't try to establish any such link between moral well-doing and the will of God, or of the gods. This is a perfectly fair criticism, and explains why the question of the alleged link between religious belief and moral practice is considered primarily in relation to theistic, rather than non-theistic religions (see below). The dividing point, interestingly enough, is the area of the globe in which the world's major religions originated. There have been only two of these: Asia, and the Middle East. From Asia emerged Hinduism, Buddhism, Sikhism, Confucianism, Taoism, Shintoism; from Asia Minor, Judaism, Christianity, Islam, and – if it can be included in the major world religions – Zoroastrianism. Unless you count such isms as Communism and capitalism to be religions – and that would be stretching the definition of the word so widely as to be virtually meaningless – four of the world's five continents remain unrepresented in this list: Europe, North and South America, Africa, and Australasia.

It would be interesting to speculate why this fascinating geographical phenomenon has occurred, but that is beyond the confines of this book. Our concern is with the moral effects of the teachings of the different religions. But before embarking on a discussion of this issue, and the problems to which it gives rise, it is necessary to define a number of terms so as to clarify the distinctions on a philosophical basis.

(a) Pantheism

This word is derived from the Greek words 'pan', meaning 'all' and 'theos' meaning 'God'. As the word therefore implies, pantheism is the belief that God, or godness, or divinity, is to be found in everything that lives: not only in human beings, but in animals, birds, fish, insects, plants, and trees. Even a blade of grass contains, on this view, its special share of divinity. It should not be confused with animism, which is the belief that material objects such as rocks, streams, or pools are animated with their own individual spirits. Pantheism is an ancient belief and, taken to extremes, can bring about what to most of us may appear odd behaviour: the Jainite monks in India, three thousand years ago (and this practice continues among some groups to this day) swept the ground before them as they walked in order to avoid, as far as possible, walking on an insect, and wore a gauze over their faces to avoid accidentally breathing in or swallowing a fly. In the present world there are people known as fruitarians who will eat nothing but fruit, vegetables, nuts, and corn, and are starker than the vegans in that they will eat only the fruit of the plant and will not destroy the main plant itself. Many poets have expressed pantheistic views in their verse, an outstanding example being Shelley's poem 'Adonais', written on the death of his friend and fellow-poet, Keats, which includes the following lines:

He is made one with Nature: there is heard
His voice in all her music, from the moan
Of thunder, to the song of night's sweet bird;
He is a presence to be felt and known

In darkness and in light, from herb and stone,
Spreading itself where'er that Power may move
Which has withdrawn his being to its own . . .
He is a portion of the loveliness
Which once he made more lovely . . .

Shelley described himself as an atheist, but, if this poem reflects his truly-held belief, he was a pantheist. Perhaps he meant to describe himself as a 'non-theist'.

The problem with pantheism, so far as deciding between right and wrong conduct is concerned, is that, because everything that lives is viewed as divine, it is difficult to distinguish between good and bad when reflecting on individual behaviour. This is true of all species in general, but of the human species in particular. If all that is associated with being human is viewed as divine, it is logically impossible to single out any particular form of conduct for condemnation or for praise: all conduct is an expression of the divine nature, and therefore, in the words of one Hindu school which we shall briefly consider, 'beyond good and evil' (interestingly, though used in a different sense, the title of one of Nietzsche's works). Who is to say, and on what basis does he say it, that, while one person's self-sacrifice on the part of another is 'right', another's violent behaviour towards somebody else is 'wrong'? The rightness or wrongness of behaviour is relative, so that, for the pantheist, the issue of the alleged relationship between belief in God and one's sense of moral obligation simply does not arise. One man's 'right' may be another's 'wrong'.

(b) Deism

With this word (derived from the Latin 'deus', meaning 'God') we have to be careful since historically it has been used to express a variety of forms of belief. For our purposes we shall concentrate on its usage during the time of the Enlightenment in the seventeenth and eighteenth centuries in Western Europe, since this particular usage is the most relevant to our present discussion, and offers a distinctive theory of the relationship between God and the world. These deists were men of science, or men influenced by the scientific explorations and discoveries of the period – the age in which the discoveries of Copernicus, Galileo, Newton, and others had shattered the Aristotelian image of a universe with the earth at its centre. As a result of the new image which emerged – born in the realisation that the universe was infinitely vaster and more complex than had previously been held by all except an enlightened few – it was felt necessary on intellectual grounds to dispense with the cosy idea of God as an intimate counsellor of human beings and replace this with the image of

God as the supreme, perfect Being who had devised and then created the universe. Belief in God was therefore retained, since otherwise it would have seemed impossible to explain how the universe came into being, or how our world, culminating in the advent of homo sapiens, arrived as it did. (Darwin, Huxley, and the theory of evolution were still to come.) But God was viewed as a non-interfering God, a *deus ex machina*; and, as a master watchmaker may make a perfect watch which, because it is perfect, will thereafter require no further attention, so God, the master Architect, had created a perfect mechanical universe which, being perfect, required no further intervention from its designer. (After all, if God is by definition perfect, he could hardly create anything less than perfect, whether the issue be considered from the uncritical viewpoint of the believer or the hypercritical viewpoint of the logician.)

The picture of God that deism offers us is that of a Being who, having initiated the whole process of matter in motion, culminating in human life on the planet earth, then retired for a well-earned rest lasting for the remainder of eternity. It is the God of the person who says 'well, there must be someone out there, mustn't there, else how did all this come about?'; it is a God who is an intellectual device, made necessary to explain what is otherwise inexplicable (though of course it hasn't explained it at all but has simply pushed the problem a stage further away). Most importantly of all for the present discussion, it is a God who does not intervene in or intrude on our moral decisions. He is the object of awe and adoration because of the immensity of what He has achieved; but for such a God the mundane activities of people's lives are beneath consideration. As the psalmist wrote (8, 3–4):

When I look at thy heavens, the work of thy fingers,
   the moon and the stars which thou hast established;
what is man that thou art mindful of him,
   and the son of man that thou dost care for him?

The Book of Psalms, like much of the Old Testament, expresses the hope that God really is concerned with 'our goings-out and our comings-in'; the thorough-going deist dispensed altogether with this idea, and in practice this view is not far removed from disbelief, or agnosticism (q.v.).

(c) Theism

According to this view, God is not only the almighty, omniscient creator of the universe, but also continues to be present in the lives of those whom He has created. The theist views God as a constant counsellor and comforter, a friend and a guide. He is therefore involved in the world He has made, and concerned about the moral choices of human beings, His creatures. He has shown them what is right, so that they have no excuse for ignorance on moral matters. This image of God takes no account of the logical problem arising from the association of omnipotence and benevolence as characteristics of the Creator of a world which evinces a considerable amount of natural disorder and human evil, neither of which appears to square with the foregoing features. The problem of evil dominates all theological discussion and holy writings, from Genesis to Revelation and on to the Koran, and will be the basis of a case study at the end of the chapter. The Book of Job represents the peak of philosophical/theological discussion of the problem, written in magnificent prose, and ends with an archetypal theistic statement by Job: 'I had heard of thee with the hearing of mine ear; but now mine eye seeth thee. Wherefore, I abhor myself and repent, in dust and ashes.' (42, 5/6)

It is clearly this theistic interpretation of the deity which raises most directly the question of the logical link between our understanding of the will of God and our own sense of moral obligation. A matter of interest is the fact that the major religions of the world which embraced this view were those which evolved in the Middle East – Judaeism, Christianity, and Islam. It is therefore the ethical views presented by these three religions that I shall have primarily in mind throughout this chapter, though special attention will be paid to Christianity, since it is the religion with which I am most familiar, as will probably be the case with most readers. I shall not be arguing the case for or against either the existence of God or the theistic interpretation of His nature. We shall assume that both of these views are beyond dispute, and consider the ethical implications of the stance, using as source material primarily the holy books of these religions and, secondarily, affirmations by their leading exponents.

Three other words and their meaning should first be noted. (i) *Panentheism* literally means 'all in God', and is a combination of pantheism and theism. From pantheism it takes the view that God exists in and through all living things; but so far as the pantheistic interpretation is concerned, this represents the limits of God's existence. Panentheism asserts that God is all this and more: He is able, so to speak, to stand or exist outside what we define as life, being therefore both the underlying essence of all that we know to exist, but not confined by this; for the panentheist there can be no boundaries to God's existence.

The other two words can be compared and contrasted side by side. (ii) *Atheism* means, literally, 'no God', while (iii) *agnosticism*, from the Greek 'gnosis', meaning 'knowledge' with the prefix 'a' meaning 'no' or 'not', means 'no knowledge'. The difference between the two becomes clear if they are considered in terms of belief, or lack of it. The atheist affirms, positively and absolutely, that there is no God; the agnostic takes a less forthright line, arguing that the evidence for or against is inconclusive.

The atheist will say, 'I believe that there is no God'; the agnostic, 'I don't believe there is a God'. These may at first sight seem similar statements, but, when you think about them carefully, there is a subtle and profound difference between the two stances. My experience is that, while a considerable number of people are happy, like T. H. Huxley, who coined the word, to describe themselves as agnostics (Buddha was probably one) few are prepared to take the more radical step, illustrated in the writings of Bertrand Russell, of declaring themselves to be actual atheists, and there is still a good deal of repugnance in people's reaction to the word. The reaction of most of the United States, for instance, remains as it was when Russell was a visiting professor there, and atheism is treated as a disease comparable to syphilis or the bubonic plague.

THEISM AND ETHICS: IS THERE A LOGICAL CONNECTION?

As has already been noted in Chapter Four, a considerable number of people, if asked whence they derive their knowledge of right and wrong behaviour, will answer, quite simply, 'from God.' For many of these people the philosophical agonisings already described in this book seem pointless, if not absurd. If God exists as an omnipotent, omniscient Being, then we have the obvious answer to our quandaries, moral as well as intellectual. All we need to do is to obey the will of God, and we shan't go far wrong.

The problems created by this viewpoint have already been hinted at in Chapter 4 (pp.75–8), but we must now explore these in more detail. The question we face is whether there is a clear philosophical link between the statements 'God wills me to do x' and 'I ought to do x'. There are two ways of interpreting the former of these: either x is right because God wills it, or God wills x because it is right. The implications of both of these must be examined.

X is right because God wills it

On this view, God is seen as the creator of morality, the instigator of ethical principles, the one who determines what conduct shall be adjudged right, and what wrong. He is the absolute authority in these matters, and His followers are therefore in duty bound to behave as He has directed.

There are four main problems with this point of view.

(i) It portrays God as a purely arbitrary being. Behaviour is not right or wrong for any *reason*, (not, that is, because of human reasoning) but simply on His say-so. He has decreed certain forms of behaviour as being in accordance with His will, but He could, had He wished, just as easily have decreed otherwise. Forms of behaviour which are generally looked upon as being virtuous would then have been viewed as vicious, and vices virtues.

(ii) From this follows the fact that this view leaves no room for exploration of either moral principles or moral actions on the part of human beings. The individual is left with no initiative to weigh up the pros and cons of forms of behaviour: rather, he assumes the role of a servant, even a slave, taking orders and obeying without question. It seems impossible to describe this as mature moral behaviour. What 'mature moral behaviour' means in this context will be explored in detail in the next chapter, but it may be briefly stated at this point that two qualities which seem to be imperative are *freedom* and *reason*. The moral agent can hardly be described as making a decision if no choice is available to him. For example, the prisoner who cleans out his cell on orders from a guard can hardly expect to receive praise for this; likewise the soldier who stands to attention on the corporal's command. Blind obedience, desirable though it may be at times (in the middle of a battle, for instance), is not an element of moral behaviour, because it reduces the agent to an automaton.

Similarly, it seems essential that the person who makes a moral choice should be able to give reasons to explain why he chose course x rather than course y. In one sense, admittedly, he could be said to be giving a reason when he replies, 'I chose x rather than y because that was God's command'. But that is hardly what is normally meant by 'giving reasons', any more than is the answer 'because I felt like it', or 'because the coin came down heads rather than tails'. The question which must be put, and to which some sort of rational reply should be made, is, what factors brought you to consider action x preferable, morally speaking, to action y? And – perhaps even more significant – how would you defend that action against one who did not acknowledge the existence of the God whom you aver to be the source of any rule you may be obeying?

(iii) The next problem relates to that last question. If God is the sole creator and source of morality, it follows logically that only those who acknowledge Him as such can be described as behaving morally. The atheist or agnostic, however outwardly 'moral' he may seem to be, must be judged either to be acting in some kind of limbo or no man's land, with his behaviour described, at best, as neutral; or, even worse, he may be accused of simply living off the 'spiritual and moral capital' offered to him by, or revealed to him through, those who do believe, and have created a moral ethos in the community in which the atheist participates whether he acknowledges it or not. (This may sound a peculiar argument, but I have heard it used extensively in both Britain and – especially – the United States.)

This whole argument seems to be unrealistic. It simply will not do to affirm that atheists, or non-believers, are either immoral, amoral, or learning morality at second hand from surrounding believers, or from believers of an earlier generation. We must all have met people raised in a non-religious environment whose lives are just as morally acceptable as are those of people raised in a religious context. Sometimes, in fact, the boot is on the other foot. The South African Nationalist leader, the atheist, Nelson Mandela, was prepared to spend decades of his life in prison rather than modify his opposition to that country's apartheid policy. We thus have the example of an atheist sacrificing his freedom rather than compromise himself on the apartheid policy, viewed by many people outside South Africa as the most unjust and inhumane form of government since that of Nazi Germany; but those who defended it were starkly religious Afrikaners who believed, sincerely and devoutly, that apartheid was God's will.

(iv) This leads to what is, perhaps, the most difficult problem of all for those who take the obedience-to-the-will-of-God approach: one would have thought that, if this is to be the be-all and end-all of moral behaviour, there would have been unambiguous information as to precisely what His will required of us. After all, if we were to be punished for breaking the law of our country, those who administer justice would be able to point to the law as it is written, and to indicate in what respect we had broken it. If there were any ambiguity in the law, this would be recognised and removed by the legislature. With God's law we are not so fortunate; by a careful selection of texts from the scriptures, which are believed to be the basic source of our understanding of the will of God, we can conscientiously follow diametrically opposing paths on most of the great moral issues, such as war and peace, drinking alcohol, sex, and, as we have seen, race. It seems, for example, disconcerting to read, on the one hand 'drink our wine with a merry heart; for God has already approved what you do' (Eccles. 9,7) and, on the other, 'Wine is a mocker, strong drink a brawler, and whoever is led astray by it is not wise' (Prov. 20,1). If the law of the land were presented to us with such inconsistencies, the country would be in a state of chaos.

Apologists for the will-of-God theory argue that we must understand the scriptures as interpreted by the Church – by the Fathers, and Elders, and Councils. Through their pronouncements, it is suggested, what appear to simple minds to be anomalies are put in context and ironed out. This answer might help to allay uncertainty if the Church's pronouncements over the centuries had shown any degree of consistency: but this is not the case. To read Church history is to read of leaders and councils in constant contention with each other (on theological, as well as moral, matters, of course). On issues as central and important to many individuals as birth control, taking up arms, and women's rights and responsibilities we have what can be described only as a mishmash. One wonders, for instance, to what extent in our own time the leaders of the

Roman Catholic Church will be able to find agreement on any issue with leaders of the fundamentalist sects, such as Baptists or Pentecostalists.

Even if we add the clause that the individual's conscience must be the final arbiter as to what is God's will, we are still left with the problem, mentioned in Chapter Four, as to what exactly the conscience is, and what the factors are which lead any individual to make a conscientious decision. There is the added problem that the conscience shares with the scriptures and Church councils the fact that it speaks ambiguously. Some of the world's most dreadful deeds have been performed with a perfectly clear conscience: the burning of heretics, the hanging of child thieves, the stoning to death of adulterers: all have been committed by men who conscientiously believed that their behaviour was willed by the Almighty.

God wills x because it is right

On this view, God is no longer seen as the creator of morality but as the omniscient mentor who points us, so to speak, in the right direction. He knows what is best for us, and, if we are wise, we mortal beings will take advantage of His expertise, as students will make use of the insights offered to them by an authority in their field of study.

This is a more philosophically acceptable interpretation of the problem, even though it still retains the inherent weakness, already outlined, of the ambiguity expressed in those areas which allegedly contain God's Counsel. More important for those who wish to retain the notion of the will of God as basic for moral decision-making, it effectively makes God redundant. What exactly are we asserting when we say that God wills x because it is right? If the statement is carefully analysed, it becomes clear that x is independent of God's judgment: whether He says so or not, x is right, and the moral agent can, if he so chooses, explore for himself the possibilities raised by any moral dilemma and reach his own conclusion on the basis of his own judgment. God's omniscience may be treated either as merely a confirming characteristic of the problem, or ignored entirely, as a student of psychology may ignore the works of Freud. Critics of such a modus operandi may argue that the agent would thereby be depriving himself of wise and authoritative guidance, and maybe this would be true: but the point we're discussing is not whether it is wise to equate my sense of right and wrong with the will of God but whether there is a logical link between the two. Since, on this second interpretation of that alleged link, forms of behaviour are accepted as right or wrong whether God says so or not, this link manifestly does not exist. Some people may find it helpful to use religious sources in their quest for right behaviour, but others may justifiably say that they will rely solely on their own initiative, experience, reason, and feelings in order to reach a satisfactory answer in their moral quest; for them, God is superfluous.

And it would be a wild judgment to assert that the behaviour of those who have thus chosen their moral standards has been generally worse than that of those who link their behaviour with their religious beliefs. The evidence, as we shall see in a moment, suggests that the situation is sometimes quite the reverse of this.

It may be argued that if, as Christians suggest, *agape* (three syllables), or love, stands as the highest motive for human behaviour, and if, as the Christian, at least, believes, the life of Jesus expressed this perfectly, then it behoves us to make him the model of our own behaviour. Three comments can be made on this. Firstly, the value and centrality of love in human relationships stand secure independently of Christian teaching or of any religious teaching whatever. Its expression in the New Testament certainly reinforced its worth; but it was advocated also in the Old Testament, and is to be found in Buddhist, Hindu, and Taoist teaching. It is also to be found as the basic motivation of atheists and agnostics, of humanists and heretics: Christians have no unique claim here – 'Love they neighbour as thyself' was written a thousand years before either Jesus or St Paul arrived on the scene. (See pp.306–9 for an analysis of the word 'love'.)

Secondly, and purely practically: if the Christian theological assertions about the nature of Jesus are true – that he was the divine Son of God – then, to put it mildly, he had an advantage over the rest of the human race so enormous as to place him in a category all on his own and make the idea of imitating him quite absurd – more absurd than expecting an infant to write a sequel to Wittgenstein's *Tractatus Logico-Philosophicus*, or take on Jack Nicklaus on the golf course. The theological affirmation that, despite his divinity, Jesus was fully human like the rest of us, 'tempted like as we are', does nothing to erase the problem. If he was divine he was special, and can consequently have no contribution to make to the resolution of moral dilemmas faced by the remainder of the human race.

Finally, even if we set these two objections aside, it still does not follow from a philosophical point of view that Jesus's followers should aim to live as he did. To say this is to commit the naturalistic fallacy mentioned in Chapter Four. In effect, the argument takes the form of a syllogism:

Love is the perfect basis for behaviour
Jesus expressed love perfectly
we should try to live like Jesus.

Few will deny that it would not harm society if more people did so live, assuming for the sake of the argument that the second of these statements is true: but there is no *logical* justification for the bottom line. Only if we begin by stating something like 'every individual ought to try and imitate perfection when he sees it' can the conclusion be logically arrived at, otherwise we are guilty of trying to derive an 'ought' from an 'is'; and if we do add this extra statement at the beginning, we are still left with the question: from whence is *that* ought-statement derived?

The conclusion here seems clear-cut: while many people actually make a connection in their minds between their religious beliefs and moral behaviour, there is no logical link between the two. In the end, religion and ethics belong to two quite different levels, or areas, of experience.

Theistic religion as the sanction for morality

Many readers may at this point acknowledge the validity of the argument so far, but will contend that, while no demonstrable *logical* connection between moral behaviour and religious belief can be established, there remains a *practical* connection. As a simple matter of fact it will be said, millions of people for at least three millennia have made the connection in their own lives. Whatever may be demonstrated by philosophical analysts, they have lived in the conviction that what they believed to be right or wrong behaviour had been sanctioned by God. The Ten Commandments are consequently viewed by these people not as rules for nomads concocted by Moses but as a direct expression of the will of Jehovah; the Gospels are not held as semi-reliable documents written by simple-minded people, but as the living embodiment of the Word (*logos*) of God. Whether or not these are logical judgments is therefore irrelevant: great people and simple people have throughout the centuries made the connection and have demonstrated the truth of their convictions by the fact that in practice, that is, in their behaviour, the convictions work. 'By their fruits shall ye know them', or, put negatively in the words of a latter-day apologist for Christianity, C. S. Lewis, 'We only learn to behave ourselves in the presence of God; and when the sense of that presence is removed, mankind tends to lark about'.

Since we are dealing here with the private beliefs of individuals which are not open to the process of verification, it is impossible to discuss this matter philosophically. All one can ask is whether the historical facts support the contention as just expressed. Much will depend here on where one looks, and how comprehensively. By a careful selection of names over the centuries, a Christian, or Islamic, or Jewish apologist could no doubt paint a picture of honesty, compassion, and generally acceptable behaviour. The question remains, however, whether (a) those societies which rejected the concept of a link between God's will and man's sense of moral obligation were in fact morally 'lower' than those which affirmed such a link; and (b) the example of communities which on the whole have confessed a theistic belief reveal themselves as 'good fruit', in the sense that they did, on the whole, 'behave themselves'.

To discuss these questions at length is beyond the scope of this book, (see Chapter Four under 'God' for an earlier reflection) and I will content myself with two brief statements. The first is a quotation from an article in the *Encyclopaedia of Philosophy* by P. H. Nowell-Smith, entitled 'Religion and Morality' (p. 150). The author is comparing the Judaeo-Christian tradition with those of Greece, Rome, and China. He writes:

In these three civilisations morality and religion were to a large extent independent of each other, and the line between a man's moral duties to his fellow men and his religious duties to the gods or the shades of his departed ancestors was not blurred, as it was by the Jews and Christians. Yet the moral principles of these three civilisations were not, on the whole, lower than ours; indeed they were, in their main outlines, identical.

As for point (b) raised above: I can state only that after sixteen years as an ordained minister of the Church, and with several degrees in and books on theology behind me, I have over the ensuing years become increasingly convinced that Christianity, and theism generally, is more a force for harm than for good. With its emphases – both in its sacred writings and its affirmations through the centuries – on the impotence of the individual vis-à-vis the omnipotent deity, its exclusivity which condemns non-believers to the outer darkness, its life-denying condemnation of natural human pleasures, and its incipient appeal to human greed with its continual promises of rewards in heaven, it seems now to me that Christianity, as represented by both its founder, Jesus, and its followers over the centuries, far from adding force to the idea that religious belief and moral practice are linked, has demonstrated that such a link is, to put it mildly, unlikely. There have been 'moral' Christians: but the connection has, I believe, been quite accidental.

MORALITY AND EASTERN THOUGHT

We conclude this study with a brief consideration of the approach to moral issues expressed in certain Eastern philosophies. Whether you consider them to be religions or not will depend on your choice of essentials from the list given at the start of the chapter. There is no theism in these philosophies, no belief in a personal, omnipotent God who can intervene in and direct a person's life. Instead, we have expressions of pantheism, deism, agnosticism, even atheism. They represent an approach to living so different from that of the West that most books on philosophy ignore them entirely (and even here they are receiving no more than a passing reference). But perhaps just a few paragraphs will suffice to indicate that any study of philosophy which ignores the East would be like studying the history of Communism without reference to China.

A few generalisations may help to bring into focus the differences of emphasis between East and West. As will have become apparent from earlier chapters, Western philosophy sets great store on logic and reason: man's capacity to think is viewed as his highest and noblest quality. The problems of ethics which we have looked at in this book have been presented (I hope) on a *rational* basis: you have been asked to *reason* your way through a series of moral dilemmas. The part played by other aspects of the human personality – such as emotion, or will-power – has not been overlooked: but the act of studying moral philosophy must have been basically one of *thinking* (which should have done you no lasting harm!)

Allied with reason is the Western desire to be up and doing. The typical Westerner wishes to be active, even aggressive, involved in affairs, creating, manufacturing. The United States epitomises this: there is a country brimful of workaholics, all seeking to get ahead of their neighbours on the ladder of achievement, which is assessed in terms of income. 'Better nouveau riche than never riche' could be their motto, and I have written the following revision of the Lord's Prayer for them and their European counterparts:

Paternal Banker
Which art in Wall Street:
Dollar be thine aim;
Thy profits come,
Thy perks belong To my account, as they do in Wall Street.
And give me this day my daily interest;
And forgive me when not in credit,
As I make bankrupt all my debtors;
And lead me not into altruism,
But deliver me from a social conscience.
For Thine is the capital, the lucre, and the rake-off
Till I rest on my pickings. Amen.

(Even the biro with which I wrote those words reflects their message. It has inscribed on it two numbers –11501 and 42424 – with the statement: 'IF BOTH NUMBERS MATCH YOU COULD BE THE INSTANT

WINNER OF 50,000 DOLLARS'. Is this what is meant by writing for profit?)

Western philosophy and, with it, theistic religion is geared to changing things. Westerners have sent missionaries to foreign parts to persuade the people of those parts to change their ways, their customs, their morals. Westerners have engaged in wars on ideological grounds, and have countenanced revolutions, both industrial and social. It is totally unsurprising that the religion which accommodated itself to the West with scarcely a ripple on the surface was Christianity, with its aggressive proselytising zeal (akin to that of the Muslims, of course, but theirs was a different arena of influence). 'In this sign conquer' dreamed Constantine of the Cross, and today it is difficult to know whether to speak of Western or Christian culture.

What, then, of the East? While reason is by no means excluded in their philosophical processes, it is acknowledged as only one of several faculties which make human beings human. Intuition, emotion, insight are all viewed as equal partners with reason in the process of arriving at a point of view, or deciding how to behave, just as they are when painting a picture, composing a song, or arranging a vase of flowers. In contrast to Western activity (or activeness) they advocate passivity. *Being* is more important than *doing* and infinitely more than *having*. They emphasise a basic dichotomy in life which the West, until recently, has generally lost sight of: the Yang and the Yin, the active and the passive, the male and the female, the dominant and the submissive. Unless these are in harmony, it is believed, life will be distorted and unfulfilled.

Time is viewed as illusory. Our *karma* (an important word in Eastern philosophy) sets us inexorably at our starting-point in life, but from that point the choices we make are made freely. This gives an eternal dimension to the present – the ever present *now* – and means that there is no need to hurry, to go rushing into revolutionary change, since change is an illusion. Against the Western emphasis on individual self-awareness the philosophers of Asia taught that individual consciousness must eventually (and in some moments of insight some sense that it may already) be caught up in the vast stream of the universal consciousness (Brahman, the Tao), or we lose our consciousness in the blissful state of *Nirvana*. This is the state beyond desire, and is achieved, according to Buddha, by meditation rather than disputation, withdrawal rather than involvement, peace within oneself rather than power over others or obedience to a superior Being.

Buddhism

The concept of Nirvana was central to the teachings of *Buddha* (BC 563–483). The name means 'the enlightened one', and his real name was

Gautama Sakyamuni. He summarised human experience in his Four Noble Truths:

1 To live means to suffer. In this world a certain amount of suffering is inevitable.
2 The origin of suffering – for oneself and for others – lies in craving or grasping after such things as wealth or power.
3 The cessation of suffering is possible through the discarding of selfish goals: in effect, by removing from our vocabulary such words as 'me' or 'mine'.
4 The way to this cessation, which can lead to enlightenment, is what is known as the Noble Eightfold Path or, simply, the middle path. This will lead to Nirvana, which means, literally, the 'blowing-out' as of a flame: the state beyond desire.

The eight steps included attitudes of mind and forms of behaviour (for instance, no killing was allowed, so a Buddhist could not be a soldier or a butcher) but the central feature was contemplation, through which alone a state of peace and joy could be attained. This contemplation would lead a person to realise that all events in space and time occur through the operating of regulating principles. Fire burns, the lotus blooms, tigers hunt. Every action implacably brings its fruit in due time – bitter or sweet: and human free choice determines which will occur ('Karma' means, literally, 'action', meaning the consequences of previous actions). Behaviour like taking life, violence, stealing, lying, and so on are all against man's true interest and prejudicial to the attainment of Nirvana, for which a right way of life is a precondition.

Many of the issues discussed in this book would have been viewed by Buddha as either too obvious for discussion, or pointless. Since the goal of all human aspiration is Nirvana, questions like the nature of values, ends and means, absolutism and relativism, are solved. Nirvana is the only ultimate value, the end to which all else should be subordinated, and so the only absolute. The question of the origin of the sense of ought does not arise. Why the universe exists in such a way that choices have to be made is an unanswerable question. The man struck by a poisoned arrow does not waste time guessing what the arrow is made of or where it comes from: he rushes for an antidote. In a world of suffering, it is therefore mad to speculate on the reasons why things are as they are, instead of rushing to end suffering by taking the noble path.

Taoism

This idea of a path, or way, was found also in China, a country into which Buddhism spread, particularly after its adherents were driven from India by the Moslems. 'Tao' means 'Way', and is associated with

Lao Tsu, a teacher who is alleged to have lived in the sixth century BC and to have been the author of the most revered of Taoist writings, the *Tao Te Ching*. Whether or not Lao Tsu was an actual person (the name means 'Great Master') and, if so, the actual author of these writings, is unimportant: they exist, and express a particular philosophy.

The *Tao Te Ching* means 'Classic of the Way and Power', which indicates something of the mystical nature of its themes. This mysticism centres on the inner harmony which a person achieves through his awareness of being part of the underlying principle of the universe (something akin to the Greek *logos*), the inexpressible source of living: a pantheistic philosophy, perhaps, though no Taoist would use that word. The writings are cryptic in expression, appealing to the whole of a reader's personality, not just to his reason. For those trained solely in the Western way of presenting a case – through logic and rational argument – much of the *Tao Te Ching* may seem incomprehensible and even self-contradictory. But if the reader reads slowly, and allows the words to penetrate beyond the purely rational faculties, he may discover that there is more to 'a philosophy of life' than can be dealt with in an examination paper. The following passage is typical:

Under heaven all can see beauty only because there is ugliness.
All can know good as good only because there is evil.
Therefore having and not having arise together.
Difficult and easy complement each other.
Long and short contrast each other;
High and low rest upon each other;
Voice and sound harmonise each other;
Front and back follow each other.
(trans. Gia-Fu Feng and Jane English, 1972)

Taoism lays great emphasis on passivity, on 'letting things be'. The universe pre-existed man by billions of years, and will continue to be after all agonies of moral choice have died away. The wise man will therefore leave such matters to those still bound by temporal considerations and will himself exist (to use a by now familiar phase) 'beyond good and evil'. Towards governments his attitude will be indifferent if not anarchic; towards wealth and prestige, disinterest; towards social norms, unconcern. The *Tao Te Ching* says:

Do you think you can take over the universe and improve it?
I do not believe it can be done.

The universe is sacred. You cannot improve it.
If you try to change it you will ruin it.
If you try to hold it, you will lose it.

This emphasis on the Yin rather than the Yang is central to Taoism.

Hinduism: Advaita Vedanta

Hinduism spans three millennia, and has many forms. Among the most advanced is one expressed in the Middle Ages by the 'master', Shankara. 'Vedanta' means the ultimate significance of the early writings called 'Veda'. 'Advaita' is one of its main trends. There is a host of literature on Hinduism, and if you are interested you could well find helpful the suggested further reading at the end of the book.

Although Shankara developed his thoughts with a complicated apparatus of logical argument which sounds Western in its approach, unlike Plato and most Western thinkers he does not start with ideas or words but with human experience in its fulness, with varying states of consciousness. Four main states are recognised: dreamless sleep, dreaming, waking (or empirical consciousness), and 'the fourth' – the indescribable state of objectless self-awareness in which the individual spirit realises its identity with the 'ground of its being', a phrase employed by Kierkegaard (and further illustrating a common element between certain expressions of existentialism and certain elements in Asian thought).

Corresponding to the four states are four levels of truth. In sleep there is ignorance of subjects and objects. In dreams this ignorance is 'sublated' (contradicted or corrected at a higher level) by the dreamer's awareness of both himself and the dream-objects. Dreaming consciousness is sublated by waking consciousness, which sharply divides the experiencing subject from the social world of reality. For the enlightened – and on the timescale of Hindu cosmology, with its infinite number of reincarnations, everyone will eventually become enlightened – the dual experience of waking is itself sublated by the non-dual mystic contemplation.

This probably sounds very complicated, but the philosophy perhaps becomes clearer through studying Vedanta ethics, the key to which is its view of truth. The Western tradition (which we have explored in most of the earlier chapters) sees truth and falsehood like a game of chess. The game is played on the restricted surface of the board, on which all squares are either black or white. Each piece moves according to pre-determined rules and, although players have a free choice amongst the permitted moves, some moves are 'good' as they lead to taking one of the

194

opponent's pieces, and a succession of good moves may lead to winning the game. A player may not know the best move to make next, but there is no ambiguity about the rules, and all players agree about what counts as taking a piece and winning a game.

Advaita Vedanta goes beyond both the simple idea that statements are true or false and the subjectivist view that there is no truth except what is 'true for me'. For Vedanta there is one supreme goal, realisation of the Absolute, which is the ultimate truth. This is the top of the mountain, which all travellers (whether they know it or not) are bound for. But, though the goal is the same for everyone, each traveller must start from wherever he happens to find himself (like the *Geworfenheit* of Heidegger, with the difference that for Vedanta, as throughout Hinduism generally, the starting-point is fixed by *karma*). No two people are in exactly the same spot, and in seeking the goal there is not only one path up the mountain. In fact, there are not only many paths, some broad and much used, others made by a single individual, but they seem to go in different directions, and even for a while to go down instead of up (a not unnatural phenomenon on mountains). People may be in all sorts of places and seemingly moving apart, but still in fact be moving to the same peak. Even along the same path one position may be right for one person because it is higher than where he was before, but it may be wrong for another who starts from a different point. Places on the map are in themselves neither good nor bad, right or wrong, but for any particular individual to move to a certain place is either good or bad, according to whether it takes him nearer to or further from the goal: what matters is not position but direction, not where you are but which way you are going. This is the relativism mentioned earlier.

Translated into the terms of Western moral philosophy – and some of these terms have no equivalent in Sanskrit – *there are no absolute moral laws, no objective standards, no categorical imperatives, no universal duties*. But there are different ways, notably the ways of the well-trodden paths of the ancient philosophies or religions, but also modern secular ideologies and the private paths of individuals: and within each school and ideology there are rules and conventions. Normally the individual moves in the right direction by living in accordance with these ideologies, not merely by following the rules blindly, but by entering more deeply into their inner essence. This does not exclude the possibility that some individuals may feel impelled to deviate from the tradition in which they find themselves, perhaps by reforming it, by starting a new movement, or affiliating to another one, or by following a lonely course of their own. Apart from the individual concerned, and conceivably some spiritual teacher of great insight, nobody else can judge for certain whether he is moving in the right direction.

For all its breadth and complexity, Vedanta has, then, a very clear message to individuals. You can only live *your* life. Where you are and what sort of person you are is no accident. Follow the path you are in as long as you feel able to; or, as the Quaker and pacifist, George Fox, said to a soldier: 'Wear thy sword as long as thou canst'. Because there is a goal you will, sooner or later, somehow or other, be drawn towards it. When this time comes you will not need clever arguments, you will not need to drain your subconscious emotions or follow the peer-group consensus. At the right moment the guru appears: not necessarily as a wise man, but perhaps through a critical personal event, a book, a work of art, or a natural scene (guru means, quite literally, from darkness (gu) to light (ru)).

The goal itself, according to Vedanta, is in no way a form of moral ideal, a sort of perfect personality; the goal transcends the 'pairs of opposites' which run throughout everyday life – heat and cold, hatred and love, pleasure and pain, good and bad. The enlightened man is not totally good but 'beyond good and evil' (the same phrase as Nietzsche's, but quite differently used). Good and evil are tied to a purpose; the enlightened man has fulfilled his purpose: he has nothing more to attain.

The teaching of Vedanta was given prominence in the nineteenth century by the advocacy of the Indian writer Ramakrishna, and, in our own time, even more so, by Radhakrishnan. Other Westerners have begun to discover not only Vedanta, but also that the philosophies of Buddhism and Taoism are by no means void of consequence for the West. Even though we may find some of the Eastern emphases difficult to accommodate into our psyches (there seem, for example, to be some social evils such as apartheid which demand practical application of energy rather than contemplation) there is, I hope, enough, even in the brief glimpses of the East reflected in this section, to cause any thoughtful Westerner to look favourably on the possibilities of dialogue with his Eastern counterpart. It is a dialogue which is long overdue: it is pursued at length in my *East of Existentialism*.

CASE STUDY 26: EASTERN AND MIDDLE EASTERN PHILOSOPHIES AND THE PROBLEM OF SUFFERING

One constant theme in this chapter has been man's experience of suffering and his reaction to it, philosophically and otherwise. Any person who holds the view that life has a pattern, a purpose, a discernible design must come to terms, one way or another, with the fact of suffering. Only those who die young are likely to avoid it, directly or indirectly. We shall in this study outline first the areas or types of suffering which have caused the problem; some of the answers given at different times by apologists for particular beliefs; and the alternatives facing a person as ways of coming to terms with suffering.

Which theory, or combination of theories, seems to you the most sensible for a human being, faced with the inevitability of suffering, to adopt? Would you wish to add to the variety of viewpoints presented?

1 Types of suffering we may encounter

(a) Natural – 'acts of God' in legal terminology: floods, earthquakes, fire, volcanic eruptions, etc.

(b) Disease, including (i) those associated with forms of human behaviour, such as syphilis or lung cancer, and (ii) where there is no apparent connection with human behaviour, such as meningitis or arthritis.

(c) Accidents, including (i) those associated with the fact of living, such as drowning, falling, choking, etc., and (ii) those associated with human activity – road accidents, atomic radiation, electrocution, etc.

(d) Suffering deliberately inflicted by one person, or set of persons, on another – exploitation, starvation, incarceration, torture, murder, etc.

(e) Suffering caused by human stupidity, insensitivity, or greed – loneliness, rejection, psychopathic disorders, etc.

2 The purpose of suffering

Through history, people of differing religious or philosophical persuasions have attempted to give a coherent explanation of the *role of suffering*, directing their attention to some, if not all, of the above. Among what they have come up with are:

(a) God's punishment for the sins of the parents, and sometimes even earlier generations (many references in the Old Testament to the effect of sin 'on your children and your children's children unto the third or fourth generation'): seems somewhat unfair on the children, to say nothing of the great-great-grandchildren.

(b) God's punishment on the individual who has sinned (Billy Graham on film star Jayne Mansfield, decapitated in a car smash; Moral Majority leader Jerry Falwell on AIDS and homosexuality; Ian Paisley, extreme Northern Irish Protestant, on attempted assassination of Pope John Paul II, etc.). All seem somewhat arbitrary: not *every* homosexual gets AIDS; not *every* promiscuous person has his/her head severed; not *every* Pope gets shot at. There is, admittedly, more consistency in God's alleged behaviour at the time of the Flood, when He decided to get rid of the lot of them, with minimal exceptions, and start again, but this behaviour seems extreme. (This answer should not just be treated frivolously; there are many people throughout the world living lives of inner torment because they believe that the wrath of God has descended or is due to descend upon them.)

(c) Man brings suffering on himself: sometimes true (wars, certain diseases, nuclear radiation, pain as a result of mental cruelty – lack of love – etc.) but not true of all diseases, or of 'acts of God', unless you say that people shouldn't live near volcanoes, or areas where hurricanes or earthquakes, or famines are likely to occur.

(d) To increase compassion in others (Mother Teresa on the Ethiopian famine (p.54)). What would be the Ethiopian view of this theory that people are a means to an end rather than an end in themselves?

(e) Suffering purifies the sufferer, giving him a more mature, reflective, and more broadly sympathetic view of life and other people; the person who hasn't experienced suffering remains an innocent, and therefore shallow, person. – Impossible to generalise: some people grow in this way through suffering, others become cynical and bitter. If suffering is simply accepted as a fact of life, as seems to be the case, there seems no more reason to engage in this special pleading on its behalf than for the fact of losing one's youth, or lacking certain physical or mental skills.

(f) To test the believer's faith. It is no doubt the case that if the holding of a certain set of beliefs ensured the absence of suffering, those beliefs would have universal appeal. This answer is a disguise for the more general view, expressed by adherents of all the theistic religions, that we don't really know why God, assuming Him to be benevolent, allows the faithful to suffer, but that this ignorance on our part is brought about simply because, unlike the Almighty, we can't see the whole scene. If we could see, as God sees, *sub specie aeternitatis* (from the standpoint of eternity) then we should understand, and cease to question. This is the philosophy expressed in the Book of Job in the Old Testament, and its argument is probably the most honest of the theistic arguments and, incidentally, the nearest that any theistic work comes to the Eastern approach as expressed, for instance, in Buddhism or the Vedanta.

(g) A test for the next incarnation: bear suffering patiently now, and life will be better in your reincarnation (Buddhism, Hinduism). This no doubt enables some people to endure suffering more contentedly than might otherwise be the case; but since the doctrine of reincarnation is totally unverifiable, this must be interpreted as a mental exercise to cushion off some of the misery of suffering. Did it enable the thousands of people in Bhopal in India who suffered agonisingly as a result of the leakage from the chemical plant nearby – some of whom must have held this belief – to achieve greater equanimity?

(h) One school of thought, the Waldorf School, founded by Rudolf

Steiner, tackles the problem for any teleological view of life raised by the existence of severely subnormal – particularly mentally subnormal – people. Based on the doctrine of reincarnation, the view is held that, because such handicapped people have no responsibilities and have to be cared for by others throughout their lives, this particular incarnation represents for them, a 'holiday' incarnation, a break from the responsibilities normally encountered in life. The same problem arises here as with the previous answer: the unverifiability of the doctrine of reincarnation. The handicapped are in any case running a grave risk on this 'holiday': they may encounter communities which spurn them and treat them cruelly, and not as in a caring community like the Waldorf.

(i) Suffering is necessary if great achievements are to be made. Words like 'heroism', 'endurance', 'loyalty', 'strength of character', etc., would have little or no meaning without the presence of suffering to which such qualities are a reaction. This is really an extension of Heidegger's view that only the inevitability of death motivates people to do *anything* worthwhile. It is sound as a descriptive statement of the nature of human existence: is it any comfort to the parents who lose their teenage son through cancer, or the husband whose wife is murdered because he is a Catholic and she a Protestant?

(j) Suffering is vicarious: one person can suffer, or die, for another or for others (Judaism, Christianity). There have been notable examples of this throughout history, symbolised in the legend of Hiawatha who died self-sacrificially but from whose grave maize began to grow. Voluntary self-sacrifice has constituted a poignant element in human life, creating one of its deepest mysteries, and perhaps it is a central fact of evolution (bees dying to save their hives, the pheasant exposing itself to save its offspring, the soldier who fights on in what he knows will be a deadly encounter in order to give his comrades time to regroup, etc.). But most human suffering is involuntary, and this argument, valid though it is in its own context, is irrelevant to the main problem. Most people who suffer do not *choose* to do so.

(k) Human suffering reflects the nature of God, who is a suffering God. It is therefore part of the central mystery of life. This is a theological (theistic) argument which cannot be discussed philosophically. Even if it is assumed to be true, it still doesn't explain why some people suffer almost infinitely more than others. Are we to say that a person who has lived a hard-working and satisfying life, has children of whom both parents can be fond and proud, and dies peacefully in his sleep, has experienced less of life's mysteries than has one with a sickly constitution, an unhappy marriage, children who reject him, and a painful, drawn-out death?

The idea seems morbid. (It also incidentally suggests that the theist cannot logically claim that God is (i) omnipotent and (ii) benevolent. Either He *can* remove suffering but *won't*, or He *wants* to remove suffering but *can't*. He is thus either a monster, or is impotent.)

3 Attitudes to suffering

(a) Accept it as an inevitable element in a world from which you can be eventually released: try not to let it worry you (Buddha).

(b) Bear it patiently, in the expectation of a better deal next time round (Hinduism).

(c) Resignation: accept its inevitability without complaint, and make the best of it (Stoicism).

(d) Fight it: you may have to accept it, but need not passively give in to it (Yin) or lose the surge of pride within you (Yang). 'Curse God and die' (Job); 'Do not go gentle into that good night: Rage, rage against the dying of the light' (Dylan Thomas on his dying father).

(e) Where suffering can be alleviated (by social reform, medical research, refusal to sacrifice human safety for the sake of technological development) do all that you can to bring this about (humanism, Confucius).

(f) Accept that to live at all is to live dangerously, that life is risky, that the chances of life's occurring in the universe are a billion-to-one against, so be glad that you have existed at all. If everyone lived maimed, deprived lives the problem would not arise: it is the contrast between those who are happier because of their circumstances and those who are sadder that brings the issue into focus. So come to terms with the unfairness of life, and make the best of your chances (existentialism).

(g) Accept that life is unfair, but look forward to compensation in heaven (Christianity, Islam).

(h) Ignore it, along with all other worldly cares and concerns, and find happiness through realising you are part of the universal stream, the eternal essence of life, alongside which the pangs of mortal existence are transitory in their duration and illusory in their significance (Tao).

CASE STUDY 27: WHAT IS RELIGION?

Refer to the list of characteristics of religion, on pages 177–8.

(a) Which of these, if any, do you consider to be essential?

(b) Which can be dispensed with as long as the others are present?

(c) Which ones have greater weight than others in counting towards being a religion?

(d) Which combination(s) would, in your view, constitute a quorum sufficient to entitle one to use the word?

CASE STUDY 28: SEXUAL MORALITY: is there any uniformity of attitude?

There is a great diversity in the marriage rules of different societies. In some, polygamy is encouraged, in others it is forbidden. In some, divorce is easy for husbands, in others it is difficult or impossible. In some, marriage to a person to whom one is closely related is banned, in others, this is the only kind of marriage which is allowed. In some, widows must remarry, in others they must commit suicide, or return to their parental home. In some a woman must be a virgin at the time of marriage, in others it is an advantage if she has already had a child. Preliterate societies in fact show an amazing variety of sexual practices (polyandry, incest, paedophilia, etc.) and major civilisations and religions have incompatible codes (homosexuality encouraged in classical Greece, banning of divorce in Islam and Roman Catholicism, etc.). A single civilisation may also have different standards at different times (compare Victorian England with the 1960s) and within a single society there are likely to be different standards between classes, areas, and subcultures (compare the so-called 'soft south' with the more rigorous north in England, or the 'Bible Belt' with the San Francisco Bay area in America).

Are there any individual precepts about sexual behaviour which are recognised universally? One may point to incest, adultery, and homosexuality as likely examples, but there are exceptions to all these. The following may be considered as general principles which are observed in all societies: you may wish to challenge whether this is so.

1 All societies have some arrangement by which women become in some sense the exclusive property of men.
2 All have rules about who is responsible for bringing up children.
3 All forbid irregular sexual contact with married women.
4 All have some prohibitions on sexual relations within certain degrees of kinship.
5 All regard some forms of sexual behaviour as perversions.
6 All have severe sanctions to enforce these rules.

Do these uniformities point to some underlying universal human need to preserve love and security? Or do they merely illustrate different attempts to solve problems caused by economic needs in hostile environments? Is the universal subjugation of women (a) an accident of history; (b) a consequence of some male conspiracy; or (c) a natural law, to break which would disturb the balance of society and threaten the survival of the species?

More to the point is the consideration of whether birth control on the one hand and the AIDS fear on the other have created a totally new situation which makes historical generalities about sexual behaviour quite irrelevant.

See how you react to the following questions:

1 Has the development of contraceptives changed the whole basis of sexual morality, or has it simply made sexual morality more complicated?

2 In societies where women are taking over many – and perhaps, eventually, all – of the traditionally male roles, is there the need for a re-think of customary practices and arrangements?

3 Should sex, marriage, and the care of children now be separated?

4 How far is the institution of marriage and the traditional male–female sexual partnership challenged by such processes as artificial insemination, etc.? What are likely to be the consequences, in this field, of separating child-birth from sex?

5 Is there an evolutionary trend away from reproductive sex toward sex for pleasure?

6 Should there be laws against any kind of sexual behaviour? If so, what?

7 Should there be changes in existing laws such as
   (a) Stricter enforcement of the age of consent (how?)
   (b) Total removal of the age of consent – resulting, perhaps, in
   (c) Lowering of the age of marriage (child brides as in some Islamic countries: less desirable than leaving 12- and 13-year-old girls to hang around in discotheques and amusement arcades as in Christian countries?)
   (d) Sterilising the mentally and socially handicapped, including psychotically violent criminals.
   (e) The abolition of marriage on a civil basis, leaving it solely as a religious event for those who desire it.

8 Does the advent of AIDS mean that sex should be viewed as life-long between the same two partners?

9 Which is most natural: monogamy, polygamy/polyandry, or promiscuity?

CASE STUDY 29: MORAL EMPHASES IN THE WORLD'S RELIGIONS

There was an example, on p.34, of a moral issue about which the major religions of the world speak with different voices: the eating of the flesh of certain animals. This is just one example of the wide range of approaches taken by these religions, in their official pronouncements, to moral problems. Below are a series of stances made by various religions on some of these problems. See if you can come up with (i) a consistent principle among the practices; and (ii) emphases that make you more respectful to one of these religions than to the others.

1 Christians have no specific rules about **eating animal flesh**. Many Buddhists are vegetarian, though certain of them will eat meat purchased from a butcher, though they would not kill an animal themselves. Jews and Hindus refrain from certain meats. Jainites eat no meat at all.

2 **On waging war**, Christianity has generally followed St Paul's teaching (Romans 13) that, the State being God's servant on earth, it is the Christian's duty to defend it (though this religion has produced some noted pacifists). Buddhists preach *ahimsa* or non-violence, and through history have seldom been involved in religious wars. Islam proclaims Jihad, or Holy War, against non-believers, the infidels. Judaism is equally belligerent. Zen was popular among both the samurai, and the World War II kamikazi pilots and soldiers who committed hara-kiri. The *Bhagavadgita*, the Hindus' most respected religious text, outlines one man's spiritual enlightenment before proceeding into battle.

3 Jews and Christians have no universal sanctions against **drinking alcohol**. Islam forbids it. Buddha included it with all that the body enjoys as requiring strict self-control in its use.

4 Christianity, which originally spread among people who believed that the world was shortly to end, has nothing to say about **sex** except that, on the whole, it should be avoided. Jainite monks and nuns are forbidden to touch each other. Tantric Hindus believe that the bliss of sexual intercourse is the closest that human beings come to the even greater bliss of cosmic enlightenment and union with the Ground of Being (Brahman): the *Karma Sutra* is a holy book. In Taoism there is an emphasis on the union of the forces of yin and yang, most surely realised when there is a union of male and female, whether they are lifelong partners or not. Only Taoism consistently treats the female as totally equal to the male.

5 The highest expressions of Hinduism and of Zen Buddhism speak of

an enlightened state which is 'beyond good and evil'. Do you find this a more mature approach to morality than that which simply divides forms of behaviour into 'right' and 'wrong'?

Issues in moral and practical philosophy

Chapter Nine

Moral maturity

What is a morally mature adult? On the face of it, this is a straightforward question, which suggests that there is an equally straightforward reply. We have already seen, however, that the word 'mature' is an evaluative word which can be defined in a number of different ways. A person may be described as mature if he has learned, and follows, the rules relating to any particular group of which he is a member or participant – at home, or school, at college, or work, in a club, or local community, in a country or even simply as a member of the human race. A person may be described as mature who has learned the meaning and value of discipline and observes this in his behaviour; it will be evinced not only in groups which 'specialise' in discipline, such as the army, the police force, or the church, but in the smaller everyday matters of being punctual, telling the truth, keeping promises, and not cheating. These are all *outward* signs of what most people would describe as mature behaviour; the question is whether there is not more to moral maturity than this.

While there are a number of rival definitions of the word to that just described, the word that encapsulates a wide range of these is *autonomy*. In Chapter Twelve this will be discussed apropos of educational aims in particular; here we shall discuss it in relation to the moral agent in general. The question is whether moral behaviour based solely on obedience to authority, and which, by repetition over the years, has become habitual, can genuinely be described as mature behaviour. I am not thinking here of the person who has spent some years in pondering over the merits and demerits of particular life-styles, and has concluded that, for reasons that convince him, one of these is preferable to the others; rather, of people who, through indolence, lack of inclination, or, sometimes, lack of opportunity, have slotted early in life into a certain moral groove, and have proceeded to follow in that groove with, apparently, a fair degree of equanimity and usually with their neighbours' approval. I think of the youth raised in a military family who follows in the family tradition and never for a moment questions the military values which pervade the air he breathes; or of the girl – a relative of mine born at the start of the century – who was put by her parents into a convent in her mid-teens because of the stringent economic conditions of Ireland at that time, and has remained there for life: has she ever had any inducement to question the religious values which underlie her Order? Both of these may appear extreme examples, but in their stark way they invite the question: how many people in the run-of-the-mill walks of life can truly affirm that they are morally autonomous: that the views they present, where these are similar to those of their peers, are views that they have personally arrived at after a process of reflection based on experience? I'm not suggesting that those who have been unwilling so to reflect are never praiseworthy; only that they are praiseworthy as members of an electorate are praiseworthy who consistently vote the same way – but only because that's how they've been brought up to vote; praiseworthy as a child is praiseworthy who automatically washes his hands before meals; praiseworthy as a housetrained pet is praiseworthy.

I am aware that this is a value judgment on my part, but I take it as axiomatic that moral maturity means more than obeying orders consistently; more than accepting unquestioningly ('Ours not to reason why') the authority of another person, or group, or Being; more than patriotism, or any other ism, political or religious, which hands down rules from 'on high' with the expectation that the adherent will follow and teach them just because they're in the book; more, even, than loyalty, which may be totally misguided: Genghis Khan, Adolf Hitler, Josef Stalin, all had their loyal followers. The morally mature person is one who knows when to disobey an order, to disregard authority, to break a rule, to desert a leader: such a person is autonomous, as the person who is never out of step cannot hope to be. My judgment is that, whatever other qualities are required in order to be morally mature, autonomy is a *sine qua non*: it may not be sufficient, but it is necessary.

AUTONOMY

What, then, is an autonomous person? What qualities are required if any moral agent is to be so characterised? Three factors seem paramount: firstly, it must be possible for the agent to *give reasons* for his behaviour; this must involve, secondly, *freedom of choice* on his part; and, thirdly, the agent's own *disposition* must be taken into account. (All three of these are articulated by John Wilson in his section of *Introduction to Moral Education*, and all require some analysis.)

1. Reason

To make a moral judgment is to consider choices, and this process involves the use of reason. This implies that morality can be defined in part as action based on the right reasons and applying fundamental principles. What these principles are has to be discovered by thoughtful enquiry, which is saying no more than that the individual must learn to enunciate them for himself, because he accepts them as true, rather than because he has been authoritatively informed that this is the case. The fact that certain moral principles *seem* to be objectively or self-evidently true (that is, true independently of any individual's judgment about their validity) such as keeping a promise or paying a debt is in no way destroyed or undermined by encouraging the moral agent to discover this for himself.

As we saw in the second chapter, the moral agent finds himself faced with two sets of rules: basic rules, or principles, and procedural rules, or the application of these principles to actual situations. The basic rules – justice, equality, sympathy, and so on – seem to have a givenness, or at least a universality, about them, which leaves little room for dispute. The procedural rules, on the other hand, may be right or wrong according to the circumstances. The basic rule of a parent in relation to his children is likely to be that all shall be treated fairly. Where one child displays intellectual and other skills far in excess of those shown by the rest of the family, however, the parent may well decide to treat this one with a greater degree of rigour than the others. 'To whom much is given, much shall be required' (Luke 12, 48). There may well be some debate as to whether this behaviour is fair or not.

The application of these procedural rules is likely in many cases to mean no more than that the agent observes how others have behaved in similar circumstances, and agree with their decision: but this act of agreement involves the use of reason (to be autonomous doesn't mean making moral decisions which are always out on a limb). On the other hand, he may disagree with the commonly accepted application of the basic rule, and follow a different path. Where this occurs, he may well be challenged as to the grounds for his contrary behaviour, and his answer will, again, involve the use of reason. By this process, forms of behaviour which may have been frowned on, if not barred by law, in one generation may be acceptable to the next. The attitude to homo-sexuality is one example of the occurrence of such change (though some still hold the earlier view that these practices, being 'unnatural', should remain illegal). Experiments on human embryos create an area of current – and no doubt continuing – controversy. The process of moving from an immature moral stance to one that is more mature is in part one of establishing priorities among rules: determining which rules are basic and which procedural; where two basic rules clash (justice versus benevolence, for instance), which should be given the greater weight; and under what circumstances procedural rules should be modified or abandoned altogether. For the child, as we shall see, even procedural rules are likely to be treated as fixed and unchange-able because this gives him a sense of security; part of the process of becoming adult is that of abandoning this crutch and walking unaided. The road to autonomy is no joyride. (See Case Studies 30 and 42.)

What kind of reasoning is required if this road is to be pursued? One philosopher who has written extensively on this theme is John Wilson of the University of Oxford, whose ideas, while later adumbrated and expanded in other works, are contained in the book already mentioned (p. 208). He suggests the following paradigm as a basis for moral reasoning (the shorthand words to label each factor are his own):

(a) *Ingredients:* (i) PHIL: Identity with others; recognising that, in any moral decision making, others are involved besides yourself. This means not only respect for and fairness towards others, but a willingness to go beyond the strict call of justice, to have a caring attitude to others (agape – see Chapter Thirteen).

(ii) EMP: an awareness of the emotions, both conscious and unconscious, of other people and of oneself; learning to see things from the point of view of others, to feel not only *for* them (sympathy) but *with* them (empathy); understanding, and taking into account, one's own motives in the decision-making process. All this means developing the ability to think oneself *into* another person, however boring or unsympathetic a person he may be: trying to look at life from inside him, and judge his behaviour accordingly. This is not easy and some, perhaps with more imagination or sensitivity than others, will progress further than others along this road, as some find literacy or numeracy easier to achieve than others. Even the process of reaching an understanding of one's own feelings is not easy: even to ourselves we will always remain somewhat of a mystery; but one should keep on practising, as one does in other fields, like keeping physically fit, or learning a language, or mastering a musical instrument.

(iii) GIG: straightforward knowledge; this requires not only an understanding of the facts of a problem – knowing *that* – but also an awareness of the options realistically available when tackling the problem, and which is likely to be the most effective – knowing *how*. The first of these is clearly essential when making moral decisions, and may require a good deal of hard work on the moral agent's part. To make a decision based on the wrong facts, or a misunderstanding of the facts, can be disastrous, as evidenced by the events recorded at Beddgelert, where a blood-soaked dog was killed by its master in the mistaken belief that the blood was that of the master's daughter.[1] Equally, forms of behaviour which may be right for one particular person or set of circumstances may be counterproductive for another. Dealing, for instance, with a manic

---

[1] The blood, as all visitors to the dog's shrine in this North Wales village will know, was that of a wolf which the dog had slain when it had attacked the daughter.

talker whose contribution in any group is always a continuous monologue may mean ignoring him, or it may require someone to tell him pointedly – even if this hurts him deeply – to shut up or get out.

(b) *Procedure:* (iv) KRAT: reaching a decision about what to do. This will require a combination of PHIL, EMP, and GIG; it means that the moral agent must be alert to a problem, willing to think it through responsibly, and reach a commitment for action. This means that there must be also the motivation to take action: in the example above for instance, one individual may conclude that the only way to deal with the problem is to talk sharply to the windbag, but may either be so unconcerned about the dynamic of that particular group or be so lacking in courage that he remains silent. The actual making of a commitment and acting on it Wilson calls (v) DIK: many people reach – often laboriously – the decision about what ought to be done in a particular situation, but hold back from involving themselves in the (sometimes painful) process of actually doing it. It does not come easy to some, for instance, to say to another person what they think needs to be said if they know that their words will be wounding in their effect.

Wilson has had to bear the brunt of ridicule from some of his colleagues, not least because of the odd-sounding monosyllables that he has coined as a summary of his paradigm. This reaction seems misplaced: Wilson has been bold enough to accept the challenge posed by those who ask what moral reasoning means, and has made a comprehensive attempt to provide an answer. However, one is forced to ask how relevant his framework is for a wide range of moral problems. One can see how it applies to the example he chooses – driving a car: an awareness of other drivers' interests and intentions is a major requirement in the prevention of road accidents. It is difficult, however, to see how this formula could apply to the person trying to reach a decision in time of war on whether he should join the armed forces or take the pacifist position. The paradigm may serve as a reminder of considerations which should not be overlooked, but the ingredients provided seem inadequate, or too general, for the reaching of a decision. Apart from the eternal dilemma of being sure of the facts in time of war (GIG) there is the more important problem, raised by the introduction of PHIL and EMP, of deciding which group of people one should be sympathetic or empathetic with. In the Second World War, for instance, there was the aggressor (Germany), the people overrun by the aggressor (Poland, Belgium, France, Holland, etc.) and, for the British in 1940, one's own nation facing the aggressor single-handed. The pacifist point of view was that one could hardly express either PHIL or EMP towards the Germans by blowing off the soldiers' heads, and blowing up their families' homes; yet not to behave in this way meant doing nothing in the interests of the subjugated nations. The incredibly complex tangle of the Middle East, involving the perennial problem of Jews versus Arabs (and sometimes, as in the Gulf War of 1991, Arabs versus Arabs) illustrates the universality – in time and place – of the dilemma. Case study 35 (pp. 265–9) pursues this theme: at this stage it is enough to state that the complex problems of international warfare, exacerbated now by nuclear power, are hardly to be resolved by use of a simple paradigm.

At the other extreme, some moral dilemmas seem too limited in their field of application to require the use of a formula which now appears overcomplicated. For many people it is the cause of much inward agonising to decide whether to watch television or to study, whether to smoke in the privacy of the home, whether to read pornographic literature, and so on. In situations like these, while GIG may not be irrelevant, it is difficult to see that PHIL or EMP are greatly involved other than tangentially. Even with obvious drawbacks, however, there remain many issues to which Wilson's formula has a relevant application, as may be illustrated in one of the Case Studies (30) after this chapter.

2. Freedom

The second requirement, Wilson suggests, for the morally mature person follows logically from the first. The process of giving reasons and acting in accordance with the conclusions reached means that the agent must be free both to decide on the rights and wrongs of an issue and free, accordingly, to act. We discuss in Chapter Ten the general philosophical issues of freewill versus determinism; here we are concerned only with the implications of freedom in the field of moral development. Moral maturity implies that a person has not only thought through a problem, reached a conclusion, and acted on it, but also that, whatever conclusion he reached, and however he behaved, he did so of his own volition. In other words, while he could have acted differently, he chose not to. If it is the case that George Washington, as history informs us, 'could not tell a lie', then truth-telling in his case can hardly be presented as an indication of his moral maturity: the person who *can* tell a lie (in the sense of being able to live with himself afterwards) but chooses not to do so would, in this field, be evincing a higher degree of maturity.

Since a person cannot choose whether to be free or not, (which is no more than saying that whether a person has or has not been conditioned in a particular way he is not the one to be held responsible for this state) this requirement has far-reaching implications for education in general and for moral education in particular. If it is the case that autonomy is the key to moral maturity, then what must be avoided, by parents and teachers alike, is any deliberate attempt to indoctrinate the growing child. It would obviously be hopelessly unrealistic to expect any child to grow up without being influenced by the views and values of those surrounding him. Every idea is an incitement, an element in a natural conditioning process, and some moulding of children's minds is therefore inevitable: what is not inevitable, and should be viewed as totally undesirable if the aim is to produce morally mature people, is the formulation of a certain set of values within a fixed framework, and the conscious imposition of these on the developing young person. That person may as a result be able eventually to speak authoritatively and persuasively on the values to which he has been conditioned; but the holding of strong, unambiguous views on moral issues, and the ability to express them articulately, does not imply that the person so speaking is morally mature. In fact, the reverse is likely to be the case: the person who thinks he has found the answer to all moral dilemmas simply hasn't looked far enough; where moral issues are concerned, only the immature are convinced that they are right and that those who hold any kind of alternative views are wrong. No doubt the protean newt, which cannot see because it lives in darkness, if able to speak would affirm that there is no such thing as the sun – and would say so with absolute confidence, born of a life-long experience; but it would be no more futile to debate the sun's existence with such a newt than to discuss alternative views of morals with neo-Nazis, Jehovah's Witnesses, the Life organisation, Militant socialists, or Bible-waving Protestants (see Case Study 10).

It seems beyond question that a person who reaches moral decisions out of prejudice ('I hate blacks'), or through fear ('I'll suffer in hell if I do that') or in response solely to authority ('I must do as my leader/teacher/parent/priest says') is in the same position in the moral rating league as the illiterate or innumerate are in their respective leagues. This does not mean that they lose all respect as persons, any more than do the illiterate or innumerate: only that their contribution to any moral discussion should not be given the attentive hearing which those who are totally confident of their own infallibility usually receive. The conditioning process may well produce people who, when others vacillate because of the complexities of a problem, offer a firmness of conviction which the insecure may feel glad to anchor themselves to: but it is an unrealistic, artificial security similar to that of airline passengers still comfortably strapped to their seats as the plane flies into the side of a mountain. To be free does not mean, as is the criticism often made by products of the school of conviction, to be free-and-easy: it means recognising the infinite complications of existence (because people are infinitely varied) and realising that there can be no blueprint for moral behaviour. The morally mature person is free to adjust his behaviour according to the needs of the particular individual or individuals involved in any moral dilemma. To be a libertarian doesn't mean – as popular usage would have it – to be without standards.

3. Disposition

The third requirement for moral maturity, Wilson suggests, is *right disposition*. This means not only what people do and why they do it, and what courses of action they have considered but found wanting, but what they feel within themselves. Wilson illustrates what he means by paraphrasing Aristotle:

But virtuous actions are not done in a virtuous – a just or temperate – way merely because they have the appropriate quality. The doer must be in a certain frame of mind when he does them. Three conditions are involved: (1) the agent must act in full consciousness of what he is doing; (2) he must will his action, and will it for its own sake; (3) the act must proceed from a fixed and unchangeable disposition.

This last quality is difficult to describe: how does one define 'disposition'? Two examples may indicate what it is, and why it is important when assessing moral maturity as indicated by a person's behaviour. One may occur in a divorce court, where one spouse is attempting to indicate cruelty by the other as a ground for separation. He or she may find it impossible to specify either a time or place when or where a particular overt act of cruelty occurred; all that can be done is to affirm that the 'guilty' partner registered a regular feeling of animosity towards the other, so establishing an overwhelming sense of malevolence in the partnership, on the one hand, and fear, perhaps, on the other – qualities which, while probably recognised by any children of the relationship, may never have been identified by relatives or friends. Thus a marriage which might on the surface have appeared to be satisfactory, in which neither partner apparently denied the other freedom, or acted unreasonably toward the other, was in fact a totally unsatisfactory relationship. (The same could be true within the confines of a monastic order where the observance of each day's outward and visible forms can hide from non-trained eyes an inner, invisible venom.)

A second example was given earlier in the book: the person who buys a round of drinks in such a way that one or more of the recipients must feel demeaned by the process. Variations in inflection of voice in the words 'Oh, and a pint for him' can make an insult of a gift.

Habit The question that arises here is how far the moral agent can be expected to be responsible for his dispositions. The answer seems to be suggested by what R. S. Peters[1] has to say about habit. He argues that the moral educator, whether parent or teacher, will not be diminishing a person's autonomy by attempting to establish habits in those in his charge. Habits, by their nature, relate to the broader, general issues of morality when these are observed habitually: when, for instance, a person shows respect for others without having to be continually working out whether this kind of attitude is justified or not, he is then more free to use his reason on the more precise, more novel, and usually more complicated issues which he may have to face, such as how to end a relationship with a sexual partner without causing him or her unnecessary pain or loss of self-regard. In this respect, facing up to life's moral issues is like driving a car. After a while, most of a driver's actions are taken without thought: gear changing, accelerating and decelerating, and so on, so that one can make a reasonably long journey without consciously making a decision; but when an emergency arises, such as the sudden slowing down of the vehicle ahead, or the unexpected emergence of a pedestrian from the side, all the attention can be concentrated into dealing with that crisis. A learner driver will find even the most elementary aspects of driving exhausting: eventually he will be able to preserve his energies for those special occasions. To those who contend that the formulation of habits in a person lessens his freedom of choice, Peters argues that habits are not beyond the bounds of reason; by serious contemplation they can be broken, and new habits formed. 'Habits need not be exercised out of force of habit.'

From immaturity to maturity The process by which a child moves from a state of moral immaturity to one of maturity has been copiously studied and described. Two researchers in particular may be briefly mentioned here. The pioneer work in the field was undertaken by the French educational psychologist, Piaget. He distinguished two kinds of morality in children: an earlier morality based on the authority of others (the technical word for this is heteronymous) and, round about the age of 12, a more mature autonomous morality; he described this shift as one from a state of 'moral realism' to a condition of 'moral relativism', a morality based on respect for others, and described by Piaget as a form of internalised morality of cooperation. The immature idea of rules is that they are absolute and unchangeable rather than, as the mature person sees them, human devices which are useful if, and only if, they serve their human purpose. Other distinctions outlined by Piaget may be tabled as follows:

[1] 'Reason and Habit', in *Moral Education in a Changing Society*, ed. W. R. Niblett

Immature	*Mature*
Rules derived from an absolute authority	Rules derived from the need for cooperation and interaction between people
Motive, intention, not taken into account in assessing the moral worth of an action: deviation from the rule is itself enough	Motive and intention important in judgment of behaviour; rule breaking, disregard of authority, not viewed as necessarily bad
Punishment retributive – 'an eye for an eye'	Punishment reformative – to enable the offender to make a worthier contribution to society
Acts judged by physical consequences (a dozen accidental fouls viewed as worse than one deliberate foul)	Acts judged by intention (one deliberate foul worse than any number of accidental fouls)
Absolutist about behaviour	Relativist, in one way or another
In doubt, defer to adults	Knows there are divergent views of right and wrong
Sanctions central: behaviour judged bad according to the punishment it brings	Actions bad because they harm others
Reciprocity (akin to Kant's universalisability) not a reason for behaviour	Reciprocity often a reason, whether simply along the lines of the golden rule or as a process of empathy
Contiguity: misfortune occurring after misbehaviour seen as a punishment ('post hoc, ergo propter hoc' see pp.235–6)	No confusion of natural accidents with punishment

This process of studying the shift from immature to mature moral behaviour has been given further direction by the researches of the American educational psychologist, Louis Kohlberg. His analysis led him to conclude that there are three stages of development, from views of morality based on sanctions to the assessment of actions in terms of moral standards. These stages, or levels, divide into six types:

Level I Premoral:
    Type 1: orientated towards punishment and obedience
    Type 2: seeing happiness as an end (early instrumental hedonism)
Level II Morality of conventional role, and conformity to it:
    Type 3: need to maintain good relations and the approval of others
    Type 4: authority as the sanction for and support of morality

Level III Morality of self-accepted moral principles:
  Type 5: morality of contract and the idea of individual rights
  Type 6: morality of individual principles of conscience

Kohlberg's findings were that types 1 and 2 lessen over the years, types 3 and 4 continue until about the age of 13, after which types 5 and 6 increasingly operate. Kohlberg also argued that, having moved from one type to the next, children never regress: this is an interesting issue for the study of child behaviour, but too specific to be pursued here. One comment on Kohlberg's findings is apposite:

It would appear that in younger children moral conduct is based primarily on fear and perhaps also on a lack of arousal or opportunity to transgress whilst among older children good behaviour and acceptance of the society's rules is more likely to be based on moral beliefs, on a desire to avoid guilt feelings and upon 'strength of character', or in Freudian terms on ego factors.
(K. Connolly, *Moral Development and the Handicapped Child*, the Spastics Society)

It may be added that, if this schema is sound, adults who have not moved from the earlier to the later types – and such people are to be found – must be judged as morally immature.

MORAL EDUCATION

It has been assumed throughout this chapter that it is possible to conceive of a morally mature person, and this assumption will be maintained. The question follows whether it is possible also to conceive of a process by which the shift from the early to the later stages of moral development may be facilitated? Is *moral education* viable?

The debate on this theme, which has been comprehensive and extensive, has tended to revolve itself around three issues: the relation between religion and morals, the analysis of the sense of moral obligation, and the appropriate methods for promoting certain moral attitudes, generally those of liberal humanism. There has, however, been little attempt to analyse the role of moral education in society: is it feasible to speak of training people morally, as we train them in literacy or numeracy? Should the move from moral immaturity to moral maturity (Level I to Level III in Kohlberg's paradigm) be viewed as a process that occurs naturally, or is there something that schools (in particular) can do about it? Having suggested that there is no logical connection between religious belief and moral convictions, and that the part played by reason in the moral decision-making process is only one of several requirements, what should be the policy for education in this field?

The fact is that the basis of morality, as a necessary means for the survival of society, is in no way diminished by the exposure of the limitations or illusions of supernatural sanctions. Society persists because it is in the interests of most individuals that it should continue to do so. Let's face it, ultimately the sanction for morality is that society must and will use violence against those whose conduct threatens it. It is wholly unnecessary to teach children to feel guilty about stealing when they know that if they steal they will stand a good chance of being placed in prison. (This is not to suggest that fear of punishment is a sign of maturity in moral behaviour: quite the reverse, as both Piaget and Kohlberg indicate; but it would be unrealistic to deny that it operates in the minds of many, for whom the eleventh and chief commandment is: Thou shalt not be found out.) *The question then is not whether moral standards have in practice declined but whether moral maturity is increasing*; and the problem here has been intensified by two new complications. Firstly, life in the metropolitan city makes it necessary for society to impose ever greater restrictions on individual freedom, and the greater the number of restrictions, the harder it is to enforce them all. Secondly, the world has become technologically one unit. It seems that the nation-states themselves must surrender their freedom in the interests of the survival of humanity, and the machinery for imposing this, despite the existence of the United Nations Organisation and earlier campaigns for world government, has not yet been devised. More than ever, therefore, moral education in some form seems to be required among young people.

Tasks for moral education In general, four tasks appear for moral education. The first, and perhaps most urgent, is the negative one of *destroying vestiges of superstitious views of morality*. The biggest obstacle to progress is not moral weakness or wickedness but the ignorance which enslaves people to concepts of 'right' or 'wrong' which are little more than taboos. These concepts are not only false but harmful. A vast amount of wholly unnecessary misery is, for instance, caused by bondage to the belief (usually on the part of old people) that it is wrong to be 'obligated' by receiving charity in the form of benefits to which citizens – and, particularly, older citizens – are entitled; another taboo area is that of religious objections to birth control, abortion, and (though less common) blood transfusions. Children properly instructed in the rational social basis of morality need never fall into such errors.

The second task is *to make pupils aware of the existing consensus on morality*. It is fashionable in some quarters to deny that such a consensus exists. There are, of course, controversial issues, but on a wide range of issues we (that is, human beings of all nations and races) are virtually unanimous. We are all (or almost all) against war, murder, theft from individuals, cruelty – especially to children and animals – social inequality, racial intolerance, religious bigotry, and authoritarianism. We are all (or almost all) in favour of compassion, kindness, liberation for oppressed minorities, conservation and protection of the environment, individual and, in particular, sexual freedom. Readers of popular newspapers in many countries throughout the world may argue that the stories presented don't encourage this optimism, but here it is necessary to become sophisticated enough to know that it is news of human follies and vices which sells newspapers, not reports on virtuous behaviour. The teacher can counteract the distortions of the press by informing more comprehensively and fairly both as to what the prevailing values are and as to the sanctions imposed on those who violate them.

The third, and perhaps most difficult, task is to *extrapolate from present values and try to forecast those which will emerge* in the world in which the pupils will soon be playing a positive part. If the teacher plays the prophet he risks being wrong, but this tension between conformity to present society and preparation for a new society is endemic to education, as will be further discussed in Chapter Twelve. The need to create effective world institutions, the overthrow of systems based on the economic power of an exploiting class, and the creation of a genuine (as distinct from a hypocritical) permissive society are obvious candidates for future developments in society.

Finally, the teacher may try to educate pupils to *make responsible choices between the mores of different sub-groups*. The adolescent seeking identity is confronted by the pressures of a commercialised consumer society and of the idiot herd as well as the opportunities for working towards constructive change. The teacher cannot choose for the pupil, but he can give him the information which will enable him to choose for himself as rival claims are made, some more raucously than others, from this tower of Babel.

CASE STUDY 30: ASSESSING ONE'S AUTONOMY

The following are real-life situations causing moral dilemmas; all have occurred, or been written about, during the preparation of this book. Discuss them bearing in mind that you are exploring your autonomy, meaning 'having one's own name', which in turn implies that you are not mouthing the views of, for example, your parents, your friends, or your local community group. Obviously, the views of these three groups will not always coincide; but this exercise, if your answers are as honest as you can make them, should give you some idea of how independent you are of the mores of each of these groups. As indicated in the text, this will not necessarily imply that you have achieved autonomy (you may auton-omously agree with one or more groups) but it should give you a rough guide as to how far you are prepared to take your own line on moral issues.

In each of the following examples, ask yourself the question: what would I do (or in some cases, perhaps, what have I done) in these circumstances? Try using Wilson's paradigm (pp.210–11) and see how helpful – or otherwise – it turns out to be on these issues.

(a) A community of hippies encamps on some nearby ground. You are asked to sign a petition for their removal. (Perhaps it's your own or your parents' ground.)

(b) You are a non-smoker attending a committee meeting. A motion is presented to ban smoking during the meeting. There is an open window at one end of the committee room.

(c) You slightly dent the door of a parked car while reversing. Neither its owner nor anyone else is around. You have a notebook and pen handy.

(d) You are a social worker called out on strike by your union because of a genuine grievance. You have clients who desperately need you.

(e) You are rung up in the early hours to collect from the local police jail a flatmate who has been taken there in a drunken condition. This has happened several times before, when you have agreed to get up and go.

(f) The college/office/works bore joins your table at lunch and starts his usual interminable drone.

(g) You are a police officer and discover that your neighbour's 13-year-old daughter is having, with her parents' apparent approval, an affair with a 19-year-old boyfriend.

(h) You are on your college/works disciplinary committee. A colleague has been caught stealing a book/cigarette lighter accidentally left behind by another person. It is the culprit's second offence, and it is proposed to expel/sack him.

(i) You are a middle-of-the-road member of the Labour Party, and your local branch, which you attend regularly, has been inundated by adherents of the ultra-left. However hard you protest, you are invariably outvoted.

(j) You are a doctor whose patient has syphilis. You ask him to tell his wife about this but he refuses. She is also your patient.

(k) Your neighbour sometimes plays his record-player loudly late at night. You ask him to tone it down as you retire early as a rule, but, somewhat offensively, he refuses.

(l) Your feelings towards your sexual partner have cooled. You know that he/she would be shattered if the relationship ended.

(m) The landlord of your local pub regularly breaks the law by serving alcohol to youngsters whom you know to be only in their early teens.

(n) A friend/colleague tells a crudely racialist/sexist joke.

(o) You are an alcoholic, and chief executive of an advertising agency. The opportunity arises for your firm to get the contract for a large distilling firm. You have the authority to block the contract.

(p) You are an animal rights enthusiast. A doctor lives in your town who works in the vivisection laboratory of the local university. The local animal rights activists invite you to join them in a demonstration outside his home, which you feel could turn nasty.

(q) A male colleague states openly that he enjoys looking at, and is sexually aroused by, pictures and photographs of beautiful nude women. A female colleague describes this as typical male depravity which must be made socially unacceptable.

CASE STUDY 31: WONDERWOMAN AND SUPERMAN

The following is a review, written by the author, of a book entitled *Wonderwoman and Superman*, subtitled 'The Ethics of Human Biotechnology', by John Harris (Oxford University Press). Read it through and then discuss the questions that follow.

If Henry VIII and Catherine of Aragon had had access to twentieth-century biotechnology, it is likely that they would have had the son Henry wanted for the sake of England's political stability. The break with Rome need not have occurred, later wives would have been superfluous to requirements (saving the rolling of several heads) and Elizabeth would probably not have become Queen.

Today, with the acceleration of understanding in embryo research, our present royals could (as is probably the case) ensure the continuation of the line by storing frozen Windsor embryos in a secret vault, for use against the wiping out of visible members of the family by twenty-first-century republican revolutionaries. This may seem a startling consideration, but, as John Harris points out, the revolution in molecular biology will in fact enable us not only to preserve human life forms for decades or more after the decease of their progenitors but also to change, modify, or control the forms themselves. Defects can be removed, illnesses like heart disease abolished, and organs be available for transplant at any moment. Whatever legislators may decide, in a society ruled by market forces, if a mortgage could be paid off for the price of an eye, there are those who will find the offer irresistible.

Harris writes as though there was a certain inevitability about the process. 'The decision before us now,' he suggests, 'is not whether or not to use this power but how and to what extent.' . . . We seem to be well on the way to creating the eponymous wonderwoman and superman as we cease leaving the evolutionary process to natural forces and take control by, for, and of ourselves. The Brave New World has dawned. Is it a dawn to rejoice over, or should we be closing the shutters to its malevolent rays, banishing the geneticists to Outer Mongolia, destroying embryo banks, outlawing foetal research? Harris recognises that many people will feel alien to research in this field, not only on religious grounds ('humans playing God') but also because it bears with it a dreadful responsibility which, misused or misunderstood, could lead to disaster.

2,500 years ago, Lao Tzu, in the *Tao Te Ching*, suggested that it was absurd to try to improve on nature, and many today, Catholic or Charismatic, New Age or New Statesman, will echo these feelings. But Harris argues that, just as we cannot undo nuclear weapons by 'forgetting' how to make them, so the knowledge of how to manufacture new life forms will remain whether we feel that this means we are facing a Golden Age of Superfolk, or standing at the edge of the Abyss, preparing to make one final outrageous Mephistophelian leap.

How does this prospect affect you? Should these matters be left to 'God' or to 'nature', or are they now in the hands of mature, responsible human beings?

Chapter Ten

Free will

Cancer: (June 22–July 23) At 10.44 am, as the sun shines in your sign, so summer begins and the solstice declares it's time for you to display your talents and exude a confidence in yourself.

– Daily newspaper

This typical quotation from a morning horoscope illustrates in a somewhat extreme way an important fact about many people's approach to living. There seems to be a strong desire, perhaps not openly expressed but lurking just beneath the consciousness, to view life in general and one's own life in particular as containing some kind of order: a pattern, or plan, with a sort of golden thread running through it. Writers throughout the ages have discussed such concepts as 'human destiny', 'inexorable fate', 'the meaning of life'. Underlying all these concepts is the assumption – again, often tacit – that we are unavoidably caught up in a process over which we as individuals – and perhaps as a race – have no final control.

The effect of this view on human behaviour varies from person to person. The belief in inexorable destiny has been expressed by many a tyrant to justify his tyranny; and by many a coward to excuse his inactivity; it has produced the spirit of optimism, expressed in the myth of Prometheus, raging against his lot and defying his fate; or, on a human plane, Browning's call to 'Grow old along with me, The best is yet to be.' It has also produced the spirit of resignation, or impotence: the 'philosophical' attitude of the Stoics, or the hedonism of the 'eat-drink-and-be-merry-for-tomorrow-we-die' school. Nowhere has the view that 'what will be, will be' been more hauntingly expressed than in the *Rubaiyat* of Omar Khayyam, written in Persia around the start of the twelfth century: these stanzas are typical:

> The Moving Finger writes: and, having writ,
> Moves on: nor all thy Piety nor Wit
> Shall lure it back to cancel half a Line,
> Nor all thy Tears wash out a Word of it.

And that inverted Bowl we call The Sky,
Whereunder crawling coop't we live and die,
Lift not thy hands to *It* for help - for It
Rolls impotently on as Thou or I.

There is, then, a deterministic element in the approach to life made by a fair number of people. The aim of this chapter is to explore how viable this stance is as we experience life's encounters and their moral dilemmas. As we saw when discussing existentialism, it may be easier, less harrowing, to take the view that 'que sera, sera'; it may even sometimes be psychologically sustaining to believe this – as did numberless men in the trenches in the First World War: you would die if your name was on the bullet, and not otherwise. Our concern is not with the effects of taking a deterministic stance (which, if the stance is itself misguided or unnatural, would have no more validity as a *modus vivendi* than the fantasies and convictions which overtake the mind when clouded by alcohol) but whether it is a viable stance to take, philosophically speaking. Putting the issue at its most direct: how free are we? The answer which anybody gives to this question will indicate a good deal about him. It is in fact one of the key questions of philosophy (which is probably why so many books have been written on the subject, as you will discover if you peruse the philosophy shelves in your local library – unless, like mine, the only philosophy works are about ESP.)

Meaning of 'freedom' The word 'free' is full of complications and ambiguities. For most people the problem is either 'how do I get free?' (from prison, from my spouse, from debt) or 'what do I do with the freedom I have?' (how do I spend my holidays, my free time, my money; or how do I choose my job, my partner, my religion, or my party?) People ask the question – without any kind of philosophical overtones – are you free tonight? is she free to marry me? when will you be free of your commitments? Seldom does anyone seriously ask, am *I* free? (I have put the question to numerous friends, and invariably they have answered it with reference to the law of the land.) For better or for worse, it is therefore one of the distinctive roles of the philosopher to ask the question, is man free?

The only way to find out what freedom means is to look at the ways people talk about it. There is a trap here which western philosophers from Plato onwards have fallen into, and it is necessary to point this out with as much clarity as can be mustered before we take a step further. This is to talk as if somehow, somewhere over and above the way people actually use the word, there is another timeless 'ideal', or meaning. Modern English-speaking philosophers call this meaning a 'concept'.

The 'concept' fallacy

Hearing or reading the word 'concept' should, as I've already warned several times, so I really mean it, ring an alarm bell in the head of any alert student: it always means danger, and often signals entry into a disaster area. 'Concept' is sometimes used to mean simply 'word' or 'definition'; at other times it seems to mean 'idea'. Danger lies in the sliding from one meaning to the other, so that a particular and often partisan idea is made to seem true by definition. On the basis of an idea of, say, education, one out of several current meanings of the word is sanctioned exclusively and others ruled out of order (see Chapter Twelve). In this slippery way substantive conclusions about what is to be taught in schools are made to 'follow' from what is no more than an arbitrary manipulation of a word. (A more sinister manipulation has in recent years debased the word 'liberal' in the USA.) Most of our evaluative words – like duty, equality, purity, courage, perfection, etc. – have been described as concepts at one time or another. So far as freedom is concerned, one could follow some philosophers – not only Plato, but Descartes, Hobbes, Leibniz, and others – and solve the 'problem of freedom' by starting with an idea of freedom which is called 'the concept of freedom'. The assumptions underlying this 'concept' may be summarised as follows:

(i)   there is a basic, discoverable reality called freedom
(ii) though discoverable, it is concealed, or underlying
(iii) it is different from, though related to, the surface of things
(iv) its discovery will enable us to describe human nature and establish whether we have free will
(v)   truth about reality is unchanging, and independent of us as would-be describers of it.

All this may seem somewhat pretentious to anyone not versed in philosophical thought processes; the important thing is to be aware that philosophers' ideas have no more privileged access to truth than ideas devised and offered from a different perspective. Philosophers' usage of words is neither more nor less valid than anybody else's, and these assumptions about the 'concept' of freedom are no exception to this. There is, to put it bluntly, no point in looking for the 'concept of freedom' since there is no reason for supposing that any such creature exists. A word is not a token of some unchangeable metaphysical 'idea'. In fact, as Wittgenstein has pointed out, no word exists on its own, in a vacuum or in some supermind: even a dictionary can tell the meaning only by either using cognate words or offering examples. Words in real life come only in bunches – sentences, phrases, or whatever – as part of communication between two or more people. The meaning of one word depends on its place in the bunch, and on the nature of the relationship between those using it.

So the philosopher's insistence on saying 'I don't want to know the meaning of freedom in one particular conversation or text, I want *the* meaning of freedom' must be treated with the same incredulity as one would a person who insisted 'I don't want to know the cause of asthma, or jaundice, or gravel, but just the cause of illness'; or 'I'm not asking why this plane crashed or that ship was wrecked: I want to know the cause of accidents in general'. Just as there is no one cause of illness or accidents in general, so there is no one meaning of the word 'free'. Different people mean different things at different times.

To give an exhaustive answer to the question 'what is freedom?' would, therefore, mean looking at all the times people had ever used the word. Even this would not tell anybody anything about 'the world' or 'reality' in general over and above the particular instances. The problem is seen to be quite unimaginably complicated once the cultural tribalism of the English – including English philosophers – is acknowledged. English philosophers (and this book probably bears the guilt as much as most) seem to think, for instance, that to analyse the meaning of the English word 'good' tells them all there is worth knowing about goodness without bothering to look at words in Arabic, Japanese, or Sanskrit. Similarly with freedom. The range and meanings of the English word 'freedom', with its emotional and literary associations, is by no means identical with those of the Welsh word 'rhyddid', the French 'liberté', or the Russian 'svoboda', to name but three. (The Russian word is so different from the English in its usage that it led President Reagan – not noted for his understanding of the philosophy of language – to declare publicly that the Russians had no word for freedom, with the implication that this was for the same reason that the Eskimos have no word for sand or the Arabs for snow.)

Most of the problems about who or what is free are practical problems about the facts. Is this 'free offer' really free? The only way to answer is to read the small print and see how much you have to pay for something else to get the 'free offer'. Rousseau's concept (note the word) of freedom won't help. He began his *Le Contrat Social* with the famous words, 'Man is born free but everywhere he is in chains'. By this he referred to his own theory, based on a belief in reincarnation, that a child comes into the world free from evil, from selfishness, or from wickedness of any kind. Only as the stifling tendons of society ('shades of the prison-house' – Wordsworth) with all its greed and envy and animosity increasingly grip the growing child does he lose this initial freedom. But this theory is logically unsound. If everyone enters the world as a free, pure, individual, at what point did people as a plurality lose this freedom and purity? The whole, on this theory, is more than (or less than or different from) the sum of its parts, which implies that a new factor has entered among the constituents. What is this factor? Rousseau does not answer this question.

Other examples of the use of the word can commonly be found. What does 'free collective bargaining' mean? Free from flying pickets, free from lock-outs by employers, free from government interference or TUC guidelines? It may mean any or all or none of these. The only way to find out is not to chase a mythical 'concept' of freedom but to see what the people who use the phrase actually mean. The judge who tells the prisoner 'You're a free man' after a 'Not guilty' verdict is not pronouncing on his psychological ability to choose between two or more courses of action: he is just saying, 'You don't have to go (back) to jail.' In these and lots of other examples it may not always be easy to find out if people are telling the truth or if they have really thought out what they mean, but there is no particular problem about the meanings.

Where we do find controversy which is at least partly about what 'freedom' means is in politics. Defenders of Western parliamentary systems say that countries like the United States, Britain, and West Germany are 'free' but countries like Russia (even post-1989), China, and Cuba are not. Communists say that communist countries are 'free' while capitalist countries are not. Anarchists say that all governments deny freedom to their subjects. These claims seem reducible to the question of the different uses of the word 'free'. Western politicians, when they say that their countries are free, mean that voters can choose between candidates of two or more parties, and that their citizens need not fear arbitrary arrest (a lessening freedom in our time, one feels). When communist politicians say that their countries are free they mean that workers are free from the threat of unemployment and are free to enjoy benefits like state health services and welfare schemes. When anarchists attack capitalism and communism alike they point to the existence of laws and coercion by armed forces and police as a denial of the individual's freedom to do what he likes. The difficulty is that unsophisticated people may not be aware of the different meanings intended and may be swayed by the emotive appeal of language.

So far as obedience to the law is concerned, there is one sense in which I am free to act as I will, another in which I'm not. I am free to dump my garden rubbish wherever I will: but if I am seen doing this in certain places, and my action is reported to the relevant authority, I can expect to pay the requisite penalty (in my case, recently, a £10 fine). There is in my village a bridge which has been for centuries a useful short-cut from one part of the area to another. Recently this bridge has been closed to traffic, through pressure brought by members of the local preservation society, because repairs necessitated to this bridge by the flow of traffic over it would mean changing its facade and destroying its historic value. The bridge is still there; it has no physical barriers – only a sign forbidding vehicles to cross. Am I free to drive across it? I *can* do so, but *may* not (the meaning emerges more starkly in German: 'ich kann, aber darf nicht').

Over the past century, belief that criminals were free to have acted otherwise than they did, and should be punished on this assumption, has been eroded in the name of sociology, psychology, and criminology, and, to a lesser extent, forensic medicine. None of these studies has proved that criminals are not free, but they have with more or less plausibility shown that the incidence of criminal acts can be predicted from a knowledge of housing conditions, family situations, and a variety of genetic and environmental factors. Those found to have committed criminal acts are therefore held – by social scientists and psychiatrists if not by courts – not to have acted freely, and so to need treatment rather than punishment. It seems that if the facts are as stated by social scientists and psychiatrists it would be more efficient to attack the problem of reducing the amount of criminal behaviour by changing social conditions (and perhaps by sterilising some potential parents) than by punishing offenders. (See Case Study 33.)

Moral freedom

Few topics have attracted philosophers as much as that of man's freedom to make moral decisions; and few are more difficult to resolve. It is an area of debate which illustrates a central aspect of philosophy which was mentioned in several of the earliest chapters of this book: no final proof, either for or against freewill, can be presented. In the end we can do no more than either live our lives *as though* we are free – with all the implications that brings – or as not free: and the variety of routes by which this second conclusion has been reached must be considered. It may help to clear the ground if I offer a preliminary remark which will indicate my own stance on the matter. There would be no problem about moral freedom if man were not free. The point is not just that, if man's actions were wholly unfree, it would be very odd that he should imagine himself free and bother to argue about it. Nor is it simply that the activity of arguing for or against freedom itself presupposes that the debaters are free to accept or reject arguments. It is rather that *people arguing for or against freedom know what they're arguing about only because they experience freedom*. Arguments about freedom in a determined or fixed world would be impossible for the same reason as arguments about colours would be impossible in a world where everyone was born blind. Arguments about whether people have moral freedom are in fact as pointless as arguments about the possibility of vision in a world where nobody is blind.

Only in Western philosophy has anyone questioned man's moral freedom. This may seem an odd statement in the light of (for example) the Indian doctrine of karma. But this doctrine refers, as we saw in Chapter Eight, to the individual's status, role in life, and place on the moral ladder at birth. Certainly none of these, according to the idea of karma, can be altered. But while the moral choices we face now are, according to the doctrine, brought about inexorably by the endless chain of past events, that chain includes past free choices; and with all those choices behind us, we are still free to choose at this moment between two or more alternatives. The fact is that men no more need to prove that they are free than they need to prove that they are alive or hungry or in pain or in love. In one sense, none of these apparently obvious aspects of ourselves can be proved: I could not even prove to you that I am not a robot, or that the rest of the universe is no more than a figment of my imagination (in which case, of course, there would be no point in trying to prove anything to you because you would just be part of that figment), nor that I wasn't created, or didn't come into existence, five minutes ago, bearing with me a memory that suggests that I have in fact lived much longer. None of these can be proved, but anyone who made any decisions in life on the basis that these remain open questions (except when participating in certain types of philosophy seminars) would, justifiably in my view, be put into an asylum for those suffering from softening of the brain. (From a perusal of this book you may be forgiven for thinking that this might be a very crowded asylum!)

There is, therefore, no answer to the problem of whether man has moral freedom, because there is no such problem; and if general agreement could be reached about this, we could end this discussion here and turn to something else. The fact that we are not doing so indicates that this conclusion has been rejected by enough people and at enough length to necessitate further examination of the issue. Put specifically: what are the grounds for holding the alternative, determinist, view?

Determinism

Determinism is the view that, when making moral decisions, the choice I make is fixed, in whole or in part, by previous events, decisions, or conditions: the decision could have been different only if what went before had been different. Before considering some of the different fields in which this position has been held, let me acknowledge immediately that of course there are in life many features which bear out this statement. I am, for instance, subject to natural laws. If I jump out of an aeroplane I shall go down, not up; prick my finger and I shall bleed; if I bathe naked on the Costa Brava, certain parts of my anatomy, hitherto unexposed to the sun at any time, will painfully remind me that they must not be taken for granted. Equally, it would seem absurd to question the fact that, because of the part played by habit in people's lives, human behaviour can often be predicted with a fair degree of certainty. I would bet a year's salary, for instance, that my neighbour when gardening, even in the middle of a heatwave, will wear his wellingtons; that my son will have the Scrabble board ready when I return from a meeting at 5 p.m.

next Sunday; and that my mother will phone me at the end of 'Songs of Praise' on TV at 7.15 that evening.

Even in the elusive area of moral decision-making, it is possible to predict what decisions will be made much of the time by people we know well, or know a lot about. The pacifist is unlikely, in any circumstances, to opt for a policy of violence, or a member of the Ku Klux Klan for racial equality. You won't find many Roman Catholics supporting abortion on demand, or members of women's rights movements beauty contests. We all of us create some kind of moral mould for ourselves, and the more others get to know us, the more accurately they will be able to predict our behaviour in any set of circumstances.

These concessions, however, will not satisfy the genuine determinist. He looks for an overall pattern, capable of universal explanation, and his approach has been expressed in various fields. There is no space to explore these in detail, but some may be briefly mentioned, though there is a risk of distortion because of the brevity.

Theological determinism is the teaching found in early orthodox Islam and the Augustinian tradition in Christianity (pursued by Calvin in particular) that because God is all-powerful and all-knowing everything that happens must be willed by Him and known to Him in advance. If, then, God knows what I am going to do before I do it and has actually decreed what I am to do, there seems little point in saying that I have free choice. Few Muslims and almost no other Christian theologians have been willing to accept this conclusion because it contradicts other doctrines of their religions which teach the possibility of choosing to obey or disobey God's laws. The sort of answer proposed has usually been that God's knowledge is not like human free knowledge of something in the future but is eternal, as God sees all time at once, and that God's will does not dictate what man shall choose but allows him free choice. The philosophically interesting point about this is that religious thinkers have felt it important not to impugn free will.

One philosopher who expressed a form of theological determinism in his writings was the German, *Gottfried Leibniz* (1646–1716). His view was that all the phenomena of the world, things as they appear, can be reduced to simple, indivisible elements which he described as 'monads'. These monads should be understood as being essentially force or energy, each a world in itself, reflecting the activities of all other monads but not acting upon them causally: they seek their own perfection through a 'preestablished harmony' instituted by God 'the Prime Monad'. Leibniz's explanation is:

The phrase 'preestablished harmony' is a term of art, I confess; but it is not a phrase without content, since it is explained very intelligibly. The nature of every simple substance, soul, or true monad, is such that each subsequent state is a consequence of the preceding one; in this lies the cause of the harmony. For God needs only to make a simple substance once to be from the beginning a representation of the universe, according to its point of view; it follows from this alone that it will be so perpetually, and that all simple substances will always have a harmony among themselves, because they always represent the same universe . . .. The concept of an individual substance includes once for all everything which can ever happen to it and . . . in considering this concept one will be able to say everything that can truly be said about the individual.

So each substance, or soul, or monad, by containing in itself from the beginning of its existence all that it will ever be, is as the acorn which 'contains' the oak, or the egg which 'contains' the eagle. Leibniz argued that the harmony in the universe is not a result of blind chance but of God's choice to establish a world in which the best and most complete combination of monads, or essences, would result. This is, he claimed, 'the best of all possible worlds' because God has chosen the most perfect, hypothetically simple but phenomenologically rich. (This optimism was ridiculed by Voltaire in *Candide*: and note the word 'concept' in the quotation above (cf. p. 225)). It follows from this that human beings, who are aggregates of monads, have no choice in their own development. Leibniz was anxious not to appear deterministic in his philosophy, but this paragraph from his *Discourse on Metaphysics* seems difficult to interpret otherwise:

God determines our will to the choice of that which appears best, but without necessitating it in the least. It has the power of acting differently or even suspending its action entirely, both choices being and remaining possible. Nevertheless it is true, and even assured from all eternity, that certain souls will not make use of this power in such and such situations. And since from the time when I began to exist it was possible to say of me truly that this or that would happen to me, it must be acknowledged that these predicates were laws included in the complete notion of me which makes that which is called I, which is the foundation of the interconnection of all my different states, and which was perfectly known to God from all eternity.

For Leibniz a person is a mystery in the process of being inexorably unfolded; each choice he makes unfolds that mystery a little further. There could be no starker contrast than this to the views of Sartre, who viewed each person as 'a mystery in broad daylight', still remaining mysterious after making countless choices because each choice, having no 'reason' for being as it is, is 'absurd'.

(Leibniz's view that God pre-established the entire series of events in His universe seems to lead to the view that God is responsible for the evil, as well as the good, in that universe. You may wish to consider this in relation to the case study on the problem of evil in Chapter Eight.)

Psychological determinism is the belief that we all possess certain mental qualities – neuroses, psychoses, drives, phobias, and so on – which govern our lives. The psychological determinist like Freud assumes that we are all therefore at the mercy of mental factors which are beyond our conscious comprehension. This doctrine is open to two objections. Firstly, because we are unconscious of these so-called determining factors, their very existence, let alone their influence, must, by definition, be matters solely of speculation. The claims for psychological determinism are unverifiable, as are the claims of those putting it into practice: psychoanalysts. Pending such verifiability, it must remain in the area of what Sir Karl Popper has termed 'pseudoscience'. I acknowledge that issues relating to the free will–determinism debate are not open to proof either way; but, to me at least, any argument for determinism based on concepts (note the word) of an unconscious control through the psyche seems the most unsubstantiated and insubstantial of all.

Secondly, it is a matter of common human experience that, whether caused by unconscious factors or not, our psychological make-up is one that need not be seen as 'fixed' indefinitely (though in some people it may well appear so) but a state which can be changed. Just as a person can learn to control his palate (by acquiring a taste for olives, or losing a taste for sweet things, for instance) so a person can learn to control the psychological aspects of himself, especially as he increasingly understands how these can be affected by physical, or chemical, changes in himself. The timid person can learn to withdraw from his shell and become more assertive; the bombastic can learn to control his overweening desire to assert himself, and so become less overbearing; the 'phobias' which we feel can be overcome through the deliberate application of willpower: fear of the dark, of open spaces, of confined spaces, of spiders, wasps, rats, mice, hobgoblins, and foul fiends: of all these it is possible to say 'I am determined to overcome this fear' – and to be successful in the result.

Historical determinism is the belief that history is governed by economic or other forces which make certain developments inevitable. This theory seems to be the result of wanting to see pattern and purpose in history rather than merely an accidental collocation of happenings; and this desire seems to coincide with that of wishing to study history scientifically. We saw in the first chapter how different historians have studied the same sets of past events and from them have created totally divergent patterns or pictures, giving at least the impression that historical writings are more an imaginative work of fiction than pieces of scientific exploration. (This is not to belittle history: quite the reverse.) The problem is confounded whenever any historian has attempted to forecast the future. If historical determinism has even a whiff of truth about it, one would expect to find a few insights from other historians which might prepare us for what is to come. But even Marxist theory, the main representative of this brand of determinism, has achieved only mixed success in predicting what will happen. More important, those who profess to believe in the inevitability of the historic process appeal to members of the working class (in particular) in language and with underlying assumptions which would make no sense at all if they were not free to accept or reject Marxist leadership. If the Marxist interpretation of history is true, what is the point of wasting time trying to persuade people that this is the case? If it were so, they would need no persuasion, since they would be seeing it happen. The very act of attempting to persuade seems to be one of wilfully making things happen, which is the reverse of determinism. How Marxists themselves can patch up the apparent contradiction is disputable, but the significant point remains that determinists do not in fact carry through their determinism systematically.

Environmental determinism is the tendency to see human actions as in principle predictable through knowledge of the supposed 'laws' of social science. As usually presented this is not so much a teaching that no decisions are free as a tendency in practice to ignore the possibility of freedom. It would be absurd to deny that our environment through one form or another has affected our lives, and continues to do so. Even Sartre, the high priest of libertarianism, came to recognise that some people are born into such deprived situations and conditions that it is desperately difficult for them to achieve any opportunity for expressing freedom of choice. If every ounce of energy has to be spent purely on surviving, there is virtually no scope for the expression of moral freedom. But this is a comment on – a condemnation of, in fact – social conditions which many people believe should not be allowed to occur, for the very reason that it denies men freedom of expression.

This form of determinism also has the same inherent weakness as historical determinism: it shows very little success in *predicting* human actions, and certainly not such success as need concern anyone wishing to defend free will. The fact that sociologists can make a rough guess at the number of suicides next year does not push anyone off the Bay Bridge. The practical problem is not whether any human actions are free, but – granted the common-sense belief in the possibility of freedom – whether, in particular cases, this freedom has been impaired. One can accept this without in any way supporting a determinist philosophy.

233

Mechanistic, or scientific determinism is the claim that all events throughout the universe happen according to laws which can in principle be known by scientific methods. It is a view which first came into vogue in the seventeenth century, following the Copernican revolution, and constitutes an expression of one of the central themes of the 'Age of Enlightenment'. To describe the material world as behaving in accordance with certain mechanical laws may not seem too deterministic a philosophy, since our concern is with human behaviour, not that of 'dead' matter. But there emerged a school of philosophy which asserted not only that reality consists of nothing more than matter in motion, but also that human beings are part of this, and so are subject to the same mechanistic laws as everything else. Hobbes, whose life spanned the seventeenth century, stated this case in his book *Of Liberty and Necessity*, in which he vigorously affirmed that man's will was not free:

I make not only the *effect* but also the election of that particular effect necessary, inasmuch as the will itself and each propension of a man during his deliberation is as much necessitated as anything else whatsoever. . . . It be not in his will to choose his fancy, or choose his election and will.

Thus one could not say, as Plato said, and as Descartes, Hobbes's contemporary, said, that, because human beings are mental as well as material beings, and because the mental is not subject to mechanical laws, the human will *must* be free because the will belongs with the mental, not the material, aspect of the person. Hobbes was a monist, a materialist, who rejected the claim that human beings possess any special quality which exempts them from the laws of matter: and this includes even his thought processes.

His claim to the contrary, which has been supported by numerous scientists and philosophers in the succeeding centuries, derives whatever credibility it has from the success of scientists in finding out facts, making predictions, and changing the natural course of events through technology. It is the elevation of a methodological principle – every event has a cause – to the status of dogma. Scientists, as scientists, assume that things happen as determined by antecedent fixed causes, and, as scientists, argue that this goes for moral decisions too. In everyday life scientists, like everyone else, take it for granted that many things happen because people freely decide to make them happen when they might freely have chosen otherwise.

If there were a straightforward contradiction between free will and science, then without any doubt it is science (or at least the claim that science is true) which would have to be abandoned, because free will is part of the basic facts of human experience against which scientific findings are judged. In fact the contradiction is not between free will and science, but between free will and an arbitrary extension of a scientific assumption to a field where it does not belong.

In these latest paragraphs, the word 'causal' has been introduced without comment, and this important 'concept' must now be examined.

Causation and determinism

In the mechanical world we constantly observe sequences of events which always occur in conjunction with each other; that is to say, when event A occurs it is invariably followed by event B. Night follows day, and day follows night; as days grow shorter, leaves turn brown; I bite an apple and perceive a particular flavour on my palate; in a circular mountain range I give a shout and, a second or two later, hear the echo of my voice; I hit a billiard ball on its right-hand side and it moves to the left; and so on. Two questions arise from our experience of 'constant conjunction': (a) does one cause the other (which causes something else, which in turn has a further causal effect, and so on ad infinitum)? and (b) does the fact of causality, if it is established, mean that everything in the universe is therefore determined, so that, granted a knowledge of all the relevant facts of the present situation, we could accurately foretell all that will happen within the universe into the indefinite future? An issue that arises with both these questions is, whatever be the case with the mechanical universe, is it also true, as Hobbes affirmed, of human (especially moral) behaviour?

(a) Hume on causality The philosopher Hume maintained that the constant conjunction of events does not imply causality. Experience – our perception of events – may lead us to infer that this is so, but reasoning or reflection may assure us that we are wrong to jump to such conclusions. It may seem, for instance, that, because night always follows day and day, night, each is caused by the other; but reason explains both as being jointly caused by the earth's rotation. To conclude otherwise would be to be guilty of the fallacy of *post hoc ergo propter hoc* (after x therefore caused by x) – or putting two and two together and making five.

This is a fallacy constantly fallen into by specialist groups who make comments on various facets of human affairs – politicians, sociologists, criminologists, journalists, and so on. 'Since this government came to power . . .' on the lips of a politician can be expected to lead to an artificial juxtaposition of circumstances which seems to upgrade the speaker's party and downgrade the opponent's. People worried about crime statistics will quote a previous event of their choice to 'prove' why certain crimes are rising, or falling. ('Since the abolition of capital punishment, terrorist crimes have increased fourfold in the British

Isles.') A woman in Blackburn market (where they talk about very little else other than 'post hoc ergo propter hoc') once assured me that England's performances at successive Olympic Games had declined with the decline in church attendance; and my elderly aunt in Scotland believed sincerely that every time she dropped a spoon she was due to have a visitor (since she had regular visitors she was usually confirmed in this prediction).

One can have great fun with this particular fallacy ('before Reagan became US President AIDS had never been heard of'), but there are also serious uses (or misuses?) made of it. The Hopi Indians in America perform a ritual every morning just before sunrise, in the firm belief that the sun would not otherwise rise at all. Since they have never failed to perform the ritual, and since the sun has never failed to rise, they feel confirmed in their belief. This naivety illustrate's Hume's argument in an obvious way: but he contended that even in areas where perceptions were universal, though a particular combination of events had always occurred, this did not prove conclusively that the same combination would occur next time, or for the indefinite future.

The contrary of every matter of fact is still possible: . . . . That the sun will not rise tomorrow is no less intelligible a proposition and implies no more contradiction than the affirmation that it will rise. We should in vain, therefore, attempt to demonstrate its falsehood.

The bread, which I formerly ate, nourished me . . . but does it follow that other bread must also nourish me at another time?

(*Enquiry*, IV I)

Bertrand Russell, in his *History of Western Philosophy* (p. 643) suggests that Hume is obliged to answer this question in the negative:

Hume is not content with reducing the evidence of a causal connection to experience of frequent conjunction; he proceeds to argue that such experience does not justify the expectation of similar conjunctions in the future. For example, when . . . I see an apple, past experience makes me expect that it will taste like an apple, and not like roast beef; but there is no rational justification for this expectation.

This whole discussion may appear to be a typical piece of philosophical finickiness, and at one level one would be sympathetic with this judgment. But the point that Hume is making is a very important one: that

236

our association of cause and effect plays a considerable part in the process by which we establish our values, which will in turn influence our way of behaving towards other people. Since the mind seems to desire order rather than chaos, design rather than accident, it therefore tends to make a pattern of what may well be in reality disjointed events, however frequently repeated in conjunction with each other. This process, which is one of inductive reasoning, (reaching a general conclusion from a series of individual examples) may in certain circumstances be desirable, if not essential (market researchers and opinion pollsters do it continually). If we lived our lives as though the sun might not rise tomorrow, little forward planning would be possible. Hume is simply reminding us that because, for instance, the laws of motion may change, or because of some inter-galactical 'catastrophe', there may be no 'tomorrow'. He is effectually countering the mechanistic views of Hobbes and his supporters, and so prepares us for the unexpected. The chicken that runs every morning to the farmer, looking forward to being fed, is likely one morning to be surprised (to put it at its mildest) to find that it has its head chopped off instead.

(b) *Is any cause inevitable?* Nothing that Hume wrote is intended to deny the obvious truth that every event has some cause. The idea of an 'uncaused first cause' which is expressed in certain theological affirmations is illogical; so also it would be to affirm that 'nothing' caused the door to open, or a person to trip up, or the *Marie Celeste* to lose its crew. The important question is not whether any event has a cause, nor whether we have rightly judged the nature of any particular cause, nor even whether the cause-and-effect syndrome is a permanent feature of various sets of circumstances; the question raised by the determinists is whether any particular cause of an event was itself inevitable.

So far as the mechanical universe is concerned, we may well conclude that this is so. The cause of the door's suddenly opening is a draught; study the meteorological conditions and the cause of the draught may be established; and if it were worth our while, we could follow weather conditions back and recognise a continuous causal connection. This connection is in no way lost by accepting the incidence of 'accidents', such as the volcanic eruption in Washington in the early 1980s which affected the climate of the northern hemisphere for some years thereafter. It is possible to live quite equably with the idea of the universe as a vast, infinitely complicated machine of inter-connected causes and effects, because all are so numerous and complicated that the process remains, and is likely always to remain, on the whole, a mystery. (Many quantum physicists deny that the laws of nature are causally determined, and assert only the statistical *probability* of occurrences at the sub-atomic level.)

The libertarian need have no qualms about accepting causality as in the nature of the universe as a whole; where he parts company with the determinist is on the question of human decision-making. Is human decision-making an 'event'? More specifically, is the thought which led to the decision an event? If so, is it subject to the same inexorable laws of cause and effect as the mechanical universe in which the decisions are made? The determinist will affirm that this is in fact the case, and that if we understood adequately the workings of the human mind we should recognise the cause of the emergence of a particular idea, and the cause of that cause, and so on, so that we would be compelled to conclude that all thought and behaviour was as inevitable as the movement of the billiard ball.

If this were true, it is difficult to see how many factors about human behaviour which receive well-nigh universal consent can continue to be maintained. If every decision is caused inexorably, it seems harsh to blame the agent for making the 'wrong' decision (meaning that most of the others disapprove of it) or to praise him for making the 'right' decision (that is, one generally approved of). Whatever determinists may say to the contrary, this belief, if firmly and sincerely held, must lead people to be somewhat – if not totally – fatalistic in their view of life in general and their own role in it in particular. It must remove, or at least water down, any sense of urgency to improve social conditions and individual situations. The determinist may justifiably argue that, even granted that these are, or will be, the consequences of accepting his philosophy, this is no argument against the validity of the thesis. Maybe the natural way of life is to 'take things as they come', though the behaviourist (scientific determinist) B.F. Skinner effectively denied this by setting up groups of small communities.

These are deep waters for which there is neither time nor (being honest with myself) inclination to pursue further. There is enough literature on the matter to keep any student busy for the rest of his life (and I'm referring to young, as well as mature, students). The principal objection to determinism has already been stated: I am conscious, when I deliberate carefully over a forthcoming decision, that I am free to choose. The billiard ball must take a leftward direction if hit on the right; but it is I who decide whether to hit it on the right or on the left. It is I who make up my mind whether to aim to put it in the top pocket or the middle pocket. An observer may criticise my decision on the grounds that the alternative offered better prospects for continuing my break: but the decision was mine, and I could have chosen otherwise. I am not arguing that every decision I make is as free as this, nor whether, say, a man who commits a criminal act was free, in that particular situation, to have behaved otherwise. I am simply affirming that my own experience assures me that not all my behaviour through life has been determined, and that the determinist case is invalid. Their argument that this is a piece of self-deception on my part, as on the part of all other libertarians such as the existentialists, is one that I cannot disprove, any more than I can prove to others that I have toothache or have fallen in love.

Conclusion   There is, then, as we have seen, no one meaning of words like 'free' or 'freedom' and there is no one meaning of 'the problem of freedom'. The difficulties listed in this chapter are only a few of those that arise, but they are sufficiently representative to enable one to conclude that difficulties about freedom are of two kinds. There are *verbal difficulties*, where the same word is used in more than one sense or where language is vague, muddled, or inconsistent. In theory, these can be sorted out quite easily by patient analysis; in practice, some people have a vested interest in distortion and lack of clarity. Then there are *difficulties caused by lack of information*, some of which can, at least in principle, be cleared up, whilst others probably stem from inherent limitations of knowledge. An important example of this last class is the difficulty of knowing in particular cases whether a person was free to have acted otherwise than he did: and this is the key issue.

It seems clear to me that freedom of choice, including freedom of moral choice, is available to all, but that many people experience from an early age pressures virtually beyond their control which force them into some kind of moral groove from which they find difficulty in breaking free; and also that some people find a sense of security within the groove, as many old people do in a sheltered home, preferring institutional restrictions to the risk of personal responsibility; but the possibility of greater freedom remains open to them if they are prepared to take it.

The image of the human being offered by the determinist is that of a tramcar, its wheels fixed in a set of grooves, capable of moving only in the direction taken by the grooves and the overhead power cables. The alternative, libertarian, image is that of an omnibus, limited by its supply of petrol and subject to the natural laws of wear and tear, but free to move in any direction, to make U-turns, to follow the main route, or take a side route. Perhaps the image which most fits the reality of the human situation is that of the trolley-bus: free, because it runs on the road surface like any other vehicle, to move about within certain limits, but limited by its overhead cable as to the main directions it can take. Thus I shall certainly never rule Britain, or be a beauty queen, or become President of the United States; it is unlikely that I shall become prime minister, sail the Atlantic single-handed, or make a million (though these are not impossible, like the first set of examples); it is more possible, but still not to be expected, that I shall become a film star, or principal of a college, or write a bestseller; and, with sights set ever lower, the range of opportunities continues to widen. In the end I find that, within certain limitations, there is much more that I am free to do than might at first appear. The same, with variations in the range of opportunity, is true, I

believe, of everyone. Man is more than a highly intelligent animal: his
autonomy makes him so.

APPENDIX: A BREAKDOWN OF SCHOOLS

For your information, and to enable you to see how wide is the range of
emphases where free will is concerned, here is a list (to which other
names could be added) of varieties of schools of libertarianism and
determinism.

1 **Rational libertarianism** (*R. M. Hare*):
   True freedom is choosing to act in accordance with enlightened
   reason (altruism).
2 **Noumenal libertarianism** (*Kant*):
   Phenomena (the appearances of everyday life studied in science) are
   under the sway of mechanical causality.
   Noumena (things in themselves) are inaccessible to science: they
   include man's free will – a good will is the only thing which is good
   in itself.
3 **Irrational libertarianism** (*Camus*):
   Any purpose superior to the individual world would restrict his
   freedom, so the free man exercises his freedom by gratuitous,
   spontaneous acts subject to no law or constraint (cf. also the novel
   The Dice Man).
4 **Psychological libertarianism** (*Laing, Janov*):
   Most people are bound by compulsions derived from society or
   from traumas in infancy, but freedom can be achieved by a
   psychological breakthrough (insight/primal therapy).
5 **Political libertarianism** (*Ayn Rand*):
   Inner moral freedom is threatened by political tendencies (e.g. the
   welfare state, socialism) which stifle initiative and weaken self-
   reliance: true freedom is freedom to be selfish, and demands a free
   capitalist society.
6 **Immoral libertarianism** (*Calvin*):
   Man was created free to serve God, but after the Fall he has become
   totally depraved so that he is free to do evil but not to do good.
7 **Deterministic libertarianism** (*G. Ryle*):
   What we do is determined by prior states of the human organism,
   but we freely choose to do what is determined.
8 **Qualified libertarianism** (*Shankara: the Vedanta*):
   At any given moment man is free to choose between two or more
   alternatives, but what these alternatives are is determined by
   the endless chain of past events including past free choices
   (karma).

9 **Astral determinism** (*Jaimini*):
What happens in anyone's life is pre-determined by the position of the planets, stars, etc., at the moment of birth (fatalism).
10 **Historical quasi-determinism** (*Marx*):
The general course of events follows from the operation of economic and social laws which can be understood but not altered, but individuals are free to achieve a heightened consciousness and to work for or against revolutionary change.
11 **Social quasi-determinism** (*Durkheim*):
Human behaviour conforms to laws which enable it to be predicted, but sociology is not concerned with individual psychology.
12 **Scientific determinism** (*Skinner*):
Science methodologically assumes that all events, including human actions, are part of a universal network of cause and effect, so that all behaviour can be seen as response to stimuli.

CASE STUDY 32: ARE YOU FREE?

As we saw in the text, the question of how free we are to choose how we shall behave in any given situation is not quite so straightforward as may at first appear. Listed below are situations in which there is a prima-facie case for freedom of action: but is one really free to choose in these situations? Consider the problems we face:

1 Influence of **social pressures**, for example *telling the truth*. No problem about this? How about your first visit to your likely future in-laws whom, for your partner's sake (if for no other reason) you must impress? They present you (accidentally) with your least favourite meal, cook it execrably, and then ask you if you enjoyed it. How much does the injunction 'Thou shalt not bear false witness' influence you in this situation?
2 Influence of **upbringing**: *telling a lie*. You need to lie to save the reputation of a friend; in fact, you know that it will be the kindest thing to do. But you are the straightforward sort and you know that your face will contradict everything you say.
3 The influence of **common politeness**. A student finds a lecture both boring and irrelevant to his studies, and realises that there are still 35 minutes to go. He is free to walk out (there are no heavies at the door) but . . .
4 The influence of **convention**. During a heatwave, you attend a residential course where everyone else is dressed formally (dark suits for both men and women). You are free to turn up dressed in T-shirt and shorts – or are you?
5 Influence of **respect for persons**. (The following situation is one actually faced by the author.) In the school where you teach you are –

with everybody's knowledge – at daggers drawn with the head teacher. One of your colleagues wins the jackpot on the pools and, in front of a score of witnesses, offers you half of it if, with the whole school watching, you empty your lunch over the head teacher's head next time you're sitting at top table. The money would be enough to save you from ever having to work again.

Can you add to this list? That is, can you give examples of situations where in one sense you are free to behave in a certain way but in fact your hands are tied? What does this say about the question of freewill? How far do you go along with these words of Tennyson, which could be interpreted as a paraphrase of Leibniz: 'We needs must choose the highest when we see it.' Do you think anyone ever behaves in a worse way than the best *as he sees it*?

CASE STUDY 33: CRIME AND PUNISHMENT

Below is a set of questions aimed to start you reflecting on the vexed problem of the criminal in society and the causes and treatment of his socially unacceptable activity.

1 If *crime* is breaking the law –
    (a) What is the law?
    (b) Who makes law?
    (c) Is law breaking always a Bad Thing?
2 Why do people take up crime?
    (a) Born that way (in the genes)?
    (b) Family conditioning? (How then could one son of a burglar
        follow in his father's footsteps while the other becomes an
        accountant: or would you say that both had followed father, but
        one chose a more socially acceptable way?)
    (c) Influence of peer group ('got in with the wrong sort')?
    (d) Bloody-mindedness (holds a grudge against society)?
    (e) Poverty – forced into crime in order to survive? (Not all poor
        people become criminals.)
    (f) Compulsion – crime provides means of obtaining drugs, etc.?
    (g) Adventure – excitement of taking risks?
    (h) Security – prison becomes home?
3 Why punish crime?
    ('All punishment is mischief; all punishment is itself evil' –
    Bentham)
    (a) To repay wrong-doing (retributive)? – the deontological
        approach: all crime carries its punishment as the other side of the
        coin – an 'eye for an eye' (Kant). Connection clear if death the

punishment for murder: what, on this basis, should be the punishment for rape, or fraud, blackmail, or robbery?

(b) To discourage others (deterrent)? – a teleological approach. Does punishment deter – e.g. capital punishment for murder? (Compare incidents of murder in those US states practising capital punishment with those that don't.) Do prisons deter? (Population ever-increasing. A large percentage are recidivists.)

(c) To protect society? – teleological.

(d) To educate wrong-doers (reformative)? – teleological. Accepting that this rules out capital punishment, is there any evidence that prisons reform? (Over 50 percent of first-time prisoners return to prison for at least a second time.)

4 What are the *criteria* for deciding types of punishment?
  (a) 'The greatest good of the greatest number'?
  (b) The welfare of the criminal?
  (c) Scarcity of resources?
  (d) Consistency?
  (e) The feelings of victims or their families?
  (f) Tradition?
  (g) Desire to express public attitudes?

5 What are prisons?
  (a) Places of custody for those on remand?
  (b) Secure units to protect the public?
  (c) Therapeutic institutions?
  (d) Homes for the inadequate?
  (e) 'Colleges' of crime?

6 How could prisons be changed?
  (a) Allow wives/girlfriends to visit regularly? (Much homosexuality in prisons.)
  (b) Allow prisoners to learn and/or follow a worthwhile trade to help eliminate boredom?
  (c) Introduce more warders to supervise prisoners outside their cells for longer periods?
  (d) Build more human places of confinement? (All these would require massive injections of cash: which area should it come from – the National Health Service? Education? Defence?)
  (e) Create a 'devil's island' (say the Isle of Man – a holiday island west of Liverpool) and leave prisoners to fend for themselves?
  (f) Reduce sentences?
  (g) Increase sentences?

7 What are the alternatives to prison?
  (a) Brain operations to make violent people mild?
  (b) Compulsory injections of drugs with similar effects?
  (c) Change society so that crime ceases to exist? (What do you do

with existing criminals? Which society has ever abolished crime?)

(d) Make long spells of work in the community compulsory? – how many supervisors would be needed?

(e) Deport criminals? – are there any more Australias in the world?

(f) Ignore crime and criminals altogether? – would society survive?

(See also Case Study 13, pp. 96–8.)

Chapter Eleven

Ethics and politics

To discuss moral issues in relation to politics will appear to some as misplaced as eulogising the virtues of total abstinence in a brewery, or those of virginity in a brothel. Politics is popularly held to be a 'dirty business', operated by wheeler-dealers and time-servers. It has been defined as 'the art of the possible' and, more cynically, 'the art of the second-best'; its practitioners bear the image in the eyes of many of unprincipled lusters after power, where power, in the words of Henry Kissinger when he was American Secretary of State, 'is a great aphrodisiac'. Yet politics has not only thrown up rogues, liars, pawns, and idiots but also eminent people who have made moral issues matters of national, if not international, debate. Some of the noblest contributors to history have been politicians; and some of the finest philosophical ideas have been penned by politicians. Italy produced Garibaldi as well as Mussolini; Germany Bismarck as well as Hitler; even Rome produced its Hadrians and Trajans besides its Caligulas and Neros. The English-speaking world has produced perhaps an even larger proportion of philosopher-politicians, from Jefferson and – though he, tragically, never became president – Adlai Stevenson in America to Burke, Mill, and Disraeli in Britain. It would be quite wrong, therefore, to generalise from holders of the highest elected offices in Britain and America during, say, the 1980s that politics is only for blinkered bullies. Since politicians are people, they will naturally reflect the gamut of human virtues and vices, and if the latter seem to be dominant at a particular time it seems reasonable to expect a swing of the pendulum towards virtue to take place sooner or later. 'Man', said Aristotle, 'is a political animal'; his saying so does not make it so, of course, but his words seem to carry enough truth to justify a brief examination of politics insofar as moral issues are involved.

Forms of Government

It will clear the way for discussion of the main issues of this chapter if we first outline some of the various ways by which government has taken shape in different countries and periods. The Greek word *arche* means (in one of its senses) 'rule', and *kratein* 'to rule'. One or other of these occurs as the second half of each word that follows, to which the first half is the identifying variant.

Autocracy (*autos* = 'self'): government by a single ruler; the same system is found in a

Monarchy (*monos* = 'alone'): in current usage this signifies rule by a hereditary king or queen, while an autocracy is normally ruled by a dictator who has gained his absolute power by his own efforts, one way or another.

Oligarchy (*oligos* = 'a few'): rule by a few, as by the triumvirate after the murder of Julius Caesar.

Patriarchy (*pater* = 'father'): rule by fathers (or the older and more respected members of a tribe or community, such as among the Aborigines).

Aristocracy (*aristos* = 'finest' or 'best'): government by nobles as, effectively, for long periods in pre-Revolutionary France or pre-Tudor England.

Plutocracy (*ploutos* = 'wealth'): rule by the rich. There are cynics who so describe the American system, since the 'log cabin to White House' syndrome seems to be a thing of the past.

Bureaucracy (using the French word for 'office' on this occasion, since there is no Greek equivalent): government by public officials or civil servants. To refer again to our guest cynic, it may be said that this is how Britain is governed since, while elected ministers come and go, civil servants go on – and on – through successive parliaments.

Theocracy: literally 'rule by God', derivatively, rule by God's representatives – the priests or their equivalent (in post Shah-ist Iran, the Ayatollahs, in Geneva of the Reformation, the elders or presbyters). Etymologically similar to this is

Hierarchy (*hieros* = 'holy'): in modern popular usage this word has lost its original meaning and now refers to the upper echelons of any community or company, organisation, or profession. Interestingly, the word still retains its 'tread softly as I'm holier than you' ethos.

Gerontocracy (*geron* = 'old man'): government by the aged. Until the advent of Gorbachev in Soviet Russia, and for decades after the Communist victory in China in 1948, both these countries could have been described in this way.

Stratocracy (*stratos* = 'an army'): government by military rule; plenty of examples of these in the modern world.

Meritocracy (*meritum* = 'desert' in Latin): a modern word, coined in the title of the book *The Rise of the Meritocracy*, meaning rule by the most able/learned/highly-esteemed. It is a 'snarl' rather than a 'purr' word, suggesting that the process by which people reach the highest positions of responsibility is based on the philosophy 'To them that have shall be given'.

Democracy (*demos* = 'the people'): government by the people. This form of government will be discussed at some length in the text, with a case study on people's rights. At this point all that needs to be noted is that, for this system to work effectively, there should be constant changes of those who govern so that the 'us-them' syndrome, comprising, on the one hand, those who govern and, on the other, those who are governed, should be minimised as far as possible if not totally eliminated. This process is, of course, more viable in a small than in a large organisation of people. (I belong to an organisation which steadfastly refuses to establish any kind of hierarchy; its method of achieving this is by the (unwritten) rule that the chairperson and secretary of local meetings shall hold his/her post for a maximum of three months.)

These are just a few examples of the types of government which the world has experienced and is still experiencing. You may wish to add to the list and could, in fact, have fun in doing so, especially if you have a sound knowledge of Greek (a useful weapon when tackling philosophy). Rule by teachers is 'pedagogarchy', by a woman is 'gynarchy', though 'gynecocracy' means government by women in the plural. ('Porcocracy' would presumably be government by male chauvinists, 'ludocracy', by playboys; 'pornogarchy' and 'idiotocracy' are almost (though not quite – consult an etymological dictionary) self-explanatory; but how about 'pharmacarchy' or 'oinopotocracy'?)

For purposes of clarification, the different forms of government have been categorised separately, but in practice the chances are that two or more types will overlap. An autocrat, for example, is likely to be rich, if not noble; gerontocracy could still be democratic, and bureaucracy could masquerade under any of the other forms. One form of government (though in this case that phrase is totally inapplicable) which is and will always remain in a category apart from the rest is anarchy, meaning, literally, 'no rule'. There has been a variety of expressions of this over the past three centuries.

Government and the philosophers

Many countries in the world – from Western Europe to North America via Australasia – claim to be democratically governed. We shall first examine how the idea of democracy developed in the thinking of a succession of philosophers from Plato to Mill (selected primarily because of the variations in their thought); then we shall take a close look at what democracy means in practice, and ask whether the idea is capable of being expressed in the political structures of the modern world.

Plato's Republic The idea of democracy was popularised over two millennia ago by Plato in what is arguably the most famous of all philosophical works: *The Republic*, in which the author expounded his views on politics, education, morality, marriage, metaphysics, art, poetry, psychology, theology, and justice. The American writer and philosopher, R. W. Emerson, said of *The Republic*: 'Burn the libraries, for their value is in this book.' To study philosophy without reading it would be like studying Christianity without consulting the Old Testament, or Western music without J. S. Bach.

The ideal republic as envisaged by Plato contains three streams or strata among its citizens: the philosopher-kings who rule the state, having been selected because of their superior intellectual skills; the soldiers, who defend the state; and the workers – farmers, tool-makers, merchants, and so on – who perform all the menial chores, having failed the academic tests. Plato chose the most academically brilliant to be guardians of the state because he believed that the firmest hope for sound and just government was through rule by the enlightened. He wrote, 'Until wisdom and political leadership meet in the same man . . . cities will never cease from ill, nor the human race.'

Plato's picture of Utopia is often described as democratic, but this was hardly the case. It certainly avoided the perils of autocracy, plutocracy, and aristocracy: to become a ruler involved the practising of innate intellectual skills, developed through years of rigorous training: the position was not hereditary, and wealth could not buy a place among the élite. But the word *élite* gives the game away: the post of guardian was open to only a select minority of the citizens, and in no way represented a cross-section of those ruled. So with guardianship accessible only to the few (to use the classification given earlier), it was an oligarchic meritocracy, more democratic than some forms of government, but not representative of democracy as it was later to be described, if not enacted.

It would be interesting to speculate on whether democracy, as enacted in western countries, would be more efficient if its servants were obliged to be academically qualified in some way. To be a member of Parliament was described by R. L. Stevenson as the only profession for which no qualification is required – and that goes for the American Senate and House of Representatives too (not to mention the President). In theory this sounds like a reasonable requirement, but in practice several problems would quickly come to the fore. Firstly, government is concerned with decision-making, and there seems little evidence to suggest that academics are specially qualified to do this. (Having sat on many academic boards which have usually been little more than academics bored, I wonder if academic expertise and the ability to make practical commitments are not opposing skills.) Secondly, while academic ability may normally reflect intelligence, it is no indicator of common sense: in most cases (again, in my experience) the reverse occurs. Thirdly, cleverness does not guarantee breadth of sympathy with others, which must be a high priority for any in government: some of the world's most evil men, whether in politics or in business, have been undoubtedly clever. Fourthly, there is the problem of who would set and assess the test (and of who would select the assessors, assuming that this could hardly be a role of the legislature itself). Finally – and this remains the gravest question mark over Plato's entire proposal – such a selective process, by excluding a large proportion of the population, would never be representative of the population as a whole, and would effectively be not dissimilar to the British parliament when only landowners had the vote. Bearing in mind that about half the population in Plato's republic – as in contemporary Athens – were slaves, with no rights at all, some may view his proposals as little more than a genuflection towards democracy.

Hobbes's Leviathan　We have already seen (Chapter Two) how *Hobbes's* view of government emanated from his view of human nature, about which he was forthright and unambiguous. Because he viewed man as an integral part of a mechanistic universe, he believed that the philosopher or social scientist could treat human actions and desires in the same way that the physicist treats weights and measures. Arguing inductively from himself to mankind as a whole, he described man as naturally and fundamentally selfish, quarrelsome, power-hungry, cruel, and perverse. In a state of anarchy people would therefore destroy each other. To avoid this, a compromise had to be made: man's natural right to do as he pleased had to give way to a natural law that the species must avoid self-destruction. This could be achieved only by a form of contract in which the individuals of any state sacrificed a portion of their autonomy to an independent public authority; only in this way could peace between the citizens be both assured and maintained, since any private agreement between two individuals would, Hobbes asserted, otherwise be broken as soon as one of the parties saw this as an advantageous procedure. Through this contract – and only through this contract: earlier writers had viewed the state as part of the state of nature – the state comes into being.

Hobbes, in his masterpiece, *Leviathan*, argued that the ideal form of government was a monarchy, or autocracy, since a democracy or oligarchy would involve decision-making by people with, inevitably, conflicting interests. The people's task was therefore to elect the first sovereign, after which the rules of succession would ensure that no further elections would be required. Hobbes added that, once a majority vote had been cast for the ruler, 'everyone, both he that voted for it and he that voted against it, shall authorise all the actions and judgments of that man . . . as if they were his own.' The person elected in this way would then fulfil his side of the contract by maintaining law and order among those whom he ruled, and by performing whatever other actions might be needed to ensure that the social fabric was secured and sustained. The authority of this person would, Hobbes believed, have been fatally curtailed if the ruler were made answerable to the electors by (for instance) having to submit himself to a reselection process every few years, or by having to operate within a constitution which allowed rivals to challenge him if he acted contrarily to popular wishes (by raising extra taxes, for example). Though Hobbes was himself sceptical about religion, one can understand how his political theory lent support to the concept of 'the divine right of kings'; he certainly would have found life difficult without the support of the Stuarts, especially Charles II; it was Hobbes's misfortune (though not quite as strongly so as Charles the First's) to encounter those who believed they were of the divine left, so that during the Commonwealth interregnum he had to flee the country.

Hobbes's defence of strong, single-handed (and, it goes without saying, single-minded) government is an extension of the view put forward a century earlier by the Italian, Machiavelli, who, in his book *The Prince*, had, with brutal frankness, propounded the idea that politics – by which he then meant European politics – rested largely on force and selfishness. The main direct effect of Hobbes's ideas was to establish the sovereignty of the nation-state. Indirectly, and, from the philosophical viewpoint, of greater interest, is the support he gave to individualism: the power of the state and the authority of the law are justified, according to this belief, only because they contribute to the security of individual human beings. The only grounds for any individual's surrendering part of his personal autonomy are that the obedience and respect for authority thus required are less painful to the individual – and so more to his advantage in the long term – than would be any refusal on his part to take this step.

It is easy to see why any dictator – assuming he were literate enough to manage this – would delight in the pages of Hobbes's *Leviathan*: and why many a prime minister of democratic countries must often secretly have longed for the power that Hobbes envisaged for the ruler. Even liberals have been occasionally seduced, despairing of situations brought about by some of the less desirable aspects of democracy (described by G. B. Shaw as substituting 'election by the incompetent many for appointment by the corrupt few'); it is in fact a pleasurable pastime to fantasise about what bills one would introduce, granted absolute power. Experience of this form of government, however, indicates that, while occasionally it may throw up a wise and beneficent ruler, it is likelier – and more natural, if Hobbes is right – to produce one who uses his power not for the benefit of his subjects but solely in order to feather his own nest. For every Pitt there are a dozen Thatchers, for every Lincoln there are a thousand Reagans. Perhaps at certain stages of development a state is best served by an autocracy (post-colonial Africa may well exemplify this): but, it seems, the corrupting influence of power on the individual, and especially when that individual establishes a dynasty, is quite obvious even without Lord Acton's dictum: power tends to corrupt and absolute power corrupts absolutely. If, as Plato asserted, 'democracy turns into despotism' what hope is there for a system which starts off with all the trappings of despotism?

Locke Much nearer to the current view in the West about the ideal form of government is *John Locke* (1632–1704) who, if we were studying epistemology, would loom large in this book. His views on government were based on the principle that the contract between government and citizens should be one which had the full consent of the governed; that they should be free to express dissent; and that consequently no government should survive which had lost the support of the majority of those who experienced the effects of its jurisdiction. *Men make and break their rulers.* No citizen, Locke argued, should be 'subjected to the political power of another without his own consent'. Against Hobbes's view that natural law required an autocratic government in the long-term interests of its citizens, Locke contended that no man or government 'has the arbitrary power over the life, liberty, or possessions of another'. If, reading Locke, echoes are heard of the American Declaration of Independence, this is no accident: Locke wrote with the state of the American colonies in mind, and Thomas Jefferson, who wrote the Declaration, was well-versed in Locke.

Effectively, Locke enunciated a view of government which may be described as democracy, since it was an advocacy of government with authority based solely on the support of the majority. This may not seem to us a particularly revolutionary idea, but for many of Locke's contemporaries it was virtually treasonable. Such power in the hands of the citizens implied, for instance, that when oppressed by tyrannical rule, the people have the right to revolution. We shall return later to the question of rights; the issue with which Locke presents us is how laudable is the notion, if not the actual practice, of rule based in its authority on the support of the majority.

Democracy It must be acknowledged at once that there is a prima facie case for supporting this system of government. The fact that a ruler or group of rulers must at all times be answerable to the people for their decisions must be seen as likely to produce as great a degree of satisfaction as is possible in a species with no two samples exactly alike. The case for this is even stronger in conditions of universal suffrage over a certain age than it was in Locke's time when only a small minority of the population had this right. The people whom Locke believed the government had to serve and please were only the landed gentry and other property-owners: none of the poor of the land, and no women, were represented, so that his form of democracy still remained open to the objection made to Plato's republic: it did not represent a full cross-section of the citizens who came under its rule. But at least Locke was proposing some sanctions or brakes on the rulers, and this must be seen as a desirable development.

There are (at least) three problems relating to the practice of rule by majority support which must, however, be borne in mind. Firstly, there is the fact of the existence of the so-called *silent majority*: those who have no deep political convictions, and no desire to become involved in any aspect of political activity. These people don't mind who rules, so long as, on the whole, they are left in peace. Occasionally, as, perhaps, when the Social Democratic party was formed in Britain, they may be stirred out of their lethargy: but they hold no particular political ideology. Since this group (and its size is inestimable) will generally go along with whichever political theory is the flavour of the month, it means that in effect the real debate in a democracy – the expression of support for or objection to the rulers of the day – is left to the political activists, who are only a minority of the electorate as a whole.

Secondly, and allied to the first problem, the ideal of democracy has to contend with the *power of the mass media* of communication to influence people's minds and affect how they vote. In recent years, in both Britain and America (and probably in most other democratic countries) the image presented by proponents of political schools on television has been one – if not the most important – of the factors affecting how citizens vote. Locke would hardly have been amused to learn that a presidential election in the America of his dreams was won and lost because one of the contenders in a series of television debates between the two protagonists had a five o'clock shadow, and reminded the audience of a 'baddie' in a western film. The attitude to their readers taken by the bulk of the popular press in Britain – if the 'stories' with which they choose to fill their pages are any guide – is one of unconcealed and cynical contempt. The editor of one of them, Cecil Harmsworth King (as he then was) of the *Daily Mirror*, when criticised for the low level of intellect assumed in its readers by his paper, simply remarked that the trouble with intellectuals was that they did not understand just how crass, how ignorant, how prejudiced, and how incapable of any real thought on any matter were the majority of newspaper readers. Those were harsh words, and were fiercely debated at the time; but a country with four million daily readers of the *Sun* (to name but one national newspaper that one would wish to hide from overseas visitors) might have made Locke think again before enthusing so strongly about the consent of the majority. He would hardly have viewed as healthy a consensus expressed by four million parrots, taught by a handful of aliens.

The third problem with majority rule is the one that is philosophically the most important. Even granted that all those who constitute the majority have actually thought through the various political issues, so that their support is active rather than tacit, there remains the question of the representation of the *rights of the minority*. Hobbes had argued that, once the ruler had been (s)elected, he must represent all the citizens, not just those who supported him. This sounds fine in theory, but in practice the situation has often been frustrating, to put it mildly. The fact that a particular policy reflects the views of the majority does not, so argue the minority, guarantee the 'rightness' of the opinion, even if 'rightness' is defined in Hobbesian terms as 'in the best interests of the state'. For decades, for example, a substantial minority of British people held the belief that Britain should impose economic sanctions on South Africa. This belief grew both on moral grounds – the inhumane treatment of blacks by whites in that country being ethically indefensible – and on practical grounds – if nothing was done this would not be forgotten when, as would inevitably happen eventually, there was majority rule in South Africa, and relationships with Britain reviewed (it is the latter consideration which would have weighed the more strongly with Hobbes). The minority were ignored on this issue, (ironically concerning a government which, by itself representing only a minority of the population, illustrated the viewpoint that, while the majority may sometimes be wrong, the minority may not always be right).

Mill On Liberty   The question of minority rights was taken up, both in his writings and in parliament itself, by *John Stuart Mill*. His argument was in essence very basic and very simple: if democracy is to be an expression of the wishes of all the governed, then this must include those who, on any issue, could or would not go along with the will of the majority. Mill put this viewpoint with penetrating clarity in his most famous book, *On Liberty* (perhaps, among writings on political philosophy, the chief rival to *The Republic* in its lucidity, scope, and liberalism: you could profitably take time off from this present reading to browse through it: you would probably be surprised to discover how many familiar 'quotations' it contains). Two sentences from the second chapter should indicate the motif of the work:

If all mankind minus one were of one opinion, and only one person were of the contrary opinion, mankind would be no more justified in silencing that one person than he, if he had the power, would be justified in silencing mankind . . .

We can never be sure that the opinion we are endeavouring to stifle is false opinion; and if we were sure, stifling it would be an evil still.

These words are of course reminiscent of Voltaire a century earlier: 'I disapprove of what you say, but will defend to the death your right to say it'. Mill's *On Liberty* makes four basic points about minorities in the state.

1 The majority may be wrong.
2 Even if the majority is right, the minority may have a contribution to make.
3 If the majority is wrong, it represents a danger to the wellbeing of the people.
4 The minority should therefore have freedom of speech.

With the first three statements few are likely to be at odds; the main problem is not political but philosophical: the nature of the authority required in order to state emphatically that the majority is wrong. History has often censured the deeds of a state whose majority gave their support, as it has judged the majority in eighteenth-century Britain who supported the slave trade, or the majority of Germans in the 1930s and 40s who turned a blind eye to the extermination camps: but, at the time, how can anyone be sure that an accepted view or policy is wrong? We are up against the same problem faced by the individual, and discussed in Chapter Four, as to how he can be sure about the moral worth of his behaviour. (Some historical judgments against a state's behaviour have nothing to do with morals, of course. The groundnuts scheme in post-war Britain was altruistic in its aim and therefore, presumably, commendable; but it has been universally condemned for the near-total incompetence of its operation.)

Mill's final statement can be taken to mean freedom to communicate ideas in any way – orally or in writing. There are two possible opposing reactions which may spring from it. On the one hand, it may be *objected to* on the grounds that, if only for security reasons, it would be impolitic to allow every conceivable opinion to be expressed, since such utterances are likely to lead sooner or later to action on the part of some who agree with these opinions – action which could be detrimental to the state. There must be few countries in the world without their proportion of citizens deprived by imprisonment of their right to express their opinion. (Mill might have been Life President of Amnesty International, on the grounds that a government which could deal with opinions contrary to its policies only by stifling those opinions because it feared that the citizens would fall in line with them, had already lost its right to rule.)

The second reaction would be *to agree* that perhaps it is desirable, on the whole, to allow freedom of speech on political matters in a democracy but to question whether this freedom could be extended into every sphere of human thought and behaviour. We might (just) agree that it is better to allow fascists to express their views in public places (even though these views include the advocacy of the deprivation of many basic rights to a large proportion of the community) since otherwise we should seem to be acting intolerantly in the name of tolerance (quite a dilemma, really): but there must be some limit to the extent to which society as a whole can allow individuals to behave according to their innermost desires; it seems unlikely, for instance, that we shall ever tolerate the necrophiliac, and the law, in Western states at least, has disallowed pederasty and paedophilia. On issues like these the public attitude has been that there are certain forms of personal satisfaction which cannot be sanctioned because of the damage they do, or are likely to do, to the neutral parties involved. Mill himself allowed for this:

The liberty of the individual must be thus far limited: he must not make himself a nuisance to other people.

The trouble is, of course, that while this sentiment may seem reasonable, it does not answer the basic problem because of the questions it begs. Am I to take umbrage because a visitor to the estate on which I live has parked his car in the space outside my house, thus forcing me either to take somebody else's space or pay to park my car in a garage a quarter of a mile away? Though nobody else is affected, the visitor's action is certainly a nuisance to *me*, but the issue is hardly the kind that Mill had in mind. The fact is that situations which in some cause no more than a shrug of the shoulder in others cause paroxysms of rage. I have a neighbour who called the police to descend on a couple, living in a flat opposite, who hung out the washing on their veranda – on the grounds that the couple were thereby breaking the terms of their contract which expressly forbade any 'alteration to the frontage' of their accommodation. The phrase 'make no nuisance' in legal terms means 'do not urinate in public places', and most of us would probably both observe this ourselves and expect it from others: but people have been known to do themselves immense physical damage by observing the code in places where relief was not available except by breaking the law. (The way in which the British, in particular, do everything possible, both in their phraseology and secretive actions, to disguise the fact that bodily functions of this nature actually occur – with the implication that respectable people don't stoop to such activities – is one of the quirks of the nation. Incontinence causes more genuine torment to old people than any other aspect of growing old, and this torment, irrational though it may seem, is an inevitable consequence of the ethos of a society that seems to put potty-training as the first priority in the rearing of children.)

To return to Mill: the point that he was trying to establish was that the state which tried to deny freedom of expression to the non-conformists in its midst on the grounds that some of these might present a threat to its own safety was in danger of becoming a state of faceless people mouthing platitudes in unison. George Orwell's *1984*, with its depiction of brainwashed citizens, admirably indicates the depths to which a nation can sink – and in some cases has sunk – under bureaucracy, with its desire to have everything and everybody pigeon-holed tidily, with nobody (to change the metaphor) rocking the boat. Alas for the citizen of such a state who is accidentally filed as deceased and tries to prove that he is still alive. The final – rather long – sentence of *On Liberty* makes the point in these words:

The worth of a State, in the long run, is the worth of the individuals composing it; and a State which postpones the interests of *their* mental expansion and elevation to a little more of administrative skill, or of that semblance of it which practice gives, in the details of business; a State which dwarfs its men, in order that they may be more docile instruments in its hands even for beneficial purposes – will find that with small men no really great thing can be accomplished: and that the perfection of machinery to which it has sacrificed everything will in the end avail it nothing, for want of the vital power which, in order that the machine might work more smoothly, it has preferred to banish.

On this level, having taken into account all the provisos for those whose nonconformity is directly harmful to others, these words must be viewed as prophetic.

Human rights

A word that has cropped up several times in previous paragraphs is *rights*. The most famous expression of these in political terms is in the American Declaration of Independence, which includes these words:

We hold these truths to be self-evident: that all men are created equal; that they are endowed by their Creator with certain unalienable rights; that among these are life, liberty, and the pursuit of happiness. That, to secure these rights, governments are instituted among men, deriving their just powers from the consent of the governed; that, whenever any form of government becomes destructive of these ends, it is the right of the people to alter or abolish it, and to institute a new government, laying its foundation on such principles, and organising its powers in such form, as to them shall seem most likely to effect their safety and happiness.

These words seem difficult to contradict, not only because of their resonance but because of the – apparent – fundamental validity of the argument. Who will dare to assert that all human beings do not possess the right to life, to be free, the right not to be forced to suffer inner torment (a quality expressed negatively but perhaps clarifying some of the vagueness of the word 'happiness' – see Chapter Six)? On the face of it, any discussion of rights will be straightforward; on analysis, it emerges as a very tricky word indeed, to be used only with the utmost caution. Three questions must be briefly considered: *what are rights? where do they originate? and what do they involve?*

1. The nature of 'rights'   What does it mean to say that anyone has the right to anything? We talk of 'conjugal rights', 'parental rights', 'civil rights'; people campaign for the 'rights of the unborn', 'animal rights', and even a 'tree's right' not to be felled in its prime. Implied in these assertions are at least the following:

(a) It would be morally wrong to deprive anyone (or anything, in some cases) of such rights without sufficient justification.
(b) It would be wrong because of the harm it would do to his/her/its interests.
(c) A definition of rights might therefore be: *a valid claim that certain treatment is owed to oneself and to others.*

Each of these statements sounds straightforward enough, but on analysis it will be seen that each suffers from a fatal (so far as clarity is concerned) flaw: in each there is a vague, evaluative word, begging so many questions that it is difficult to see how much progress can be made. In the first statement we have the word 'sufficient'; we have already seen, apropos of my neighbour, that one person's 'sufficient justification' to deprive another of his rights (in the example used, freedom to hang out washing) is another's intolerable imposition on people's freedom; (it is a moot point whether, by hanging out washing, the couple had in fact broken the regulation in their contract about altering the frontage of their home). The question of what constitutes sufficient justification in virtually all circumstances is an open one, for the simple reason that there is unlikely to be a consensus on any matter.

In the second statement appears the equally vague word 'interests'. How are these to be assessed, and who is to make the assessment? Are we to think in the short term or in the long term, of 'his' interests as they affect him personally or as those around him might be affected? Answers in both cases could vary enormously. One of my sons, for example, complains now that I was not more vigorous in making him do his homework regularly when he was at school. At the time, rightly or wrongly, I felt it pointless to watch over him constantly like a martinet when his mind was on rock concerts, playing the guitar, and discovering girls (in that order). It seemed to me that it would be counter-productive to try to persuade a 16-year-old, full of the joys of spring, to settle down to Shakespeare, economic statistics, and French irregular verbs: but today he complains that he is not sufficiently qualified for the jobs he wants to do. Equally, do I encourage him to remain silent about the pettiness of the neighbours (already described) on the grounds that it would be in his interests to learn to 'live and let live', when, deep down, I feel that it is I who am making a rather shameful compromise by remaining silent? How can one person judge where another's interests really lie in any case? Can one even be sure of what are one's own 'best interests'?

The word 'valid' in the definitional statement (c) raises the same kind of problem. Could a mass murderer make a valid claim that he had a right to go on living? a hijacker that he had the right to liberty? the school leaver with no qualifications that he had the right to continuing education? the unemployed that he had the right to work? the person with the boring, unfulfilling job that he had the right to happiness at work? How valid is the claim in each of these cases? Further, how does this definition affect those who cannot express or claim rights for themselves – the mentally defective, young children, animals, and so on? Have these groups more, fewer, or the same rights as everybody else? The situation is fraught with difficulties, because those facing the problem will not be doing so from the same perspective as others, or with the same values in mind. What is a right to me may be an optional extra to you. A 'natural right' to you may be to me no more than a desirable luxury.

Your attitude to rights will be tested in a lengthy case study which presents an extensive range of situations in which the question arises (see Case Study 36). These include problems relating to civil rights, which are integral to the theme of this chapter. Where these rights are concerned, it seems that the natural inclination of government is to underplay them as much as possible (since this makes life easier for government) while that of the individual is (or would be, if he took the time and trouble) to emphasise and speak out about them as much as possible. Between these two extremes some kind of compromise may be expected to be found, but there remain contentious issues like the individual right to privacy versus government's right to security. Should any government have the right to tap a person's phone, assuming that there is good reason to believe that the individual is a subversive (always bearing in mind that one person's subversive is another's prophet of enlightenment)?

Revolutionists' rights An issue even more pregnant with dire implications is that of the right of the governed to revolt against the government where this is no longer seen to be acting in the interests of the majority of the citizens, and no democratic way (that is, via the ballot box) presents itself as a means of bringing about change. Marx, as we saw when discussing historical determinism, believed this to be not only the citizens' rights in those circumstances, but an inevitable process, even if it could come about only through violence and bloodshed. 'You can't make an omelette without breaking eggs,' Trotsky remarked. More mellifluently but, as events showed, with similarly violent consequences, the American Declaration of Independence stated: 'When a long train of abuses and usurpations, pursuing invariably the same object, evinces a design to reduce them under absolute despotism, it is their right, it is their duty, to throw off such government, and to provide new guards for their future security.' The rights referred to were those of the Americans, and the throwing off meant, euphemistically, the bloody War of Independence, whose aims were supported by such noteworthy defenders of human rights as Edmund Burke and Thomas Paine.

Few people, except, perhaps, absolute pacifists, will oppose the view that, where government has become tyrannical, and change can be effected only through (inevitably) bloody revolution, this must, however reluctantly, be undertaken: the blame would lie primarily at the door of the tyrant. Even the pacifist Bonhoeffer was driven by Hitler's excesses to participate in the plot on his life. What must here be borne in mind is the difference between what political philosophers call government *de jure* and government *de facto*. (The distinction between these two will be discussed in Chapter Twelve with regard to the teacher's authority in the education process.) In effect, it distinguishes between government which has the legal right to govern – de jure, or in law – and one which actually has the authority or power to express this right in practice – de facto, or in reality. One does not guarantee the other. The American, French, and Russian Revolutions all occurred because the governments of the day had ceased to concern themselves with the interests of the majority of those governed. Effectively, they were no longer governing (that is to say, they were governing de jure, but not de facto). Even in a democracy this can occur: any American President in the last year of office will be described as a 'lame duck' president because he must be replaced within the year, so that his power is considerably diminished if not (as with President Carter) almost entirely eliminated.

One further point should be added here. Whether the overthrowing of a government by violent means is described (as the overthrowers might well describe it) as suicide on the government's part or (as the overthrown might describe it) as murder on the revolutionaries' part, there can be no guarantee in advance that its replacement will be less tyrannical. The American Revolution was, in this respect, the successful one of the three; the French Revolution (if this is not a case of 'post hoc ergo propter hoc') led to Robespierre, the guillotine, and, eventually, Napoleon; the Russian Revolution to the bloodbaths of Stalin, trained in the same kind of theological seminary as the Borgias. The weakness of Marx's political philosophy is that, while he correctly predicted the process of communist revolution, he was wrong about the consequences. There has been no new Age of Enlightenment with the advent of communist states, and, with the notable exception of Cuba, no removal of the 'us–them' syndrome between government and governed. The

Marxist argument that this is irrelevant because those states which claim to be Marxist are not really so is as circular as arguing that a person cannot be called a Christian if he doesn't behave like one.

(A case study on pacifism – no. 35 – will allow the question to be raised as to whether violence is ever justified, whatever the cause: ends v. means again.)

2. The origin of rights   The question of the source of rights is an equally tricky one to settle. The phrase 'natural rights' has cropped up already, and, on the face of it, this may seem satisfactory, at least when discussing such basic rights as the right to life, or to happiness, or to freedom. Few people are likely not to want these for themselves, and few would go out of their way to prevent others from enjoying them. This case is not weakened by the fact that sometimes people take their own lives, or sacrifice their happiness on behalf of others, or put their freedom at risk. The would-be suicide may well contend that his proposed action no more removes the fact of his right to life than does the proud refusal of a pensioner to accept state supplementary benefits mean that his right to them does not exist. The same is true, apropos of other 'natural' rights, of the woman who sacrifices the chance of marriage in order to care for her elderly parents, or of the freedom fighter who, like Nelson Mandela when imprisoned in South Africa, accepts the loss of his freedom to say what he pleases, go where he pleases, and see whom he pleases.

If, however, a right is a natural consequence of simply being a member of the human race, it would seem to follow from this that such a right is inalienable: no circumstances would justify its denial to a person. Yet manifestly there are circumstances in which it would be generally agreed by the community at large that certain individuals had, by their behaviour, forfeited one or more of these rights. The rapist, the murderer, the kidnapper, the hijacker, the child molester: few would defend the right of these to 'liberty and the pursuit of happiness', and many would argue that, in some extreme cases, the right to life had itself been forfeited. Perhaps a reasonably valid summary of the general view might be that those people who have wilfully prevented others, at some time, from enjoying their rights have themselves abrogated their own claim to these. If this is the case, it means that the deontological view of Kant, that wrong-doing carries within itself its own nemesis, is widely held. *How natural, then, are natural rights?* (Does the word mean the same in each part of that sentence?)

The problem of the source of certain other rights is more easily tackled. The rights to unemployment benefit, to drive a car, to own a house, or to vote for or against the government of the day, are all rights conferred by a nation's legal system, and vary in detail from country to country. The right to vote is less significant in countries where there is only one name on the ballot sheet than where there is a genuine choice; in certain periods, such as times of war or of grave petrol shortage, one's right to drive a motor vehicle may be curtailed; and the right to own a house loses much of its significance if there are no houses to be bought. But while questions like these will continually occur where legal rights are concerned, so that occasionally laws will have to be changed, they are straightforward in a way that so-called natural rights are not.

The problem is confounded at times when certain rights, while less basic than those mentioned as natural rights, are presented by some advocates as belonging nonetheless in this category: the right to work and the right to education are two frequently-quoted examples of these. It would be confusing to describe rights like these as either legal or natural. In the English-speaking world, to look no further, there is no legal right to work; and while in Britain every child has the legal right to attend an educational institution at public expense until the age of sixteen, this does not necessarily mean, as we shall see further in the next chapter, that he has been educated. There are in fact those who affirm that since many jobs require few, if any, skills (the ability to hoe, for example – a task that was the bane of my life during my farming days – requires no more than that the operative shall be able to (a) stand, (b) move a lightweight implement back and forth, and (c) see as far as the ground at his feet: nothing very demanding in those requirements) there is consequently little point in spending time and cash on superfluous training. It seems that both of these 'rights', along with numerous others, are conventions which are presented to people according to society's needs. These needs vary from time to time and from place to place, so that the opportunities for employment, and the particular skills required, will vary accordingly. There is, for instance, no point in teaching literacy to members of a primitive society which survives by learning and applying such skills as hunting, fishing, fighting, house-building, and so on.

The challenge to those who believe in natural rights is whether these also arc in the end social conventions, more universally applied, perhaps, than other rights, but liable to be withdrawn in extreme circumstances. It is interesting that, just as different states allow their citizens different legal rights, so the most basic right, the right to life, is applied with varying degrees of absoluteness throughout the world. In some countries, particularly around the Middle East, a citizen may lose his right just for making jokes, let alone political criticism, about the ruler; in others a person found guilty of mass torturing of children, rape, and murder would still be able to retain this right. It seems therefore that rights arise from the needs and values of a particular community: that no rights exist in 'nature', but that they have to be acknowledged and conferred by others.

3. The 'meaning' of rights   The third question was expressed earlier as that of what rights *involved*, but a more accurate expression would have been to ask what they *imply*. The answer to this is almost included in the question. Rights imply obligations; I cannot (or, at least, should not) claim a right for myself which I am not prepared to allow to others. If I claim the right to type away at the final draft of this book into the early hours, thus occasionally disturbing neighbours, I am hardly in a position to complain if, during a hot summer's day, I can hardly hear what I'm thinking because of the shrieks of their children playing in the pool. If a man claims the right to be unfaithful to his spouse, he is in no place to become censorious if she does likewise. Occasionally it may be argued that this obligation does not apply – that special circumstances confer on a particular person a right which cannot be universalised. For example, I claim the right to express critical views on theological and biblical affirmations, but only on the basis of decades of study in those fields; the person who makes similar criticisms without having done a certain amount of research in the fields seems to me not to possess the same right of assertion. But perhaps here I am confusing 'right' with 'authority' – a concept to be discussed in the next chapter.

Referenda and PR   It seems, therefore, that Mill's ideals are incapable of being given total expression in any state. However democratically motivated a government may be, there are some people whom it will never please, and some – probably a larger group – who will never feel themselves to be represented. The holding of national referenda on certain issues of national importance may seem to be one way of minimising this discontent, by multiplying the number of decision makers; but there will still remain the minority who were defeated in the referendum, and the cynic would suggest that most of those who voted for it did so under the influence of a handful of newspaper proprietors. The story of Britain's entry into the European Community is illuminative here: as went the newspapers, so went the nation, whether during the earlier years of refusal to enter, or at the time of eventual acceptance following the referendum of 1975.

An issue like this is an example of an area where no compromise can be made in order to accommodate the minority view: the country could hardly have agreed to go 60 percent of the way into membership of the EEC while remaining 40 percent out. Many voices are raised, however, in favour of such a system of government through the process of *proportional representation*. The vociferous supporters of this electoral method are those least represented in government as a result of the 'first past the post' system. (As a certain Mandy Rice-Davies said at a famous trial: 'they would, wouldn't they?') The fact is that while this system, as it has been experienced in Britain, usually creates a government on the basis of less than 50 percent of the number of votes cast, at least those who voted for the winning party have reason to be content. Under the system of PR, where two parties are likely to have to work together through some form of compromise because no one party has an overall majority, the resultant policy will be one for which nobody has voted. It may constitute the via media between two opposing expressions of political judgment, but that does not mean that it is either right, or what the people want or need. It illustrates the fallacy of the argument of the middle way, as a result of which it can be claimed that two two's are five because a person on one side said they made a beggarly four, while, on the other side, the grandiose claim had been made that they were as many as six. But the middle way here is wrong, even though it is a middle way (and even when the middle way is right, this is not because it is the middle way).

It seems, therefore, that democracy must join justice and equality (two examples that have been discussed already) as being simply an ideal – a concept in people's minds, but no more capable of being incarnated in human activity than the other two. The word itself is often used as no more than a 'purr' word (as opposed, in the West, to such 'snarl' words as 'autocratic' or 'Marxist'); what we need to know, assuming that government should, as far as possible, reflect the views of the people governed, is how far any particular government bill or action actually does this. And even then, there might be occasions – as we saw when discussing the overwhelming desire in Britain and America for the restoration of capital punishment – when the *vox populi*, while perhaps being the *vox dei*, could not be described as the voice either of reason or of compassion. Perhaps the wisest word on the matter was spoken by Winston Churchill: 'Democracy is the worst system of government in the world, except all those other systems.'

CASE STUDY 34: TORTURE

Many nations throughout the world practise torture for political reasons: that is to say, it is viewed as a legitimate policy of government. The names of states where this happens are mentioned from time to time at the United Nations General Assembly, and the practitioners are castigated. (Amnesty International will provide details of these states.) These criticisms are usually either denied or ignored. More universally accepted at government level is the belief that, regretful though it may be, torture is occasionally necessary for security reasons, such as the extracting in a hurry of information vital to the wellbeing of the community.

The case study is aimed at allowing you to analyse your own reaction to the issue, with the final question as the 'bottom line' in both senses of the phrase.

1 Reasons offered for torture

(a) It's always been done here; it's accepted as necessary for deterring the government's adversaries; only countries which don't practise it abhor it, as people raised in vegetarian communities abhor the eating of flesh.
Why then the denials that it occurs? And why the expressions of shame when proof is produced that it does occur?

(b) If the opposition were in power they'd do the same.
Maybe, but the questions under (a) still apply.

(c) It is a sad necessity for the preservation of stable government.
Other governments survive without adopting this practice. How stable is any government which has to do it systematically?

(d) Circumstances sometimes make it the only possible procedure. If a bomb were hidden in a crowded store or on an aeroplane in flight, and security forces held the man who had planted it, they would be justified in torturing him mercilessly to make him state quickly the location of the bomb.
This could never be proved either way. If he tells under torture, he might still have told anyway. If he doesn't tell, nothing has been gained in any case. Better, then, to avoid descending into the use of barbaric behaviour.

(e) He did it to others. Now he's tasting it for himself.
Does this make you any better than him?

2 Effects of torture

(a) Physical disablement of victim.

(b) The breakdown of the victim's mind:
  (i) Permanent deep trauma from mental terror
  (ii) Loss of the mind's integrity, e.g. creates a cringing desire to please, like that of a small child, or a dog, in disgrace
  (iii) Sense of degradation and self-loathing.

(c) Dehumanises the torturer as well as the victim:
Confessions of ex-torturers suggest that:
  (i) They started their training reluctantly.
  (ii) They quickly adjusted to the underlying ethos of the training routine.
  (iii) When set to work they became totally callous about the victim's physical and mental anguish.
  (iv) They found sexual satisfaction in the process, especially, but not only, when the victims were women. (Almost all torturers are male, and women victims have described how their torturers regularly had orgasms during a session. Male school teachers have occasionally confessed to the same feelings when beating pupils.)

Retired torturers tend to justify what they did in the same way as German ex-concentration camps officials, e.g. 'I had to do it, I was under orders'; 'If I hadn't done it, someone else would', etc. Do you think this exonerates them?

3 Are we over-reacting to accounts of torture today?
  (a) Instruments of torture in the Middle Ages caused similar pain, and look just as gruesome as anything used today.
  We cannot be sure of this, but even if true this is no excuse for continuing to adopt their practices.
  (b) The highly sophisticated brain-washing techniques developed in recent years are just as, if not more, destructive of the victim's mind.
  To oppose one form of torture does not mean condoning another.
  (c) Torturing a person for information may be counter-productive. The victim may clam up, or simply tell lies; and in some countries evidence given under duress is inadmissible in court.
  All true, but torturing continues.
  (d) Drugs can and do destroy the victim's mind just as effectively.
  Tell that to the torturers.

4 What can be done to suppress torture as an instrument of policy?
  (a) Introduce sanctions against known offenders: *but how many trading partners would we then lose?*
  (b) Emphasise the individual responsibility of the torturer, so that 'obedience to higher orders' cannot be a defence. If the torturer knew that he would be treated like (e.g.) a hijacker if his crimes came to light, he might be more reluctant to be drafted that way. *This would need the cooperation of all nations, the lack of which is precisely the problem faced by UNO.*
  (c) Increase world-wide aid to victims, as for victims of natural disasters. Governments, besides Amnesty International, etc., should help.

5 Do we all secretly harbour a sadistic element in our natures?
Students in psychological experiments have given fellow students electric shocks. Could/would you never willingly cause another person pain? Honestly?

CASE STUDY 35: PACIFISM AND WAR

One group of people whom every state has to contend with are pacifists – those who refuse to take up arms in any circumstances, even to defend the state against an aggressor, because of their absolute refusal to use physical violence, either in their personal lives or as an instrument of

265

government policy. The method of treating these people varies from country to country; some look upon them as traitors, and deal with them according to their laws relating to that crime. Others have a conscience clause in their constitution, and if, after examination by a tribunal, the claimants' pacifism is deemed to be based on genuine conviction, religious or otherwise, they are registered as 'conscientious objectors'. In times of war, or in periods when all citizens have to complete a period of compulsory military service, they will be offered alternative service, such as in hospitals, mines, or in farming. A small proportion of pacifists refuse even this kind of duty, on the grounds that the state has no right to direct any of its citizens as to how they shall spend some years of their lives. What follows is a debate between a pacifist and a non-pacifist: read it, and then debate with others the questions at the end.

1 You pacifists seem to me to be totally unrealistic. If primitive tribes had not been willing to defend themselves against aggressors, they would have been annihilated. And aggression didn't stop as civilisation spread – it just got more deadly. Would you have stood back in World War II and let the Germans take over?

Yes I would. I agree that there have been wars of one kind or another since man arrived on the planet; but that doesn't justify it as an aspect of a nation's way of governing. There have been murders throughout human history but that doesn't make them a necessary aspect of human relationships. As far as Germany in 1939 was concerned, my view is that the end never justifies the means so, no, we shouldn't have fought them.

2 So you would be prepared for your country to be occupied by a foreign invader?

If need be, yes: I would put my faith in the power of love, or agape, to overcome evil.

3 Don't you think that is being too heavenly-minded for this world? After all, one of the greatest Christian theologians, Thomas Aquinas, said there were three conditions which justified war: the ruler's authority, or what he called 'auctoritas principia'; a just cause and rightful intent' – 'justa causa' and 'recta intentio'; and that it should be waged by the proper means – 'debito modo'. I know the last is question-begging, what with

I don't look on Aquinas as having spoken the last word on the question: I see his views as a distortion of New Testament teaching. I know St Paul argued that the state was the servant of God, and its citizens should be prepared to defend it. But he was writing before Nero's persecution of dissidents. Your last point puts the finger on the problem: what exactly are 'proper means'? In modern times we have access to gas, H-bombs, and chemical warfare, but Aquinas's other requirements were certainly present in Britain's declaration of war on Germany.

4 There you go again – totally unrealistic. You may destroy weapons, but you can't destroy the knowledge of how to make them. You seem to be wanting to deal with some other kind of being than man as he really is. We are naturally aggressive, and war is just one expression of this. Actually some of the noblest deeds in history have been performed in war: do you think we'd know the meaning of the word heroism without war? or courage? or honour? Some of the greatest novels have been inspired by war – look at *War and Peace* – and poems, and films, and paintings. If there were no more wars we'd have to create conditions of danger to bring out the best in people.

5 OK, but these are necessary to keep morale high, just as in other dangerous situations – being lost in the mist on a mountain, for instance – someone must ensure that the group's spirits are kept up. You talk as though all moral considerations go out of the window in wartime: but there are rules of war, such as

weapons that could destroy the entire human race. Don't tell me they wouldn't be used because they're so powerful: they exist, and not just to be put in the shop window. And because a so-called conventional war could escalate into a nuclear war, the only way of achieving peace is to ban all weapons. You can't wage war if you haven't got the means to do so.

Spin-offs like that are irrelevant. You might just as well say that because a child develops great courage and maturity as he dies of leukaemia we should accept illnesses like these as desirable; or justify the starving of millions in Africa because their misery inspires others in wealthier countries to help. *War and Peace* was written by a pacifist, and most of the poetry of war condemns it. No wonder: it may produce its heroes, but it also produces its psychopaths – men who find they enjoy killing and are licensed to do it. It produces lies, jingoistic madness, and a total destruction of the truth. Read the headlines and reports in the gutter press in Britain and America during the Gulf War and you'll see what I mean.

The Geneva Convention didn't come about from ethical considerations, but because combatants wanted to feel safe from the sort of actions it disallows. For the same reason gas wasn't used after 1918: it could backfire on the users. Any moral deeds in war are not shooting prisoners, and treating wounded prisoners – the Geneva convention, in other words: those who broke it were tried as war criminals because they hadn't observed the ethics of war: yet you speak as though there were no such thing.

performed despite, not because of, the war. The basic fact is that in war respect for others is destroyed, there is a cruel and insane waste of life, human anguish rules most people's lives (how many *families* of enlisted men remember the war days as pleasurable?). In no other situation do basic human values reach so low a depth as in war.

6 All right, so war has its nasty side – but you can't go through life ignoring the facts of human nature: Hobbes was right when he described human beings as in a state of constant warfare with each other. Not all wars have been justified – I have strong doubts about the American intervention in Vietnam, for example: but I don't know what else was possible when Hitler was overrunning Europe or Saddam Hussein doing a Genghis Khan on his neighbours. Doesn't your sympathy for the oppressed become the top priority in that case?

You can't generalise about human nature: there are just different types of human beings, with different attitudes and values. Most people dread even the thought of war, and it's only the willingness of governments to contemplate it, and put a huge slice of their budgets into preparing for it, that makes it possible. I'm not just being starry-eyed about this either. I'm campaigning for the abolition of national sovereignty – just a step further on from the sovereignty of the barons 400 years ago – and a genuine world government which would limit the possession of arms to a world police force.

7 So you're not against force in all circumstances?

No: if someone attacked my family I would restrain him with all my strength: but I wouldn't then drop a bomb on his family. And I see a fundamental difference between force operating under the control of the law as in the police force, and uncontrolled violence as in war. A world police force could well be a world peace force.

8 Well, I'm not opposed to that, but meanwhile we've somehow got to live together as harmoniously as

I don't think we'd have achieved anything by violence; the views to which Smith gave expression possible. And when you get rogue elephants, as when Ian Smith unilaterally declared Rhodesia independent in 1965, the most effective – and probably the most humane response in the long term – must be the short sharp shock treatment: in Smith's case, the overthrow and arrest of the white traitors who were depriving the bulk of the population of their rights.

would have continued to fester if he'd been suppressed. In the end, I suppose it's a question of whether one is optimistic or pessimistic about human beings. I'm an optimist, by which I mean that I think human beings will eventually realise the folly of violence. Meanwhile, we must be willing to suffer so that at length we can learn from experience, and realise that it's actually possible for people to live peaceably together.

9 I give you full marks for your idealism, and appreciate the need for people like you; but remember, you're free to say it only because a lot of people in the past were willing to fight for it at the risk of their lives.

1 Is there a role for the idealist in society?
2 Could pacifism foreseeably be adopted world-wide as a realistic policy?
3 Are human beings naturally aggressive, or is aggression just a stage in the evolutionary process? Can you distinguish between violence and force?
4 Does it make sense to contemplate war when nations possess enough weapons to wipe out the entire human species many times over?
5 If the pacifist is asking for the impossible, has he any valid contribution to make in the world's peace-making processes?
6 Should we be aiming to give the United Nations Organisation more authority by making it a genuine World Government? Would sovereign states be willing to surrender that part of their sovereignty which allows them to have national armies? (And if we start with that, why not a world currency and a world bank?)

CASE STUDY 36: HUMAN RIGHTS

Here are some descriptions of situations in which the question of rights occurs. For convenience, they are divided into rough categories. You will be concerned basically with the question either of whether a right exists or not, or, where there is a clash of rights, which has prior claim. Do you consider any right to be (a) natural or (b) bestowed by convention? If the latter, how far do you find yourself believing that existing conventions should be changed? If you do feel this, on what basis (by what right, if you like) do you reach this conclusion?

A. Personal rights   Should the following rights – all of which have been claimed at some time or other – be acknowledged?

(a) A middle-aged person dying of cancer seeks a death-inducing drug.
(b) A teenager, totally paralysed after an accident, seeks the same.
(c) The parents of a baby born with an extreme spina bifida seek the same for the baby.
(d) A foetus is discovered at 24 weeks to have Down's Syndrome. The parents seek an abortion.

B. Civil rights   In the following examples, which right should be paramount: the individual's or the other party's (or parties')?

(a) The local council wish to knock down a row of old houses to make room for a by-pass, and offer alternative accommodation to the owners. One elderly occupant, who has lived in the house all his life, refuses to leave and barricades himself indoors.
(b) A dog persistently bites visitors, making no distinction between postmen and sales reps. The local magistrates order the owner to keep the dog locked indoors, or have it destroyed. The owner loves the dog.
(c) A man is angered when visited by reps who have bought his address from a firm that specialises in selling addresses of people, taken from computer records of service card owners, HP repayers, etc.
(d) In an area noted for violent rioting, a person wishes to carry his own revolver.
(e) Believing a certain person to be a heroin smuggler/suspect in a gang rape/IRA bomber, the police tap his phone.

C. Parental Rights   Do parental rights over their children extend as far as the following? At what point should the rights of the children, or of the community as a whole, take precedence over those of the parents?

(a) A couple whose first child had to be taken into care because they battered it have a second child, and wish to look after it.
(b) A Private Member's Bill comes before the House of Commons proposing that family allowances should cease after the birth of the third child (fourth? tenth?).
(c) A similar bill is introduced, proposing the compulsory sterilisation of habitually violent criminals/the severely mentally disordered.
(d) An unemployed couple spend most of their state benefit on cigarettes and hire of videotapes. They approach the local authorities for supplementary financial support for their children.

(e) A couple allow their two small children to sit up late watching video nasties. The children are too tired to work at school.

(f) One child in a family living in a small house has pet hamsters, mice, and gerbils, to which he is devoted. His brother's asthma is found to be caused by his being allergic to fur.

(g) Parents believe in, and regularly put into practice, the maxim, 'Spare the rod and spoil the child'.

D. *The Individual and the Community*   How far has any individual the right to the following?

(a) An unemployed person is offered work, but in a town far away. He wishes to work only in his home town.

(b) A man who has spent five years' apprenticeship learning a special skill is made redundant; it is suggested that he retrain, but he likes his original job, and does not wish to do anything else.

(c) A dog attacks and kills the next-door cat. The man next door shoots the dog.

(d) A man can get sexual satisfaction only if there is an element of sadism in his love-making. His girlfriend is not a masochist.

(e) A village bus service is given the chop because it is uneconomic. The handful of elderly villagers who relied on the service for their weekly visits into town request that the service be restored.

(f)Students who disapprove of the political views of one of their tutors (who regularly airs these views outside the lecture room) demonstrate against him outside the lecture theatre.

(g) A nurse works for a publicly-funded home for old people. She finds the conditions for the residents, in her view, sub-human and degrading. Complaints to her superiors fall on deaf ears, so she writes to a national newspaper, outlining the conditions frankly as she sees them. For this she is found guilty by her superiors of unprofessional conduct, and is dismissed.

E. *Individual Rights*   Which of the following do you consider to be justifiable?

(a) The right of any person to commit suicide.

(b) The right of a lifer to be executed instead of enduring a life in jail.

(c) The right of a brother and sister, sexually attracted to each other, to make love.

(d) The right of a born-again Christian to sing hymns day and night in his thinly-walled tenement.

(e) The right of a talented young musician to practise the trumpet every evening (in his thinly-walled tenement).

(f) The right to park your car blocking a private entrance when you are desperate (for time).

(g) The right to ownership, by inheritance, of a piece of land.

271

Finally, comment on the following incident, which I witnessed some time ago; which party, in your view, had the greater right?

In a shopping centre, parking spaces are virtually unobtainable. The driver of an estate car sees another car drawing away from a lot, and drives his car forward in order to reverse into the lot (his car is too large to be driven straight in without going over the pavement, which is somewhat high). As he goes forward, indicating his intentions, a mini car driver moves straight into the vacant lot. As the mini car driver feeds the parking meter, the estate car owner approaches him and informs him that if he insists on leaving his car in that lot he will wait until he (the mini car owner) has gone and will then let the air out of all four of his tyres. The mini car driver explains, in non-judicial language, that possession is nine-tenths of the law, and that his money is in the parking meter. After he has left, the estate car owner flattens all four tyres of the mini, and drives away.

CASE STUDY 37: DEMOCRACY, AUTOCRACY, ANARCHY

These three styles of government (or non-government in the last case) between them represent the extremes which have drawn people's attention over the centuries. Each has its strengths and weaknesses.

1 In theory, as its name suggests, **democracy** uses the skills of all the community in the governing process. In practice, because of the ever-increasing numbers of the units concerned, there has had to be a commensurate amount of delegating. Even elected members of Parliament and of Congress find that the only way to make any impact is to specialise in their area of expertise. For members of the public it is virtually impossible to have more than the most generalised knowledge on any issue – often conveyed in a distorted way via the media.

2 In theory, **autocracy** is the most straightforward method of government. In particular, because the ruler never need worry about making popular decisions in a contrived way before general elections, policies can be consistent and continuous. In practice, autocrats have throughout history tended to be corrupted by their own power; and as their judgment has faltered their regimes have moved more and more into the realm of tyranny. Hobbes's 'benevolent autocrat' has proved itself an oxymoron, or contradiction in terms (like 'business ethics'?).

3 **Anarchy** is a noble ideal, expressing the view that communities of people don't need either an all-powerful sovereign or a group of people delegated to represent their points of view in decision-making places. So: no power, no corruption. In practice, this theory has run up against the inherent greed of *homo sapiens* which, as Hobbes (again)

recognised, needs to be strictly controlled if it is not to run wild. Perhaps this approach to government is most fitting for small communities united by a strong common band of belief: but even then one finds indications of dictatorship by those with the strongest claims to authority in interpreting the sources of the belief-system – not always to everyone's satisfaction, as records of these communities reveal.

For discussion or reflection: has there ever been a form of government which has avoided the dangers, while retaining the strengths, of these three? Do you think it might be possible to govern with a combination of the strengths they represent, without also falling prey to their weaknesses?

In the end, should government simply be viewed as a necessary evil which is best left to lesser mortals who enjoy exercising power, while you concentrate on ways of minimising that power?

CASE STUDY 38: THE ART OF THE POSSIBLE?

The Art of the Possible was the title of the autobiography of R.A. Butler, who during the 1950s and 1960s held virtually every post in the cabinet except that of Prime Minister. His title, he believed, aptly summed up the political process. With so many people's interests at stake – often in contention with the rest – it was impossible for anyone entering the highest echelons of government to hope to achieve more than a tiny proportion of his or her declared objectives. So the art of government became one of compromise, trying not to surrender more of one's ideals than was absolutely necessary.

Is this an acceptable view of government? Or do you think it too vague, leaving undetermined precisely what *is* possible and what is not? Shouldn't a representative of the people *make* things possible? Or is that too starry-eyed? Butler argued that any government of any persuasion could change the political scene only minimally in any one direction; hence the term 'Butskellism' – a combination of (the left-wing Tory) Butler and (the right-wing Labour leader) Gaitskell. Do you think this is preferable to the openly confrontational view expressed by Prime Minister Margaret Thatcher through the 1980s, when no attempt was made to water down the current political doctrine of monetarism, or to be leader of any of the people who was not 'one of us'?

Chapter Twelve

Ethics and education

We have discussed in Chapter Nine the possibilities and problems of moral education as a discrete subject in the school curriculum. We turn now to an issue which, while it may sound similar to that one, is in fact quite distinct: how far do or should moral principles express themselves in the education process? A generation of moral philosophers have turned their attention to this question, expressing their views both in an outpouring of books on the subject and, in a process of continuous debate, through articles and papers published in the *Journal of the Society of the Philosophy of Education*. This debate ranges over issues far too numerous to be discussed here; what we can do is to take a look at the central issue – what education is – and consider its implication for both teacher and learner. A brief sketch of some of the most distinctive contributions to the discussion made by certain philosophers over the centuries should then allow for the presentation of a number of general conclusions on the matter – conclusions which you may wish to challenge, or modify. You will have the chance to do this in Case Study 39, which follows the chapter.

The etymology of education

The word 'education' is derived from a Latin root. But which root? We have on offer both the word *educare* and the word *educere*; these words may look and sound alike, but there is between them a gulf of meaning so broad that it is difficult to imagine that they can both cohabit in the context of a school's curriculum. I know of no single issue which more profoundly divides human beings than the educare/educere issue; whether they are conservative or reformist in their views and attitudes, reactionaries or radicals, absolutists or relativists, even realists or idealists, will be reflected more in their stance on this problem of etymology and its implications than on any other matter. This may sound a wildly exorbitant claim, but a study of the two words should indicate why it is made.

Educare

The word educare means 'to train', to equip the learner with a particular skill. The skill concerned is frequently a physical skill: the manual dexterity of an engineer or surgeon, a mechanic or plasterer, and the pedal skills of a dancer or football player; but there are other skills for which training is needed, such as numeracy, or logic, or linguistic analysis, which may more aptly be described as mental skills. As all these examples suggest, the educare approach is normally linked with a particular trade or profession. Thus a person will 'train' as an accountant, a systems analyst, a plumber, a tool-maker, a nurse or a priest. Skills in logic or linguistics may be applied in a number of fields where communication skills are required, though the connection between the training and the job is less direct here than in the other cases.

There are two important implications for education in general which follow from this interpretation. The first is that the esteem of subjects taught in the curriculum of a school or college will be determined largely by the economic or social needs of the state, or community. The prime motivation for both the teacher and the learner of a subject will be that of the extent to which knowledge of this subject qualifies the learner for a particular job; and this in turn means that those skills will be given highest priority in areas where there is greatest work opportunity. Where there is a decline in the call for particular skills (such as in some branches of engineering or construction) the teaching of these will be viewed as less important as the teaching of skills for which there is a continuing or increasing demand (such as those required for computing or in certain branches of the sciences). It's worth recalling that the famous Education Act of 1870 in Britain, which made provision for elementary education for all, came about not because there was any great conviction that all people were *morally* entitled to education, but because, in the wake of the Industrial Revolution, there was a proven need, in factories and businesses, for clerks who were numerate and literate: hence the Victorian definition of education as the 'three Rs'. Education as educare will be viewed as part of a state's economic policies, and those involved in education viewed as the manservants or maidservants of the state.

The second implication is that the assessment of what is worthwhile in the curriculum will be based on what is judged to be 'useful' – in the minds of teachers and students alike. Thus physics and maths are deemed to be worthwhile subjects to pursue, since there is a continuing need, in a wide range of jobs, for people with skills in these fields; while subjects such as English literature, fine art, and sociology, while they may be 'interesting', rank low in the list of priorities because there is no direct application of any of these in the work field. It is particularly significant that the student themselves seem to catch this attitude, so that many students of the arts, the humanities and the social sciences have to

275

undergo an element of derision expressed by colleagues studying such subjects as accountancy, business studies, or aerodynamics.

Thus the educare approach to education is one geared to slotting students into an already-existing system; and the achievement of a written qualification in the form of a certificate, a diploma, or a degree in the subject becomes the *sine qua non* for the curriculum. Students may study subjects which frankly bore them in order to gain this precious piece of paper; and individual themes within the subject are studied for no other reason than that they are favourites with the examiners. With educare as the overriding consideration, the straitjacket beckons, and the student spends his years of formal learning by so moulding himself that he can wear it with ease. Since the jacket also has a set of blinkers attached, the consequence is that, unless somehow he can break out from his chosen or allotted role, the trainee will have simply prepared himself for life on a treadmill.

Educere

The word *educere* has a very different meaning. The initial 'e' (from which the 'x' has necessarily been omitted) means 'out of' or 'forth', like the 'ex' in 'exit', a word which literally means 'he (she, it) goes out'. 'Ducere' means 'to lead': so the full word means 'to lead out, or forth'. Education conducted on the educere principle will consequently be viewed as primarily one of enablement: allowing the student to explore both the world and himself; to follow up ideas and develop skills not because of any pragmatic reason (that they will be useful to society, and consequently to himself as an element in that society, though this may, incidentally, be the case) but because he personally finds these ideas and skills to be inherently valuable. The direction he takes in his studies will therefore be determined not by external motivation – qualifications, jobs, and so on – but by the internal motivation of discovering the subject to be rewarding and fulfilling in itself. The question 'what will you *do* with this when you are finished?' is both irrelevant and absurd: irrelevant because this is not the reason for studying the subject in the first place, and absurd because there is no sense in which a student with this approach will ever be 'finished' (a theme to which we shall return).

The role of the teacher adopting this approach to his duties will be that of a resource rather than a pedagogue, an encourager in a process of exploration rather than a purveyor of knowledge, a 'drawer-out' rather than a 'putter-in'. Indeed, in this philosophy, teacher and student are more partners in a common enterprise than people standing on the opposite sides of a divide. The student will be encouraged to think for himself, even to disagree with the teacher, rather than accept ideas purely on the basis of another person's authority. This may mean that, from time to time, he is forced to have to learn from his mistakes. The educere perspective views this as a healthier process than accepting without question what the other has to say. To put the issue starkly: to any extent that a person has to rely on the judgments of other people, to any extent that he is limited in his capacity for making decisions for himself, and to any extent that he is incapable of appreciating values held by other people, he is, from the educere point of view, to that extent diminished as a human being.

Autonomy   In a word, with educere as the dominant idea in education, its overriding aim will be not that of producing specialists in particular fields, but personal *autonomy*. It would be absurd on this view to suggest that because one can wave a certificate at the public one is therefore educated – as absurd as suggesting that because you have a certificate of release from a mental institution you can prove yourself sane. Having developed this autonomy, the individual should be able to see issues on a wider perspective than is likely if he has simply been trained to practise a fixed number of skills. He should have increased his imaginative powers, so that he will be able to acknowledge both the fact of the existence of views different from his own, and the strength or value of those views. Bigotry and prejudice are less likely to occur in his thinking. A bi-product of this is that he will have a contribution to make in a range of fields, where the ability to stand on one's own feet and make adjustments to situations is often called for. An element of training 'at the coal face' is always likely to be needed for such people, but they will enter many spheres of work already armed with the main qualification for the job. Many an engineering graduate, as I have often been told by a friend who heads such a firm, enters a factory with impressive qualifications after his name but finds himself incapable of adjusting to the process of change which is inevitable in such an industry. Educare has provided him with enough skills to get the job; but it will require elements of the educere approach to make any progress in it.

I have tried to be as objective as possible in delineating the two approaches, and any assessment of them must acknowledge the necessity for both in the education system. If I have been harsher in the description of educare and more eulogistic about educere, this may be attributed to the general down-playing of the latter in modern Western society. The value of being trained in some practical skill needs no defending. It is my great regret that my education was geared totally towards the humanities; this was certainly what I wanted to study, but I wish now that, as among the Semites two thousand years ago (and still today, for all I know) I had also been trained in a 'useful' skill, like car maintenance or the workings of a radio or television. Apart from anything else, I should then have saved myself a good deal of money over the years. It is also clear that for some people any sense of satisfaction or fulfilment in life is derived from the gaining of such a skill. Part of the problem in education is the 'lower end' of a school where most people have little or no sense of achievement. I have seen a despondent group of such youngsters gradually transformed by an excellent woodwork teacher who both showed them what could be done with a block of wood and enabled them to do it. For most of them this was a kind of release from slavery. Their self-image, and perhaps thereby their autonomy, was enhanced.

There are in fact certain situations in which I should be alarmed to hear that those in charge had been educated only on the educere principle. If, before an operation, I were to be told that the surgeon had never performed an operation in his life before, but had been taught over a number of years how to tackle problems, I would be making sure that my life insurance premiums had been fully paid up; and my anxiety would not be alleviated with the assurances that if I died he would bear the blame. Equally, if I were on a Boeing 747 about to fly to California and were told that this was the pilot's first flight, that he would learn the use and purpose of the instruments as he went along, and would be discharged if he did not get the passengers to their destination, I'd be inclined to settle for crossing the Atlantic by rowing boat.

The point that is being made by those who present the educere approach as the key to the nature of *education* as opposed to *training*, is that education cannot be conveniently pigeon-holed as the attainment of a particular skill, and nothing more. Education, so argue these protagonists, is continuous, involving, potentially, the whole of life. It may be freely acknowledged that educare has provided the human race with all manner of labour-saving devices, speeded-up transport systems, calculators and computers, and a range of automatic machines to take over the most repetitive and boring jobs, both at work and in the home. Good. So now we all have more spare time on our hands, the drudgery is taken out of life, women look younger at forty than they did a couple of generations ago, and we no longer need the ox-like man carrying a steel girder over each shoulder. The question then arises as to what shall be done with the extra leisure time thus gained – the time when people can *choose* what to do. Educare will not help with this, and if the answer is to spend hour after hour watching American soap operas, finding one's own company dull, and satisfying an ever-increasing craving for alcohol, it must be wondered whether we should not be better off helping Sisyphus with his boulder up his mountain. If, as B. F. Skinner said, 'education is what survives when what has been learnt has been forgotten', we may reinterpret those sentiments to state that a man shows the extent of his education by what he does in the hours in which he is under no necessity, economic or otherwise, to behave in a certain way.

The fact is that it is still possible to have everything in the world that educare can provide, and still be – on this definition – uneducated. One may have a string of houses and a fleet of cars and still be educationally illiterate; one may have degrees the length of one's arm and still be petty-minded; one may be capable of flying Concorde to every country in the world and still be a racialist; one may be able to transplant human organs and still be a sexist; one may be an expert on the preservation of the environment and still hate one's fellow human beings; one may be able to speak a dozen languages fluently, and not have anything worthwhile to say in any of them (the cynical definition of a bilingual secretary is 'one who is illiterate in two languages').

The major problem for anyone convinced of the value of the educere approach in education is that of finding a place, or time, for it in a system geared to educare. Granted that students should be encouraged to think for themselves, to work out their studies autonomously, to follow up those subjects and topics which strike a chord in their minds or capture their imaginations: how is this possible in a system dominated by syllabuses, qualifications, and the demands of the community and government? Is educere, like democracy, just an ideal in a few people's minds, a twinkle in the eye of the geography teacher engaged for the twentieth time on the course on sedimentary rocks? Before tackling that problem, we must face the central question of the role of the teacher generally in the education process and, in particular, the nature or source of his authority.

The teacher's authority

The word 'authority' (Latin root 'auctoritas') is interesting. Its meaning emerges from a consideration of the cognate word, author (auctor): an author is a pioneer, an originator, the presenter of ideas, images, characterisations, to which others respond. Others may criticise his work, even develop it further than he is able to do, but he remains the initiator, their catalyst. So he, and anyone else in authority, may be described as the one who is primary in any group, controlling certain aspects of what they do and say, if not what they think. The teacher is generally viewed as one having authority – or, if he doesn't have it, one who ought to have it. On what is this authority based, and how does it relate to the educare/educere dichotomy? There are six possible answers to this, which I shall outline in ascending order (as I see it) of relevance to the debate.

(a) Tradition People of a certain social standing and of certain professions have traditionally been accorded the respect of authority: the monarchy, the aristocracy, the clergy, members of the medical profession, and so on. Among these, certainly until well into the twentieth century, have been teachers. The authority which they were viewed to hold in any community is vividly expressed in Oliver Goldsmith's *The Deserted Village*:

There, in his noisy mansion skilled to rule
The village master taught his little school.
A man severe he was, and stern to view;
I knew him well, and every truant knew:
Well had the boding tremblers learned to trace
The day's disasters in his morning face;
Full well they laughed with counterfeited glee
At all his jokes, for many a joke had he;
Full well the busy whisper circling round
Conveyed the dismal tidings when he frowned.
Yet he was kind, or, if severe in aught,
The love he bore to learning was in fault . . .
While words of learned length and thundering sound
Amazed the gazing rustics ranged around;
And still they gazed, and still the wonder grew
That one small head could carry all he knew.

Some of these groups retain this authority today: people in Britain will still laugh uproariously at the corniest of jokes if told by a member of the royal family; and medical doctors' opinions will be treated with respect not only when they discuss medical matters, but also on such matters as morals, marriages, or metaphysics. For the clergy, with the general decline in religious belief in the western world, there has been a lessening of authority in most countries; and, with the enormous increase in the number of professions requiring higher qualifications, there has been a virtually universal loss of authority on the part of teachers. The accountant, the stockbroker, even the estate agent are all likely to be held in greater respect than the teacher. This is one tradition that has died the death of the educare syndrome.

(b) Physical authority *Kent:* You have that in your countenance that I
would fain call master.
Lear: What's that?
Kent: Authority.

(*King Lear*, I, iv)

The authority that Lear possessed at the time was that of the bully – having the power, at a stroke, to banish the trustworthy Kent and disown the only daughter that loved him. Physical authority is that of the tyrant, the dictator who controls his armies, the hijacker with a gun in his hand, the kidnapper with power over a person's life. It is the authority accorded to the toughest in the gang, to the most long-winded in discussion and the most self-assertive in behaviour. It is the authority brought about by other people's fear: fear of death or imprisonment or torture in some cases, but fear also of the lash of a person's tongue, an expression of contempt, the determination not to relinquish the floor. I have seen it expressed a thousand times in board meetings and, in days in which corporal punishment is no longer permitted in most schools, teachers may still fall back on this when all else has failed. (I still bear the marks of the withering sarcasm of my physics master at Blackburn Grammar School, who held me in contempt because I, a member of his form and House, refused to join his Air Training Corps. One of the moments of pure joy that I carry with me from my school days is the look of utter mortification on his face when I emerged as top in physics in his 'mock' 'O' level examination.)

The important point here is not that teachers don't fall back on these physical effects in order to assert their authority (they still do, if not quite as blatantly as Mr Squeers of Dotheboys Hall): what is at stake is the education process itself. It is hard to imagine that any real learning, except parrot-fashion, occurs where fear is the motive; hence any teacher who resorts to this lays himself open to the charge of acting under false pretences. How can anyone claim to be a teacher if nobody is learning what is allegedly being taught?

(c) Charismatic authority Charisma is a difficult word to define; literally, it means 'spiritual gift', and is often associated with religious evangelical fervour (it is to be found in this context in the New Testament). In this present context we can take it to mean a quality of character or of personality which others find attracting if not always attractive. It gives a person power to hold the attention of others, and perhaps cause them to wish to emulate the one who expresses it. A person with charisma will stand out in a group, impress – at least at first – where others fail to impress, and, especially in politics, capture the headlines when others, perhaps more hard-working and knowledgeable on the subject, are ignored. President Kennedy had charisma, President Carter did not: it will be interesting to see what place history eventually accords them both.

We can all probably remember charismatic teachers: those whose very presence in the classroom made the burden of attending school less onerous. However, there are two cautionary comments pertinent to this discussion. The first is the obvious one that charisma cannot be taught, bought, or learned; there is no general certificate or post-graduate qualification in the subject. If a person has it, he has it; if not, not. So the teacher born with this quality should be grateful for it – if he's aware of it – and should be humble and realistic enough to recognise it as a bonus not possessed by all. The second caution follows from this. The student may hero-worship a charismatic teacher, but this spirit of adulation may in fact militate against the need for hard graft in the learning process. Every teacher must point the way to this sooner or later, since the training of the mind is just as arduous a process as the training of the body. The charismatic teacher who puts all his trust in his own innate dynamism and ability to hold the attention of others must fight hard to avoid both the temptation to shine and the temptation to decline (which may lead to the temptation to whine). Education, like life, can be glorious fun: but the fun is best appreciated in a context of routine.

(d) *Delegated authority*   At this point we return to a notion raised in the previous chapter: authority *de jure* as opposed to authority de facto. Delegated authority is authority de jure, that is, the authority a person expresses not because of the kind of person he is but because of the position he holds. The returning officer at an election count will begin his reading of the result with the words 'By the authority invested in me . . .'; a minister of religion will normally be granted the authority to legalise weddings in his church; and perhaps the best example of this type of authority is the policeman: what we recall after any encounter with such a person is not the face but the uniform, and he gains our respect not because of any personal attributes but because of what he represents: the law. Many people with *de jure* authority may well have a certain natural authority independently of the office they hold: authority *de facto*; others certainly do not possess this kind of authority, and we must all be familiar with the pipsqueak public official who can – and does – throw his weight around in his official capacity, but beyond that is a nonentity. How far does a teacher's authority spring from his being formally recognised by the Ministry of Education? This recognition will gain him admittance to the classroom; it should give him a certain amount of self-confidence; but it is to be doubted if any student has ever embarked on the learning process solely because he was instructed to do so by a person with the requisite qualifications. In fact, of all the possible sources of authority for a teacher, this one seems the most irrelevant when applied to the class- or lecture-room situation. The tutor may have a string of degrees plus a teaching certificate, bearing the full support of the Department of Education and Science, the Local Education Authority, the National Union of Teachers, the head teacher of the school (and MI5 and the CIA for all I know), but still be a disaster at the 'coal face'. *De facto* authority does not proceed automatically from authority *de jure*, as the Holy Spirit is alleged in the Creeds to proceed from the Father and the Son: this kind of authority is not bestowed, but has to be earned. (It is not earned by simply presenting an imposing presence to the students, as in an Irish Convent School I once visited: in each classroom was an ultrahigh chair, reached only by ascending six or seven steps. When I asked the nun in charge why the teachers used such ugly monstrosities – though I expressed my question, as I recall, somewhat more neutrally – she replied in a surprised tone: 'So that the children will look up to us, of course.')

(e) Academic authority The answer which would probably receive greatest public support (if not from the teaching profession itself) in this quest is that a teacher's authority arises from his academic expertise. He is heard because he knows his subject, and may even be 'an authority' in his field. Those who take the educare view of education are likely to rank this quality high on their list of priorities for a teacher. It is certainly the case that expertise in a field will play a considerable part in determining how far any teacher expresses authority. 'Why are you there and me here?' a pompous middle-aged student once asked a much younger person who was his Open University tutor. 'Because I know the subject and you don't,' was the conclusive reply. Without such knowledge, any teacher is likely to find the classroom a continuous walk along a razor's edge, with the abyss of wrong information on the one side and admission of ignorance on the other.

The question at issue, however, is whether expertise in a subject is all that is needed in order to teach it: granted it may be necessary, is it sufficient? I think not. If the converse were true, it would imply that the affirmation 'if you know it you can teach it' is sound, thus making superfluous any process of teacher training. Some might suggest that this would not be an altogether bad thing, and that many a good teacher can get his subject across without having experienced an hour of training. But the same is true in other professions; there are famous actors who have never attended drama school, clergymen who have missed out on theological colleges, even healers who have never seen the inside of a medical school. But the chances are that a person trained for any of these jobs will do it more effectively than one who hasn't: 'naturals' in any profession are a small minority of the whole, and teaching is no exception. I have known scholars who are so up-to-date in their fields that the fields have difficulty keeping up with them: yet they are quite incapable of so arranging their knowledge that others are able to learn it. Academic authority will allow a person to pontificate before others, but this is no guarantee that learning will take place. And *unless something is learned, nothing is taught.* What is euphemistically described as teaching in many an academic institution – and universities must carry a major share of responsibility here – is in reality often little more than a display of erudition on somebody's part. (There may be a place in education for such displays, but it is the authority of the teacher which is under discussion.)

It can be acknowledged, then, that a teacher whose academic expertise is only partial is likely to have a hard time with his students; but it does not follow automatically that one with with great expertise will achieve what he is in the class- or lecture-room to do: to assist or enable the students to make progress with their learning. The teacher's authority lies elsewhere than simply being a fund of knowledge.

(f) Moral authority It is through his moral attitude to the enterprise of education that a teacher primarily establishes his authority. What this means must be carefully adumbrated, since the image presented by the phrase can be, to put it mildly, off-putting, reflecting such precious attitudes as that of a colleague who refused to join a one-day strike, called for by his union and professional association, on the grounds that he was a 'dedicated teacher'. Two characteristics of moral authority are central: (i) The teacher indicates, by the general tenor of the approach to his work, that the enterprise on which both he and the students are engaged is intrinsically worthwhile. The learning process, which is viewed as one of developing the mind and the imagination, is therefore seen as a value *per se*, requiring no external motivation, such as qualifications or employment prospects, in order to justify itself. Such a teacher will be committed to the educere approach to his work, even if he is teaching in a field which seems to relate primarily to educare – like the carpentry teacher already mentioned who viewed his subject, geared though it was to the students' eventual careers, as primarily one which enabled students to experience the pride of achievement (the same incentive which causes other people to lead deprived inner-city children up mountains).

How the teacher brings this about will vary from person to person. On the negative side it means avoiding the cynicism which can overtake this profession more than most. A colleague who set off to teach a class of apprentices with the words 'I'll go and cast a few more pearls before the swine' may have been making a joke, but it was a bad joke, since it reflected his general opinion of his job (he now works for a broadcasting company). Similarly, no teacher who is seriously encouraging his students to develop themselves to the full will respond, as did another former colleague to a boy who had stated that after school he wanted to 'go on the land', with the words, 'What as, laddy, manure?' Sarcasm is not only the lowest form of wit: in the classroom or lecture theatre it is a sure sign to the students that the teacher no longer believes that what he is doing is worthwhile. There is, moreover, no necessity for this seriousness of purpose to be reflected in pomposity of style; one can be relaxed in manner without showing the indifference of the cynic, which will soon be spotted by students of all ages.

(ii) The second characteristic of a teacher's moral authority is the ability to motivate students to study, without falling back on the refuge of 'this is a favourite with the examiners'. As with the first characteristic, this requires an enthusiasm for his work which may be caught by the students. (Educere suggests that education as a whole is caught, not taught.) The teacher who is bored by what he teaches is likely to bore his students and so reduce this element of his authority; with enthusiasm, he stands a chance of maintaining their interest long enough to get them involved in, if not totally committed to, that particular aspect of the educational enterprise.

The most important factor in bringing about motivation in the learner – so far, at any rate, as the teacher is concerned – is the relationship between teacher and student. This issue has been admirably discussed at length in R. S. Peters's *Ethics and Education*, and here it is necessary only to touch briefly on its implications. Basically, it involves the ability on the teacher's part to empathise with the students. He must realise that while students can and should be stretched, they must not be stretched too far lest the connecting line breaks. The best teachers are those who, however scholarly they may be, can make their deepest insights clear to those who cannot possibly have their resources for the simple reason that they haven't yet had the time to build them up. Heidegger's lectures, referred to in Chapter Seven, were gnomic utterances, like a prophet speaking in tongues, but students went away filled with awe rather than knowledge. Russell, on the other hand, could make his years of work on, say, scepticism sound like reflections on one's favourite novel: we went away not conscious of the cleverness of the lecturer but fascinated by the subject. It would be worth any teacher's while to recall, from time to time, how he felt about his subject-matter as a beginner: he might then be more in tune with the students' perplexities. The process of getting on to the students' wavelengths and adapting the subject-matter accordingly will need more thought in preparation than is required in just reading a scholarly tome, for which the real audience are the subscribers to one or other learned journal. (This is especially true of books on philosophy.)

Good teaching therefore requires more than knowledge of a subject; to this knowledge must be added a sense of sympathy with those to be taught, with the realisation that they, as well as the teacher, have rights in the educational process: in this case, the right to be taught, in effect, in their own language. This is a moral requirement of the teacher and, independently of his qualifications, scholarship, or even charisma, will provide him with his authority in the field. Ironically, on this basis, authority is an issue which is hardly likely to occur to either the teacher or the students.

Historical considerations

A number of philosophers have contributed over the centuries to the central moral issues in education: who is it for, and how should it proceed? A brief resumé of some of their ideas may facilitate us in making a judgment on the basic question raised in this chapter.

Plato As hinted at in Chapter Eleven, Plato taught that, while education was in theory open to all (except the slaves, of course) in practice the majority of students, by failing at one stage or another, would be judged unfit to travel the length of the line. His philosophy of education may not unfairly be described as the cultivation of excellence. This view is naturally criticised by egalitarians in the community on the grounds that this is unfair to slower learners, and that in any case social factors play a major part in determining how far any student progresses along the educational line. To this Plato may well have replied along the lines of a poem I wrote some years ago in order to act as a catalyst at an educational teach-in; its inclusion at this point may be justified on the grounds of fairness rather than its aesthetic qualities:

> The other day Tom Dudgeon died
> And went to heaven all starry-eyed;
> He hurried to the pearly gate,
> Intent on not arriving late:
> But what was this? His wits had been suborned?
> The man who let him in was tailed and horned!
> 'Oh, my mistake,' said Tom, now apprehensive.
> 'No, not at all,' said Nick, 'we've just gone comprehensive.'

Plato he say: 'If all skilled men have to try to turn sows' ears into silk purses, who is left to make silk into silk purses?'

Whatever view be held on the structure of the educational system, the basic question remains as to whether there is ever a time when a person's education should be deemed to be at an end. This is quite feasible if the approach is that of educare: a person either qualifies for a role in society or he fails to do so: having failed, he must make do with whatever other openings remain, for which lower qualifications, or no qualifications at all, are required. The issue, then, is whether, having failed at the first hurdle, a person will have another chance to have a go at it later in life when his capacities may well have developed sufficiently for him to be more successful. The demonstrable success rate of mature students in the Open University and polytechnics in Britain, and the state universities in America, has established the viability of the 'second chance' in education.

Underlying this discussion is the philosophy, expressed by the educere view of education, that education is not a commodity but a process, or attitude of mind. On this view, the educare idea that to be qualified is synonymous with being educated is frankly naive. R. S. Peters (op. cit.) makes the perceptive remark: 'To be educated is not to have arrived, it is to travel with a different view'. What this difference is cannot be glibly defined, but it is at least a process of 'unblinkering', so that the main effect of learning is the realisation of how much more there is to learn. Perhaps it could be said that an educated person will be humble about his own capacities, appreciative of the point of view of others, imaginative and humane: the opposite, in fact, of the professor at a neighbouring university who, when invited to lecture at my university when it was still a polytechnic, replied: 'I am an academic and a gentleman: I do not lecture at polytechnics'. (He was a historian, but that hardly exonerates him). (Case study 39 will allow you to follow up this and cognate issues.)

Aquinas The name of the medieval philosopher and theologian, *Thomas Aquinas* (1224–74) has already cropped up in this book, and on the subject of education he made a profound observation, using a particularly vivid image. The relationship between teacher and student, he argued, was like that between doctor and patient. The doctor cannot make the sick patient well: all he can do is to suggest what steps the patient should take in order to be better. Whether the patient heeds the doctor's advice is then a matter solely for the patient: no doctor can heal a patient. Similarly, no teacher can give a student an education. All he can do is to indicate what steps the student should take in order to become more educated. He may suggest questions to answer, avenues to explore, people to consult, books to read: he may even make things easier for the student by providing him with a summary of the salient facts on any issue. But whether the student follows up these suggestions by researching as advised, or learning the facts so as to proceed further, is the decision of the student. *The teacher cannot 'learn' the student*; teaching, in fact, cannot take place if nobody wishes to learn, just as a patient's chances of recovery are reduced if not totally removed if he does not wish to be well.

Plato himself had made a similar comment. 'Knowledge that is acquired under compulsion has no hold on the mind. Therefore do not use compulsion, but let early education be rather a sort of amusement.' The implications of that second sentence were to be expressed in Rousseau's *Emile*, to which we shall shortly give attention. The truth of the first sentence, on which Aquinas's views are, in effect, a commentary, has not found easy acceptance, even among educationists. Many teachers appear satisfied with themselves by simply covering in the allotted time all the subjects on the particular syllabus; yet this does not guarantee that any learning has occurred, except that of memorising enough facts to pass an exam. Just as one can lead a horse to water without making him drink, so one can lead a student to the classroom without making him think. This is not to say that the teacher who is aware of the all-importance of motivation in the learning process will have a hundred percent success rate. Whatever people may do to bring about internal motivation in others, whether this be parents with their children, doctors with their patients, missionaries with non-believers, or teachers with students, they must be realistic enough to acknowledge that failures occur. The anorexic will refuse even the most delectable of food.

Rousseau *Rousseau*, as we have seen, believed in reincarnation and the natural goodness of people. His educational theory was based on this view; he showed in *Emile* how to preserve this natural goodness by 'guarding the heart against vice and the mind against error'. The vice, and the error, he believed, grew out of the greed and selfishness of society. A child's education should therefore be guided by the aim of preserving him for as long as possible from society's values. For the first twelve years of his life, a child should be allowed simply to grow and develop physically, in harmony with nature in all its purity, and shielded from the books which, having been written by people inevitably tainted by the world, must begin to pollute him. Even after twelve, the main source of his educational development must be the observation of nature, beginning with curricula in astronomy, science, arts, and crafts, and only in the later teens proceeding to the more 'social' subjects, such as history, politics, and economics.

The effect of *Emile* on Rousseau's contemporary Kant was that he forgot, for once in his life, to take his afternoon walk (which in turn caused all his neighbours to check their clocks). The idea of 'education through nature' was not new (Lao Tsu had advocated it in China over two millennia earlier) but it had never been given such direct and literate expression before *Emile*. This philosophy stands out firmly against any theory of education as indoctrination, and any view of teaching based on the belief that this involves no more than drilling facts into students. Rousseau would have been as horrified by the nun teaching from her chair near the ceiling as he would have been delighted by the encouragement given to students to make their own curricula and discipline instanced in the 'progressive' schools of Britain and America.

Dewey One further contributor should be mentioned before the attempt is made to draw together the varying strands of this discussion. The American philosopher John Dewey (1859–1952 – it seems that being a philosopher is more a guarantee of long life than being, say, a musician) has probably had a larger impact on educational theory and practice than any other person over the last century. His views epitomise the most practicable insights of the other philosophers we have reviewed, and are as good an extension of the educere interpretation of education as we are likely to find.

Dewey dispensed altogether with the idea that an educational institution is a talking shop, a place where blackboards or OHP slides are filled up by one person to be transcribed by others, where notes are transferred from the lecturers' notebooks to the students' notebooks without necessarily going through the heads of either. Instead, he viewed the school as a social system which is the framework and an essential element of the curriculum. Learning takes place within this social context, and the students are therefore expected to play their part in determining both the form and values of that context. He advocated school councils, on which the students would have the authority to share in deciding the school's activities, both social and academic, and in its expression of discipline. Having such responsibilities, he believed, would give students a greater motivation to learn: learning was secondary to living.

The learning process he believed to be 'learning by doing'; and this would be achieved by the inductive method of science rather than by the absorption of facts from books or lectures. This is the 'problem-solving' approach to education, described by Karl Popper in his book on the philosophy of science, *Conjectures and Refutations* (mentioned in Chapter One). According to Popper, the whole of scientific enquiry has been a process of producing a hypothesis and attempting to disprove it. Dewey, in his *Logic, the Theory of Inquiry*, argued that this should be true of all intellectual enquiry, and described the process of problem-solving as having the following five steps:

1. The indeterminate situation. Where the equilibrium between an organism and its environment has become disturbed, inquiry is introduced in order to restore it.
2. The institution of a problem. The inquirer recognises that this lack of equilibrium creates a problem that needs his attention.
3. Setting up a hypothesis. The inquirer anticipates what will happen when certain forces are brought to bear upon this disturbance, and the symbols with which he expresses his idea, or hypothesis, become the conceptual elements in this new stage of the inquiry.
4. Reasoning. The hypothesis is then tested deductively; as with scientific experimentation, if these tests do not work, a further hypothesis must be sought.
5. The construction of judgment. The inquiry is concluded as the equilibrium is restored: the problem is solved, and the student can turn his attention to a further indeterminate situation.

In the situation to which this philosophy of learning gives rise, the teacher's role is as we have seen, to be an aid, not a fund of knowledge. In the words of Pope's *Essay on Man*:

> Men should be taught as though you taught them not,
> And things unknown forthtold as things forgot.

If it is the case that a school is not merely a 'teaching shop' but a place where values and attitudes are transmitted, then the whole question of the meaning of education becomes willy-nilly, a political issue on which a stand must be taken. If, as I suggested in Chapter Nine, it is also the case that 'every idea is an incitement' it follows that everyone engaged in the ideas-sharing process is potentially a revolutionary. So to the extent that schools and colleges actually encourage people to think, they must be inherently dangerous institutions for any establishment, whose fundamental fear was expressed by Shakespeare: 'He thinks too much: such men are dangerous'. Education, as both Russell and Sartre (to name but two philosophers) remarked, ought to be fostering the wish for truth, not expounding the conviction that some particular creed – religious, political, or otherwise – is the truth. Perhaps when today's philosophers have stopped discussing the meaning of meaning they may, like some of their most eminent forebears, take to the market-places and be thorns in the establishment's flesh. (The American philosopher, Noam Chomsky, is a superb example here.)

In this chapter I have, I guess, come off the non-committal fence of the start of the book. In an age in which economic considerations seem to determine the *practice* of 'ought' if not its *meaning*, this commitment should be recognised as inevitable. The teaching of philosophy has, on these grounds, been curtailed if not totally eliminated in many educational institutions, and in many others the subject is under threat. (My own institution, for instance, banned it without consultation from a summer school programme on the grounds that it was not a 'useful' subject like handling finance or learning a foreign language, and therefore would not have enough takers to be financially viable: this may have been an accurate judgment on the controllers' part.) The strength of feeling in this chapter is born, therefore, of the convictions, firstly, that subjects like philosophy – the humanities, the arts, the social sciences to a lesser extent – have been generally downgraded by those in authority so that they are underestimated by the bulk of modern students.

Secondly, I am angered and saddened by what I believe to be many of the signs of a new Dark Age. I applaud the succinct expressiveness of Emerson:

A man is the whole encyclopedia of facts. The creation of a thousand forests is in one acorn, and Egypt, Greece, Rome, Gaul, Britain, America, lie folded already in the first man.

My fear is that Western civilisation has embarked on a process of folding man up again and destroying this heritage, by neglect if not by direct action. A nation that esteems accountants and estate agents more highly than it does teachers or scholars has indeed become a nation of shopkeepers; and it is hard to view with equanimity the consequence of this for many people, young and old: as one door shuts, another one closes.

The case studies which follow have been designed to allow you to examine some of the provocative issues for yourself: explode, if you wish, but at least work them through.

CASE STUDY 39: EDUCATION

A. What is it for?
1 Child-minding – but is it the cheapest way?
2 Teaching basic skills – but does it do this? How else could (and do) children learn?
3 Preparation for jobs – but what jobs?
4 Transmission of the culture and values of society – but who decides what this means? Should they be transmitted or transformed?
5 Selecting and grooming of the elite – but what about the rest?
6 Development of personality – who is competent to do this?

B. Who should decide what kind of education we have?
1 'Society', because tax-payers pay for education – but who speaks for 'society', and how much control do they exercise?
2 Parents – what are the limits of their rights?
3 Children and young people – but what if they reject what is on offer?
4 Professional 'educators' – but who decides what group of 'experts' is right?

C. How long should formal education last?
1 Until a child is 'fed up' with school – but does he know best?
2 Until children have learned what they need for their future employment – but this could mean just teaching them literacy and/or numeracy, and perhaps no education at all.
3 Until a compulsory school-leaving age – but what is to be done with those who have ceased to learn, because they don't want to learn, long before that?
4 For as long as any individual wishes – this would mean further or higher education on demand: can we afford 'open' tertiary education?

D. How should education be paid for?
1 Taxes – why should these be paid by the childless, or by those who (perhaps at personal sacrifice) pay for private education?
2 Privately – what will happen to children of very poor families?
3 A mixture of 1 and 2 (vouchers?).
4 Industrial or commercial sponsorship – what would happen to

291

subjects like literature or history which have no obvious link with these?

5 Loans – how long to repay? what if the student never becomes a wage-earner?

E. In general:

1 Is small beautiful in education?
2 Are some of our schools, colleges, polytechnics, universities too big?
3 Is education a right? What should be done with those who refuse it?
4 Should more, or less, money be spent on the education of slow learners or the handicapped?

CASE STUDY 40: PEACE STUDIES IN THE CURRICULUM

Peace education has emerged in recent years as a subject for study in schools. This case study is intended to encourage you to discuss problems which have revealed themselves in the process, particularly as they hinge on issues raised in the previous chapter.

1 Some local authorities have either banned the subject or have had it modified; many others have expressed 'deep concern' about the teaching of the subject. On the face of it, this expression of antagonism seems odd: war studies are conspicuous in history courses and, if the Old Testament forms part of the RE syllabuses, considerable attention may well have to be paid by the students to the extensive amount of smiting and being smitten, slaying and being slain, which dominates Old Testament history. Why, then, the suspicion of peace studies?

(a) Political – fear that it will be taught by 'left-wingers'? Is this a justifiable fear, or a phobia?
(b) Authoritarianism – fear that the establishment might be criticised? (You may think that this would not be altogether harmful, but is it not in the nature of establishments to minimise opportunities for criticism – anywhere?)
(c) Prejudice/patriotism – the fear that students may begin to doubt whether 'dulce et decorum est pro patria mori', and reject the attitude of 'my country, right or wrong'? (If you feel that this is already an outdated view, take a look at the opinion polls and views expressed in popular newspapers as recently as in the Falklands War in 1982, or the Gulf War of 1991.
(d) Greed – the advent of peace would hit the pockets of the millions for whom war is a prosperous enterprise, either directly by

manufacturing and trading in weapons of war, or indirectly by holding shares in relevant companies?

Has the word 'peace' become a dirty word in certain circles? ('peace' = communism, anarchy, red brigades, revolutions, arson, rape, murder, bringing down the mighty from their seats and sending the rich empty away, etc.?)

2 As an exercise, try to devise a syllabus in peace studies (say an hour a week for a year) for fifth-formers – 15–16-year-olds. Bear in mind the following central aspects which relate the syllabus to the curriculum as a whole:

(a) What are your aims/objectives? ('Broadening of knowledge', modifying the 'normal' attitudes of approval towards war, countering the cult of violence, etc.)
(b) What topics would you include/exclude?
(c) How should the subject be taught? Through discussion? – who would introduce it, using what sources of information? Through role play? Could you be sure that the person in charge had the skill to devise this?
(d) Who should teach it? The form teacher irrespective of his specialist subject? the RE teacher? a part-time specialist? (specialist in what?); a series of visitors with authority in specific fields? (who will organise these, and on what basis should he decide who to invite?)
(e) Who would monitor the course, and how would you ensure impartiality? Should the course be left unassessed? What might then be the dangers, so far as both teachers and students are concerned?

3 Assuming that trends in classroom discussions on this theme are likely to include a fair amount of criticism of government policy, is this the kind of responsibility that school teachers, paid out of public money, should be (a) allowed and (b) expected to bear? Even assuming that members of a school's teaching staff have enough strength of purpose and authoritative knowledge on world affairs to be able to teach the subject to the standards required, and acknowledging that in many subjects, such as history, art, literature, geography etc., a degree of bias (or special interest) is inevitable in a teacher, is it the teacher's place to be a culture-change agent? Can any teacher ultimately avoid playing the tune paid for by the piper?

You may contend that because Religious Education is a compulsory part of the curriculum in Britain's state schools, the pass has already been sold since, theoretically at least, the acceptance of this subject implies the truth of certain unproven hypotheses which affect how people behave: assumptions are therefore made to which many object. If you are critical of the privileged position of this subject, you should be exploring ways of undermining this position, and so combatting a historical 'thrust'. The case for peace studies will have to be justified independently.

An alternative topic to which the same order of questions could be applied: *Sex Education in schools*.

CASE STUDY 41: CONTROVERSY IN THE CLASSROOM

Many educational authorities have objected to the introduction of Peace Studies into the classroom, not on the ground that they preferred 'War Studies' (some would say that that was the subtext of the history syllabus) but because its teachers tended to be of a particular political persuasion (left-wing, to be precise).

How far do you consider it right that schools should be allowed to introduce controversial subjects into their curriculum? One noted example of this is Sex Education, which has always had to face the opposition of multitudes of parents and 'concerned citizens' on the grounds that it 'encourages children to experiment in this field'. Do you think that is true? And even if it is, does it justify the banning of the subject except, perhaps, as a slot in the biology syllabus?

If you can, try to make some cross-cultural and cross-national comparisons about attitudes to teaching this subject. How far do you think that people of the UK and of the USA are tight-lipped about it because their upbringing and religious traditions reflect an intense (unhealthy?) Puritanism?

You probably experienced the teaching of Religious Instruction at school. How far did you feel that this subject, like Peace Studies and Sex Education, was in the category of 'controversial' because it expressed only one point of view among many, was no longer held by the majority of the population, and related to an area about which, in its consequences historically, there remains at best a huge question mark?

If it is the case that 'every idea is an incitement', does it seem right that views on subjects which affect us all, but are not held by all, should be removed from the classroom altogether? Is education suffering from terminal anaemia?

Chapter Thirteen

Phi beta kappa
The philosophy of experience

At the start of this book, I raised the question of the nature of philosophy, and concluded that it was both a specific methodological approach to learning and an area of study which strictly belonged nowhere else in the educational curriculum. Both of these features link up with the Greek origin of the word, since both involve a pursuit of wisdom. The meaning, here, of 'wisdom' is quite simple. On the one hand, it is taking a generally closer look at the use and meaning of words and sentences than is required – or normally happens – in everyday communication, whether between individuals or through the media. On the other hand, philosophy, when examining certain subject areas such as metaphysics or ethics, takes a longer view, a broader perspective, than may be looked for in most other fields of debate. It is possible to be an intolerant philosopher, but this attitude of mind hardly fits the subject since intolerance springs from a background of prejudice, bigotry, and ignorance. The most insufferable people in the universe are those who know nothing but express their views as though they know it all: if such views have occasionally been punctured in this book, I make no apology: millions of people throughout the world are living deprived, hopeless, shattered lives because of others' ignorance and prejudice, and if the philosopher will not expose these twin menaces to human happiness, it is difficult to know where else to turn.

Behind this (I hope) innocuous-sounding description there lies, however, an underlying assumption about the nature of philosophy and the role of the philosopher in society which, to put it mildly, will be reacted to by most current expositors of the subject with somewhat less than acclamation. For them the study of philosophy begins and ends with the analysis of meaning, a process which is serviced primarily by the discipline of logic. The high priest of this school is Ludwig Wittgenstein, arguably the greatest philosopher of modern times (he was certainly the only philosopher whom Bertrand Russell acknowledged as at least his equal) and unquestionably one of the most influential men of this century, in philosophy or any other sphere. It is impossible not to be profoundly excited both with the man and with his writings. Inasmuch as the possession of language is what makes homo sapiens unique among all the multifarious species, he has made a major contribution to our under-standing of ourselves.

The point at issue, however, is not whether linguistic analysis is important – of course it is – but whether it is, as some of its proponents claim, (and in his earlier years Wittgenstein was among these) the sole, or even main, subject for philosophical enquiry. People do exist who think this. I referred in Chapter Seven to the many exponents of philosophical expertise who refuse to acknowledge existentialism as a philosophy. There are others who say exactly the same about utilitarianism; and no doubt many other themes considered in this book would be refused their philosophical imprimatur. The shortcomings of this attitude were wittily pointed out by Bertrand Russell, himself a major logician and analyser of language, in his book *Portraits from Memory*. He describes how he once asked a shopkeeper the shortest way to Winchester. The shopkeeper called to a man in the back premises:

'Gentleman wants to know the shortest way to Winchester.'
'Winchester?' an unseen voice replied.
'Aye.'
'Way to Winchester?'
'Aye.'
'Shortest way?'
'Aye.'
'Dunno.'

Russell adds: 'He wanted to get the nature of the question clear, but took no interest in answering it. This is exactly what modern philosophy does for the earnest seeker after truth. Is it surprising that young people turn to other studies?'

Philosophy must be more than linguistic analysis, if it is not to be classified as no more than a rather sophisticated word-game. Is it enough simply to add that the results of analysis will be that the subject will take the longer view, the broader perspective, which I mentioned at the start of the chapter? This is certainly a step further forward: to recognise that there are perspectives on moral issues which are quite different from one's own must (and this is, I admit, a value judgment) constitute a healthier state of affairs than one which admits of no possible alternative outlook than one's own. At its best this latter outlook closes the mind, consciously or otherwise, to the realities of the situation, as the flat-earthers seem genuinely able to blot out from their consciousness any evidence that the earth is round. At its worst, this state of mind leads to fanaticism or psychopathy, qualities which may occasionally move mountains but seldom in the desired direction.

If this is true, being philosophical is as that phrase suggests: not living solely for the moment, having the capacity not to be overwhelmed by every gust of wind that blows, or to be seduced by every whim or fancy that besets one. This is the philosophy born of maturity, which is not to be equated with longevity. The difference between maturity and immaturity in this context is like the difference between enjoying cricket and enjoying baseball (and enjoying test match cricket over five days rather than one-day cricket), or between enjoying snooker and enjoying pool. (One thing's for sure: if you ever make a fortune and want to lose it quickly you could do worse than investing it in test match cricket in the United States.)

I hope that, on the whole, this kind of approach characterises the treatment of the issues raised in this book. Perhaps the fact that you have reached this far is a sign that I have been at least partially successful in achieving this aim. The question that remains is whether, even if our analysis were perfect and our perspective infinite, we should have done justice to philosophy. This would certainly mean that the subject could be put into a more compact pigeon-hole than appeared to be the case in the opening chapter. But can philosophy be so circumscribed? This final chapter is written in the profound belief that this is not the case: that in addition to speaking of 'doing philosophy' (analysis) or 'being philosophical' (tolerant, or stoical), we should also be using the phrase 'philosophy of life'.

This brings us to the title of this chapter, which may have struck you as an odd way to conclude any book, even one on philosophy. The words phi, beta, and kappa are simply a transliteration of the three Greek letters θ, β and κ being the initial letters of the statement 'philosophia biou kubernetes': *philosophy is the guide* (literally steersman – or steersperson) *of life*. This is the motto of a student society (fraternity or sorority) founded in 1776 at the William and Mary College in Virginia, USA. (The tradition of using initial Greek letters in this way continues among student societies in most American universities and colleges.) There remains an ambiguity as to what the word philosophy in that context actually means (few people's lives would receive much direction from a study of philosophical logic, for instance, or from analysis along the lines of Wittgenstein's *Tractatus*) but the general implication seems to me quite clear and totally commendable: the wise man learns from his experiences in life and behaves accordingly. As these experiences are confirmed or modified by subsequent experiences, so his philosophy is strengthened, or changes tack (to retain the steersman image).

Philosophy of experience

We thus arrive at what may be termed a *philosophy of experience* – a phrase I prefer to the uglier 'experientialism'. The standpoint of this philosophy is extremely simple. It is that, as far as I am concerned, there

297

is or can be only my experience, but there is *all* my experience – thinking and feeling, willing and loving, believing and hoping, and so on, both in public and in private. At first glance this seems so obvious as to be not worth saying, but philosophers – especially Western philosophers – seem persistently to forget it. Many of them fall back on the notion of 'concepts' (an aberration discussed apropos of freedom, in Chapter Ten) and some of them have even held that one cannot discuss philosophically any issue which does not render itself subject to the cool, mathematical precision of logic. As a result, much recent philosophy, as taught in universities, polytechnics, and colleges, has ignored most of the most serious questions that people ask, such as the theme of this book: what is right and what is wrong? For this reason, it is impossible to designate as a 'philosophy of experience' that tradition in western philosophy known as *'empiricism'*, even though its advocates claimed that this philosophy was based on experience. The reason for this criticism is that empiricists restricted knowledge to that which can be perceived by the five senses, and determined by mathematical and logical reasoning.

Critique of Empiricism   Empiricists have probably not wanted to deny that people have a wider range of experience than seeing red patches and so on, but they (Locke, Berkeley, Hume, and their successors) have shown a constant prejudice against the affective side of human consciousness, and thereby have lost sight of facets of the human being which are in fact unavoidable if not central. No doubt, they seem to say, man is a dreamer, a lover, an idealist, a creature of emotions and fantasies, but philosophy is concerned only with the serious side of life, the rational intellect and what it can prove.

Clearly – and this book should, I hope, provide enough examples of this to suggest that it is self-evidently the case – the side of life on which empiricists lay such stress must be taken into account whenever we make moral decisions; indeed it is hard to think of any situation in which the evidence provided by reason and the senses would be irrelevant. What I'm objecting to is not the giving of these elements a *part* in the interpretation of experience, but giving them an *exclusive* part. This is to make a caricature of homo sapiens. In real life it is just not true that people only know something when they act like the empiricists' model scientist, verifying their hypotheses by observation. I know a joke is funny, that I can trust my friend, that I am in love, that a speaker is insincere, that a couple are not getting on together, that a landscape is beautiful, that wilful cruelty is wrong. In my knowledge there is usually a place for perception through the senses – I would not know that the joke was funny if I had not heard it or read it – but the cognitive experience goes far beyond the senses. The self-imposed restriction of the empiricists makes their philosophy boring and sterile.

Some hoary 'problems' of philosophy disappear once the artificial restriction of knowledge is dropped. One of these problems – the question of freedom – was discussed in Chapter Ten. As I stated then, *I know that I am at least sometimes free.* So does everyone else, including the determinist philosopher. Once it is admitted that experience includes the direct knowledge of freedom, it is irrelevant and absurd to try to prove or disprove it by empirical or any other means. Experience is the only evidence there ever could be, and if experience seems to be contradicted by some philosophical or scientific theory, then it is the theory which must be changed or abandoned.

Experience and interpretation   The philosophy of experience does not and cannot have an exhaustive list of categories. Nobody is in a position to lay down in advance the kinds of experience people can have, or to rule out some types of experience which people say they have had. The only way to find out what life is like is to live it. When individuals talk about their experience in art or religion or dreams or any mode of perception outside the accepted normal, their testimony has a right to be heard. They may, of course, be lying, or misinterpreting their experience. So may the scientist who conveniently 'adjusts' the results of his experiment. Fraudulent mediums, for example, do not disprove the possibility of spiritualism any more than the Piltdown hoax discredits palaeontology.

It is important that a rider be added here, lest much of what I am now saying appears out of key with remarks made continually in earlier chapters, like my comment on the man who claimed to have spoken with Jesus in his car. One difference between the philosophy of experience and simply living from day to day is that a philosopher is cautious, because he is aware that people often talk about their experience in a misleading way. Coincidences are interpreted as portents, and out-of-the-way events, like the lightning which struck and severely damaged York Minster in 1984, as of divine origin (in that event, an indication of God's displeasure over the appointment of the radical David Jenkins to the bishopric of neighbouring Durham). So it is vital to recognise at this point what is often overlooked: *experience is self-authenticating; interpretation of experience is not.*

Obviously, 'experience' and 'interpretation', like all such abstract words, are not simply names for identifiable, abstract things. They are not related like a bag of nails and a sticker with the name and price on. Learning the names of things is itself an important part of experience, and is the way in which we learn to see the world in one way rather than another, to divide things in this way rather than that. There are many different, though usually not incompatible, ways of seeing the world. From the standpoint of the philosophy of experience there is no privileged world-view, in the light of which others can be judged, just as there is no privileged view of human nature, or the source of moral awareness, or of what is 'good' or 'bad' in the arts. It does not follow that all individual interpretations in any of these – or many other – areas are equally valid. For a start, and to look at the issue at its most elemental, any statement about one's experience has to be made in a public language: if it were in a private language it could not be an act of communication. And a public language is, amongst other things, a set of rules, which must not change too quickly for the audience to understand the speaker. One of the philosopher's jobs, as has already been noted several times, is to watch the way words are used, and to ring a sound of alarm when people are in danger of being misled. Particular attention was paid to this in Chapter Three.

Another – I believe, more important – job for the philosopher is to look at experience as a whole. If I am not just a mind that can follow rules of logic, or a seer of red patches, what sort of a being am I that I have such varied types of experience? If different cultures see the world in such diverse ways – and the varieties of ways simply of viewing moral issues have filled many pages in this book – what sort of a world is it that is compatible with so many interpretations?

Meaning in experience

Trying to find meaning is not an academic exercise, not a question set by an armchair examiner, nor a question of words, much less of 'concepts'. Without claiming to speak for you or anyone else, *I cannot live without living for something.* At a certain level there is an element of the obvious about that remark. There are features of my life – as in the lives of virtually everyone else – which draw me or drive me: my work, certain relationships, various pleasures, the need to be needed and, sometimes, to be wanted. But the issue can be taken deeper than this. It is not a matter of caprice that I spend so much of my time trying to get and stay warm, comfortable, well fed, secure, and so on, nor is it any of my own making that I prefer to tell and be told the truth, that I like independence, freedom from criticism, certain company at some times and solitude at others, peace of mind. What is not quite so obvious until I begin to think about it is that all these and a great many other traits of character, tastes, habits, values, and purposes are at root forms of one simple fundamental urge: *the urge* to be happy. All my experience is subordinated to this end.

Happiness

This is not to state that I am innately hedonistic (though others may say this of me!) We saw when discussing utilitarianism that the word has a much more profound meaning than just that of pleasure. In fact I have often, along with numberless other people, participated in activities which are totally unpleasant, if not utterly painful: but the end in view has been happiness. Just as some people queue all night in the cold for a cup final ticket or a bargain at the sales, so I have spent interminable hours slogging up mountains, and have missed out on a year's normal social activity in order to write this book. Even things which might seem, from an observer's perspective, to create unhappiness, such as sacrificing one's life for a friend or for a cause, could be not incompatible with this intention.

The urge to be happy and not just to be cheerful and more or less content, but to be deeply and fully happy, is as much a part of my nature as it is part of the nature of plants to respond to the attraction of the sun. The way other people talk and behave strongly suggests to me that they too want more than anything else to be happy, even though in my eyes some of them go a strange way about achieving it, and even though numerous eminent theologians, and some philosophers, contend that this should not be so, or is not so. It does not, however, follow that people know how to reach happiness.

The elusiveness of happiness There seems to be a contradiction in the conditions of life in that the movement which seeks happiness is constantly being frustrated. It is not simply that I happen to experience some things which are painful, and fail to experience some things which are joyful. Sometimes it is easy to say, 'If only I could win the pools, or get a better job, or live somewhere else, everything would be all right.' But the truth is always that everything would *not* be all right. The proportion of pain and pleasure, joy and sorrow, might be changed, but happiness would still be fatally marred. It is not so much the temporary content of the states of experience which is unsatisfying, as their nature: they are cursed with the inevitable destruction of time, which clouds and threatens and finally buries all that is desirable.

If experience is so radically bitter (and it was Brecht who wrote 'only the unaware are happy': ignorance is bliss) and if life as it daily shows itself on the stage of consciousness is all there is, then the yearning for perfect happiness, however deeply ingrained, is a perverted instinct or a gilded death wish. It is not comfortable to discover an irremovable contradiction in the heart of life, but a philosophy based on experience cannot rule out a priori such a contradiction. There are no dogmas or principles independent of experience which assert that life (or the universe) must make sense, must be conformable to reason. For the philosophy of experience the only way to find out whether a thing is so or not is to look and see. Of course, very often I cannot look and see, and I must act (if I have to act at all) out of faith or despair. In the end all our moral decisions spring from one or other of these qualities. What I cannot do, if I am to be true to experience, is to act from faith and pretend that I act from knowledge. So experience leaves no room for doubt: *true and perfect happiness is not possible.*

Still, I cannot abandon the craving for happiness. Even if I know it to be totally futile I could no more stop trying to find it than a bird with its wings clipped can stop trying to fly. *It is a psychological impossibility to accept a condition of unhappiness.* This is one of the most obvious facets of people's behaviour, and yet few western philosophers seem to think it is important, though Aristotle was a superb exception to this. There are three easily available ways of seeking happiness in a world pervaded by misery. Each has numerous forms, and it is possible to try more than one at the same time. The ways may be called 'making the best of it', 'trying to make the world a better place', and 'dropping out'. All have found expression, one way or another, in schools of philosophy commented on in earlier chapters. (You may like to reflect on which schools are akin to which of the three approaches.)

Making the best of it (a) 'Making the best of it' means concentrating one's attention on the good, the joyful, the pleasant. Folk wisdom, expressed sometimes in religion, and, at a more sophisticated level, in the philosophy of Stoicism, has passed from generation to generation the virtue of 'being philosophical' about things. 'Count your blessing.' 'Look on the bright side.' 'However badly off you are, there's always someone worse off than you.' 'I'm sorry you've lost your left hand but it might have been worse: at least you're right-handed.' 'If you think your food's awful, remember the starving millions.' No doubt this technique works: one can put up with misfortune more easily if one is convinced that one is relatively well off, just as one can be discontented in prosperity if others are more prosperous (a fact of life which keeps people who work in the advertising industry in employment).

'Making the best of it' works at a different level when the adversity is thought of as part of a higher purpose. 'These things are sent to try us.' 'It doesn't do to have it good all the time.' 'Rain before seven, fine before eleven.' Once one accepts Murphy's first law as true: 'If things can go wrong, they will', it's amazing with what equanimity life's frustrations can be faced. At another level again, it is possible actually not to feel a pain (physical or mental) if one's attention is diverted. The sportsman in the game, the soldier on the battlefield, the rescue team on the mountain, may not notice their injuries, or be aware of their worries and fears, at the time. Hypnosis and yoga carry this principle further. 'Making the best of it' gives human ingenuity a chance to make life tolerable. Some of its 'coping strategies' could be taught in schools and colleges where they would do more to relieve suffering than most of the subjects now taught.

Making the world a better place (b) 'Making the best of it' adjusts the imbalance between what I desire and what I find by changing the way I perceive things. It transforms my experience by applying my will to my own imagination and feelings. 'Trying to make the world a better place' also works at changing my experience, but it does so by trying to change what Heidegger called 'my field' – the 'not-I'. There are innumerable variations of this gambit, but they may very roughly be placed in three classes. The first class says, 'The world is my oyster'. It tries to change the world by grabbing more of the good things in the world – riches, power, fame, pleasure, all kinds of expressions of personal ambition. Hobbes reckoned this was the primary expression of human nature. The second class submerges individual happiness in a group identity. It has slogans like 'My country, right or wrong', 'Up the workers', or 'Skinheads rule OK'. A drawback of this is the frequent rift between groups, but it has the advantage that the burden of responsibility is lifted from the individual; if I fail in my personal ambition it may seem to be my fault; if my group fails it is someone else's fault: and the group is not so obviously mortal. The third class says things like 'nuclear disarmament now', 'Christ for the world', 'unite to build socialism', 'fight world hunger'. Here the individual is professedly, perhaps really, ready to renounce his own interests in favour of the wellbeing of an indefinitely large group: workers of the world, generations yet unborn, or animals. 'Trying to make the world a better place' is not, at least directly, a way of distracting one's attention from evils, but a way of making life bearable by actively trying to combat evils, whether the evils are the uneven distribution of the world's goods, racialism, or the threat to the survival of the whale. Without a cause of some kind, many people would find life empty.

Dropping out (c) The third way, dropping out, is not concerned either with minimising the unhappiness of experience or with changing it. One obvious way of achieving this is through drugs ('the quickest way out of Manchester is a bottle of whisky') but there are many kinds of 'dropping out' which, without deliberately altering the chemistry of the body (including the brain) by introducing a foreign element, enable the subject to find a way out of a waking state permeated by sorrow and a sense of deprivation, into a new kind of consciousness not limited by the frustrations of day-to-day experience. From the standpoint of the philosophy of experience – what philosophers term the 'phenomenological' perspective – one cannot lay down any hard-and-fast rules for these paranormal states of consciousness. Externally, they can be distinguished by the ways in which they are produced; but one can say nothing directly about what is outside one's own experience: one can only report the reports of people who have had the experience, and that is a poor second-best. Some, like drugs, affect only the individual concerned; sexual ecstasy generally occurs between two people; charismatic and similar phenomena typically happen in crowds; that much can be observed. But the success or failure of any of these altered states of consciousness in meeting the challenge of unhappiness cannot be judged objectively. *Morphine may make a dying criminal of its user, but whether the relief it gives is worth it, none but the addict knows.*

(d) Apart from these three ways, a fourth way is to find life intolerable and to refuse to tolerate it. This is the way of suicide, either physical suicide by ending the series of states of experience in death, or psychic suicide, by crippling the waking state through the retreat to madness.

Philosophies which set up some kind of abstraction as an idol – abstractions like the concept of duty or the will of God – can effortlessly devise criteria for judging the different ways of coping with life in a radically unsatisfactory world, commending some, tolerating or condemning others. The philosophy of experience can only record the ways in which a particular individual has coped with life and his own feelings. This may sound like a counsel of despair, but in fact it is the only firm foundation. Since individual experience is all anyone can have, nobody can learn, except from his own experience, which includes other people's communication of their individual experience. Buddha's meeting with an old man, a sick man, a corpse, and a monk set him on the road to enlightenment with an urgency which no metaphysical analysis could copy. To say that truth is relative and subjective is not to say that there is no truth, or that attitudes to life are entirely arbitrary. I may say that there are few forms of behaviour which can be applauded or condemned in all conceivable circumstances, but this does not mean that there is no difference between right and wrong, only that this difference cannot be demonstrated by recourse to a golden rule, or a process of logical analysis.

All this may seem far removed from the main theme of this book – the problem of morality, the theory of right and wrong conduct – but for me the issues just raised must be relevant, or the whole study of moral philosophy emerges as no more than an academic exercise, valuable because it helps to train the mind, but divorced from the lives – the hopes, and fears, and joys, and miseries – of everyday people: a category which includes scientists and philosophers (at least, when they're at home). Inevitably, sections of the book have required an examination of some of the traditional problems of moral and practical philosophy without any emphasis on the phi beta kappa approach. I want now to select three of the emphases expressed, in order to indicate which contributions, in this infinitely extensive field, seem to me to have most to offer in the interpretation of my experience. I shall introduce, while making the third point, the name of a philosopher who merits more space than he can be afforded. One final extrapolation will then be made. If the points so emphasised seem to be at times inconsistent with each other, perhaps even self-contradictory, then this must simply be viewed as an expression of how life is. We don't live our lives on the basis of syllogisms.

1. Existentialism

From existentialist thought, I extract the view – which for me is a product of experience over many years – that my life is my own, and nobody else's, and so, when making moral and related decisions, I am free to choose how to behave. Just as the environmentalists, a decade or more ago, produced the vivid phrase 'spaceship earth' to describe the world, so, on that spaceship, I am a universe of individual consciousness and autonomous responsibility. This means that I am in personal charge of myself, and have only myself to blame if my decisions turn out to have been the wrong ones. Others may give their advice and support (I have been cursed with more than my fair share of the first, and similarly blessed with the second) but in the end it is my foot which steps in a certain direction, and I who choose the direction. If I may be very personal: for years I was advised, counselled, cautioned, warned by those around me that my consumption of alcohol was financially, physically, mentally, and socially unhealthy for me. All their comments were totally futile: only when I 'came to myself' and knew in my own experience the horror of what I had become was it possible to begin again and follow the one simple rule of the alcoholic: don't take the first drink.

Freedom of behaviour follows naturally as an expression of this autonomy. There are limits to this freedom, as we have seen; but, whatever pressures may be placed upon me when I am facing a moral decision – pressures from those around me, pressures of habit, pressures arising from limitations in choice, and so on – how I behave is my choice, however desperately at times I may long to find a scapegoat. Whatever contribution may have been made by others, whatever information I have been provided with, whatever considerations I may have gleaned from schools of moral philosophy, there comes a moment when the die must be cast: and my hand alone is making the cast. Just as the trainee pilot can fly for hours accompanied by an instructor but must eventually reach the moment when he is alone in the cockpit, or as a medical student must eventually, if he is to become a surgeon, stand alone with his instruments over the patient, so I as a moral agent stand alone at the moment of decision; and if the decision is wrong I must carry the can.

My experience convinces me that the one concept above all others devised by man which is destructive of both these central characteristics of my personal universe – my autonomy and my freedom of choice – is theism. However else perfect happiness is to be found, it cannot be found with the idea of an omnipotent Judge waiting at the end of the road; however else I am to achieve autonomy, it cannot happen if there is One who has imposed the rules out of His fund of omniscience – and this remains the case even if He has left it to me to decode these rules; however I may express my freedom, it cannot be done if in the end I have to say, 'I, yet not I, but Christ; or Allah; or Jehovah'. I agree absolutely with these words of J. S. Mill:

When I am told that I must believe (in God), and at the same time call this being by the names which express and affirm the highest human morality, I say in plain terms that I will not. Whatever power such a being may have over me, there is one thing that he shall not do: he shall not compel me to worship him. I will call no being good, who is not what I mean when I apply that epithet to my fellow creatures; and if such a being can sentence me to hell for calling him so, to hell I will go.

('An Examination of Sir William Hamilton's Philosophy', quoted in J. Hospers, *Human Conduct*, pp. 186f.)

2. Love

The second emphasis which experience brings me to wish to make as a basic guide, as well as aim, in the process of moral decision making is on love. The claim is often made, by both believers and others, that this is the unique contribution made by Christianity to the process of making decisions. This claim is, as I stated in Chapter Eight, nonsense: the commandment 'Love thy neighbour as thyself' was expressed in the book of Leviticus, written hundreds of years before the birth of Christianity. It is also found in the non-theistic religions – in Buddhism, Hinduism, Taoism, and others. It was Buddha who said:

Hatred does not put an end to hatred; hatred ceases by love.
Love can overcome hatred; goodness can triumph over evil.
Face the stingy man with generosity; treat the liar with truth.
Treat others as you do yourself.

There is nothing specifically 'religious' about love, and it is not made into a religious quality because it is described in certain holy books. It is in fact a thoroughly human quality, to which humanists and atheists, pantheists and agnostics, can respond just as fully as theists.

We have to be clear what is meant by the word love. In English it can often be confusing because it describes a wide range of emotions. I can state without fear of being misunderstood, that I love my wife, my job, my brother-in-law, my pipe, cricket, California, and nubile women. But in that process I am in fact acknowledging the existence of numerous different drives in my life, and it is not satisfactory that the same word should be used to describe them all. The Germans in fact have made a joke to illustrate the confusion this situation can cause (and being a German joke, it is no laughing matter, as I remarked earlier):

Der schlimmste Feind – merk' dir es wohl –
Er ist der böse Alkohol;
Doch in der Bibel steht geschrieben:
Du sollst auch deine Feinde lieben.

(The worst enemy – mark this well –
It is the wicked alcohol;
But in the Bible it is written:
'Thou shalt also love thine enemies'.)

In Greek there are four words, for each of which 'love' can be a translation. Firstly, there is *eros*, from which our word 'erotic' is derived. This is sensual love: the love of a person lusting after a member of the opposite sex, or after food, or even a new car. It is the love of possession.

Secondly, there is the word *storge*, which means family affection or, more precisely (since sometimes relatives don't experience this emotion even though they may sign letters to each other 'with love') family ties. Though it would be a rare family in which all members felt emotionally bound to each other, this word reflects the fact that blood is thicker than water; however little in common there may be between different members of a family – in-laws and outlaws included – they are still 'family'.

Thirdly, there is the word *philia* which means liking, kindred feelings, friendship. In English we have recognised its use in the word philosophy, but there are many others, like philanthropy, philology, and so on, which use this prefix to mean 'lover of. . . .'. It expresses the affinity which develops between people with similar values, temperaments, or interests. Where philia exists between people they can be totally at ease in each other's company. It is difficult to know why philia should develop between person X and person Y and not between person X and person Z; or why person X may feel philia towards persons Y and Z, yet persons Y and Z may not be able to stand each other. The classical example of this is that of the woman (or man, but we'll stick with the single example) who loves (philia plus storge) her mother as well as her husband (philia plus eros), yet mother-in-law and son-in-law feel only animosity towards each other. Perhaps this is a case of the *storge* of one being alienated from the *eros* of the other: but we must have all had at some time the embarrassing experience of introducing two of our friends to each other, and discovering that they don't get on together.

There is a certain 'givenness' about philia; it seems that we cannot choose either to like or dislike another person. These responses seem to occur as a result of personality and other factors (chemistry, perhaps) over which we have no control. A well-known ditty aptly expresses this arbitrariness:

I do not like thee, Dr Fell:
The reason why I cannot tell;
But this I know, and know quite well:
I do not like thee, Dr Fell.

Agape The fourth word for love in the Greek language is the word *agape* (three syllables); it has its equivalent in Hebrew, Sanskrit, Hindi, and other languages, but not in English. Yet it is the word which all the great teachers have had in mind when describing ideal human behaviour. Unlike philia, agape is not based on any natural affinity between people. It is an attitude towards others summed up in such words as sympathy, compassion, understanding, empathy. It means considering another's best interests, learning (with whatever hesitation or difficulty) to look at issues from another's point of view. It means being willing to tolerate, and live with, differences between oneself and others. And it operates by free choice.

In this feature lies the great departure of agape from philia. It does not mean liking other people: liking, as we saw, is a purely arbitrary matter. Agape goes beyond the purely psychological, physiological fact of natural affinity, and can operate between people where no philia is present: *you can love a person you don't like*. Sartre, in his play *No Exit*, introduced the famous line, 'Hell is other people'. The answer of those who live by agape is that, however alienated from another person one may be, through agape life together can be bearable. In other words, it simply (from the point of view of agape) will not do to assert that because another person is so different from oneself in temperament it is therefore impossible to establish any kind of relationship with him. With agape as the basic motive, hell will not necessarily become heaven between two people, but at least their relationship will become endurable. Agape is the love of a family towards an aged cantankerous member, of a soldier for an enemy dying in his arms, of a teacher for a temperamental adolescent in the class. It is the noblest quality human beings can express.

In her book *The Sovereignty of Good*, Iris Murdoch discusses the problem of defining 'the Good', a concept which she places higher than all others. She writes:

Is there not . . . something about the conception of a refined love which is practically identical with goodness? Will not 'Act lovingly' translate 'Act perfectly', whereas 'Act rationally' will not? It is tempting to say so.

(p. 102)

Only in the West does she need to add that concessional last sentence; and only a person unconversant with the Greek original would water down the above sentiments, when arguing that the Good and human love cannot be equated, by adding 'human love is usually self-assertive'. In some of its expressions this is certainly the case; but the assertive side of love finds a different word as its symbol in the Greek language. Agape is not self-assertive, except when compassion for another requires it (and even then, because the intention is to act in another's best interests, the phrase *self*-assertiveness is hardly apposite).

The quest for happiness may therefore be seen as the search for agape as the bond between human beings in all aspects of their relationships. The achieving of it cannot be described in precise words, any more than the Nirvana of Buddhism, or the Way of Tao can be described. I think we can emphasise one element which it must however contain – an element hinted at in Iris Murdoch's implicit criticism of self-assertiveness: the *Yin* element – the receptive, the reflective, the complex and intuitive – must be recognised alongside the aggressive, logical, rational *Yang* element having a role in human relationships generally, and in arriving at moral decisions in particular. This implies, I think, that any process of moral decision-making based on some form of authoritarianism must be laid aside. This will mean excluding as a basis for moral judgment not only the concepts of God or of duty, but the code of a peer group or a family. Any behaviour based on external commands (implicitly or explicitly) falls short of the ideal. Agape grows from within a person, it must be experienced by each individual within his own universe, and then followed as, in effect, a natural process. This process cannot happen amid the raucous moralisings of those who gain some perverted kind of satisfaction by imposing their moral convictions on others, in a domineering, Yang-like fashion.

3. I-thou

The third element, which is closely linked with the second, and is a central feature in much of Eastern thought, may appear to be contradictory to what I said apropos of existentialism. While I am conscious of myself as an individual universe, responsible to and for myself, creating my own nature by the decisions I make, and so on, and looking for an end to unhappiness somewhat along the lines of Buddhist thought, I am also, at times, aware that I am not really in isolation from the other personal universes around me. Occasionally, this realisation is very vivid, and I experience something akin to the 'I–thou' relationship described by the Jewish existentialist Martin Buber (1878–1965) in his book of that name. He gives an example of one such situation:

In the deadly crush of an air-raid shelter the glances of two strangers suddenly meet for a second in astonishing and unrelated mutuality; when the All Clear sounds it is forgotten; and yet it did happen, in a realm that existed only for that moment.

It is in such moments that the happiness I seek seems most real: moments when the individual I is sublated by and into the not-I, when the need for individual assertiveness has gone, and I am become part of a stream. If *Taoism* expresses even a tiny element of truth, then I can know that this stream flows into a mightier river, and thence into a universal sea.

Spinoza   Most Western philosophers have paid little attention to this approach to morality, but there is one outstanding exception who has so far received no mention in this book: the Dutch philosopher Spinoza (1632–77). Many of his ideas, such as his deterministic view of life, have been discussed (and sometimes discarded) in earlier chapters. He himself was excommunicated by the Jews, into whose faith he was born, and condemned as an atheist by the Christians among whom he lived. His book *Ethics* is one of the most important in the history of moral philosophy, yet is one of the most difficult to comprehend. Bertrand Russell,[1] never over-generous in his praise of other philosophers, wrote of him: 'Spinoza is the noblest and most lovable of the great philosophers. Intellectually, some others have surpassed him, but ethically he is supreme.'

Spinoza's *Ethics* includes much more than what is normally contained under that title: he gives his view of the whole of reality, and of human nature in relation to it. For him there was only one reality, which may be termed either 'God' or 'Nature'. Though 'God' frequently occurs in his discourse, it is a pantheistic rather than theistic view which he holds, and of all the Western philosophers he has most in common with such Eastern teachers as were mentioned in Chapter Eight. He supported the view that happiness was the goal of all human endeavour, and argued that this could be achieved – if at all – only when man conformed willingly with his place in the universe. For this to happen, he must move beyond the world of sense data (what he termed 'opinion') and of intellect and abstract logic ('reason') to one of 'intuition', in which the

---

[1] *History of Western Philosophy*, p. 552

mind has a vision of the whole of reality. Man is by nature, he believed, both body and mind: he does not *have* a body and a mind, but he is both at once, so that what affects one affects the other. Human perfection lies in being fully what one is by nature: a unified entity.

He divided human emotions into the 'passive' and the 'active': the former originate from outside the person, the latter from within. The path to freedom and to happiness is to be identified by the transition from the passive to the active emotions, by personal autonomy and the strength of purpose not to be the prey of external factors. Virtue means 'acting according to the laws of our own nature', happiness the ability to preserve our own being. This may sound like a doctrine of self-containment along Nietzschean lines, but Spinoza well knew that we depend on those outside us – the not-I – not only for our preservation, but also for our perfection. 'Nothing', he wrote, 'is more useful to man than man.' Those who have perceived this 'desire nothing for themselves that they do not desire for other men'. He was a contemporary of Hobbes (though, as you may note, a considerably more short-lived one) but disagreed with his view that man is by nature an egotistic anarchist; he believed that if he would accept his oneness with the whole of Nature he would realise that 'whatever conduces to the universal fellowship of men, that is to say, whatever causes men to live in harmony with one another, is profitable, and, on the contrary, whatever brings discord into the State is evil'. For example, the impulse to compel other men to believe as we do, by bullying or bigotry, must be replaced by a joy in sharing another's insights.

Although appallingly treated by his contemporaries in the name of God, Spinoza pleaded for the intellectual love of God as the supreme means of achieving blessedness. It must be borne in mind that his view of God was not that of the divine law-giver and Judge, offering His creatures reward and punishment after death, but the universal life-force in which every creature shares. He wrote: 'Blessedness is not the reward of virtue, but is virtue itself; nor do we delight in blessedness because we restrain our lusts; but, on the contrary, because we delight in it, therefore are we able to restrain them.' He concludes the *Ethics* with these memorable and oft-quoted words:

From what has been said we see what is the strength of the wise man and how much he surpasses the ignorant who is driven forward by lust alone. For the ignorant man is not only agitated by external causes in many ways and never enjoys true peace of soul, but lives also ignorant, as it were, both of God and of things, and as soon as he ceases to suffer ceases also to be. On the other hand, the wise man . . . is scarcely ever moved in his mind, but, being conscious by a certain external necessity of himself, of God, and of things, never ceases to be and always enjoys true peace of soul. If the way which, as I have shown, leads hither seems very difficult, it can nevertheless be found. . . . All noble things are as difficult as they are rare.

It may be argued that not everyone can assume this universal and timeless perspective on life – 'sub specie aeternitatis' (from the viewpoint of eternity) because sometimes, and, for some people, most times, there is an issue to be resolved here and now. I accept that the comment, made in the midst of a problem which is causing me irritation if not complete despair, 'Don't worry: it'll all be the same in a hundred years' time' has sometimes brought the utterer, if he did but know it, close to his demise. Nonetheless, I sense that, in my life-long search for perfect happiness, the ability to reflect on my individual problems as an infinitesimal part of the universe can give those problems a perspective which, while not removing them, enables me to view them rationally and positively. In Russell's words, 'Such reflections may not suffice to constitute a religion, but in a painful world they are a help towards sanity and an antidote to the paralysis of utter despair.'[1]

This mention of despair brings me back to the question introduced earlier in the chapter. Could it be that Spinoza had discovered the answer to the apparent paradox that, while we long for happiness, this cannot be obtained, except intermittently, or partially? If all the devices suggested earlier – 'making the best of it', 'trying to improve the world', dropping out, and suicide – are, as in my experience they are, ultimately incapable of dealing with the root evil of time, are we simply to accept that nature has played us a dirty trick by implanting in us a thirst which cannot be satisfied? If there is to be a way out of this impasse, it must be a way in someone's experience, past, present, or future: if it were on some platonic world of ideas it would be inaccessible, and therefore no way for me.

A fourth state   What does seem to be documented in the experience of some human beings is a state beyond that of being consciously awake, as this latter state is beyond that of dreaming. When one wakes from a dream, there is a moment when one is simply dreaming, followed by a moment when the dream is invaded but not quite destroyed by waking up, and then a moment when one is awake, and the dream consciousness is sublated, known for what it is. At the second moment the dreamer does not know that he is awake – he is not fully awake, but his dream consciousness includes a hint of what is to come. The philosophy of experience says to the individual: 'Are there moments in your waking life which seem like hints of another and higher state?'

To look for a higher state is not encouraged in the Western world for –

[1] Op. cit., p. 562

I think – two reasons. Firstly, we seem to have created a civilisation which centres on the world of toys, or what is otherwise claimed to be technology; the making and selling of these toys has made the whole of our civilisation into a race of shopkeepers, and the pleasures these provide have been seducing other civilisations, and eroding the indigenous and elemental distinctiveness of their philosophy. Secondly, many people in the West are tied up with claims of empiricism, discussed earlier, that experience must mean no more than what can be perceived by the five senses (or 'science', as such knowledge is often called). We have acknowledged at various points in this book that certain issues cannot be discussed because the claims made by their defenders are not open to verification, and we shall be wise to maintain this safeguard in our discussions. The question at issue is not whether a verification process should or should not be discarded, but whether the means or tools of verification as maintained generally throughout the West are themselves adequate to account for all the phenomena of experience. Once it is acknowledged that the only bounds of experience are *what actually happens*, the claims of empiricism are shattered.

Experience is bigger than is normally recognised in the West, for at least three reasons. Firstly, it spans time. I feel not only the present but the past in a plethora of subtle ways, of which the word 'memory' gives a poor idea (perhaps Jung's 'collective unconscious' is a more comprehensive expression of what I mean), and I feel also the future pulling just as strongly, its force no less real. Secondly, though my experience is wholly mine, it is made up of truths contributed by the 'not-I', and particularly by other people. As a mother teaches her child not just by articulating factually correct propositions (!) but by being herself, teaches it to love by loving it, so I learn and my experience grows all the time I meet others. Such learning is not easily put into words, though some novelists, playwrights, and poets have made distinguished attempts to achieve this. Thirdly, experience is not only what is known to science or taught in schools or held up as entertainment and culture. The moments of deepest insight are seldom linked with the blinkered truths, or half-truths, of society. In particular, the educare approach to education, which dominates our schools system, seems more geared to surrounding our children with the 'shades of the prison-house' of Wordsworth's *Ode on the Intimations of Immortality* than with the means of release and fulfilment.

If we accept this as at least a working hypothesis, it seems impossible to write off as deceivers or deceived those who have claimed to have experienced the state beyond that of conscious wakefulness. From Buddha, with his attainment of Nirvana, through the Vedanta school of Hinduism with its experience 'beyond good and evil', through the mystics of various religions, Spinoza's expression of the unity of Nature, and de Chardin's description of the neosphere beyond our normally experienced biosphere (cf. Chapter 4, p. 89), accounts of this extra state are to be found. Perhaps the most famous in our own time is that of the physicist, Fritjof Capra, in his remarkable book *The Tao of Physics*. In the preface, he describes the experience which set him on the road to exploring the relationship between modern physics – specifically quantum physics – and the insights of Eastern philosophy.

Five years ago, I had a beautiful experience which set me on a road which has led to the writing of this book. I was sitting by the ocean one late summer afternoon, watching the waves rolling in and feeling the rhythm of my breathing, when I suddenly became aware of my whole environment as being engaged in a gigantic cosmic dance. Being a physicist, I knew that the sand, rocks, water and air around me were made of vibrating molecules and atoms, and that these consisted of particles which interacted with one another by creating and destroying other particles. I knew also that the Earth's atmosphere was continually bombarded by showers of 'cosmic rays', particles of high energy undergoing multiple collisions as they penetrated the air. All this was familiar to me from my research in high-energy physics, but until that moment I had only experienced it through graphs, diagrams, and mathematical theories. As I sat on that beach my former experiences came to life; I 'saw' cascades of energy coming down from outer space, in which particles were created and destroyed in rhythmic pulses; I 'saw' the atoms of the elements and those of my body participating in this cosmic dance of energy; I felt its rhythm and I 'heard' its sound, and at that moment I *knew* that this was the Dance of Shiva, the Lord of Dancers worshipped by the Hindus.

If such words as these, and of others who have claimed to have 'awakened' to a new state seem to speak to you from your own future, or if some living teacher communicates the urge to move on, then you may be on the brink of a new consciousness, which will put the waking state in perspective by going beyond it.

All this should not be seen as implying that the issues discussed in this book are either unimportant or wrongly construed. If this were the case, then I have been misusing my time in writing, and you in reading, about them! As I said in the second chapter, we cannot avoid the making of moral decisions, and it is important to reflect on the means whereby we should set about accomplishing this. The trouble with a very large proportion of books on moral philosophy is that they are aridly academic, divorcing themselves from people as they really are. People are not logically constructed computers, but creatures of passions and mixed motives, inconsistent and blinkered; and limits for these people are often much lower than those assumed by numerous writers on ethics. By appealing only to the cognitive side of human beings, and ignoring – or virtually ignoring – the affective, these writers may have been acting with the most laudable of intentions, but in effect they are describing only cut-out people in a fantasy world.

The phi beta kappa approach to philosophy is one which does not look upon a person as simply a brain to be stimulated but as a real entity who responds to problems in a variety of ways with a mixture of faculties. It is with this whole person that philosophy must be concerned – a being with instincts as well as senses, with moods and hunches as well as knowledge, with a heart as well as a brain. If philosophical writing can rediscover this comprehensive approach expressed by philosophers, of both West and East, two-and-a-half millennia ago, and never wholly lost sight of through the centuries, then perhaps it can reassume its ancient role as the central guide in human exploration. To use the image of Ezekiel (Chapter 37): the breath of experience must enter into the dry bones in order that they may once again be vibrant. Philosophy will then be living; and many more of us will be living philosophy.

CASE STUDY 42: THE VALUE OF LIFE

The theme of this lengthy case study underlies many of the issues raised throughout this book. Some of the most intense dilemmas facing the human race relate to the question of the value of life – when it begins, to what extent it should be preserved, whether it must in all circumstances be the prime consideration, and so on. Under the following set of subheadings you can debate these searching issues. In the process, see if you discover that any insight from one or other of the schools of philosophy, or ethical considerations, presented in the book emerges in your mind as having a high priority when deciding what should or should not be done. You may then wish to pursue a discussion of the problems in greater depth; if so, you could do worse than begin with a book entitled *The Value of Life* by John Harris (Routledge & Kegan Paul, 1985, pbk 1988). I know no other book which deals with medical ethics so comprehensively.

1 When is a person a person?
  (a) At conception?
  (b) At 'quickening' – when the womb has 'accepted' the foetus?
  (c) When the foetus receives a soul: but apart from its unverifiability, must not any decision about the soul's beginnings be arbitrary?
  (d) At birth?
  (e) When the infant is able to respond to and communicate with others?

315

A foetus and neonate becomes a person 'when it is capable of valuing its own existence' – Harris: is this right? If so, what are the implications?

2 In vitro fertilisation

(A process whereby, when a blockage prevents conception in the normal manner, a woman's ova are removed and fertilised 'in vitro' – i.e. in a glass or test-tube – by the partner's sperm; the embryo is then implanted in the woman: a process normally for the benefit of childless couples.)

(a) Should more health resources be put into this process? (Childlessness is now recognised as an illness by many medical organisations; roughly one couple in five have this illness.)
(b) If so, where would you make cuts in services?
(c) Assuming that demand for this service continues to be greater than the supply, how would you establish priorities?
  (i) Ability to pay privately? (A four-figure sum is involved.)
  (ii) Length of period of childlessness?
  (iii) Age of the couple?
  (iv) Value/esteem of the couple to, and in the eyes of, the community?
  (v) First come first served?
(d) What should be done with the superfluous embryos? (There are likely to be a number of these, even if the first implantation fails, and a second is tried some weeks or months later.)
  (i) Destroy them (human embryos: would this be murder?).
  (ii) Use for medical research, specifically to gain knowledge about diseases in foetuses, and then destroy them (up to what age of embryo/foetus should such experimentation be allowed?).
  (iii) Retain in state of deep freeze for posterity (e.g. pending a nuclear holocaust; as a precaution against the father's later becoming impotent, for example after certain treatment for cancer; father a soldier; etc.). How does the idea of your having a child born in the twenty-second century strike you?
(e) When, because of physical infirmity, the mother is incapable of bearing the child, should it be possible (i.e. legal) to use a surrogate mother? If so, is there any moral objection to paying the surrogate for the inconvenience? If not, is there any moral objection to the establishment of agencies to bring childless couples and willing surrogates together, as dating agencies bring together potential sex partners?

3 Abortion: when should it be legally allowed?

(a) Never?

(b) Only after conception following rape?

(c) If the mother is likely to die in child-birth?

(d) If the mother's mental condition is directly affected by the pregnancy?

(e) If there would be grave social problems (e.g. a large family already, with a low income, children already in care through parents' cruelty)?

(f) On demand: the woman's right supreme?

4 Euthanasia: when should it be allowed?

(a) Never?

(b) When it means letting nature take its course – turning off life support machines?

(c) When death is near, and the final stage of life is painful and otherwise distressing? (Euthanasia = 'good death'.)

(d) When death is not necessarily near, but the quality of life is nearly zero (brain damage, total paralysis, senile dementia, etc.)? (Can any third party judge/assess another's quality of life?)

(e) Of an infant, when its life potential is virtually zero? (See question on (d).)

(f) On demand: the right of each individual to choose not to go on living? (See 5 for possible problems.)

5 If euthanasia were legalised, who should make the decision to speed up death? (If a combination of the following, which combination?)

(a) The individual concerned? (Even during temporary depression or other mental disturbance which may be impermanent?)

(b) The next of kin? (Possible ulterior motives – inheritance, convenience, etc.?)

(c) The medical expert(s) involved? (Would they wish to carry this responsibility?)

(d) An ethical committee? (Who would be elected to this, and by whom: and if one member took the 4(a) line above, would there ever be a genuine debate?)

6 Should compulsory sterilisation be legalised? If so, for which groups?

(a) The mentally subnormal? (How subnormal: don't many subnormal couples cope with offspring?)

(b) The morally subnormal such as violent psychopaths who are likely to injure their children?

(c) The socially subnormal, i.e. those who cannot cope with relationships or cannot organise the basics of life? (Who is to determine who fits into this category: what are the criteria to be?)

(d) Single-parent mothers? (Is there concrete evidence that children are gravely disadvantaged without a father's presence?)

(e) Gay people? (Similar question.)

7 What constitutes a valuable/worthwhile life?

(a) Any life? (Is nothing worse than death? Even being used for vicious experiments as in Nazi concentration camps?)

(b) Possession of full mental faculties? (Can we be sure that even a severely subnormal person does not or cannot 'value its own existence'?)

(c) Being wanted/needed by somebody else? (Same question as (b).)

(d) Achieving one's 'potential'? (A question-begging concept: does one miss what has never been gained? Isn't there value in second-best – or even lower?)

8 Some general questions

(a) Is a 'potential' person (a foetus) a person?

(b) If question 1 is answered with 1(a) as the guiding belief does this imply that contraception must be viewed as a form of killing, since it prevents any possibility of life's beginning at this moment?

(c) If the answer is guided by 1(e), is there any distinction, other than in degree, between abortion and infanticide?

(d) Is the important issue (cf. Harris, op. cit.) not when life begins, but when it begins to matter?

(e) Is the right to sire and bear children a universal inalienable human right? If so, does this mean you would put no restriction whatsoever on any couple? If not (and this implies that compulsion of some kind will be brought to bear on potential parents, whether by sterilisation or by keeping them apart from each other) who should be given the authority to decide (i) who falls into this category and (ii) how to deal with them?

CASE STUDY 43: ANIMAL RIGHTS

The case for animal rights is based on the belief that (a) so far as we can judge by their behaviour, animals are sentient beings, experiencing fear, pain, loneliness, hunger, and other effects of deprivation as do human beings. Consequently, (b) whatever rights we accord to human beings (an issue discussed in Chapter Eleven) cannot be denied to animals. The grounds for ceasing to experiment on animals, whether these are for testing drugs – the effects of modern weapons, or cosmetics, together with the vegetarian philosophy, must be adjudged shaky or firm according to the validity of these twin assumptions.

In this case study, I shall in effect put the animal rights supporter in the dock, and pose a series of questions. They are questions to which I have so far failed to receive answers that satisfy me, though (I hope, as on all issues) I retain an open mind. It is difficult to do so on this issue because of the emotive way in which the arguments *for* animal rights are often (not always) presented: as with anti-abortion, this issue seems to attract the lunatic fringe of British society. I recall once answering a question about town foxes on BBC Radio Four's programme *Any Questions?* One such fox had, the previous week, decapitated our pet rabbit, and I suggested that, while I didn't believe in weapons, I could happily shoot the next fox that ventured in our garden. This was the only answer in the programme to which I received private correspondence, all vituperative, some obscene. Among the mildest was the comment from one lady in Minehead that she would like to have *me* in the sights of her rifle, adding (and this worried me more) that she would add my name to her prayer list the following Sunday. It is therefore with some trepidation that I proceed with my questions. (For me, no. 12 is basic.)

1 Are animals aware of their own mortality? (Our knowledge of the certain fact of death is a determinant motive of much human behaviour, and the cause of phobias, neuroses, and other mental disorders. Are animals different in degree or in kind?)
2 If it is different in kind, that is, animals are not conscious of the fact of death in any way that remotely resembles human awareness, is not the sting taken out of a segment of the animal rights argument?
3 If it is different only in degree, how would one set about demonstrating (e.g.) that any elderly animal was aware that it hadn't got long for this world? Are there indications of 'intimations of mortality'?
4 Granted that animals feel pain, can we not accept that (a) as with human beings – in time of war, for instance – pain is sometimes necessary for the greater good and (b) provided the scientists keep pain to a minimum, their work on animals is an example of seeking this greater good? Do not scientists realise as much as animal rights activists that cruel science is bad science, because animals in pain are out of control and therefore unreliable subjects for an investigation?
5 While acknowledging that the subjects of animal experiments have no choice about their role, is this not also true of soldiers in time of war? How much freedom of choice do most people give, for instance, their pet dogs (even if they don't dress them up like mannequins)?
6 If it is the case that polio has been eliminated among human beings through drugs tested on animals; and if diabetes is controlled through insulin, every batch of which has to be tested on mice in order to be certain of its strength, does not this justify the existence of animal laboratories? Would it not have been good that

thalidomide had been tested on animals before being given to pregnant women, thus preventing the birth of limbless babies? (It's not an answer to this question to query the nation's policy on drugs in relation to health. That is a wider and different issue. To state that one is against animal experiments because drugs should not be used is like denying a promiscuous girl the pill on the grounds that she should be celibate.)

7 Since war is a fact of life, and new weapons are constantly being invented, isn't it better to test the effect of these on animals, in order to understand better how to treat a human being wounded by one of them?

8 If there is a possibility that a cosmetic like a shampoo could blind a child, isn't it preferable to test these on animals first? (Again, it is no answer to state that such shampoos, or other possibly toxic cosmetics, should not exist. They do, and society, if it is to be responsible, must organise safeguards.)

9 Isn't much of the reaction to animal experiments emotional – we don't like the look of the animal in that condition? Isn't this reaction similar to that of any observer of a human being undergoing major surgery? Or a patient with tubes protruding from various orifices?

10 Would feeling run so high if experiments were made, not on familiar and lovable animals such as dogs, cats, rabbits, and mice, but on less appealing animals like jackals, hyenas, vipers, or skunks?

11 If the Commandment 'Thou shalt not kill' is applied absolutely to all animals, are we to include the locust, the tapeworm, and the tsetse fly?

12 (The question raising the most searching judgment of value): Isn't it better to have been bred for an experiment, or bred for slaughter to become food for human consumption, than never to have been bred at all?

14 If vegetarianism were adopted by all, either voluntarily or by law, what would happen to the existing stock of animals? Assuming (which I know cannot be universally assumed) that there is no objection to the consumption of dairy produce, how are we to cope with the mating and calving which necessarily precedes this? Are wild boars and bulls to be left to roam the countryside? Is husbandry to cease? If not, what is to be done with existing animals? How realistic, how moral even, is vegetarianism (as a philosophy)?

14 Since the whole of nature is a system of predator and prey, isn't it natural for homo sapiens to consume other species? Even if we *can* survive on lettuce and carrots, why should we?

15 Would anyone *in their right mind* wilfully cause pain – even to animals?

16 In a world in which basic human rights are denied to half the population, isn't it self-indulgent to be so preoccupied with animals?

CASE STUDY 44: TOO MANY PEOPLE?

Let us assume that you have read this book from cover to final case study (this one), and that you read at an average pace of 20 pages an hour. If you have accomplished this in one sitting (hardly likely, but let us go on assuming), then it will have taken you 15 hours. While you have been completing this daunting exercise, the world's population has risen by over 160,000: the population of Bournemouth, Brighton, or Bolton in the UK, or of Kansas City, USA, Sydney, Australia, or Quebec in Canada. Put it another way: try counting out seconds with the words 'three more, three more, three more': that is the rate at which the world's population is expanding (increase of live births over deaths).

The distribution is instructive. If the world in the year 2000 is imagined as a global village, then 58 will be Asian, 13 African, 10 Latin American, 9 European, 5 North American, and 5 Russian. Every year there are an extra 97 million mouths to feed; by the year 2025 (well within the expectation of most student readers) the present world population of 5.25 billion will have risen to about 8 billion.

This means that every year about 38 million new jobs will have to be created; it means an ever-increasing drain on energy and natural resources (for example, oil will run out by about 2025). A major concern is the environment: because of the need to increase food supply mathematically, an area of tropical forest the size of Belgium and Austria combined is cleared every year. Alongside this destruction of our inherited wealth (crucial for the health of the world) are the destructive technologies and wasteful life-styles of the wealthy nations, which are copied, as soon as they are able, by developing countries.

With these facts and figures in mind, ask yourself these questions:

1 To what extent do issues raised in this book fade into insignificance when faced with this monumental problem? (For example, our concern about embryo research, abortion (one in four of the world's pregnancies end in this way), euthanasia, smoking, or addiction to other drugs?)
2 How far do you feel that the population explosion is the prime underlying cause of all our moral dilemmas: war, violence, abuse of the environment, factory farming, crime, etc.?
3 Is it incumbent on us to change our life-styles drastically in the face of the threat posed by this explosion? For example, governments become concerned if there is stagnancy in the market, lack of cash

flow, when people are not out and about spending what they have earned. Should we not be happy about this, because, on the world scale, it is better for people to do without than to be constantly grabbing luxuries by the armful?

4 What are the implications for our habits of eating, transport, home buying (often necessitating transport to place of work)? Should we be reverting to a village mentality, with simpler lives, less dependent on material possessions? ('How're you gonna keep them down at the farm After they've seen Paris?' as the World War I song puts it.)

5 Can the human race survive, or are we facing global social and economic collapse? (Three more, three more. . . .)

Appendices

1 POSTSCRIPT TO CASE STUDY 16, CHAPTER FIVE: WHO SHALL LIVE?

One famous renal surgeon in the north of England stated that, faced with the dilemma presented in the case study, his priority, both for access to kidney machines and for kidney transplants, was to give preference to *a married person with children over a married person without children, and to the latter over a single person without responsibilities*. 'After that,' he added, 'I would be prepared to toss a coin. I wouldn't choose between a university don and a man who carries bricks.' He found the notion of a lay panel 'abhorrent'. The doctor's own prejudices were enough without bringing in anybody else's. Who would select the panels, and on what criteria? No group was capable of sitting in judgment on its fellow men. If there had to be a panel, he said he would like to see a bookmaker among its members, as well as a clergyman.

This priority may not gain universal approval, but it has the inestimable advantage over many others that it must result in a choice based on objective data, not one based on a subjective evaluation of a person's worth (though, of course, the establishing of priorities based on a patient's marital status is itself a subjective decision).

2 POSTSCRIPT TO CASE STUDY 24, CHAPTER SEVEN: WHO'S TO BLAME?

The dialogue in the play continues as follows:
Pearl: Well I say the girl's most responsible.
Beatie: Why?
Pearl: Well, she made the choice didn't she?
Frank: Yes, but the old ferryman made her take off her clothes.
Pearl: But she didn't hev to.
Frank: Blust woman, she were in love!

Beatie: Good ole Frank.

Jenny: Hell if I know.

Beatie: Jimmy?

Jimmy: Don't ask me gal – I follow decisions, I aren't making none.

Beatie: Father?

Mr Bryant: I don't know what you're on about.

Beatie: Mother?

Mrs Bryant: Drink your tea gal – never you mind what I think. (*This is what they're waiting for.*)

Pearl: Well – what do Ronnie say?

Beatie: He say the gal is responsible only for makin' the decision to strip off and go across and that she do that because she's in love. After that she's the victim of two phoney men – one who don't love her but take advantage of her and one who say he love her but didn't love her enough to help her, and that the man who say he love her but don't do nothin' to help her is most responsible because he were the last one she could turn to.

Jenny: He've got it all worked out then!

Beatie (*Jumping on a chair thrusting her fist into the air like Ronnie, and glorying in what is the beginning of a hysteric outburst of his quotes*): 'No one do that bad that you can't forgive them.'

Pearl: He's sure of himself then?

Beatie: 'We can't be sure of everything but certain basic things we must be sure about or we'll die.'

(Perhaps the most important moral question ever asked is from the Old Testament: 'Am I my brother's keeper?')

Glossary of terms

As was pointed out when discussing the word 'libertarian', certain words are used differently, or more precisely, in philosophy than in common speech. Most of these words should have been defined, or otherwise explained, in the text. The following are some that may have slipped the net.

A priori: an idea is described as a priori when it is not derived from observation; it is thus an example of deductive reasoning (q.v.) or arguing from cause to effect. The alternative is *a posteriori*, an idea derived from observation; this is an example of inductive reasoning.

Aesthetics: the theory of beauty.

Behaviourism: a psychological method which views people solely as material objects which behave in certain fixed ways, and disregards the subject's 'consciousness' or introspection (q.v.) in explaining this behaviour.

Cognitive: Concerned with those aspects of the mind connected with the gaining of knowledge or forming beliefs (which may vary from being false, through various shades of possibility and probability, to being true). Contrasted with *affective*, or being concerned with the feelings, emotions, and affections.

Deduction: an argument in which the conclusion follows necessarily from the premises; normally this involves extracting a specific truth from a general: if, for example, all x contain y, and z is an x, then z contains y. An **inductive** argument normally operates in the reverse direction, i.e. from a specific example a general principle is inferred (such as forecasting the result of a general election from an opinion poll). The conclusion of a deductive argument must be certain; the conclusion formed from an inductive argument can only be probable.

Epistemology: the theory of knowledge – its definition, varieties (shading into beliefs), sources, and limits.

Essential: anything's essential attributes (which constitute its *essence*) are those it must have in order to be the thing it is. Other attributes are called *accidents*. Music is essential to an opera: the orchestra, conductor, producer, etc., are accidents.

Hedonism – defined in the text, but note the difference between psychological hedonism and ethical hedonism: the former states that the attaining of pleasure (and avoiding of pain) *is* the aim of all human action, the latter, that it *ought to be*.

Hypothesis: (Greek: proposal): a proposition presented not as true but as possibly true, and can be tested by its consequences and in relation to known facts. A 'working hypothesis' is one which has not been so tested, but is accepted as true for the purposes of a particular discussion or argument. Many statements in astronomy are hypothetical, such as 'Assume the universe started with a big bang . . .', etc.

Idealism: In common speech, an idealist is one with high, often unattainable ideals; in philosophy it is (a) the theory that only minds or mental states (or both, if the two are not equated) exist. The Irish bishop, George Berkeley (1685–1753), is the chief exponent of this view; and (b) the theory of Plato that our values – justice, love, etc. – reflect the ideal or *Form* of these in heaven. This is known as Plato's Theory of Forms.

Introspection: A person's self-awareness, including his own mental processes as they are occurring.

Intuition: Knowledge gained by direct apprehension, rather than by inference from knowledge of something else. In ethics, the theory that moral truths are understood directly as true via a special faculty of moral knowledge.

Materialism: in common speech, the belief that the acquiring of physical possessions is the most worthwhile goal in life. In philosophy, the belief that the universe consists of nothing else but matter.

Mechanism: the theory that every event in the universe happens according to fixed, universal laws; thus every event has a cause and effect, and knowledge of these can in theory be indefinitely extended. Opposed to *teleology* which expresses the view that events should be understood and explained according to their purpose, rather than their cause. In biology, mechanism is the view that every living organism can be explained in terms of its chemical and physical components; opposed to *vitalism*, which holds that each organism contains some 'vital principle', such as 'spirit', in addition.

Metaphysics: (Greek *meta*, after, *phusis*, nature): the investigation of the nature of the universe as a whole and of those general principles (if any) which are true of everything that exists.

Monism: the belief that there is only one kind of substance in the universe, as opposed to *dualism*, which holds that there are two. Usually equated with *materialism* (q.v.) but, as was noted under *idealism* (q.v.), there have been exceptions.

Mores: how a group behaves.

Nihilism: originally used in nineteenth-century Russia, when it was accepted that any means were justified if the result was the destruction of existing conditions. In ethics, nihilism is the denial of all traditional values and moral truths.

Subject: an observer, thinker, experiencer; *object*: what he is aware of. What is 'subjective' proceeds from the subject; 'objective' refers to what is independent of the subject or his awareness.

Optimism: in philosophy (see under *Leibniz*, Chapter Ten, pp.230f.) the belief that this is the best of all possible worlds.

Phenomenon: whatever is observable.

Positivism: the view that the description of phenomena, and the order in which they occur, is all that human beings can know. Value judgments, statements of belief, expressions of appreciation in the arts, etc., fall outside these limits.

Pragmatism: In common speech, a pragmatic test of anything is a test of its usefulness. In philosophy, it is a test of how a theory works in practice, rather than whether or not it is verifiably true. For example, belief in God is justified, according to pragmatists, if it 'works' (e.g., in giving strength, direction, comfort, sanity, etc.) for the believer. See William James, *The Meaning of Truth*.

Prima facie: literally, at first sight; usually implies that the conclusion arrived at from what is observed is the obvious (commonsensical) conclusion. Thus if a man is found dead with a knife between his shoulder blades there is a prima facie case of murder; if he is found hanging, this will not be the case.

Rationalism: has two meanings, both mentioned, if not directly, in the text. (a) the view that no beliefs should be accepted on the basis of authority, or by faith, but only if they can be justified by reason. (b) As opposed to *empiricism* (see Chapter Thirteen) the view that knowledge can be attained by reason, independently of sense-perception; the view (with differing emphases) of Descartes, Spinoza, and Leibniz.

Sense: rarely used in philosophy as in such common phrases as 'good sense'. Usually implies the five senses, and *'sensible'* means what can be perceived through these senses. *Perception* is often used synonymously with *sensation*, but there is a tendency to use sensation as sense experience without any interpretation, while perception adds the interpretation. Thus, I sense that the atmosphere has become heavy, and perceive an approaching thunderstorm.

Solipsism: (not used in the text, but a useful word to have up your sleeve): the belief that nothing else exists except me.

Stoical: (from the Greek *stoa*, (or 'porch'), in Athens, where the followers of Zeno were taught): the belief that one should accept one's fate without expression of antagonism or regret. Originally linked with the belief in a divine plan which cannot be altered, it now describes anyone who suffers without complaint, or exercises strong self-control.

Universal: a quality or relation which may be common to many things, such as hardness, benevolence. The particular instances of a universal are called 'particulars'. If I state 'this bread has gone hard' I mean that, whereas the bread was originally a particular of the universal *softness*, it is now a particular of the universal *hardness*.

Validity: an argument is valid if it obeys the rules of logic; it is *sound* if its statements are true. Thus the deductive (q.v.) argument. 'All Lancastrians are great cricketers; I am a Lancastrian; therefore I am a great cricketer' is valid but not sound. The form of this argument is called a 'syllogism'.

In the text I have used some foreign words/phrases which may be new to you:

au fond: basically, fundamentally

cor ad cor loquitor: heart speaks to heart

deus ex machina: the God outside, or beyond: not involved in the minutiae of human life

ex cathedra: literally 'from the chair', as of a pronouncement by the Pope: speaking officially

faute de mieux: in the absence of anything (anyone) better

modus operandi: method of procedure

pace: by leave of, with all due deference to: expressing disagreement courteously (pronounced pah-say)

modus vivendi: a way of cooperating or living harmoniously together; often signifies a compromise

per se: by its nature, or in itself

reductio ad absurdem: literally, reducing (an argument or situation) to an absurdity. In academic debate or human behaviour, the application of a principle or practice of a rule of behaviour so strictly that the *terminus ad quem* (final stage, or destination) is ridiculous. The *reductio ad absurdem* of taking the New Testament literally is the demonstration in public worship, by certain religious freaks in the USA, of the fulfilment of the promise made in Mark 16.18. The *reductio ad absurdem* of the rule not to be provocative in dress is the Islamic yashmak, the nun's habit, and the Victorian custom of covering up the bare legs of the piano. The *reductio ad absurdem* of 'Thou shalt not kill' is Jainites' sweeping the path before them clear of insects, or fruitarians declining to mow the lawn.

sine qua non: essential characteristic(s): music is a *sine qua non* of opera

tant pis: so much the worse, too bad (or 'hard luck')

ABBREVIATIONS USED IN TEXT

British readers will be familiar with most, if not all of these, but they may be somewhat bewildering to overseas readers

ESP: Extra-sensory perception
IRA: Irish Republican Army
MP: Member of Parliament
NF: National Front – an ultra right-wing racist political organisation
NHS: National Health Service
RE: Religious Education
TCCB: Test and Counties Cricket Board: the supreme administrative body for the sport in the UK

Further reading

There seems little point in providing an extensive bibliography, impressive though it might look. Most of the books which *I've* found useful are mentioned in their relevant contexts. If you get through them, you'll be well on the way to becoming *au fait* (at home) with the way philosophers present arguments and pursue discussions.

It is important to read some of the classical original works, and not just confine yourself to books about great works. Because the work is an original, and is classical, it doesn't necessarily follow that it's incomprehensible. I've hinted at some which fall into this latter category, so you would be able to appreciate what *not* to start with. The works by Plato and Mill should provide a relatively painless access to these originals, and the narrations by Russell (on the whole field of Western philosophy, Hospers (on moral philosophy), and Barrett (on one school of philosophy) all illustrate the teacher's authority as described in Chapter Twelve.

There are plenty of books on applied philosophy coming off the presses and I would simply draw attention to one that is both comprehensive and clear: Jonathan Glover's *Causing Death and Saving Lives*. On the question of animal rights, you could start with *In Defence of Animals*, edited by Peter Singer. On moral education, a comprehensive account is found in M. Downey and A. V. Kelly, *Moral Education, Theory and Practice*. If you are interested in the debate on theism (Chapter Eight) take a look at *Christian Ethics Re-examined* by Margaret Knight, together with Anthony Flew, *God and Philosophy*. For Eastern philosophy it is difficult to know where to start, but I. C. Sharma, *Ethical Philosophies of India* or M. Hiriyanna, *Outlines of Indian Philosophy*, together with A. Bahm, *Comparative Philosophy* and Fung's *Short History of Chinese Philosophy*, will keep you going for a while. Don't miss A. Huxley's *The Perennial Philosophy*, mentioned in the text.

On Western ethics generally, despite my strictures on some of the writers, I suggest you read J. Mackie, *Ethics*, J. Harrison, *Our Knowledge of Right and Wrong*, M. Warnock, *Ethics Since 1900*, W. Frankena, *Ethics*, J. D. Mabbott, *An Introduction to Ethics*, and A. McIntyre's book mentioned in the text. The three books by R.M. Hare, Professor of Moral Philosophy at the University of Oxford, must not be avoided:

The Language of Morals, Moral Reasoning, and (especially) *Freedom and Reason.* If you're interested in reading an account of one man's experiences under the influence of the (non-addictive) drug mescalin (an example, perhaps, of the 'dropping out' approach to life's shortcomings) read A. Huxley, *The Doors of Perception.* Don't forget to see how you get on with the *Tao Te Ching*; and Stuart Hampshire's *Spinoza* is a fine account of a great man. If your local library doesn't subscribe to the *Journal of Applied Philosophy,* you could start a campaign to persuade them otherwise.

The publication of this Second Edition allows me to recommend books which have either been published since or were overlooked at the time.

On specific moral dilemmas:

(a) Euthanasia: *Ending Lives,* by R. Campbell and D. Collinson.
(b) Capital Punishment: *Moral Theory and Capital Punishment,* by T. Sorrell.
(c) Abortion: *Beginning Lives,* by R. Hursthouse.
(d) Moral values and the meaning of life: *The Quest for Meaning,* by O. Hanfling. (All the above published by Blackham, and are text books for the Open University course 'Life and Death' (A310)).
(e) Embryo research and related matters of medical ethics: *Wonderwoman and Superman,* by J. Harris (Oxford).

A highly readable outline of an issue which is self-explanatory is: *Seven Theories of Human Nature,* by L. Stevenson (Oxford).

On existentialism: *Six Existentialist Thinkers,* by H.J. Blackham (Routledge).

On many of the issues raised in this book: *The Rational Foundation of Ethics,* by T.L.S. Sprigge (Routledge). A masterly handbook (or 'crib') is *50 Major Philosophers,* by D. Collinson (Routledge).

Other reference books worth having by you: A. Flew (ed.), *A Dictionary of Philosophy* (Pan); A.R. Lacy, *A Dictionary of Philosophy*; and, for a general introduction to philosophy which is highly readable: N. Warburton, *Philosophy, the Basics* (Routledge).

Finally, a reference book which I've found highly informative is the *Fontana Dictionary of Modern Thought,* edited by A. Bullock and O. Stallybrass.

Index of names

Index of subjects